"The greatest civilian soldie
— General John J. Pershing, describing Sergeant Alvin York,
who later received the Congressional Medal of Honor,
Prauthoy, France, 1919

"What you did was the greatest thing accomplished by any private soldier of all the armies of Europe."
— Marshal Ferdinand Foch, Supreme Allied Commander
in World War I, upon awarding Sergeant York the Croix
de Guerre with Palm, St. Silva, France, 1919

"This exemplar of the American fighting man died in 1964, all but
forgotten."
— *Life* magazine, describing Sergeant York in a special issue
on American heroes, 1997

"One of my great blessings is to have spent most of my life in the company of heroes. The classical definition of a hero is a person who puts
him or herself at risk to benefit others. That certainly defines Sergeant
Alvin York—not just for the Medal of Honor he was awarded for his
skill, marksmanship, and courage in battle—but for the way he lived
the rest of his life. Real heroes, like Sgt. York, are selfless, not selfish.
John Perry's biography of this remarkable, self-sacrificing American
hero is an inspiring read in these uncertain times."
— LtCol Oliver L. North USMC (Ret), best-selling author
of *The Rifleman* and host of the *Real American Heroes* series

"*Sgt. York: His Life, Legend, and Legacy* is the story of a military legend
and enduring role model. When it counted most, Alvin York ran to the
sound of gunfire and accomplished one of the greatest feats in American war history. He went on to live the same way, fighting for the kids
in his area to have the educational opportunity he never had. America
needs what Alvin had and other godly men have now more than ever.
After reading it, you will want every man and boy in your circle to
know this story."
— Lt. General William G. "Jerry" Boykin - US Army (Retired),
executive director of Family Research Council

Sgt. York

His Life, Legend, and Legacy

Sgt. York

HIS LIFE, LEGEND, AND LEGACY

The remarkable story of Sergeant Alvin C. York

JOHN PERRY

FIDELIS
PUBLISHING

FIDELIS PUBLISHING

ISBN: 978-1-7358563-2-2
ISBN (eBook): 978-1-7358563-3-9

Sgt. York: His Life, Legend & Legacy
The remarkable story of Sergeant Alvin C. York
© 2021 John Perry

Cover Design by Diana Lawrence
Interior Design by Lisa Parnell

For information about special discounts for bulk purchases, please contact Bulk Books.com, call 1-888-959-5153 or email - cs@bulkbooks.com

Fidelis Publishing, LLC Sterling, VA • Nashville, TN fidelispublishing.com

"We Would See Jesus" – words by Anna B. Warner (1827–1915), music by John B. Dykes (1823–1876)

"O Master, Let Me Walk with Thee" – Washington Gladden (1836–1918)

Front cover photograph by Signal Corps, U.S. Army, Public domain, via Wikimedia Commons

Manufactured in Canada

10 9 8 7 6 5 4 3 2 1

This book is dedicated to my father,

THOMAS PERRY,

whose love of history and heroes fills every page.

It is also dedicated to

CHARLTON OGBURN,

who taught me by example that true stories, well written,
are the best stories of all.

Contents

Acknowledgments

As so many wonderful projects do, this book started with dessert. Acquisitions editor Matt Jacobson had invited me to lunch at the Capitol Grill in the Hermitage Hotel, a block from the state capitol in Nashville, to discuss a writing project. Somewhere in the middle of our peerless crème brûlée I mentioned this was the hotel where Sergeant Alvin York signed his Hollywood movie contract for the 1941 movie about his life.

Wide-eyed, Matt leaned over the table and commanded, "What do you know about Sergeant York?" By the end of the meal we had a book in the works and it wasn't the one we met to talk about (though we did that one as well).

My biography of Sgt. Alvin York has remained a steady seller ever since and is still the only full-scale biography of this great American soldier and patriot. Now thanks to Gary Terashita, Oliver North, and their team at Fidelis Publishing, York's inspiring story continues to remind us all of the timeless value of faith, patriotism, and self-sacrifice. A cursory glance at today's headlines is proof we need these reminders more than ever.

One of my first lessons in beginning this project was that the truth is a slippery slope. Two people remember the same event quite differently; reference sources frequently contradict each other; in an honest effort to be helpful, people will repeat even the most tenuous supposition as though it were a historical fact. I recall talking with one group who finally agreed absolutely on the details of a particular event, but never could agree whether it was before World War II or after.

Matt Jacobson mightily championed the cause of Sergeant York from the first. Bob Krupp—who may have been the only book editor in America who was also a nationally ranked weight lifter—made valuable editorial contributions, particularly regarding the chronology of the chapters.

Andrew Cheatham, my indefatigable and endlessly cheerful research associate, accompanied me on three extended trips to Sergeant York's hometown, made many helpful suggestions during the interviews, and labored tirelessly in libraries, archives, courthouses, and newspaper offices for the good of the cause.

General Jack Newcomb, former director of the Sergeant York Historical Association (later the Sergeant York Patriotic Foundation), was instrumental in introducing me to the York story in the first place, for which I will always be grateful. W. Lipscomb Davis Jr., founder and former chairman of the SYHA, kindly loaned me his father's fascinating scrapbook tracing York's first speaking tour, and was a great encouragement to me as the book progressed.

York family members and others in Fentress County, Tennessee, were unfailingly generous with their time. Andrew Jackson York—active, jovial, and ever hospitable at the age of ninety—still lives across from the old York homeplace on the Wolf River where he was born. The house is now a state historical site, which Andy is proud to show to visitors as he answers their endless questions and poses for photos. He and his late wife, Helen, generously loaned their family photos for this project. Andy's sister and Sgt. York's youngest child, Betsy Ross York Lowrey, also shared wonderful memories of life in the York household.

Their brother George Edward Buxton York, who passed away in 2018 after a long and colorful life, was another enthusiastic contributor to his father's story. Thanks as well to the late Woodrow Wilson York for a brief but informative telephone interview.

It was a special treat to get a call from Elva Jean York Clouse, the sergeant's niece and at the time his oldest living relative, who heard about the project and wanted to help. Ernest Buck, once principal of the York Institute, forged a living link with history by sharing his eyewitness account of Sergeant York's wedding, which he attended as a boy of six. He also sent me on my way with a handful of prize-winning tomatoes.

Wilma Reagan Pinckley, a member of the first York Institute graduating class and widow of the sergeant's doctor, generously offered archival newspaper articles and other information taken from her own books about the history of Fentress County.

Leo Hatfield, whose memory for detail was astonishing, added depth and feeling to this work with stories of his and York's hunting trips and other adventures together. Bradley Cook also helped brighten the narrative with remembrances of York's land dealings, the early days of York Chapel, and much more.

Thanks are in order to others for their invaluable help during my long months of research: Mancil Johnson at the Tennessee Technological University archives in Cookeville, Tennessee; Dr. Doug Young, principal of the York Institute, for his valuable insights; Brenda Williams, librarian at the York Institute, for her many courtesies; Faye Stephens at the Fentress County courthouse for guiding me through a maze of legal records; Billy and Pat Conatser for their hospitality during my stays in Pall Mall; and to Miller Leonard for helping with Fentress County logistics early on.

Far from the Tennessee hills, I own a debt of gratitude to Leith Adams at the Warner Bros. film archive; to Stuart Ng and others at the USC Library for their efficiency and encouragement; to Ken Wales for his introduction to the corporate side of Hollywood (and his whirlwind tour of the Warner Bros. lot); and to the courteous and resourceful people at the reference library of the Motion Picture Academy of Arts and Sciences. I must also mention my chance meeting with a friendly stranger outside the USC Library. When I said I was researching the movie *Sergeant York*, he ex-claimed, "I was in *Sergeant York*!" He explained how a casting director scoured the fraternities for tall blond students to cast as Germans in the trenches and shared wonderful details about his days on the set. Thanks as well to Sofa Entertainment for permission to use a quotation from *The Ed Sullivan Show*.

Near the end of the trail I came across an unexpected delight in the person of Arthur Story Bushing, son of Arthur Samuel Bushing, York's longtime friend and supporter. I saw him give a masterful interview on an archival videotape at Tennessee Tech. On a wild hunch I contacted directory assistance in Maryville, Tennessee, where Dr. Bushing was teaching at the time of his interview in 1988, then called the only Arthur Bushing in town. From the time he answered the phone that day, he contributed mightily to this effort. After he died years later, his desk drawers yielded yet another wave of York treasures in the form of letters to and from the sergeant and luminaries including President Truman.

In years since I first spoke with them, many of these kind and gracious people have crossed to the other shore—General Newcomb, Lipscomb Davis, Wilma Pinckley (who endowed the Jamestown library, now named in her honor), and others. I hope the memory of their lives will remain strong through the stories preserved here.

During those years my children, whom I previously acknowledged for their happy greetings and cheerful spirits, have grown up and established families of their own. The world moves on. And yet the life and legacy of Sgt. Alvin York are as powerful and inspiring as ever. His is a timeless example of the best of the American spirit.

Soli deo gloria.

John Perry
Veterans Day, 2020
Nashville, Tennessee

Note to the Reader
from Andrew Jackson York

This biography of my daddy will tell you what he was really like. Sgt. York was a war hero who was awarded the Medal of Honor. But to him the most important part of his life was that he was a Christian who loved the Lord and served Him faithfully.

Every generation of Americans has its heroes—people whose sacrifice and patriotism make our country great. When America entered World War II, I was eleven years old and everybody knew about Sgt. Alvin C. York. He was a conscientious objector in World War I who went to fight anyway because he was convinced that God wanted him to. He led a miraculous victory on the battlefield in France, and the story became a hit movie the summer before Pearl Harbor. It helped remind us all what we were fighting for.

Now I'm on the other side of ninety and Daddy has been gone for more than fifty years. While classic movie fans still remember Gary Cooper playing Sgt. York on film, not many remember the real man behind the story. To me, we need his example of sacrifice and patriotism today more than ever.

John Perry spent many months in the Wolf River Valley interviewing me and others about my daddy's life. He got the story from people who knew it best. And he got it right. I appreciate his work and hope you enjoy this book.

Andrew Jackson York
Pall Mall, Tennessee
May 11, 2020

Author's Note

The quotations in this book are taken verbatim, in virtually every case, from letters, interviews, and the sources listed in the bibliography. I have not subjected them to editorial standardization or peppered them with commentary. As a result, inconsistencies will appear to the careful reader which will, I hope, enhance the experience rather than hinder it. When Corporal York signs a letter to his sweetheart as "Private Alvin C. York," or when York's mother recalls a "one-room log cabin" that had three rooms and weatherboard siding added over the years, it gives another dimension to the story I found too enjoyable to keep to myself.

York's and Gracie's spelling and grammar are as they appeared originally, revealing their lack of formal education. York's gets better over time, owing to his traveling, speaking, and reading, while Gracie's remains much the same. I have not indicated upper/lower case alterations or ellipses unless a significant change in meaning is involved.

York consistently wrote the letter B as a capital whenever it was at the beginning of a word. It was a handwriting quirk, not an issue of punctuation worthy of repetition. This predictable trait, and one or two other similar ones, have been normalized.

Chapter One

Three Hours Fifteen Minutes

The battle for the Argonne Forest began before dawn on September 26, 1918. The weather was miserable: rain alternating with drizzle in a chill wind. The sun, beginning its attempt at daylight, would soon reveal sullen clouds the same color as the mud stretching out in every direction from the ranks of soldiers along the road. An opening artillery bombardment split the leaden sky with lethal flashes, the sharp, ragged reports echoing across the quiet countryside of northeastern France. Immediately following, French forces, under General Henri J. E. Gouraud, stepped off to lead the advance.

Five minutes later, at precisely 5:30 a.m., General John J. "Blackjack" Pershing's First Army of fresh American conscripts engaged, advancing quickly up the Meuse River and plunging into the forest growth beyond. They could see enemy soldiers up ahead running away from them. Some of the American doughboys were enraged that the retreating Germans wouldn't stand and defend their ground and yelled across the field for them to "wait up and fight it out!"

The Germans gave way easily until the Americans were deep among the towering trees of the Argonne. The attackers advanced five miles northwest along the banks of the Meuse and two miles into the forest

the first day. The quick march ended there. Closely massed trees, cling-
ing undergrowth, and rough terrain in the Argonne created an effective
natural barrier between the Allies and the vital railroad the Germans
desperately needed to defend. By filling the forest with barbed wire and
other obstacles and scattering machine gun emplacements throughout,
the Germans produced an impediment even the freshest and strongest
Allies would have to pay dearly to remove.

An excellent network of railroads was one of the key elements in
Germany's success throughout the war, allowing the rapid transport of
men and supplies both up and down the front and to and from the
great manufacturing centers of the German heartland. The system was
also crucial for quick redeployment of troops along the front or for a
rapid and orderly retreat. Disrupting the rail network now, deduced
Allied commander Marshal Ferdinand Foch, would throw Germany
into a panic from which it could not recover.

The main line ran parallel to the front for more than three hundred
miles, from Bruges, Belgium, near the North Sea, southeast to Strasbourg, France, on the Rhine River. At each of three principal junctions
along the way, a heavily traveled line of supply and escape ran northeast
into Germany. The northern- and western-most of these junctions was
at Maubeuge, near the city of Aulnoye, from where a line went through
Liège to Cologne. On down the main track, near Mézières and Sedan,
a second northeast-bound line connected the front to Luxembourg and
Coblenz, where the Moselle emptied into the Rhine. The third, a southern line, took a picturesque route from Strasbourg, following the Rhine
Valley all the way through Mannheim to Mainz.

The Allied offensive called for a gargantuan pincer action against
this network, with the British First and Third Armies leading the attack
eastward at Aulnoye, cutting off German escape to Cologne; and the
American First and French Fourth Armies advancing northward to
Mézières and Sedan, stopping the enemy retreat toward Luxembourg
or Coblenz. (The third junction at Strasbourg, heavily defended and
well behind German lines, would be left alone.) Fracturing the German
railroad at the Aulnoye and Mézières-Sedan junctions would also dis-
rupt movement at the front, as well as blocking the soldiers' retreat.
Sending troops back and forth along the line of battle some other way

would cost the German command dearly in time, horses, and fuel, all in short supply.

The Americans were about halfway through the Argonne Forest when the offensive stalled on October 1. After a rest and resupplying the front with fresh troops, the advance resumed on October 4, the same day the 2nd Battalion, 328th Infantry, 82nd American Division received orders to prepare for action. They were held in reserve, camping at the Zona Woods on October 3, then moved to the edge of the Argonne on the fourth. The next morning, October 5, the battalion lined up on the main road to march into the center of the forest where the Germans made their stand.

Among the soldiers of Company G, 2nd Battalion, was a strapping six-footer with a red moustache and an unruly shock of red hair whose friends back home called him "Big 'Un." Like his daddy, he was a farmer and blacksmith, and until he was drafted he'd hardly ventured out of the Tennessee county where he was born. He was a corporal, Corporal Alvin C. York, and was a squad leader despite an official statement in his military file that he entered the service as a conscientious objector. His exemplary deportment, natural leadership ability, and outstanding marksmanship overshadowed any lingering doubt his superiors may have had about his resolve on the battlefield.

Corporal York had left his widowed mother and ten brothers and sisters behind in the Valley of the Three Forks of the Wolf, a beautiful and isolated place rimmed by mountains covered in hickory, oak, chestnut, and beech. He also left behind the girl he hoped to marry. She was eighteen, fair-skinned, and slender, with dancing blue eyes, and hair the color of mountain honey.

Since leaving home, Corporal York had written to his love, his Miss Gracie, almost every day. His writing was poor, the result of schooling lasting only a few weeks over a few summers when there was no tobacco to tend or hay to stack. But his heart was full and tender and blossoming, and he poured his love out onto the page unhindered by the finer points of spelling or grammar.

Near the front he usually wrote postcards or single-page notes. From the relative safety of the rear, he wrote for hours, laboring over his penmanship and composing letters of six to eight pages or more. He had one final chance to write Gracie from behind the lines on October 2. As usual, he jumped from one topic to another as interruptions and distractions of the field intervened. But more than anything, his thoughts were on how much he loved and missed her.

> *Say dear there isnt a day but what I am thinking of you. Well darling you said something a bout you had just combed your Hair. I wish I could have bin there with you. I think your hair is nice. . . . It has rained over here nearly every day for a month or so and is looking like winter now. Its cool here. And I wish you knowed where I was sleeping, ho ho. . . . O darling my love is for you and there is no other girl can take your place with me. You are the girl I love and I promised you that you would be my wife and I mean just what I told you. Well dear you said you didnt want me to write to* ——— *any more. I have just wrote her a few letters. But I guess you are right. You say you are not talking to no one nor writing to no one, so I guess you was right when you said that you thought I ought to quit writing to eney other girl for I ought to do by you as I wish you to do by me. So I wont write eney more now, ho ho. . . . Say dear in regard to your watch, I cant get to go to town where there is any watches and of course there is no watches in the front lines, ho ho. . . . Say dear the Americans is whipping the germans as fast as they can catch them, ho ho. They are on the run now. All the time; and have bin for some time and I think they will continue to run until the war is over. The Allies captured 50,000 thousand Turks over in Palestine in the last few days. So I think the Germans will haft to quit before long. . . . Well you stay with Mother and be a good girl and take care of yourself until I come back to you. Then you shall be mine. So that's all this time. Answer soon to your loving sweetheart, as ever yours,*

> *Pvt. Alvin C. York*
> *Co. G 328th Inf.,*
> *American E. F.,*
> *A. P. O. 742 France*

*Good bye, God bless you and keep you is my prayer. So
that's all. My kisses and best is with you.*

The roads Company G followed to the front were rivers of mud.
Even though there was little of the shelling that turned other battle-
grounds into seas of muck, the combination of frequent rain and the
enormous amount of traffic produced by hundreds of thousands of pairs
of boots and their attendant artillery wagons, supply vans, ambulances,
couriers, horses, mules, and trucks quickly made roads throughout the
region all but impassable.

Field pieces slid into ditches, to be retrieved by fifty weary men.
Broken-down trucks blocked the way, with passing doughboys swarm-
ing around them on either side, swearing at the mechanics in attendance and the mechanics swearing back. Horses dropped dead from
exhaustion and were left where they fell, men unfastening the traces
and pulling the loads themselves. MPs ran constantly from the scene of
one bottleneck to another, unsnarling traffic jams that stopped progress
for half an hour at a time.

Along a road not far from the one the 328th was traveling, soldiers had come upon a remarkable roadblock a few days before. On
September 29 French Premier Georges Clemenceau arrived at Souilly,
demanding to visit the hilltop city of Montfaucon, liberated from
German occupation only two days before. General Pershing explained
the road to Montfaucon was also the only route for reserves and supplies to reach the fighting ahead and the only way for the wounded and
battle-weary to escape. Premier Clemenceau could not expect to make
an easy trip and would in fact hamper troop movements as one more
component of the traffic jam.

Clemenceau would not be dissuaded. He wanted to see and feel the
victory in person and set off down the road in his elegant limousine to
do precisely that. The closer he got to the front, the slower the traffic
moved, and the more the impeccably-dressed premier was appalled by
the pandemonium. One of the many passing soldiers making his way
around the enormous car pointedly deduced it was "just another damn
politician blocking a lifeline with a black limousine."

After alternately standing still and inching ahead for six hours, Clemenceau realized he would never get to Montfaucon. Now his problem was getting back to Souilly. The road was narrow and muddy, and the limousine was closely surrounded on every side by traffic like a rock in a river. He summoned a squad of doughboys over to his window and curtly commanded them to hoist the car into the air, turn it around, and set it back down facing the opposite direction. The soldiers dropped their gear, wearily grabbed the mud-caked fenders and running boards, and did as they were told. Fuming, Clemenceau retraced his way back to Pershing's headquarters.

Like the premier, Corporal Alvin York also found the closer he got to the front, the more frantic the traffic became. The view became more grisly as well, with wounded being carried past him toward the rear, and dead men and horses to step around. He had seen dead soldiers before but the sheer number of them now gave him a new sense of urgency and resolve. True, he was an elder in a church that believed all war was forbidden by the Bible. Yet the Bible also said, "Blessed are the peacemakers." He had thought the matter out carefully in the months since he was drafted. If it took killing to secure a just peace, then killing would be acceptable to God.

Germans began shelling the road, and warplanes appeared overhead. Looking up briefly as he ran for cover, York found himself reciting softly aloud:

> *O Jesus, the great rock of foundation*
> *Whereon my feet were set with sovereign grace*
> *Through shells or death with all their agitation,*
> *Thou wilt protect me if I will only trust in Thy grace.*
> *Bless Thy Holy Name.*

As they approached the German lines, the men rested in ditches or foxholes by day and traveled by night. The chilling drizzle fell constantly. York was still not close enough to the battlefront to encounter machine gun fire but the shelling was relentless. The whine of the missile, the flash of light, the thunderous blast, and a concussion felt in the chest were his constant tormentors.

Men were dismembered and killed before his eyes. Training their field pieces on the American machine gun battalion on the other side of the road from where York marched, the Germans killed dozens as the corporal and the rest of his company looked on, horrified but continuing to move forward. The enemy artillery was firing from out of sight miles away; the Americans were dead. There was nothing Company G could do and stopping would only make them an easier target. York prayed for the soldiers, both German and American, and walked on.

The flash and growl of ordinance reminded him of the summer thunderstorms in the Valley of the Three Forks of the Wolf. But instead of virgin hickory, beech, and chestnut woods, he was surrounded here by mud and death and despair. Shelling was beginning to thin the forest where the 328th marched. Huge trees splintered and uprooted reminded him at first of a cyclone. *No,* he thought, *it's more like Armageddon.*

Advancing still closer to the enemy, York saw even more wounded being carried to dressing stations in the rear. Other casualties lay helpless beside the road, moaning and twitching as medics raced from one to the other trying to save as many as they could. Beside them lay more of the dead, eyes and mouths open wide, their last moment alive frozen in a snapshot of terror.

Company G and the rest of the 82nd Division penetrated to the northern section of the forest. They spent the day of October 7, lying alongside the road in the rain and mud, watching the 1st Division battle for what the field maps designated as Hill 223. This hill and its neighboring villages of Châtel and Chéhéry were near the edge of the Argonne, along the Aire River. To the west of the hill ran the narrow gauge Decauville Railroad, which the Germans depended on both to supply this stretch of the front and to take iron ore and casualties out. In a small-scale version of Foch's master plan, the American objective was to advance down the western slope of Hill 223, cross the plain at its base, and take the Decauville line. At 3:00 p.m., the German Division Headquarters received a message from the front by carrier pigeon reporting, "the enemy has penetrated our lines . . . and is advancing in dense waves."

Once Hill 223 was secured by the 1st Battalion, Company G's commander, Captain E. C. B. Danforth, received orders along with the rest of the 2nd Battalion to advance to a line just behind the crest of the hill and use it as a jumping-off point for an attack on the railroad. The orders, issued at 9:45 p.m. on October 7, by Major Trammell Scott, adjutant to the commanding general, charged the battalion with "the duty of driving hard straight west to cross the railroad at its nearest point." The hour of attack, H-hour, would be 5:00 a.m., beginning with a rolling artillery barrage. Forty-five minutes after midnight, a second order was issued delaying H-hour until 6:00 a.m., to give the artillery more time to get into position along the crowded, muddy, treacherous roads.

By 3:45 a.m. on October 8, the 2nd Battalion had crossed the Aire on temporary footbridges and taken up a position on the eastern slope of Hill 223. It was dark and raining, the air heavy with American and German shouting and the relentless din of gunfire. The Germans sent poison gas over, but the Allies kept slogging forward, grappling for gas masks among their soggy gear as they went.

As the men waited for H-hour just below the crest of Hill 223, they could at least be grateful for the fact they saw no trench warfare as such in the Meuse-Argonne. The trees, underbrush, and rolling landscape of the region provided acceptable protection from enemy fire, making trenches unnecessary. They would have been impractical besides, with the position of the battlefront changing as often as it did. Here and there men did make use of a few shallow trenches the French dug and left behind three years before. They also spent plenty of time in ditches by the side of the road and enhanced natural dips and sinkholes with shovels and spades. Still at least they were above ground, advancing, feeling like they were going somewhere.

The 2nd Battalion saw 6:00 a.m. come and go without a sound from the artillery. The morning dawned damp and cold and a thick fog covered the plain beyond their hill. An extra hour had evidently not been time enough to move the guns into place along the sloppy traffic-choked roads and poor visibility only added to the difficulty. The gunners weren't firing.

At 6:10, without waiting any longer for artillery support, the 2nd Battalion began its charge over the hill under cover of the swirling mist, trees, and heavy undergrowth. Company G was first on the left,

Company E on the right, with Companies F and H following behind. As soon as the enemy troops detected the advance, they opened fire with deadly result. From Hill 223 to the Decauville line was two kilometers on the French field maps—a mile and a quarter, an easy half-hour walk. To defend their lifeline, the Germans made the Americans pay for every inch. Machine gun emplacements across the plain and on flanking hillsides had a clear field of fire on the advancing soldiers from the point where they crested the hill, all the way down the slope, and across the plain to the railroad.

The first wave of Americans ran headlong into a wall of German lead. Hundreds died within minutes, the spectacle reminding Corporal York of hay falling in the path of a mowing machine. Diving to the ground, soldiers of the 2nd Battalion crawled forward using underbrush, stumps, and tree trunks for protection. As the advance faltered, Second Lieutenant Kirby P. Stewart of G Company rose to rally his men. After charging only ten yards, he was shot in the thigh. He continued to pull himself along, shouting encouragement, until a second shot struck him in the head.

Neither the 28th Division on their left, nor the 327th Infantry on their right was able to advance, and the 328th soon found itself pinned down and alone. G Company in particular was subjected to withering machine gun fire from the Germans on three sides and at last found its forward progress stopped entirely.

Company G's position was even more precarious when taken as part of the larger offensive. Both the 28th Division and the 77th Division, to the left of the 28th, were slowed to a crawl by German resistance. The 1st Division, after taking Hill 223, penetrated to the northwest, driving a half-mile salient into enemy territory. The rear of the salient was filled with troops of the 82nd, who were now in the path of a German pincer movement to cut off and isolate the 1st Division. Company G was at the left base of the salient, most exposed to enemy pressure and best positioned to render assistance. Unless the Spandaus protecting the plain between the foot of Hill 223 and the Decauville Railroad could be silenced, allowing the center and left units in the line to advance, the 1st Division would be forced to retreat or face capture and destruction.

As the fog lifted, Captain Danforth lay in the muddy underbrush considering Company G's choices. Danforth was a tall, lanky Georgian in his mid-twenties with a Harvard degree and a patient, calculating manner. He saw his duty and the duty of his men to preserve the salient to his right won at so great a price.

The captain decided to send a detachment of men from his 1st Platoon around the left flank of the Company G line, hoping they could distract the machine gunners, knock out some emplacements, or somehow interrupt the deadly fusillade. The platoon sergeant was an actor and renowned barroom fighter named Harry Parsons. With terse hand signals, Captain Danforth got Parsons's attention and described his assignment, pointing to the gun emplacements and circling his hand around in the air. Parsons in turn selected three squads for the mission under the command of Corporal Bernard Early, demoted from sergeant for misconduct and presently serving as an acting sergeant in the field. Early's squad leaders were Corporals William C. Cutting, Murray Savage, and Alvin C. York.

The squads started the morning with a total of twenty-four men. By this time there were seventeen left. With Early in the lead, the men dropped back from the firing line and then hunched single file around the left flank and into German territory. Continuing quickly and quietly, they stopped about three hundred yards behind enemy lines, on a ridge they decided was in line with the German front, to consider their next step. Some of the men wanted to attack the German flank from that point. York, Early, and others thought they should keep moving and attack from the rear. At last they decided to keep going and hit the enemy from behind. They came upon a ravine dug out to form a shallow trench and followed it into the woods.

Suddenly, out of the thick brush and remnants of fog, two German stretcher bearers appeared, white bands with red crosses on the arms of their uniforms. They and the Allies saw each other at the same time. The Germans dropped their empty stretcher and bolted into the woods. The Americans shouted for them to surrender; one stopped but the other continued running. One of the Americans fired a few shots to no effect.

Fearful the medics would sound the alarm, the seventeen Americans took off in pursuit. Jumping a little stream, running even though they could see only a few yards through the undergrowth in front of them, the men stumbled onto an encampment of twenty or thirty German soldiers. Officers, enlisted men, orderlies, runners, and stretcher bearers looked up from their breakfast to find themselves, though well behind the front, completely surrounded. Only the commander was armed; the rest had traded pistols and rifles for knives and forks.

These were members of the Prussian 210th Infantry, 45th Reserve Division, who were sent up as reinforcements but had not yet engaged in combat. If the Americans were surprised at their lack of preparedness, so was their commanding officer earlier in the day. First Lieutenant Vollmer was in charge of the 1st Battalion, 120th Landwehr Infantry, defending the Decauville rail line against the Americans as they headed down Hill 223 (identified on German maps as Castle Hill). Inspecting his position on the morning of October 8, he found his men poorly organized, with large gaps in the line and morale at low ebb. In the rear, Vollmer came upon this group from the 210th, their arms and ammunition belts laid aside, eating breakfast. When he upbraided them for their carelessness, the men insolently declared they had hiked all night and, before they did anything else, they were having something to eat.

As the Americans burst into their circle, the Germans made no resistance. Dropping their plates and putting up their hands, they shouted, *"Kamerad!"* After only a few shots, Early ordered his men to cease firing and take the Germans prisoners. As he formed his POWs into a line, a German officer shouted a command. In response, the machine gunners along the front swiveled their weapons around and started firing upon the Americans. Corporal Savage, who had been York's bunkmate, died instantly, peppered with so many rounds his uniform was almost torn off. Early survived a bullet in the arm and five in the body. Cutting fell wounded with three bullets in his left arm. In seconds the machine guns killed six men and wounded three. That left eight, and the ranking soldier among them was Corporal Alvin C. York. There were two casualties in his squad, one killed and one, Private Mario Muzzi, wounded in the shoulder. York hurriedly assembled the remnants of his and Cutting's platoons. Savage's men were all dead.

Up the line, First Lieutenant Vollmer was having problems of his own. Rumors of Americans breaking through sent troops into a panic. Some of them had been at the front since September 26, and were at the point of exhaustion; the worst off were too tired to call for chow the night before. There was a sense that the end was near and a life sacrificed now was a life wasted. (The men could not have known that after the collapse of the civil government in Berlin days before, the new chancellor, Prince Max von Baden, approached President Wilson through diplomatic channels requesting an armistice. Von Baden received Wilson's refusal on October 8.) Germans began to drift away from their positions, and finally a cavalry squadron was called in to cut off the retreat. Seeing a group headed for the rear, Vollmer approached to find another detachment of the 210th Infantry removing their sidearms and belts. He forced them back into the line at gunpoint.

Despite the wavering of some troops and reserves, the machine gunners continued pouring Spandau fire into the small circle where Corporal York was pinned down with seven privates and twenty or more prisoners. When the firefight started, Americans and Germans alike flattened themselves on the ground, behind stumps or trees. All except Corporal York. Alone in the muddy grass, a few yards from his men and their clump of captives, he assumed a prone position and kept firing. After the opening salvo, the gunners realized they would have to shoot over their own men to get at the Americans. To take aim that way, a gunner had to rise from behind his weapon for a clear sight.

Seeing their heads pop up above the machine guns reminded York of the way turkeys popped up over those logs at the shooting matches back home. A turkey was tethered behind a log forty yards from the contestant, who got one shot with his muzzle loader when the big bird's head appeared. The difference to the corporal was that German heads were a lot bigger than turkeys'. "In order to sight me or swing their machine guns at me," he later explained, "the Germans had to show their heads above the trenches [actually hillside gun emplacements], and every time I saw a head I just teched it off. I kept yelling at them to come down. I didn't want to kill any more than I had to. But it was they or I."

One after another, York quickly dropped the machine gunners, "teching them off" with a single rifle shot each. Every few rounds, he would stop shooting and call for the Germans to surrender. "That's enough now! You boys quit and come on down!" Answered with bullets, he reshouldered his Eddystone and picked off another several targets.

As the din began to subside, he rose to his feet, firing offhand with the form he used to win so many shooting contests in the Wolf River Valley: back arched, head down, firing arm elbow cocked high. The protective brush around him was all shot up by now and he figured he might as well stand for a better view. When his three clips of rifle ammunition ran out, he drew his Colt .45 and continued firing. A German company commander, Lieutenant Endriss, mounted a charge of six men with fixed bayonets against York. As the attackers emerged from the brush at twenty-five yards in a ragged single file, York put another of his Tennessee marksmanship lessons into practice. He knew from duck hunting that if he fired on the lead bird in the formation, the others would spook and scatter; but if he picked off targets from the rear forward, each one would be taken by surprise. So instead of firing at the first man in the oncoming line, York shot the last man first, dropping Endriss with a serious wound to the stomach. He then shot and killed the next-to-last attacker, the one in front of him, and on up the line. At that range, the first soldier in line got dangerously close by the time the others were dispatched. York dropped him with only a couple of arms' length to spare. A single miss out of six would have meant certain death.

The redheaded corporal stilled enough machine guns to begin preparations for escorting his captives behind American lines. Looking around at his group of prisoners on the ground, he noticed with a shock the German commander still had his pistol. York ordered him to hand it over and found it hot to the touch. The officer had fired at York from behind while York faced the bayonet charge.

With his soldiers guarding the Germans, York began leading the group toward the front, looking for the best place to turn south and maneuver back around both German and American flanks.

Lieutenant Kuebler was a platoon commander in First Lieutenant Vollmer's battalion, serving on the front at the point where the 210th Infantry was supposed to provide reinforcement. He had just received a visit from Vollmer, who was still trying to fill gaps in his line and support positions with communications fragmented and companies reduced to thirty men or fewer. Vollmer received orders—which he had little hope of carrying out—to counterattack against the American left flank at 10:30 that morning.

Occupied with incoming Allied rifle grenades and small arms fire, Lieutenant Kuebler nevertheless noticed the sound of his own machine guns growing fainter and less frequent. Taking two men with him to reconnoiter the position, he soon found himself facing a squad of Americans with fixed bayonets. Unable to see clearly in the underbrush and assuming they were the advance guard of a larger flanking force, he surrendered and joined the group of his countrymen already marching by twos in front of them.

The yelling of both the Germans and their American captors attracted the attention of Lieutenant Vollmer, who had walked back toward the ridge. Looking across the plain, he saw a line of American troops sneaking toward his flank. He sent orders to men in the immediate vicinity to open fire at once, then ordered a halt upon hearing the cry of, "Don't shoot! There are Germans in here!" Because of the undergrowth, Vollmer couldn't separate friendly targets from enemies. As he was considering what to do, York and those of his men not guarding prisoners rushed the lieutenant. He and his adjutant, Lieutenant Glass, alone and thinking they were surrounded by a large assault force, surrendered without resistance.

Gesturing to York, the commander asked, "English?"

"American," answered York.

"Good Lord!" said Vollmer.

Vollmer had worked in Chicago before the war and spoke English. Corporal York ordered him to form the whole detail of prisoners into a column of twos. As he obeyed, Vollmer offered to try and get the other defenders to surrender if the sharpshooting American agreed not to fire on any more of them. York concurred, adding that if he *didn't* get them to stop, Vollmer would be the next one to be "teched off." The German officer produced a whistle and blew the signal for a cease-fire. With one exception, men came off the ridge and out of the brush with their hands in the air. As he approached York, one soldier tossed a grenade at the corporal, which exploded well in front of its intended target. York fired once at the man and "teched him off."

York instructed Vollmer to direct them to the front. Vollmer indicated they should follow a gully through the brush, but York, suspecting a trap, insisted on a straight approach. Vollmer was placed at the head of the column. York followed, flanked by two other German officers, holding his .45 in the small of the lieutenant's back. Behind him were two growing columns of prisoners, some carrying the wounded Americans (Early, Cutting, and Muzzi), guarded at the flanks and rear by the seven remaining Company G privates (Beardsley, Konotski, Sok, Johnson, Saccina, Donohue, and Willis).

Approaching enemy defenses from behind, York realized for the first time that they had penetrated to the second German line. Now he had to pass through the real front. As they proceeded, more machine gunners turned their Spandaus around and began firing. York spoke to Vollmer. "Blow that whistle of yours or I'll take your head off, and theirs too." The German obeyed and the men at that position put down their weapons and surrendered. Again there was a single exception, and again York felled him with a shot.

By this time there were so many Germans in the group York was afraid they would be fired on by his own artillery. Overhearing snatches of the Americans' conversation as they discussed the situation, Vollmer began to wonder how many men there were in the command. Because of the confusion, gunfire, and the thick trees and brush, he had no idea how big the attacking force actually was. "How many men have you got?" he asked.

Without missing a beat, Corporal York answered, "I got a-plenty."

As he reached the American lines, York was relieved to encounter a support squad sent to help him, which could pass the word that these Boche (the English word for a hard-headed person) were under American control. Just to be sure, he stepped in front of Vollmer as soon as the Americans appeared, showing his uniform, and calling out to the oncoming soldiers.

York marched his prisoners to the battalion post of command, where the battalion adjutant, Lieutenant Woods, counted three officers and 129 enlisted men. Lieutenant Kuebler, to his chagrin, was not initially counted as an officer because he was wearing a trenchcoat with no insignia over his uniform. First Lieutenant Vollmer was listed as a major, probably because American battalion commanders were usually majors, and Vollmer had been relieved of his lieutenant shoulder boards by a souvenir-seeking captor. The other officers were Lieutenants Thoma and Glass.

Because there wasn't room for so many prisoners at the battalion post of command, York was ordered to march his prisoners to regimental headquarters. A field message was prepared to accompany them to the rear, containing the first sketchy record of Corporal York's accomplishment: "These men came from our left flank (132 in all besides wounded). Have not taken time to examine them for papers etc."

It was 9:25 a.m., October 8, 1918, three hours and fifteen minutes after York and the rest of Company G began their charge over the crest of Hill 223.

Regimental didn't have room for so many men either and sent York on to division headquarters to turn his prisoners over to the French military police at Varennes. The route was still subject to German shelling and York often double-timed the men to move them as quickly as possible through target areas to safety.

News of the prisoners preceded their arrival. When he reached Varennes, Corporal York was ordered to report to General Julian R. Lindsey. Escorted to headquarters, established in a shabby store near the center of town, the tall Tennessean saluted the brigadier.

"Well, York, I hear you have captured the whole damn German army."

"No, sir. I only got 132."

The general sent York and his men to the artillery kitchen, where they enjoyed the luxury of a hot meal at a table, without a drop of rain or an ounce of mud in sight.

Returning to Company G late that night, York wrote briefly in his diary about the events of the day, ending with a thought on his deliverance:

> So you can see here in this case of mine where God helped me out. I had bin living for God and working in the church some time before I come to the army. So I am a witness to the fact that God did help me out of that hard battle; for the bushes were shot up all around me and I never got a scratch.

Chapter Two

The Sixth Commandment

As singular as Corporal York's heroism and resourcefulness on the battlefield were, they were all the more remarkable in light of his former opposition to war on religious grounds. His was the unshakable conviction and resolve of a convert, having traded, on his knees, a wild, remorseless life for one of sincere Christian piety in the peaceful stillness of a New Year's dawn nearly four years before. And yet, he was persuaded that spiritual victories must sometimes be gained through wars of the flesh.

Alvin York read about the Great War in the Jamestown paper, which was sent the twelve miles from the county seat to his home town of Pall Mall, Tennessee, on horseback along with the mail. He talked about war with the other men who sat on the porch of Rosier C. Pile's store from time to time. A few of his friends even said they might enlist. They considered themselves descendants of an Anglo-Saxon warrior race, and they were eager for a chance to travel, make a little money, and perhaps learn a trade at government expense.

Nothing could have been further from Alvin's desires than to join the army. The Bible was against war and that meant he was against it too. His family had lived in the valley along the Wolf River for more than a hundred years and he had no interest in doing any different. He was the happiest and most settled he had ever been and knew for a fact Miss Gracie Williams, his lifelong neighbor, would consent to marry him soon, even if her father didn't approve. Alvin would build a house next to his mother's for the two of them, farm his seventy-five acres, and live a long, quiet, fulfilling life.

A little red postcard changed everything. Sent from Washington, DC, it worked its way by rail to the nearest station at Oneida, up to Jamestown by truck or wagon, and then across the mountain to Pall Mall. The card, addressed to Alvin C. York, was identical to the cards addressed to other men between the ages of eighteen and forty-five living in Fentress County, and ordered him to register with his local draft board.

Alvin considered himself a patriot and was proud of the American traditions of freedom and liberty. He was also a member of the Church of Christ in Christian Union, which opposed war as a violation of the Sixth Commandment: Thou shalt not kill. On June 5, 1917, the little red postcard trapped the big farmer between two seemingly irreconcilable views of the world. Only one man could help him decide which way to turn.

The local registrar for the draft was the same man who sorted the mailbag containing all those red cards at the homemade post office desk in the corner of his store. R. C. Pile was the draft board representative, storekeeper, postmaster, and unofficial mayor to the hundred or so residents of Pall Mall. He was also pastor and first elder at the new Church of Christ in Christian Union up the road, where Alvin was second elder. Pastor Pile had become York's employer, spiritual mentor, and friend since York's religious conversion. He was the one man who could sort out this draft question and Alvin went right away to talk with him.

York didn't want to go to war and didn't think he should be compelled by some distant authorities to do so. They couldn't know his heart. It wasn't that he was afraid of fighting; he'd certainly done plenty of that in barrooms and moonshine joints in earlier years. It wasn't that he was afraid of dying, even though both his grandfathers were casualties of the Civil War. It wasn't even his profound sadness at the thought of being separated from Gracie now that he had finally won her hand.

The issue was one of faith. "I've been converted to the gospel of peace and love and of 'Do good for evil,'" he reminded Pastor Pile, who preached every Sunday in the same little white frame church where Alvin led the singing. "Fight! Kill! I never killed nobody, even in my bad days, and I don't want to begin now."

True, even at his most violent, Alvin never shot at anyone, only toward them. He continued, the blood rising in his face as he spoke with increasing agitation and conviction, blue eyes sparkling. "I turned my back on all those rowdy things and found a heap of comfort and happiness in religion. I joined the church and took its creed with no reservations. I believe in the Bible, and the Bible says, 'Thou shalt not kill.' That's so definite a child can understand it. There's no way around it or out of it." Pile agreed to help his friend as best he could. The pastor faced the same issue to some extent himself, being a preacher who delivered draft notices.

A war was raging in Alvin York's heart. He wanted to be a good citizen and shoulder his share of the burden, but he was determined to keep the vow he made never to fight again. Over the next several weeks, he talked almost daily with Pastor Pile. Was there no way to be a good citizen and also a good Christian? Alvin spent hours alone on the wooded mountainside with his Bible, reading, studying, thinking, and praying. Once in a while he pulled the little red card out of his pocket and read it over and over, as if somehow the repetition would reveal something to him a hundred previous readings had not.

On one point the law was clear: he had no choice but to register. He could plead his case for exemption later on. York filled out the card and returned it as instructed. Across the bottom he wrote, "I don't want to fight."

Pastor Pile helped him prepare a letter to the Fentress County Draft Board requesting an exemption on religious grounds. On August 28, 1917, they submitted their formal request that York be exempted from military service as "a member of a well-recognized sect or organization, organized and existing May 18, 1917, whose then existing creed or principles forbade its members to participate in war in any form and whose religious principles are against war or participation therein in accordance with the creed or principles of said well-recognized religious sect or organization."

The reply from the Draft Board in Jamestown was direct and succinct.

```
Local Board for the County of Fentress
State of Tennessee
Jamestown, Tennessee
Serial Number 378 Order N. 218

Denied, because we do not think "The Church of
Christ in Christian Union" is a well-recognized
religious sect, etc. Also, we understand it has
no creed except the Bible, which its members
more or less interpret for themselves, and some
do not disbelieve in war—at least there is
nothing forbidding them to participate.
```

York was profoundly disappointed in the reply and couldn't help thinking that his earlier "rowdy days," well-known to members of the draft board, tainted their understanding of York's post-conversion view of war. Again with Pastor Pile's help in sorting through all the legal jargon, York filed an appeal in Nashville with the Draft Board for the Middle District of Tennessee during the first week of September, enclosing a notarized statement repeating his own stand against war based on religious teachings, and a second notarized statement from Pastor Pile affirming York's position that his religious denomination forbade war of any kind, and that if York "ceases to be a member of said religious sect or organization, or if the existing creed or religious principles of said organization are changed so as not to forbid its members participating in war in any form, or whenever the conditions entitling such person to discharge cease to exist, I will at once notify said Local Board and will also request my successor in office to give such notice."

The single sentence reply was unequivocal.

```
You are hereby notified that this District Board,
having considered your claim of appeal from the
decision of the Local Board, County of Fentress,
```

```
and having considered all affidavits and the
record with respect to said claim of appeal,
has, this 6th day of October, 1917, affirmed said
decision.
```

The first draft quota from Fentress County was called up on September 23. York knew now it would be only a matter of time. He received notice to report to the County Board in Jamestown for examination. On October 28, he made the twelve-mile trip over the southern rim of the valley to Jamestown, passing in places along where work had begun with mules, plows, and hay wagons on the Dixie Short Route, the first all-weather road through the mountains.

At twenty-nine, Alvin York was lean, strong, and in excellent health from blacksmithing and farming. He was also working some on the new road for $1.60 a day, the most money he had ever made. His freckled face was trim and darkly tanned, accented by a full, sandy-red moustache; his arms and hands were unusually strong, even for a man of his size and build. According to the examining official, he weighed 170 pounds and stood seventy-two inches tall. He passed his physical and was fit for duty.

Returning to Pall Mall, Alvin reported the news to Pastor Pile and to his mother. Mary York's ten other children could run the farm and care for her easily enough, but still she wept at the thought her boy would be sent off to war somewhere far away. As soon as he could, Alvin went to meet with his dear Gracie on the beech-shaded lane where they often stole a quiet moment together, away from the local gossips and the stern eyes of Gracie's father, Asbury Williams.

Alvin gave her the news. It meant their marriage would have to be postponed, but neither had even a flicker of a thought that perhaps they shouldn't marry. Standing alongside the honeysuckle, near a large, flat rock jutting out of the hillside beneath a massive, ancient beech, they tenderly pledged to be faithful to each other. Gracie of the blue eyes and honey hair would rebuff all advances from other men in the valley. Alvin, towering over her, his shock of red hair flaming in the late afternoon sun, would resist whatever temptations lay beyond Jamestown.

There was no doubt that in God's good time, war or no war, they would be man and wife.

There was nothing left to do. Alvin went back to his work on the highway. At night when the crisp autumn air blew against the small muslin-covered windows of the York cabin, Alvin thought about the events of the last weeks. He tried to explain his belief, based on the Bible, that killing was wrong. Just the same, he would have to go fight. Now he would surely end up in a situation where he might have to kill somebody—a man he didn't know and had no quarrel with personally. Worst of all, Pastor Pile, his friend and spiritual advisor, who didn't want him to go any more than he did, was the one to register him. *Why,* he thought, *if we say we're a Christian nation, don't we try to live in peace instead of sending people off to fight and kill?*

Alvin was not afraid to die. He believed a greater reward awaited him in heaven. But his country wanted him to do more than that; it wanted him to kill others. America said it was its right to ask that of him and God said it wasn't. He could only wait. And pray.

On November 10, Pastor Pile delivered a blue postcard to Alvin, carrying it in the middle of the day out to where York was driving steel on the roadway. The card told him to be ready to be called up on twenty-four hours' notice. Four days later York was ordered to report for duty in the Armed Services of the United States.

He thought about running away into the mountains but he never ran from anything in his life. He considered staying in Pall Mall to see what would happen but he expected in that case they'd send soldiers after him, which could start a fight in the valley—the last thing he wanted to have happen. He didn't want to fight at home or anywhere else. So he bid goodbye to his mother, his family, Pastor Pile, and his beloved Gracie, packed a suitcase, and walked the twelve dusty miles to Jamestown.

He reported for duty to the board, then spent the night with Doctor Alexander in town. The next morning, Alvin and twenty other men from Fentress County were taken to the nearest passenger train depot at Oneida, thirty-eight miles by road from Jamestown. Alvin had never been so far from home before and though apprehensive and already homesick, he was soon eagerly observing the houses, roads, cars, and other sights along the way. In spite of the reason for their journey, all the men found themselves caught up in a spirit of adventure as they traveled eastward, into the morning sun.

At the train station in Oneida, the men got their first taste of doing things the army way. Having been hustled out of town so early, they waited all evening for the southbound train. Midnight came and went, and finally at 2:00 a.m., twenty-one young men—some of whom, including Alvin, had never seen a passenger train before, much less imagined they would ever ride one—boarded the coach for Atlanta.

Having decided at last to become a soldier, Private Alvin York, serial number 1910421, resolved to be a good one, even if it meant doing things that didn't make a lot of sense. He spent the first morning of his army life at Camp Gordon, Georgia, picking up cigarette butts. "I thought that was pretty hard as I didn't smoke," he wrote in his small pocket diary, "but I did it just the same."

York had begun keeping a journal in a palm-sized red clothbound notebook he always carried. He had written little in his life before and the only two books he ever read by then were the Bible and a biography of Jesse James. Unschooled though he was, he was a man of order and intelligence. Somehow he felt compelled to record his thoughts of his army experience. On the first page he wrote, "A history of the places where I have bin," and made his first entry the day his draft registration notice came: "Pall Mall, Tennessee. Well, the first notice I received was to go and register. So I did, and then I begin to think that I was going to be called to be examined."

He made intermittent entries from then on. At Camp Gordon he wrote as time allowed, recording in a few sentences what happened and his observations. The flat, sandy country of Georgia depressed him. "There ain't no strength or seasoning in it," he recalled later. "It shore needs hills and mountains most awful bad."

He was assigned to the 21st Training Battalion, enduring the routine of army life without complaint and determined to learn. After two months of squads right and squads left and policing cigarette butts, York was transferred in February of 1918 to Company G, 328th Battalion, 82nd Division. The uniforms of the 82nd were distinguished by a shoulder patch emblazoned with two capital A's, noting its distinction as the All-American Division. The name came from the claim there were soldiers in the unit from every state.

Twenty percent of the division were foreign born and many of those had only the slimmest understanding of the king's English, much less the drawl of a Tennessee mountaineer. Isolated both by geography and tradition, Private York had never set eyes on a foreigner before his assignment to the 82nd, and the sight confused and amused him. In his diary he wrote, "They put me by some Greeks and Italians to sleep. Well, I couldn't understand them and they couldn't understand me, and I was the home-sickest boy you ever seen, ho! ho!"

Major George Edward Buxton, commander of the 328th Battalion, was a blue-blooded Rhode Islander and personal friend of Theodore Roosevelt, who already had a first-hand look at the war as an overseas correspondent for the *Providence Journal*. He was also an attentive and sensitive leader, well-equipped for the challenge of turning his international potpourri of recruits into a capable, effective fighting force.

Making headway often meant patiently justifying American military traditions as commonplace as saluting. Some young soldiers saw the salute as kowtowing: a practice for the servile and a sign of homage to the undeserving. Buxton explained the salute as a mark of respect and friendship among comrades in arms. Afterward, saluting became so popular—hands flying to the eyebrow at the slightest provocation—the major requested the boys ease up a little.

The captain in charge of Company G was a Georgian named E. C. B. Danforth. Though he was a good four or five years younger and infinitely more polished than York, the private quickly came to admire Captain Danforth both as a man and as a soldier.

York's own 1st Platoon, the working unit within Company G that slept and ate and lived together, was one of the most diverse platoons in the All-American Division. Some of the men York bunked with couldn't write their own names and had no interest in learning how until Captain Danforth informed them if they couldn't sign the pay sheet, they couldn't get paid.

Company G was a rough lot. York remembered them as "a gang of the toughest and most hard-boiled doughboys I ever heard tell of. There were bartenders, saloon bouncers, ice men, coal miners, dirt farmers, actors, mill hands, and city boys who had growed up in the back alleys and learned to scrap ever since they were knee high to a duck. They could out-swear, out-drink, and out-cuss any other crowd of men I have ever knowed."

These loud, belligerent foreigners were a mystery to Private York, but York was equally puzzling to the Poles, Slavs, Italians, and other immigrants from the industrial powerhouses of the North and Midwest who had never seen a man like this tall, redheaded, steely-eyed mountaineer. He didn't drink or smoke. He didn't cuss or fight. He didn't go AWOL. They teased him about his behavior, but he would never take the bait. "I didn't want to fight nobody," he wrote, "and least of all American doughboys." Each eventually grew to respect the other's position and the bonds among these soldier-brothers began at last to strengthen in preparation for the great and inevitable tests ahead.

There were a handful of Southern boys in York's company and a couple of them gave him some small comfort in proving there was at least one thing he knew and they didn't. The two were trying to shave with the newfangled safety razors they were issued. One tried it on his early morning beard, shaving cautiously at first, eventually sawing furiously at his whiskers without success. "Anything the government gives you for nothing ain't never no good," said the soldier within earshot of York, hurling the razor in disgust. The other doughboy met with similar results and threw his razor away as well. As they stormed off, York noticed with a chuckle they were trying to shave with the wax paper still on the blades.

At first blush, army rifles were little better than army razor blades. York's initial impression of the rifle he was issued, scribbled in his red pocket diary, was, "oh my that old gun was just full of Greece." Back in Pall Mall, York was a crack shot and repaired mountain muzzle loaders in his father's blacksmith shop. His new army rifle was easy to load and shoot but it fell far short of his standards for maintenance. After a good deal of swabbing and polishing, he finally got the weapon cleaned up for inspection.

On the firing line, he observed more differences between his own country upbringing and "them there Greeks and Italians and Poles and New York Jews," who missed not only the targets on the rifle range but the earthen backstops as well. "Of course," York said later, "it weren't no trouble nohow for me to hit them great big army targets. They were so much bigger than turkeys' heads."

To Captain Danforth and Major Buxton, Private York was a natural leader, and they made tentative plans to promote him to corporal. However, in his personnel file in Washington was a pink slip of paper reading:

```
Conscientious Objector
York, Alvin C.

Desires release as he is a conscientious
objector. A. G. 383.2 Exemp. Religious sects.
```

Could a conscientious objector be trusted in a position of leadership?

York never mentioned his religious beliefs or his objection to war to anyone after leaving Jamestown. Following his denial of an exemption appeal by the district board, he pursued the matter no further. However, without his knowledge, Private York's mother and Pastor Pile continued to petition for his release from military duty and had some success. The War Department sent a form to York at Camp Gordon filed by Pile on his behalf, affirming York's religious aversion to war. The private was instructed to sign the papers and send them back. If he signed, he would be certified as a conscientious objector and excused from military service. Pastor Pile also helped Mary York file a plea that Alvin was her sole support as a widow. That form was delivered to Camp Gordon as well.

To the astonishment of all who knew of the situation, Alvin refused to sign either form. In reasoning through his position, he became convinced there were two reasons he should not fight. First, the Bible was against it. Second, he knew from his personal experience—in saloons and from the deaths of both of his grandfathers as noncombatant casualties of the Civil War—fighting was wrong. These two points were his justification for an honest exemption; he would be excused on those terms or none at all. The conscientious objector option, now before him in black and white, grated somehow against the soldier's sense of right. He'd have to think it over some.

A sense of mutual respect was deepening between Private York and Captain Danforth. Danforth appreciated the mountain soldier's honesty and sincerity and York responded to the Georgian's insightful leadership. One day when the company was lined up in formation, the captain asked if any of the men kept a diary. There was a regulation against it, with court-martial as the consequence, for fear a man would be captured and his diary reveal confidential information to the Germans. The commander stopped before York in the line.

"I'm not saying whether I do or don't, sir," the private said.

"But you know, York, a diary will betray you and your comrades if you're ever captured."

"Sir, I didn't come to the war to be captured. I'm not going to be captured. If the Germans ever get any information out of me, they'll have to get it out of my dead body."

The captain kept walking and Private York kept his diary.

As basic training drew to a close and the winter gave way to a temperate Georgia spring, Private York knew Company G would be heading for the war soon. Before then his inner turmoil about whether to fight or not had to be resolved. He didn't have the answer and Pastor Pile was out of reach. Perhaps Captain Danforth would help him.

After stewing a little longer, York went to Danforth toward the middle of March 1918 with the whole story, explaining his desire to serve his country and how it was at cross purposes with his interpretation of the Bible. "I'll keep being a soldier if I have to," concluded York. "I'll go overseas. I'll even kill Germans if you order me to. But I don't believe in killing nohow and it worries me plenty."

There were several men in camp claiming conscientious objector status but Private York's sincerity and conviction made him different from the others in the captain's eyes. This man was not a coward, not a slacker, but a soldier truly burdened with doing right as he saw it. Danforth discussed the matter with his superior officer, Major Buxton, who suggested the two of them talk with York together.

A few nights later, York was summoned by Captain Danforth to join him in Major Buxton's quarters. Before leaving his barracks, York knelt on the wooden floor to pray for wisdom and guidance. Then he arose, picked up his Bible, and walked outside.

The major's room, like most of the other officers' quarters, was plain and small. There were no pictures or rugs, only a bed, a few camp stools, and a trunk in the corner. The one electric light bulb hanging from a cord in the middle of the ceiling shown on a few personal items, uniforms hanging or scattered about, a water pitcher and tumblers, and little else.

Major Buxton greeted his visitors with a smile and invited them to sit. "I don't want to discuss this question as a battalion commander discussing it with an officer and a private," he began. "I want to discuss it as three American citizens interested in a common cause. I respect any honest religious conviction and am here to talk through them man to man."

Turning to York, he asked the private why he was opposed to going to war.

"Because I belong to a church that disbelieves in fighting and killing, Major."

"What sort of church creed do you have that tells you this?"

"The only creed is the Bible, which I have done accepted as the inspired word of God and final authority for all men."

"What do you find in the Bible that's against war?"

"The Bible says 'Thou shalt not kill.'"

"Do you accept everything in the Bible—every sentence, every word—as completely as you accept the sixth commandment?"

"Yes, sir, I do."

Buxton turned to Luke 22 in his own Bible and read aloud. "'He that hath no sword, let him sell his cloak and buy one.' Is that in the Bible?"

York admitted it was and rejoined with another verse of his own. "If a man smite you on one cheek, turn the other to him."

Buxton nodded in agreement. "Yes, the Bible says that. But let me ask you this. Do you believe that the Christ who drove the money changers from the temple with a whip would stand up and do nothing when the helpless Belgian people were overrun and driven from their homes?"

As a student of the Scriptures, Second Elder Alvin York had met his match. He and Buxton, with Captain Danforth joining in from time to time, talked and read aloud from the Bible for more than an hour, their shadows dancing in the dim room as its single bulb swayed in the evening breeze. Without argument, the men read back and forth to each other. York believed the Lord was with him in that little room, four hundred miles and a world away from the log cabin where he once read and prayed so many hours in search of the answers they were still seeking now.

York: "When St. Peter struck off the ear of the high priest's servant, Christ put it back on and told Peter to put up his sword. They that live by the sword shall die by the sword.'"

Buxton: "'For my kingdom is not of this world; but if my kingdom were of this world, then would my servants fight.'"

York: "'Blessed are the peacemakers, for theirs is the kingdom of heaven.'"

Buxton: "'Render unto Caesar the things that are Caesar's.' We must fight for our earthly government whenever its liberties are threatened. Christians have a duty to their leaders."

York: "'Blessed are the meek, for they shall inherit the earth.'"

Buxton ended the evening with a reading from the thirty-third chapter of Ezekiel, as the prophet described the duties of the watchman to blow a warning trumpet in case of enemy attack. "'Then whosoever heareth the sound of the trumpet and taketh not warning; if the sword come, and take him away, his blood shall be upon his own head. . . . But if the watchman see the sword come, and blow not the trumpet, and the people be not warned; if the sword come and take any person from among them, he is taken away in his iniquity; but his blood I will require at the watchman's hand.'"

Was York to sound the watchman's trumpet for the innocent Belgians and French being slaughtered in their homes? At the moment he felt more confused than ever. Before rising to leave, York said a short silent prayer. As he looked up, his eyes met the major's and York realized the man's smile reminded him greatly of his father's.

"I'd like some time to think it over, Major," said York. "In the meantime I'll go on just as I have been, doing everything I'm told to do and trying to be a good soldier."

"Take all the time you like," replied Major Buxton, shaking hands, "and come to me any time you need to." The major also lent York a copy of *The History of the United States*, suggesting he read about the lives of great Christian patriots who had gone before: Washington, Adams, Madison, and others.

Captain Danforth escorted the private back to his quarters, where York lay awake praying and pondering the evening's events until reveille. The next morning he wrote in his little diary:

> *Camp Gordon, Georgia. Oh, these were trying hours for a boy like me, trying to live for God and do His blessed will, but yet I could look up and say:*
>
> *O Master, let me walk with Thee*
> *In lonely paths of service free,*
> *Tell me Thy secret, help me to bear*
> *The strain of toil, the fret of care.*
>
> *And then the Lord would bless me and help me to bear my hard toils.*

York thought constantly about his meeting with Major Buxton but with all the commotion of life at camp, he couldn't find the solitude and quiet to follow the matter through. What he needed was the still, familiar woods climbing the hills inside the Valley of the Three Forks of the Wolf.

He applied for leave and received a ten-day pass. He quickly packed his small suitcase and headed to the Camp Gordon depot, retracing his journey through Atlanta by rail. In Oneida, he was surprised to see his acquaintance and Jamestown resident Wright Frogge, who had driven a couple to dinner there. Frogge gave the private a ride as far as Jamestown, after which York walked the last twelve miles over dirt and gravel to Pall Mall and home, carrying his suitcase. There was no way to know whether he'd ever walk the road again in that direction or not.

York had memorized several of the passages Major Buxton read aloud in his quarters that night and eagerly sat down with Pastor Pile to sort things out. They talked for days on end and held church services like they did before Alvin left home. "The Lord works in marvelous ways, His wonders to perform," he reminded himself, admitting if it was His will, God could use war as an instrument for His greater good. But instead of growing more confident, Alvin was growing more confined. His mother prayed with him and promised to help him, whatever he wanted to do. In what little time he could spend with Gracie, she too offered her prayers and support.

After a few days in the valley, he was approaching a state of despair. Time was running out, he didn't have an answer, and he saw no hint of how to find one. Talking wasn't helping; Major Buxton's book about American heroes wasn't helping either. Then he recalled a place he knew in the mountains above the river where he might be able to think matters through. From there he could see the valley in a single sweep and hear nothing but the water and the wind. Because it was a long climb, hardly anyone ever went up there. It was where in the past he thought and wished and dreamed about Gracie and where he sorted through his feelings about religion after making the vows that changed his life so completely one still New Year's morning.

He left his mother's cabin for the hillside, climbing higher and higher up the northeastern face of the valley wall until he reached a rock ledge below two huge, flat-sided limestone boulders sitting upright, side by side near the top of the ridge. Some people called them the Yellow Doors; to others they were Bible Rock. It took hours to climb through the grapevines and blackberry briars. But once he reached his perch, York could look across the whole valley and follow the course of the river as it collected its three branches beneath him and meandered off to the west. Pile's Turnpike and the Poll Road wandered along here and there and farm houses dotted the vast, dark, fertile bottomland of which his great-great grandfather Coonrod was once a squire. There Alvin knelt on a patch of grass and began to pray.

He prayed the rest of the day, alone among the fragrant pines and ancient hardwoods growing around the two huge rocks above him. As the sun set across the valley, he built a fire and prayed on into the night, sometimes to himself, often aloud, accompanied by the sounds of birds singing in the trees and squirrels, rabbits, and raccoons scampering through the woods. Any other time he would have grabbed for his rifle, eager to test his marksmanship and bring home meat for the family. Tonight his mind was filled with other thoughts.

Bedtime was usually soon after dark, but as the night deepened, York never grew sleepy. He asked his Lord to have pity on him and show him the light. He begged for God's comfort and for God to tell him what he should do. He lost all track of time as, one by one, windows of the dark cabins in the valley shone with the glimmer of kerosene lamps, and smoke began to whisp from chimneys as wives and daughters stoked up the kitchen fires to get breakfast on.

Expanding later on the single brief diary entry written during his furlough, Alvin described what happened next:

> *As I prayed there alone, a great peace kind of come into my soul and a great calm come over me, and I received my assurance. He heard my prayer and He come to me on the mountainside. I didn't see Him, of course, but he was there just the same. I knowed he was there. He understood that I didn't want to be a fighter or a killing man, that I didn't want to go to war to hurt nobody nohow. And yet I wanted to do what my country wanted me to do. I wanted to serve God and my country, too. He understood all of this. He seen right inside of me, and He knowed I had been troubled and worried, not because I was afraid, but because I put Him first, even before my country, and I only wanted to do what would please Him.*
>
> *So He took pity on me and He gave me the assurance I needed. I didn't understand everything. I didn't understand how He could let me go to war and even kill and yet not hold it against me. I didn't even want to understand. It was His will and that was enough for me. So at last I begun to see the light. I begun to understand that no matter what a man is forced to do, so long as he is right in his own soul he remains a righteous man. I knowed I would go to war. I knowed I would be protected from all harm, and that so long as I believed in Him He would not allow even a hair of my head to be harmed.*

As the sun climbed over the ridge behind him, sunlight spilled down into the valley, glistening on the river. He looked at his own cabin far below, then at the Williams house. He looked across the valley to where the path to Jamestown disappeared over the southern rim. Beyond was the road to Oneida, from where twin ribbons of shining steel led to Atlanta and Camp Gordon. With a prayer of thanks, Private Alvin York rose to his feet and began his climb down, singing a hymn as he went.

> *O God, in hope that sends the shining ray,*
> *Far down the future's broadening way,*
> *In peace that only Thou canst give,*
> *With Thee, O Master, let me live.*

He said goodbye to his mother and Pastor Pile, assuring them he would return unharmed. There was time for one more brief rendezvous with Gracie underneath the big beech tree. They said little, words being inadequate for such feelings. "I'll come back for you," he promised. "God be with you, Alvin," she said, her eyes glistening with brimming tears.

Taking up his suitcase once more, Private York left for Camp Gordon on March 29, in order to be on duty by the time his leave expired two days later.

When he set out on foot for Jamestown, Private York was in high spirits. He felt certain his questions were laid to rest at last and he could do his duty in war without reservation. But after a few days back in camp listening to other men in his company talk about war and fighting, he began to feel little ripples of doubt again. He felt absolutely at ease about his own motivation and that his safety was assured. But what of the soldiers in the line with him? What of the soldiers he might kill? What were they thinking? How had they reconciled their patriotism with their spiritual beliefs?

A further challenge to his confidence came in the form of a letter from Washington. Pastor Pile had written President Wilson asking him to release York from his military duty; someone in the president's office forwarded Pile's letter to York for comment and follow-up.

The redheaded private made no reply.

On April 19, Company G left Camp Gordon for Camp Upton, New York, where they stayed, with occasional reprises of "squads right squads left," until the last day of the month. That day they traveled to Boston, where Captain Danforth formed his company up and asked each man individually if he objected to sailing for Europe and fighting the Germans. To his astonishment, Private York, after all the talking and thinking the captain knew he'd done, hesitated to answer when his time came.

"I don't object to fighting, sir," said York, "but the only thing that bothers me is, are we in the right or in the wrong?" A short conversation followed.

"'Blessed are the peacemakers,'" concluded the captain.

"If a man can make peace by fighting, he is a peacemaker," York responded.

Again the captain asked Private York if he objected to fighting.

"No, sir, I do not," York replied in a clear, confident voice.

Chapter Three

The Greatest Victory

Alvin York, fighter, had come full circle. He was a fighter once before. Growing up in Pall Mall, Alvin got into his share of scrapes like any other boy. There was nothing at first to indicate he was any more or any less responsible than his peers. Farm boys didn't have time to get into much trouble. There were cows to milk, eggs to gather, hay to stack, horses to care for, chicken corn to shell, wood to cut and carry, and endless trips to the spring for water.

York's father, William, farmed the seventy-five hillside acres York's mother inherited, a last remnant of the thousands of Wolf River bottomland acres belonging to her great-grandfather, Old Coonrod Pile. William supported his wife, Mary Brooks York, and their eleven children by farming, hunting, and blacksmithing. For years his forge was in a cave where folks said Old Coonrod lived when he first came to the valley. Later a shed was built and William moved his smithy there, earning up to fifty cents a day repairing farm equipment and rifles, and shoeing horses and mules. Alvin enjoyed helping his father, tending the fire, and working the bellows as William pounded red-hot iron into hoes, hinges, and plow points.

Even more than working together, Alvin and his father treasured the time they spent hunting. Boys in the valley learned to hunt as soon as they were old enough to hold a rifle and Alvin had already earned a reputation as a crack shot. His father taught him about hunting dogs too—how to train them, how to follow them on the scent, and how to pick one particular dog's baying out of the rest of the pack. Alvin had his own red hounds and loved nothing more than taking them out with him for a day or night in the woods.

When the notion struck him, which was often, William left his work in the smithy and took Alvin and some of his brothers out for a day of hunting. Returning late, he would send the boys to bed, then work into the night at the forge, finishing work promised for the next morning.

In the fall of 1911, William York was kicked in the chest by a mule. He may have already had pneumonia when he was injured or caught it as a result of his confinement afterward. (Some claimed pneumonia alone caused his illness; to admit to being kicked by a mule was humiliating for a man, particularly a blacksmith.) The country doctor did what he could, but on November 17, 1911, William York died. Christmas Day would have been his thirtieth wedding anniversary. His youngest child, little Lucy, was not quite two.

Alvin's older brothers, Henry and Joe, had already left home. That meant Alvin, at twenty-four, became chief provider for his mother and eight younger siblings. His father taught him well at the forge and Alvin supplemented his income as a blacksmith by hiring out as a hand to other farmers for forty cents a day. His next youngest brothers, John and Albert, ran Mother York's farm while Alvin worked at the neighbors'. After supper, York stoked the forge and worked late into the night in the smithy. If he wasn't too tired or there wasn't much blacksmithing to do, he followed his turn at the anvil with a late-night hunting jaunt, tracking his dogs through the dark woods as they bayed after a fox, raccoon, or possum.

Alvin took his new status as provider seriously. But his new life also revealed a part of his personality no one had seen before. Alvin had his share of fights growing up. Following William's death, the fights grew more frequent, and Alvin developed a weakness for alcohol. He started drinking the moonshine running in a steady torrent from stills around the valley. Whiskey was more than a tradition in the hills of Tennessee;

it was a hallowed right. Men rarely drank at meals, in front of women or with their families. But when a group of fellows of any age got together, especially on the weekends, a jug was usually within reach

Drinking was a rite of passage and Alvin no doubt sneaked his first sips as a young teenager. Within a year or two of his father's death, Alvin developed a reputation throughout the community as "a real hell-raiser when he'd been in the corn."

As memories of his father's guiding touch faded, Alvin began drinking with his friends on Saturdays, and gambled a little too. A quart of liquor cost sixty-five or seventy-five cents, and a good time was guaranteed. Everybody in the valley went to church on Sunday but even on the Sabbath, Alvin began finding time to join his little group for a drink and a game of cards. In their company, he adapted their profanity, and their habit of smoking. Men in the valley all grew up chewing tobacco—that was all right but there was something foreign and sinister about smoking that kept it out of polite society.

Drink made Alvin rowdy. The longer he drank, the rowdier he got, and with his size and strength, he began fighting with his confederates more and more frequently. Since men kept a muzzle loader and a hunting knife handy as a matter of course, Mary York began to fear Alvin's temper would get him killed. After a typical binge, he stumbled home to the York cabin, its two simple rooms always kept neat and clean, with muslin curtains on the windows and newspapers lining the walls for warmth. Mother York was there to warn and admonish him, to beg him to stop drinking. She knew that, like his father, Alvin never left a fight unfinished. And she feared one day Alvin would get into a fight he couldn't handle.

Seven miles north on the gravel road out of the valley was the Kentucky line. There, lined up at intervals along that invisible rule running east and west near Static and Bald Rock, were ramshackle saloons called blind tigers. A blind tiger was where a man could get the most drunk for the least money. The owners of blind tigers paid their federal taxes and had their federal license to dispense liquor. But they didn't pay state taxes and weren't licensed in either of the states whose border they were built across. Down the middle of the floor was painted a white stripe marking the state boundary. Tennesseans came in through Tennessee

doors and drank their whiskey and hard cider in Kentucky. Kentuckians entered through Kentucky doors and refreshed themselves on the
Tennessee side of the room. Neither state's grand jury could indict one
of its citizens for drinking untaxed liquor in another state. Nor could
the grand juries indict a saloon keeper for selling untaxed alcohol outside their jurisdiction.

Other than drinking, gambling was the featured entertainment
at blind tigers. There were frequent fist fights; sometimes knives were
drawn before the matter was settled. Alvin York reveled in the thick of
the drinking, the gambling, and the fighting. Along with a few others,
he and his brothers Henry and Albert held their own drinking contests
on the banks of Caney Creek nearby. The rules were simple. Each man
started with a quart of moonshine, then they all emptied their bottles
at the same rate. The last one standing was the winner. The prize was all
the remaining booze.

Over the next couple of years, Alvin was involved in several public
episodes—the tip of the iceberg—resulting from his drunkenness.
Coming home early one morning, riding double on a mule with his
friend Everett Delk, York saw a white flash along the creek. He leveled
his rifle and fired, killing a pet goose. Another morning, coming back·
from a blind tiger near daylight, York saw six turkeys sitting on a fence
across the road. Taking out his revolver, he dropped them all with six
shots. He was arraigned before the local court but the charges were
dropped after he paid for the birds.

York was in court another time for selling weapons illegally. Again,
he finessed his way out of being charged, claiming he was not actually
selling the rifle in question, just delivering it for someone else. One
Sunday morning he got into a knife fight over a girl. He and his adver-
sary were both hungover from a long night of moonshining, and friends
separated them before they could do each other any serious harm.

Mother York's efforts to steer Alvin in the right direction continued
in vain. She reminded him of how his father had worked so selflessly for
them. He never drank or gambled and here Alvin was wasting his life
with no regard for his father's teachings or his mother's heartache. He
was twenty-seven, wild-spirited, rude, belligerent, with no wife and no

prospects for marriage (who would have him?), and his future promised to be hard and short.

Mother York always prayed for her children, and the wilder Alvin became the more she prayed. She tried to tell him about the Good Shepherd and the Golden Rule. She might as well have been talking to a big, redheaded horse. Still, time after time when she heard Alvin stumble in and collapse into bed as the first light of day filtered into her cabin, she prayed a mother's prayer of desperate hope.

The Wolf River church Mother York attended was built by the Methodists. A simple white wooden building with a small porch and a steeple, it was the only church in the valley, and the only church many of its residents ever saw. Across the road to the east, on rolling hills of dark green, was the Wolf River Cemetery, with gravestones marking the generations of families who settled, stayed, and worked the fertile soil: Pile, Williams, Wright, Delk, Conatser, Frogge, Brooks, Mullinix, Rains.

In addition to spiritual nurturing, church events also provided a large measure of the local entertainment, particularly at revival time. In a place where outside diversions were precious and rare, a church revival was a grand occasion. Families traveled from all across the valley and up the mountains on every side. They came in buggies, hay wagons, buckboards, on horseback, and on foot. The children came, too, to play with friends and family they didn't see regularly, and their parents hoped, to sit quietly in church, and let at least something of the message soak in.

Revival sermons were straightforward and unadorned, appropriate for practical working people with no place for ivory tower theology but plenty of room for a God who would steer them through the troubles of life. And while the teaching was basic in content, it was rich in delivery. Pacing, gesturing, and stabbing the air, the visiting evangelists called Satan to task, exhorted the members of his congregation to trust in the Lord, and encouraged them to lift their eyes beyond the valley ridge to the spiritual and infinite.

After the service, families spread quilts and blankets on the ground and unpacked woven baskets laden with cold fried chicken and ham, tomatoes, cucumbers, onions, green beans, corn on the cob, fresh bread, and pies. The children were sent to the spring for water to complete the feast. On Sundays or on weeknights in the summer, the congregation would linger for hours after the service, catching up on local gossip while the children played and the older boys and girls teased each other, taking advantage of the rare pleasure of having the opposite sex close by without the distraction of chores. As the days grew shorter toward autumn, weeknight revival dinners became more abbreviated, often relocated to a house nearby, where the kerosene lamps filled the rooms with golden light, and friends crowded every available surface with plates and serving dishes.

Local news, gossip, and politics were uppermost in the minds of the people as they gathered after the service. What happened at the county seat in Jamestown received somewhat less attention. News from Nashville, 130 miles and two days away by wagon and railroad, seemed less crucial still. World events, having no bearing whatever on the lives or fortunes of the people here, were distant matters not much worth bothering about.

One world event did percolate its way into the fringes of conversations in the valley in those days, having filtered down from London and New York to Nashville on the news wire. There was a big war overseas. Details were confusing, but the short version was that the nephew of the emperor of Austria was assassinated in broad daylight, he and his wife shot dead as their automobile paraded down a city street. That triggered alliances setting off a chain of war declarations in August all over Europe.

As required by treaties and traditions, Pall Mall's ancestral kin in Great Britain declared war against Germany, Austria-Hungary, and Turkey. Other countries were jumping in on both sides. In October, the Germans and the French, failing to outflank each other as Germany invaded France, reached a stalemate along a line of battle running northwest-southeast through the French countryside north of Paris. For protection from enemy artillery and small arms fire in the flat terrain, both sides made trenches to shoot from. Because the two armies were dug in and neither could advance, the soldiers began literally living in the networks of ditches excavated on either side of the skirmish line. Trench warfare, they called it.

Meanwhile, Mary York kept up her own battle for her boy Alvin. He shot up a tree outside the church one Sunday morning, disturbing the service inside. The next week he went to a basket dinner and got drunk on moonshine. Basket dinners were supposed to be a special treat—social events where eligible young girls prepared a picnic dinner for two, and the young men bid for the lunch and company. York grew loud and rambunctious, which his family found particularly embarrassing at a time when all the other single men were on their best behavior.

One night after another long evening of drinking and fighting, Alvin lurched into the house after midnight and found his mother sitting in her rocking chair by the fire instead of in bed as she invariably was at such an hour. He never remembered her waiting up before. Her steely gaze, intensified by the firelight, stopped him in his tracks.

"Why don't you go lie down?" he asked.

"I can't lie down," Mother York answered. "I don't know what's going to become of you when you are out drinking and so I wait until you come in.

"Alvin," she continued softly, "when are you going to be a man like your father and your grandfather?"

Through all the years of scolding him about his drinking she never mentioned his father and grandfather that way before. His father's honesty and fairness were almost legendary in Pall Mall, to the point he often served as a mediator in community disputes. Alvin never knew his grandfather but heard the story of his final expressions of love for his wife and children as he faced certain death at the hands of Confederate vigilantes.

These were the ancestors whose blood ran in Alvin's veins—honest, good men who believed in what was right and lived their lives accordingly. Alvin was that way once but in the three years since his father's death, he had drifted steadily toward a life of ruin.

In the instant after his mother spoke, Alvin's mind raced wildly, replaying the years of drinking and fighting, revealing to him clearly for the first time the hollowness and hopelessness of such a life.

"God just took ahold of my life," he later recalled. "My little old mother had been praying for me for so long and I guess the Lord finally decided to answer her." He fell to his knees and put his head in his mother's lap, his thick farmer's hands held in her bony fingers toughened by long years of carding, spinning, and household duties. It was still and quiet inside the cabin, with the warmth and light from the fireplace embracing mother and son. After a moment Alvin looked up and through his own tears of joy, saw she was crying too. He could never remember seeing her cry before.

As though looking in a mirror for the first time, Alvin saw himself as a selfish, reckless, irresponsible man deserving of his mother's rebuke and his Creator's wrath. His wanton, careless life was shattered on the spot and left behind forever.

"Mother," Alvin said after a moment, "I promise you tonight that I will never drink again as long as I live. I will never smoke or chew again. I will never gamble again. I will never cuss or fight again. I will live the life God wants me to live."

Mary York smiled. "I know you will, son," she said simply. It was early on New Year's Day, 1915, the dawn of a new life for Alvin York.

York's newfound spiritual conviction made him particularly anxious to attend a revival later in the winter by a traveling evangelist named Melvin H. Russell, a minister of the Church of Christ in Christian Union. In the footsteps of a sturdy class of preachers called saddlebaggers, Russell came from Ohio through Kentucky and Indiana to teach and preach in the isolated mountains of Tennessee. The population there was sparse and poor, and there wasn't enough money to hire a full-time preacher. Saddlebaggers were circuit riders or traveling evangelists who came into town to hold revivals, usually for a week, with the last service on Sunday morning, aimed at reviving the community's religious conviction and its people's resolve to live life according to the teachings of the Bible. These men rode from one settlement to the next on horseback, saddlebags bulging with flyers, tracts, books, Bibles, and their preaching suits.

Russell arrived in the middle of winter, when days were short and farm work was less demanding, leaving more time for church attendance. By lamp-lighting time on the first night, families were washed, changed, and on their way to the little white Methodist church to hear Reverend Russell tell them about the tortures of hell and the promise of heaven through salvation. Russell was assisted each evening in the service by Pastor Pile.

Though he had been to plenty of revivals in the past, Alvin found himself spiritually moved as never before. His New Year's experience left him with a new eagerness to understand God and His plans. He wanted to know about the Bible—what it said, what it meant, how it instructed him to live his life. He was ready to begin a new life in the church. Russell impressed York with his "true speaking of the scriptures" and stories of punishment for the wicked and a place of happiness for those who are in Jesus Christ.

Other revivals had their converts, but Reverend Russell brought more people to the faith every year than any other preacher anyone could remember. A number of York's neighbors walked down the aisle of the Methodist church every year on the last day of Russell's visit. Sitting in the pew that week, Alvin asked God to forgive his years of sin and selfishness. He watched every day as neighbors walked to the front of the church to give their lives to the Lord. Plenty of the people who came forward had a lot less to be sorry for than he did.

Before the week was out, Alvin York took his own walk down the aisle of that church and publicly dedicated himself to God. Like the apostle Paul, the things he once loved he now hated. His mother, brothers, and sisters beamed as they watched him step forward; the neighbors who had endured his wild years looked on with a combination of astonishment and understanding. After all, God could change anybody's heart, and Alvin's wasn't as wild as some.

Recalling the moment in later years, York remarked, "That is the greatest victory I ever won. It's much harder to whip yourself than to whip the other fellow. And I ought to know because I done both."

There was more to being saved than avoiding sin. A saved man had to do good. Alvin York embraced his new religious convictions as only a convert could. He became active in the church and began studying the Bible. He held men and women who called themselves churchgoers to the new high standards of moral propriety he found in the Bible and embraced himself. He spoke out strongly against intemperance and sloth. He prayed enthusiastically during public worship at the Methodist church.

Before long, his personal standards of conduct and careful adherence to the standards of the Bible put him in conflict with what he considered the congregational standards of the church in Pall Mall. Alvin decided members of the congregation were a little too lax in their observance of Christian principles. For example, his old moonshiner friends attended the church, thereby symbolically registering their approval of the church view on abstinence from drinking, but they remained moonshiners nonetheless.

That sort of behavior didn't bother him when he was one of their number but his was not the same life anymore. He wanted to be a part of a church that lived up to its own standards. He became restless at what he saw as passive hypocrisy in the Methodist congregation and eventually had the opportunity to join a church more in keeping with his views.

A year after his vow to Mother York, Alvin attended another revival, this one led by Russell and two other preachers from the Church of Christ in Christian Union, headquartered in Circleville, Ohio. Russell, along with pastors W. W. Loveless and Charles Alvin, left Monticello, Kentucky, by horse and wagon on December 29, 1915. They preached that night in the settlement of Cooper, then traveled the next day to Slickford at the foot of Bald Mountain, which stood between them and their Tennessee destination. They started up the mountain at 10:00 a.m., but the road up the mountain was too steep for the horses to pull the baggage wagon. The three preachers got out, took their baggage in hand, and proceeded on foot.

By 2:00 p.m. they made it over the top and down into the valley where their host, Pastor Rosier Pile, was waiting with a wagon and team to take them the rest of the way to his home. By the time they arrived at the Pile farmhouse at four o'clock in the afternoon, it was nearly dark, and they were dirty, tired, and very hungry since they'd walked straight through lunchtime. Mrs. Pile, or "Sister Pile," as Reverend Loveless preferred to call her, was accustomed to facing a table of hungry men and laid on a winter feast of ham, potatoes, corn, pickled cucumbers, biscuits, gravy, and apple pies.

Pastor Pile had organized the revival meeting and invited the three preachers to make the arduous trip. Rosier Pile was an intelligent and hard-working man who took his positions of civic and spiritual leadership in Pall Mall seriously. He was on the short side of average height, the heavy side of average weight, and had a thinning head of straight black hair. His dark eyes were alert and missed nothing, whether he was transacting business in his store or speaking from the pulpit.

A fine crowd gathered for the service the first night. Reverend Loveless saw a redheaded man coming toward him as he walked through the church door, "tall and straight as an Indian, dressed in a blue jeans suit and colored shirt." The man walked up to him, stuck out his hand, and said, "Howdy, preacher." It was Alvin York, whom Reverend Russell remembered walking down the aisle to dedicate his life to Christ the year before. York was there to lead the singing.

Loveless preached that night from the twelfth chapter of Revelation beginning with verse seven: "There was war in heaven." Michael and his angels fought against the great serpent Satan and cast them out of heaven. "Now," Loveless said, "the Devil is down here and we have come to make war on him and his angels in Pall Mall." His words fell on eager ears, the congregation shouting out its approval and affirmation. Alvin led the group in hymns, which they sang by heart with fervent spirit and enthusiasm. The service closed with a time of prayer around the altar, followed by "hand-shaking time." Alvin's brother Joe spoke for many of the townspeople when he said to Loveless, "Preacher, we have had a lot of good preachers in these parts. But I want to tell you something: you are the preachingest preacher I ever heard preach!"

The weather was unseasonably warm and rain pelted the valley on and off throughout the revival week. One or two nights it rained so hard the meetings were canceled. "The rain made much mud," wrote Loveless, "and that red Tennessee mud would stick to our feet like wax." Loveless had his overshoes with him and carried a sliver of wood in his pocket to scrape the mud off them before stepping into the church. Despite his efforts and those of others to keep the floor clean, mud covered the floor in a solid sheet by the end of the day. Every morning church members scraped the dried mud loose with hoes, then shoveled it out the door. Once the big chunks were out, they sprinkled down what was left to keep it from becoming airborne and swept it with brooms.

Meetings were held mornings and evenings and by the time the second session of the day was underway, despite the shoveling and sweeping, all the shouting and clapping would raise such a cloud of red dust inside the church that Loveless couldn't see across the room. From time to time, he would have to quit shouting long enough to raise a window, stick his head out, and gulp in a few breaths of fresh air.

Between the morning and evening sessions, the three preachers ate a big midday dinner at a different house every day. After the meal they planned to set aside time for rest, prayer, and work on the upcoming night's sermon. But by 2:00 p.m. every day, people would start coming to the house with questions, testimonies, and prayer requests. Soon the house would be full and shouting, singing, and praying would fill it to overflowing like it did the church. To get his sermon ready, Loveless had to slip off to a grove of cedars on the mountain slope.

At the end of the revival, Loveless organized a new congregation of the Church of Christ in Christian Union in Pall Mall with twenty-seven founding members. Rosier Pile was elected as first elder, and Alvin York as second elder. York saw the new church as an opportunity to put his faith into practice, establishing the highest standards of behavior and strict observance of biblical teachings.

Their work finished, the three ministers prepared to take their leave of the valley. Because money was scarce and much of the local economy was based on barter, it was the custom to offer preachers provisions in exchange for their services. That created a challenge in this instance, since horses hadn't been able to get even the preachers' luggage over the mountain to the north, and the preachers couldn't carry a still heavier load back with them. One resident said, "Preacher, I have no money, but I have something I want to give you." He led Reverend Loveless to a back room and proudly displayed a two-bushel sack of shelled hickory nuts. "These are for you." It was heartbreaking to the minister to have to tell him that shipping his gift to the nearest railroad station, almost fifty miles away at Oneida, was more than he could afford.

In view of the special circumstances, the church collected a cash honorarium so, in addition to room, board, and transportation from the foot of Bald Mountain to Pall Mall, W. W. Loveless received a cash payment of three dollars for the week. Russell earned two dollars, and

Peters, one. It was what the people could give, offered and received with thanks and respect.

Sixty-seven individuals in all attended the meetings that week. Among them was a blue-eyed blonde of fifteen named Gracie Williams, daughter of Asbury and Nancy Williams. She was a shy girl and beautiful in a natural, simple sort of way. Like most of those in attendance, Gracie was born in the valley, and her family had lived there for generations. She had known Alvin York all her life. For much of that time she thought him crude, sinful, and unattractive. But over the last year or so she watched Alvin change from a wild carouser who spent the weekends playing poker and drinking moonshine, into a sober, responsible man who not only attended church, but led the singing in a strong, confident tenor voice.

Throughout her life she had heard people say that a few days after she was born, twelve-year-old Alvin looked down at her in her cradle and said, "Some day I'm going to marry that girl." True, he made boyish overtures to her off and on over the years, but he was sweet on plenty of girls besides her. She didn't care for Alvin, and Papa Williams cared for him even less. That York fellow was rough and always fighting, not the kind of man any responsible father would welcome into the family.

As far as Gracie was concerned, Alvin's new attitude changed everything. He didn't drink any more, or smoke, or gamble, or fight, and he was an elder in a church that stood firmly against all that. She noticed too how he spent less and less time with other girls and more time talking to her. This handsome, muscular redheaded blacksmith was often in Gracie's thoughts.

For his part, Alvin's mind was set. He had an eye for Gracie in his wilder days, but she steadfastly refused all his expressions of interest. He wasn't worthy of her, and, deep inside, he knew that. Now he was a man of honor, a man of God, elected by his fellow Christians as second elder in a new congregation.

He felt a miracle change his life and ever afterward gave his mother the credit for never giving up on him. "My mother's love led me to God," he explained, "and He showed me the light and I done followed it."

This new congregation of the Church of Christ in Christian Union built its own small white frame church, across the river and a half mile or so up the road from where the Methodist church stood. First Elder Rosier Pile assumed the role of preacher. Second Elder York led the singing. The two of them also taught Sunday school. To polish his vocal skills and learn some of the finer points of his new calling, Alvin York, former moonshiner, gambler, and rabble-rouser, walked over the mountain to Byrdstown once a week for singing lessons.

Chapter Four

Coonrod's People

Yorks lived in the Wolf River Valley almost since the river first appeared in the records of settlers who moved westward across the Appalachians. The river was named after a pioneer named Wolf who established a homestead on a small island midstream. After he defended his land against Jerry Buck, another homesteader, the place became known as Wolf's River.

The valley was part of North Carolina when, on July 10, 1788, Governor Samuel Johnson granted a tract of two thousand acres "lying on Wolf River on both sides of a path leading from the mouth of the Holston to the ford of the Wolf River" to Robert and Thomas King. Changes in jurisdiction over the land reflected the growing pains of the newly independent United States. After the Revolutionary War, North Carolina, like other states, was assessed its portion of the federal war debt based on size. To reduce its obligation, the legislature ceded the state's western area, known as Tennessee, back to the federal government. Seizing the opportunity, settlers in the region decided to organize an independent state and apply for admission to the Union.

A convention was held and on August 23, 1784, the new state of Franklin was established. Within a year, it formed its own military, established a superior court, and negotiated treaties with the Cherokees.

North Carolina, alarmed, and possibly embarrassed by its renegade citizens, retracted its decision, ruled the Franklin government unlawful and, in 1787, renewed its claim on Tennessee. The state of Franklin was abolished and its lands were temporarily restored to the tar heels.

As territories west of the new United States continued to develop, boundaries through the land beyond the Appalachians were further revised. One redrawing placed the Wolf River Valley in Kentucky for a few months. But when Tennessee became a state in 1796, Grainger County, Tennessee, held claim to the Wolf. As the Tennessee government established new county seats and reworked the boundaries of their jurisdictions, the valley became part of Overton County. When Fentress County was established in 1823 from parts of Morgan and Overton Counties, the section of Overton including the high green hills and dark, alluvial bottomland of the Wolf was ceded to Fentress.

The entire valley was included in the territory reserved by an Act of Congress for veterans of the Continental Army. Land warrants were issued as early as 1780, though the soldiers had twenty years to locate and claim their holdings. John Sevier, a colonel who won victories against the Indians at Boyd's Creek in 1779 and King's Mountain a year later, was awarded two grants totaling more than fifty thousand acres by the North Carolina legislature in 1795. This unusually generous gift in return for service under arms was especially noteworthy, considering that eight years before the same legislature imprisoned him briefly for his role in midwifing the state of Franklin and serving as its first and only governor.

Indians shared hunting rights in the valley for generations. The Shawnee, Cherokee, Creek, Chickamauga, and Chickasaw tribes crisscrossed the slopes and streams regularly in their search for game and hides. Even the Iroquois from New York ventured as far south and west as the Wolf. By 1800 the first white settlers to establish permanent homesteads on the riverbanks had come west from Virginia and the Carolinas. One of them was a hearty young man of twenty-four named Coonrod Pile.

Of Coonrod's birthplace and early life nothing was known. Settlers tended to travel more or less due west from their ancestral homes to new lives on the frontier; many Kentuckians were born in Virginia, while a large number of Tennesseans were North Carolina natives. When Coonrod (occasionally written "Conrad") Pile chose his new homeplace, he thought he was in Kentucky. He likely never knew the valley's convoluted history as part of North Carolina, Franklin, Kentucky, and Tennessee in turn.

Wherever he was from, Coonrod Pile lost no time acquiring as much of the beautiful and fertile land around him as quickly as he could. He received his first tract in a deed dated September 22, 1800, from Henry Rowan, a Continental soldier who was awarded the property as part of his federal grant. The land was on Spring Creek, later known as Caney Fork, one of three forks of the Wolf River branching eastward upstream into deep, dark green mountains, their banks lined with virgin hardwoods above an undergrowth of mountain laurel, fragrant honeysuckle, rhododendron, wild strawberries, and grapevines.

Long afterward, valley residents would point to a cave they said served as Pile's first shelter in the valley, though his 1800 deed includes "a cabin by the name of Livingston's cabin." He hunted down a deer, the story went, killed it on a rock ledge at the foot of a hill, and noticed the cave as he was gathering wood for a fire to roast the meat. Below the cave a cool mountain spring ran with clear, limestone-filtered water every season of the year. Across from the spring he built his first house, using huge rough-hewn logs up to fifty feet long. In 1808, Coonrod received his first direct government land grant from Governor John Sevier, then beginning his sixth two-year term as governor of Tennessee.

Other settlers were arriving, including one young man who moved from eastern Tennessee and settled on the Obed River, into which the Wolf emptied, just a few miles from Coonrod's growing holdings. His name was David Crockett. Twenty years Coonrod's junior, Crockett had already served under Andrew Jackson in the Creek War, been left a widower with three children, and married a second time to a widow with two children of her own. He had a farm and a house in the valley by 1817 and was an interesting contrast to his middle-aged neighbor, who was immersing himself ever deeper in land deals and commercial enterprises.

Crockett was a great marksman and an equally great speaker and storyteller. His dashing past and effervescent personality brought him acclaim that penetrated even the frontier isolation of Fentress County. He spent only a few months on the banks of the Wolf. Soon his reputation and thirst for adventure drew him away and into the free-for-all of frontier politics. He was elected to the state legislature in 1821 and served two terms before going to Washington for three terms in the House. Defeated for reelection in 1835, he again headed westward in search of new adventures, this time to Texas, where his fellow Tennessean Sam Houston was waging a war for Texas independence against Mexico. Crockett joined a band of 180-odd other soldiers and adventurers in setting up a delaying action, allowing Houston to prepare his men for battle against the enormous and well-provisioned Mexican army. Upon receiving news of the Mexican strength, Houston ordered the vanguard force to destroy their fortifications and abandon the plan. The garrison refused and held fast to the last man inside a century-old Spanish mission compound called San Antonio de Valero, also known as the Alamo for the cottonwood (*álamo*) trees growing nearby in the thin, arid soil.

Both the county Coonrod settled in and its county seat were named after James Fentress, speaker of the Tennessee House of Representatives, who signed the Act of Incorporation for the county and was thus doubly honored for his trouble. Jamestown (often called "Jimtown" by its residents) was previously known as Sand Springs after the springs bubbling up through the sandy topsoil just off the town square.

With deeds to register and ordinances to write, a new county like Fentress was certain to need the services of a versatile attorney, and one presently made himself available. John M. Clemens was born in Virginia, married in Kentucky, and moved to Jamestown to establish a law and surveying practice.

Clemens soon stood in a position of prominence in the community. He drew up the plans for the county jail and the first courthouse, constructed in 1828. By then Clemens was the circuit court clerk, and by 1830, he was also the acting attorney general for Fentress County. He amassed enormous land holdings and saw that continued development of the county would be served by locating a new post office in the northern part of the county, within the Wolf River Valley, whose residents were hampered by the hilly terrain from traveling the twelve miles to Jamestown to send and receive mail or transact any legal business. There were a number of communities in and around the valley: Wolf River, Boatland, Possum Trot, Little Crab, Red Hill. Clemens chose a location near Red Hill inside the valley and named it Pall Mall, though if he named it in honor of the elegant tree-lined London boulevard running off Trafalgar Square, he shared his inspiration with no one.

By the mid-1830s, John Clemens was a revered public official and one of the largest landholders in the county. But he was growing restless and began once again to look westward in search of business opportunities. The land around him was bought up and getting more expensive, and more business competition arrived in the form of another lawyer in town.

Clemens saw how important transportation was to the development of Fentress County. Where roads were built, development was plentiful; the absence of roads drastically slowed commercial growth. He decided the future of travel in America and the increase of his own fortune were tied to river commerce. In the summer of 1835, Clemens, along with his pregnant wife, left a successful law practice and more than one hundred thousand acres of land to move to Florida, Missouri, on the banks of the Mississippi River, from where Clemens was certain his fortune would flow, and where their son Samuel was born.

Four years later they moved up the river to Hannibal, where they lived while Samuel grew up, began a career as a newspaperman, and went on to novels, travelogues, and international lecture tours under the pen name of Mark Twain. ("Mark Twain wasn't born here," admitted local residents many years later, "but he *almost* was.") Young Samuel never saw Fentress County but wrote about it in the satirical novel *The Gilded Age* (1873), coauthored with Charles Dudley Warner. Jamestown in fact played a significant though unflattering role in the book, cast as the mythical Obedstown.

By the time Fentress County was formed, Coonrod Pile had more than twenty land grants to register in Jamestown. Late in life Old Coonrod was one of the most influential men in the region. He owned tens of thousands of acres of prime bottomland, vast tracts of timber, a general store, and a flour mill worked by his slaves (Pile, like Clemens, was a slave owner). Part of the key to his prosperity was never to produce more of anything than he could sell to his neighbors. There was no way of getting a surplus to market, so he learned to spend time and effort only on what he knew he could sell or trade. He only dug enough coal for his own use; he only raised enough sheep to keep the neighborhood carders and spinners busy; he only cut timber small enough to float down the Wolf River to the Obed and cities further downstream on the Cumberland.

Pile's prosperity was reflected in his appearance. His many years of luxurious living, with slaves or hirelings doing all his manual labor, rendered him so fat he could barely walk. He grew to such an enormous size and weight that when he went out to oversee work on his farm he had to be carried in a two-wheeled cart pulled by oxen.

Old Coonrod was bold at the bargaining table and ran his properties with a firm hand. His only fear in the world was lightning. It petrified him. At the first clap of thunder, he would waddle as fast as he could to the old cave he discovered so many years before, outrunning his lumbering oxcart. There he would sit cursing the storm, to the amusement of all who happened by.

As his long life drew to a close, Coonrod wanted to ensure that all he worked for would remain to be enjoyed and enhanced by his heirs. He was so meticulous with land titles that by the time he died he had three separate claims to his property, which included homesteading rights, the transfer of the North Carolina war grant from Henry Rowan, and the Tennessee warrants he received.

Coonrod Pile died at the age of eighty-three on October 14, 1849, the most powerful man in Fentress County. He left behind a widow and eight children, one of whom, Delilah Lucinda Pile, married David Crockett's nephew, William. Another child, Elijah, married and raised eleven children on his one-eighth share of the Pile holdings. By the time Elijah's children redivided his portion of old Coonrod's farmland, their individual shares provided enough to feed their families, but they lived far below the grand scale of past days. The lawlessness of the years that followed distanced them even further from their former prosperity.

When the Civil War came, Tennessee sided with the Confederacy, though somewhat halfheartedly, being both the last state to join and the first to apply for readmission to the Union. (Personifying Tennessee's divided loyalty was Vice President Andrew Johnson, a Tennessee senator before the war, who not only retained his Union office after Tennessee seceded but served as military governor of the state upon its capture by Federal troops.) Federal sympathies were strong in Fentress County and many men left for Kentucky to join the Union Army.

Coonrod's son Elijah was too old to fight but was a Union supporter. Of Elijah's four sons, two sided with the Union, two with the Confederacy. Conrad Pile Jr., known as Rod, was, like his father, a Union-leaning non-combatant. In the autumn of 1863 he was captured and executed by Confederate troops. Jeff Pile, a Southerner at heart though never a soldier, was ambushed and killed by vigilantes not long afterward, on the way to visit another brother.

As the War ground toward its sad conclusion, General Ambrose Burnside, whose Union forces were posted to Knoxville and other areas of eastern Tennessee, moved his men through Pall Mall. One of them was a dashing horseman with thick, copper-red hair named William Brooks, who had joined the army in Michigan. When the military passed on through, Brooks stayed behind. He claimed he'd done enough soldiering. Moreover, he had fallen in love with a daughter of Elijah Pile and was determined to marry her and stay on in the valley.

The soldier won Nancy Pile's hand in marriage and accepted the gift of a modest farm from her father. William had lived in the valley for about two years when he got into an argument with a local man named Preston Huff, who many were convinced was the leader of the band that killed Nancy's brother Jeff. The next day they met again. Brooks killed Huff then disappeared.

A month later, Nancy Brooks, carrying her infant daughter Mary in her arms, went to visit friends. Evading the watchful eyes of her husband's enemies, she disappeared across the Kentucky line. Huff's friends knew Nancy Brooks would eventually write to her family in Fentress County. Months later a letter finally arrived. It was intercepted and revealed the Brooks family was living at a logging camp in the northern woods of Michigan. Extradition papers were prepared and served by a sheriff at the door of the Brooks cabin. Brooks was brought back to Jamestown a prisoner and held in the jail John Clemens designed a generation before.

Brooks never went to trial. The night he arrived, a mob took him from jail to a deserted stretch of road. They bound his feet with one end of a rope and tied the other end to a horse's tail. Brooks pleaded with the men to let him see his wife and daughter before he died. They fired a bullet into his body, spooking the horse to a gallop, dragging the dying man behind him as bystanders continued to take shots at the blood-soaked form.

Weeks later, Nancy Brooks gave birth to a healthy son, whose hair, even as a newborn, was a fiery copper-red. She named him William. Mother and infant, along with young Mary, moved in with old Elijah Pile to make the best life they could with what family and resources the war left them.

Another Union sympathizer in Fentress County, one of those who went north to Kentucky to fight against the rebels, was a forty-year-old army veteran named Uriah York. York was already a seasoned campaigner who served with General Winfield Scott, commander of U.S. forces in the Mexican war. York fought in the Battle of Chapultepec, which ended with the occupation of Mexico City by United States forces in September of 1847.

Uriah heard the Mexican War called the only war ever fought where one side never lost a battle, and the other side never won. The Civil War was far different, especially in northern Tennessee where loyalties were so sharply divided. York felt it his duty to serve his country again. So he left his family, including an infant son, William, to fight under the Stars and Stripes. He saw little action before returning home sick with the measles. Hearing rumors of his presence, a ragtag band of Southerners headed for the York homestead. Uriah learned of their approach and hid in a canebrake where he and his neighbors protected their horses from army quartermasters on both sides of the conflict. York escaped his captors, but, soaked and feverish, caught pneumonia and died.

William York grew to adulthood without a father in the house, as did Mary Brooks. Both fathers were casualties of a war that demanded much from the families along the Wolf River. The peace was unsettling in its own way, as fatherless families struggled to survive, and bogus officials commandeered farms and property for nonpayment of Union taxes during the years of the Confederacy. Vigilante groups continued their occasional raids of plunder and frontier justice. Gradually over time, the wounds began to heal. And lives in the valley began to move forward once more with the rhythm of the seasons.

On Christmas Day, 1881, William York and Mary Elizabeth Brooks were married. He was eighteen; she was fifteen. They spent their first year as man and wife living in the old Coonrod Pile home, its foundations still solid, the fifty-foot logs tight and true. Mary's mother inherited the house and seventy-five acres, which she was pleased to have her new son-in-law farm, though ownership would pass in time to her son William. Mary's own legacy came with the death of her Aunt Polly Pile, at which time she received Polly's seventy-five acres.

Aunt Polly's farm was somewhat above the fertile riverbottom land the family once owned in such abundance, though it was sufficient for crops. The only building on the farm was a log corncrib Elijah Pile built across from Old Coonrod's spring and up the mountainside. Mary York never expected to raise her family in a corncrib. But such was her legacy and she and her husband set out to make the most of it. William chinked the walls with clay, installed a puncheon floor of small logs split once with their flat sides facing up, and made the crib their home. As his family grew, he added a second room and a porch. Eventually a kitchen and sleeping loft were added as well, and lumber siding was placed over the log exterior. There he lived the rest of his life and eleven children began theirs.

Over the next nineteen years, William and Mary York had eight sons and three daughters, all of whom lived to adulthood at a time when the death of children from accident or disease was commonplace. York gained a reputation for absolute fairness in all his dealings and was often invited to settle small disputes, the two sides agreeing in advance that whatever York decided would be impartial and right. Some even took to calling him Judge York and his wisdom settled many an argument that elsewhere would be fodder for a lawsuit.

What William couldn't seem to do, though, was to make a comfortable living. He farmed the foothill his wife inherited but he was as inclined to spend a day and night hunting in the woods with his dogs and his friends as he was to spend it plowing, planting, manuring, hoeing, or harvesting. Most of the bear and deer the Indians once hunted had left for less populated valleys, though rabbits, squirrels, and many foxes remained. When a dog picked up the scent of a fox, he let out a cry the other dogs instantly echoed. The sound ran chills of excitement through any hunter who heard it and reinforced the joy of being in the woods with a good rifle and a warm fire, as opposed to staring at the rear end of a horse across the handle of a plow.

To supplement his earnings, York taught himself to mend wagon wheels and shoe horses and eventually established a blacksmith shop in Coonrod's cave above what had become known as the York Spring. His reputation for fairness served him well and he had a steady business in iron and woodworking along with his farming chores. By the time his two oldest children, Henry and Joseph, were grown and gone, York had enough blacksmithing business to keep his third child on as an occasional assistant.

Alvin Cullum York grew into a muscular six-footer with copper-red hair, who could turn in a day's work to equal any man in the county. Under his father's guidance, Alvin learned the value of fairness, hard work, and the importance of accepting responsibility for getting things done. His skill in those quarters was tested sooner than either of them imagined, beginning the November day in 1911, when William York was buried in the cemetery down the hill from his house, in the shadow of the little Methodist church.

Chapter Five

Taking Aim

Like his seven brothers and three sisters, Alvin Cullum York was born in the cabin his father fashioned out of Elijah Pile's corncrib. His birthday was December 13, 1887, two and a half years after his brother Joe, three and a half years before John Samuel. As a young boy, Alvin helped his mother around the house, stacking firewood, carrying water, and seeing to the babies while Mary York cooked and tended the hearth. As he grew bigger and stronger, he began helping his father set tobacco, hoe corn, and plow behind a mule. Like other mountain boys, he was known to run from his chores on occasion, which usually produced a dose of "hickory tea" upon his return, applied to the seat of his pants with a long switch freshly cut for the purpose.

School was a luxury Wolf River families could ill afford, either in terms of money or of time away from chores. The community had one school, which was open for two or three months every summer, except for weeks when the children were needed at home for bringing in crops and foddering. Winter school was out of the question, even if there was money enough, since the creeks were too cold to wade across and nobody had a coat. The one-room schoolhouse contained no classroom texts or furniture, except benches made from split logs with pegs mortised into the bottoms for legs. If students had the luxury of pencils or chalk to write sums or spelling words, they wrote on the skin above their knees as they sat. Alvin attended several weeks of schooling every summer for four or five years. After that he was obliged to take on his share of the family work.

On a good day, his father made fifty cents blacksmithing. His mother brought in a few cents of her own by carding and spinning wool and taking in laundry. Sometimes in exchange for the washing, neighbors would give Mary York old clothes, which she would patch up to supplement what little they could buy, especially when the weather turned cold and the wind whipped in over the mountains. Everybody in the family had one fine cotton shirt but it was to be worn strictly on Sunday. In the winter, Alvin and some of his brothers wore shoes their father made in his smithy from scraps of cowhide and brass. They were so stiff in the morning they had to be warmed in front of the fire before the boys could put them on, and they still took hide off their heels when they walked.

Alvin got his first pair of store-bought Sunday shoes, size ten, when he was sixteen. They were the lightest, softest, grandest shoes he ever felt, and he laced them up with pride the following Sunday, looking forward to the chance to show them off a little at church. As he walked, he kept looking down at them and felt certain everyone else joining him on the road along the way was admiring them as much as he was. Before he reached the church, it started to rain, turning the red clay road into a sticky muck. Alvin heard a sound and looked behind him to see one of his shoe heels disappearing beneath the muddy surface. He scooped it up and put it in his pocket. Shortly the other shoe followed suit and Alvin put the second heel in his other pocket. By the time he got to church, his prized shoes were hardly worth showing off, and his shirt and pants were drenched and muddy besides.

Alvin and his father, along with most of the other men and boys in the county, spent Saturdays at the shooting matches held above the York Spring where the swell of the mountain slope made a flat table of land. The oak and beech trees were cleared from an area 150 yards long running parallel to the valley, and perhaps forty or fifty yards wide. The target end was a little wider, allowing the sunlight to fall full on the line where the marksmen drew their beads.

Fifty or more gathered on an average day, a crowd by valley standards. They carried their long rifles, powder horns, and leather pouches, which contained lead, bullet molds, cotton wadding, and percussion caps. Some drove turkey, cattle or sheep, which served as prizes. They called their heavy muzzle loaders "hog rifles," though no one could remember why. They could be longer than a man was tall and weigh fifteen pounds or more. Some of the guns were generations old, but at close range, they were still among the most accurate weapons ever designed.

Often the first event of the day was the long-range turkey shoot. A turkey was tethered by a two-foot cord to a stake at the far end of the range, 150 yards away. As it gobbled and flapped around, contestants took turns shooting at the bird. Each shot cost a dime, paid to the turkey's owner. The first man to drop the turkey received it as his prize. Shooters considered this the time to sight in their rifles and steady their nerves for a long day of competition. When a marksman had a particularly strong start, the turkey might fall on the first shot, depriving the owner of his fair return. That was a risk he took. At other times competitors were slow to find their beads and the owner cleared a dollar or more.

Once the sights were adjusted and barrels warmed, the next event was staged at a distance of forty yards. This time the turkey was tethered behind a log, so that only his head and red waddle were visible. The bird could hide behind the log, peer around it on either side, or pop his head up over the top. The marksman had to wait patiently then react in an instant when the head appeared.

The next round generated the most interest of all. Shooting for the beef cost a dollar a shot—two days' average wages at the workbench or behind the plow—but for the winner, the payoff was enough meat to feed a family for a month or more. Each contestant prepared his own target by charring a scrap of wood over a fire of twigs, then marking an X about two inches high with a knife blade. The intersecting lines cut through the burnt surface to the raw wood underneath, producing bright but extremely fine lines contrasting with the blackened area. Because marksmanship standards were so high, the men established an elaborate ritual for sighting in their rifles before every round. That way the only variable was shooting skill.

The first step in sighting in was to place the wooden targets in position, then cover the X marks with small squares of white paper. Each square had a notch cut out of the bottom, producing a triangle shape, point up, about half an inch high. This allowed the marksman to raise his foresight up the charred surface revealed in the notch until the hairline fit into the tip of the triangle. After a few practice shots, the marksman drew his bead dead on the notch and fired once. The resulting bullet hole revealed where on that particular day, with those winds and temperature, a shot perfectly sighted on the notch would make a hole in the paper. Typically the hole was an inch or less from the triangle tip. The paper was then repositioned so the center of the X carved on the charred wood behind it showed through the hole. A second smaller piece of paper was slipped under the first to hide the hole and the X it revealed. With the pieces of paper properly placed, every time the rifleman sighted his shot perfectly, it would go through the old hole, through the new paper, and hit the center of the X.

Contestants had the option of shooting from a "chunk"—any sort of rifle support such as a tree limb, stump, log, or forked stick driven into the ground—or offhand. Chunkers shot from forty yards, offhand shooters from twenty-seven. The offhand shooters looked on the rest with good-natured disdain but the concession to allow them was necessary. Otherwise, not enough men would risk a dollar to produce the minimum pot the owner of the beef required.

The technique for firing the long, heavy hog rifles developed through many years of trial and error. To a stranger it looked uncomfortable and bizarre, but there was no argument regarding its accuracy. Once the powder and ball were rammed and the percussion cap carefully primed, the marksman lifted the rifle to his shoulder. He gripped the forestock firmly and cocked the elbow of his trigger arm high in the air for balance and stability. He then brought the gun barrel up slowly from below the target, arching his back until the long, heavy weapon was in balance. He continued moving the sight up toward the tip of the triangle, held his breath, and fired.

There were no restrictions on the behavior of spectators or contestants, and pestering from the gallery was raised to an art form. Each man in turn was subject to a steady stream of commentary, advice, and ribbing as he took his place at the firing line. The hat-waving, singing, dancing, and carousing tested a man's concentration as the target tested his aim.

Just hitting the X was seldom sufficient for victory. Usually a number of men "cut center," their shot taking out the center of the X. The question then was whose shot had been closest to the exact center. After everyone fired, each contestant who claimed a chance at the prize brought his board to the judges. For each of them a rifle ball was cut in half and forced, flat side out, into the bullet hole. Using the point of a measuring compass, a tiny dent was marked in the exact center of the bullet half. Then the original knife blade marks of the X, partly torn away by the shot, were remarked across the surface of the bright, newly-cut lead. By using the compass to measure the distance between the center dent and the center of the X, the judges determined the winner.

The two best shots got a hindquarter each, with forequarters to the next two, and the fifth best receiving the tallow and hide. The beef was slaughtered and dressed on the spot, with each winner carrying home his share. It was said William York led his prize home on the hoof from time to time having made all five of the best shots. York was also frequently the judge who handled the compass, measured the shots, and made the awards.

Though the beef shoot was the centerpiece, there was still plenty more to the Saturday festivities. Shoots for sheep were held under the same conditions as the beef shoot, except these shots were six for a dollar, or "a shilling a shot" as some said, keeping the old Colonial term for a 16⅔¢ coin alive generations after the coin was gone.

Once the awards were made, the men who won nothing that day often stayed to shoot for a "pony purse," a cash prize determined by whatever amount the participants agreed to pitch in. They'd keep it up until after the long afternoon shadows ran to the horizon and disappeared completely and it finally got too dark to see the targets.

Besides the shooting matches, there were other amusements to be enjoyed in the valley. Log rollings were big community get-togethers, which served the purpose of clearing a field for planting. House or barn raisings were festive occasions as well. What each family couldn't do alone, families did together, invariably followed by feasting, music, and tall tales late into the night.

Corn huskings were popular with the men in the winter when it was too cold to shoot. Huskings could be held at night as well as by day; at night the men worked in the light of lanterns after the weak winter sun disappeared over the mountain tops. The host placed the corn he wanted husked in a huge mound in the center of the corn crib floor. Hidden at the bottom of the pile was a jug of moonshine, its mouth plugged with a corncob stopper. Men sat around the edge of the towering heap and began shucking corn, working their way to the reward in the center. If they touched an ear, they had to stop and remove the husk. Their goal was to get to the jug as quickly and with as little work as possible. The farmer's goal was to get as much work done in exchange for his liquid hospitality as possible. The result was determined by how artfully the farmer stacked his corn. With practice he could arrange the ears so that as soon as someone burrowed a hole part way through the stack, another load of corn fell from above into the opening. As the men dug toward the center, the tunnels would constantly collapse, yielding new barriers and producing more work. Anyone who was completely buried had to crawl out and start over again at the edge.

When someone finally reached the jug without causing an avalanche, the husking came to a halt amidst war whoops of victory (a sign to the women in the house that a bunch of hungry men would soon be making their way across the yard for the celebratory feast, having first sampled their reward). The leftover corn was shucked the next day by the farmer alone.

The sense of community these traditions produced was a comfort to the York family after William York died. Mother York continued to bring in a little money carding, spinning, and washing for her neighbors. Alvin, now the head of the family, put his two younger brothers John, twenty, and Albert, eighteen, to work on the farm, and looked for ways to supplement the family income.

He kept up with his blacksmithing, repairing plows and wagons, shoeing horses and mules, and even replacing worn or damaged parts on a neighbor's hog rifle from time to time. His years at the forge gave him strength enough to swing the sledgehammer with either hand, working in the modest shop his father built near the road running through the center of the valley.

If there was little prosperity in the settlement of Pall Mall, there was little true poverty. Many business transactions were in the form of barter: a turkey for a set of horseshoes, a bushel of corn to settle with the storekeeper. A valley farmer walked a flock of turkeys all the way to Louisville once to raise some cash, but that was the exception.

One of the few sources of hard currency was the thick forest covering the valley and surrounding mountains. A steady trade in wood products was possible because they could be transported out of the valley economically. Logs, lumber, barrel staves, and railroad ties could be cut and shaped by water power at the sawmill, branded on the ends with their owner's initials, then floated or rafted down the Wolf to the Obed, and on to the Cumberland.

Men who polled their rafts westward out of the valley and across the Cumberland Plateau sold their load in Nashville, the self-styled "Athens of the South," where steamboats from Louisville, St. Louis, Memphis, and New Orleans rested and rocked gently in the current, bows grounded in the soft, shallow riverbank in the absence of a dock. Pocketing their money and lingering perhaps to enjoy a sight or two in the city—the magnificent Romanesque train station, the elegant Maxwell House Hotel, the amazing electric streetcars—the men then headed eastward to begin their five-day walk back to Pall Mall.

Chapter Six

Miss Gracie

Gracie Loretta Williams and Alvin York had known each other since Gracie was born. She was the baby in the family, the last of thirteen children, born to Asbury and Alice Williams on February 7, 1900. Gracie never traveled outside the valley, so she tended to be quiet around people she didn't know well. Sometimes her shyness caused her voice to shake as she spoke, but her timidity hid a strong and resolute character. Her eyes were a clear, light blue, and she wore her dark blonde hair in two braids wound on either side of her head, sometimes interwoven with ribbons.

Though they grew up only a short walk apart, they paid no more than neighborly attention to each other until the year Gracie turned fifteen. Gracie was attracted to the tall, handsome redhead with his proud bearing, broad shoulders, and blue eyes not unlike her own. At the same time, she was repulsed by his behavior. She knew for a fact he was a drinker and a fighter and even if she could forgive these serious flaws, her father would never approve.

Asbury Williams didn't worry about the prospect of having Alvin York for a son-in-law. His daughter had more sense than that. His wife agreed their daughter should turn her attention elsewhere, as Alvin obviously had no chance of making anything of himself. They were unprepared, as Gracie's sixteenth birthday approached, for the miraculous and inexplicable change in Alvin's character. The card-playing, gun-toting, moonshine-swilling miscreant they dismissed out of hand was transformed into a sterling example of abstinence and piety. Gracie was revising her opinion of him and that had her parents plenty worried.

Alvin fell in love with Gracie before his New Year's conversion but did not pursue her because he felt he had no chance to succeed. The new Alvin York had a different view. By the time the tobacco was set and the corn was planted in the summer of 1916, he and Gracie turned their thoughts to marriage. Gracie's father would still hear nothing of the idea. In a community so small, this made courtship an imposing challenge.

To the lovers' rescue came a happy accident of geography. Upstream along the river was a footpath running between the York and Williams farms, dipping out of sight as it followed the riverbank toward the foot of the mountains. It happened to run near where Gracie sometimes walked in the late afternoon as she brought in the cows for milking. It also happened to be the direction Alvin might logically go as he headed toward the woods to hunt rabbits, squirrels, possums, or wild turkeys before sunset with his favorite red hounds. Alvin said later, he "most awful sudden found out there were a heap of squirrels along that old lane." More and more often, about the time Gracie would set out to get her cows, Alvin would whistle for his dogs, sling his hog rifle over his shoulder, and head in the same direction.

They began to meet almost every day, beyond the gaze of Asbury Williams and any curious neighbors who might happen by. And there, along a quiet lane lined with honeysuckle, shaded by ancient beech, hickory, and oak, they talked quietly of the future. Alvin gently pressed Gracie to name the day they would be married. She hesitated, worried about her father's disapproval, and affected even in love by the shyness Alvin found so comely and endearing. There was no hurry, and she wanted to be sure.

Each night after they parted and Gracie walked out of sight with her cows ambling alongside, Alvin watched her until she disappeared beyond the top of the rise, then turned and walked up the mountain to a log where he sat late into the night, his dogs on the ground around him, staring longingly down into the valley where the golden light of kerosene lamps shown from the windows of the Williams house.

Along with the rest of the able-bodied men in Fentress County, Alvin York got some good news earlier that spring. On March 23, 1916, the *Fentress County Gazette* carried a feature headed "Work Has Begun on the Dixie Short Route." A work crew had started clearing the right-of-way for a thirty-mile stretch of highway through Fentress County, a section of Federal Aid Road 28, running up the Sequatchie Valley from Alabama, across Tennessee, and on through Kentucky to St. Louis. The news was doubly good in that, first, there was a chance the years of isolation for the Wolf River Valley were coming to an end; and second, county residents who wanted the work would be given special consideration in hiring.

The article noted that Mr. Soloman, owner of the construction company, "says he is desirous of giving the local people a chance to do the working if they want to. If the people here want to keep this money in the County they now have a chance to do so. This is a good chance for any young man who wants to work to find a summer's job."

In the same issue, a Jamestown resident named C. P. Garrett wrote that the announcement of the new highway was only the tip of the iceberg of prosperity floating into Fentress County. A railroad was planned for the eastern end of the county and another proposed near the southwest corner; the lumber and coal mining businesses (lumber for export, the coal mostly for local consumption) were thriving; and now this new highway would station hungry workmen along thirty miles of right-of-way. Garrett's article concluded, "It surely looks like it is going to take a great deal of produce to supply this great host of workmen and their families. . . . The hint is simply this. Plant a few extra rows of potatoes, raise a little more garden truck of all kinds than you have during the past so you can have a little to sell. Also don't forget to set every hen that clucks, for workhands are hard on frying chickens . . . Let us get every loose dollar that's spent in the County."

Alvin was already working on Pastor Pile's farm for a dollar a day plus board, keeping up his own farm with the help of his brothers, and handling an occasional blacksmithing job. Nevertheless, the road work was appealing. It was good, steady money for anybody who didn't mind swinging an axe or sledgehammer. There were trees to fell, rocks to break and haul, dirt and gravel to grade, and more. The pay was $1.60 for a ten-hour day, making an hour's work worth about the same as a chance at a mutton hindquarter any given Saturday at "a shilling a shot."

Alvin had experience in road work. Though travelers in and out of the valley were as likely to walk along the bed of Delk Creek as anything else, there were a couple of roadways to choose from. These included Pile's Turnpike, named after the pastor's farm running alongside a portion of it, and the Poll Road. This was a public road through the valley that each able-bodied man in Pall Mall was expected to work on at least one day every year. There were no local taxes, thus no public purse to fund any road maintenance. Instead of paying a tax, which most of them couldn't have done anyway, residents paid with their labor, spending their Poll Road day clearing brush and fallen rocks out of the way, grading, or filling washed-out areas. The biggest rocks—some the size of a wagon occasionally fell from the cliffs—were left in place, the road veering around them to the left or right or splitting on both sides and leaving the rock in the middle.

Men who didn't want to put in their day's work could hire someone else to do it for them. Alvin, in addition to working off his own poll, worked off others for his neighbors on numerous occasions. His experience clearing roads and his strength as a blacksmith made York an excellent hire for the Highway 28 crew.

By the spring of 1917, Alvin was as happy as a man could be. He was strong in his faith and served his church as second elder, song leader, and Sunday school teacher. His neighbors knew him as a man of absolute honesty and transparency. He had a good job which, combined with the crops from his seventy-five acres at the foot of the mountains, yielded enough to keep himself and his family warm, clothed, fed, and secure. He had time to hunt with his prized hounds and spend Saturdays at the shooting match ground. And he was deeply and completely in love with the most beautiful, chaste, and desirable girl the Wolf River Valley ever produced. She even agreed, at last, to marry him.

Four thousand miles away in another forested valley, two ancient enemies fought to a bloody, exhausted stalemate in what the correspondents and politicians were now calling the Great War. Germany invaded France in the summer of 1914. Three years later both sides were dug in along the Hindenburg Line, a ragged scar running northwest-southeast through the countryside of northern France. Neither army could advance, neither would retreat. Temporary entrenchments to protect the opposing belligerents across the flat ground became permanent homes for tens of thousands of soldiers. Years of artillery and small arms fire felled and splintered every tree for miles and churned the soil into a gelatinous never-drying quagmire. Water and mud were constant companions. Infection, tuberculosis, trenchfoot, and other wet-weather maladies claimed more casualties than gunpowder.

The entire drama, for all its history lessons and news value, was of little interest to the residents of Pall Mall, Tennessee. That changed on April 6, 1917, when the United States of America declared war. Germany attacked France, and England went to her aid. America was stepping in to help the Brits help the French. With its factories and populations protected from the fighting by thousands of miles of salt water, America could send over a continuous supply of men and machines to eventually wear down the Boche. The Teutonic aggressors would be slammed back into place and made to pay just restitution for their imperial visions.

In particular, America got its back up over a secret message transmitted on January 19, from the German foreign secretary to his American ambassador in Washington, which was intercepted by the British. Secretary Arthur Zimmermann proposed to his fellow diplomat that if war broke out between Germany and the United States, Germany should persuade Mexico to declare war on America. In return, the victorious Germans would restore the lost territories of Texas, New Mexico, and Arizona to them.

The final straw, though, was the German declaration of unrestricted submarine warfare on January 31. After the first American ships were torpedoed, President Wilson asked for and received a declaration of war.

Diplomatically, politically, and militarily, there was a general feeling war was the right road for America to travel. Public support was high and even went so far in some communities as to ban the playing of German music and rename sauerkraut "victory cabbage."

America had seemingly limitless resources and manufacturing capability. What she didn't have though, was much of an army. Prosperous and at peace, the United States had no use for a large standing military force. Except for the brief and relatively minor Spanish-American War in 1898, America hadn't been at war since the treaty at Appomattox. In 1914 the combined strength of the standing army and national guard was just over three hundred thousand. A month after America declared war, the Selective Service Act was passed; it required men between the ages of eighteen and forty-five to register for the military draft in case they were needed for service. Before another year elapsed, more than nine million registered. Eventually twenty-four million registered, almost three million of whom were called up.

Registration cards were mailed to qualified men, who then had to report to their local draft board for a physical to determine if there was any reason they should be exempt from duty. If they passed, their names went into another pool, men found fit for military service who were subject to being inducted on twenty-four hours' notice.

One of those registration cards was sent to Alvin C. York, Pall Mall, Tennessee. It was the tinder that sparked a firestorm in the heart and spirit of a man determined to do what was right, if only he could figure out what right was.

Chapter Seven

Over There

Before dawn on the morning of May 1, 1918, the men of Company G, 2nd Battalion, 328th Infantry, fresh from basic training and ready to fight, boarded a Scandinavian transport in Boston then joined a convoy in New York Harbor for the voyage to Europe. Private Alvin York was seeing the ocean for the first time. ("I agreed with what Mark Twain said when he first saw it," he said years later. "It was a success.") Looking out past the Statue of Liberty, then through the Verrazano Narrows to the Atlantic, he had little time to be awed before the roll and pitch of the open sea began to take its toll. In his growing misery, he noted in his red pocket diary, "the Greeks, Italians, Poles and New York Jews stood the trip right smart. It sort of made up for their bad shooting."

The ship landed at Liverpool on May 16, and by May 20, the 82nd Division made its way to Southampton in preparation for the trip across the English Channel. During his few days in England, Private York marveled at the lush fields and neat, orderly houses and fences. To a man accustomed to the rough-hewn homesteads and rail fences of Appalachia, the mown lawns and precisely lain rock fences of the English countryside looked like gardens rather than farms. He figured

they must have special gardeners for every few acres to keep it all looking so perfect.

As he waited to cross to France, York began to realize this expedi-
tion was not going to be a quick trip. He and others in the company
hoped to dive into the fracas, get it over with, and get home. Homesickness was rampant and home was what the men talked about more
than anything. He had been in the army over three months without
seeing the Boche.

The order for the crossing finally came and on May 21, the
All-American Division embarked for France. Though the trip across the
channel on the HMS *Viper* took only a few hours, its effect on York was
considerable. To him it seemed more like a bucking mule than a boat,
rolling him around even worse than the Atlantic voyage. "Long before
we landed I didn't care whether we stayed up or went down, whether we
got there or didn't get there. I didn't care about anything," he reported.
He missed the sweet air and solid footing of the Tennessee mountains
more than ever.

After arriving at Le Havre, the 82nd was issued new equipment for
the battle ahead. The men turned in their American rifles for British
designs. York had grown fond of his old army rifle and was sorry to part
company with it. He cleaned and polished it enough to bring it up to
his own standards and became familiar with every piece of it through
endless inspections. It still wasn't as accurate as his Tennessee muzzle
loader at short range, but it was a lot lighter and much faster to load.
(York knew Fentress County hunters who could reload their muzzle
loaders on the run. He wondered what those Greeks and Italians would
have thought about *that*.)

The new weapons had roots on both sides of the Atlantic. With the
entry of the United States into the war, European armorers weren't able
to turn out rifles and rounds fast enough to supply the flood of doughboys heading for the front. Members of York's battalion, therefore, were
among more than a million Allied soldiers to be equipped with Eddystone rifles. They were based on the design of the 1917 British Enfield
but manufactured by Remington at its Eddystone, Pennsylvania, factory,
with modifications allowing them to accept American ammunition.

Each man was issued a gas mask. Even more than trading their training rifles for weapons of war, hooking gas masks onto their gear brought the fight suddenly closer.

They were also issued two new pairs of boots so one pair could be drying while the other was being worn. Within days virtually every soldier had thrown his second pair away, not wanting to carry the extra weight.

The troops were loaded into boxcars to begin making their way toward the front. On the outside of each car was stenciled "40 men or 8 horses." An enlisted man detailed to help load the cars went to the captain and said, "Captain, I loaded the forty men all right, but if you put the eight horses in too they'll trample the boys to death."

Traveling through the town of Eu on May 22, the men reached Floraville two days later. During their stay, the British commander, Field Marshal Haig, inspected the troops. The Americans were impressed by all the British polish and pomp and even more impressed at Haig's concern for their comfort after he asked a company cook, another tall Tennessean, if everything was all right. The cook said things were not all right because he had no salt. Turning to the quartermaster general, Field Marshall Haig asked for an explanation and was informed the last two salt ships were torpedoed by German U-boats, so there wasn't enough to go around. Haig ordered salt to be sent to the American kitchen immediately.

Still itching for their first sight of the enemy, soldiers of the 82nd were encouraged by the news that General Pershing would be inspecting them. They figured if they looked sharp and appeared ready, he'd be willing to send them to the line right away and put an end to all this waiting. General John J. "Blackjack" Pershing was only five feet nine, but, as one observer said, he was "tailor-made for monuments." Back straight, chest out, lithe and powerful at fifty-eight, he radiated supreme confidence as he stood atop the reviewing stand in a uniform custom made on London's Savile Row. York thought General Pershing seemed satisfied with them, which led the private to reflect on how far his outfit had come from the rowdy crowd he first met at Camp Gordon in March.

Continuing their slow progress eastward from the coast, the men alternately marched and traveled by train. York saw the city boys in his unit were having lots of trouble with blisters, but they kept up nonetheless. "They nursed their feet about as careful as I nursed my guns," he noted.

By June 20, they arrived at Lucey, where the men got leave and went into town for a night of entertainment. The All-American Division seemed to attract all the vin rouge, cognac, and pretty girls in France. As they moved closer to the front, the soldiers were feeling the tension building within. This particular night it all boiled to the surface. In one of the cafes, an Irish member of the platoon commented how he didn't think Poles could fight the Germans or anybody else. The Poles thought otherwise. They went at each other first with fists and then with belts, until the military guard had to be called out to restore order. Private York didn't see their behavior as bad; he saw it as a sign they were "just sort of full of life."

York seldom accompanied his comrades on their trips into the picturesque French country towns. Drinking and fighting were behind him for good. The whole time he was in France, York never had a drink, got in a fight, uttered a cuss word, or smoked a cigarette. It wasn't that he thought he was any better than any of the other boys, it was just his way of living. They did what they wanted to and so did he. His constant companions were his diary and his Bible. He wrote in one when he could and read from the other every day.

York and his platoon went for bayonet practice. The process stirred up deep feelings once again about the evils of war and whether or not it was right under any circumstances for one man to kill another. York knew the time was coming when he would be stabbing not at dummies set up by instructors but at tender, living flesh. Was it right to kill a German so he wouldn't kill you or the man behind you? York worried it was still somehow terribly wrong for human beings to take others' lives: "Though I knowed we were fighting for peace, still it made me feel queer to think I might have to cut up human beings."

On June 26, Private York and the rest of his company got their first glimpse of life on the front. After dark they marched out of the village of Rambucourt to take positions in the trenches for the first time. They could hear the rolling thunder of field artillery in the distance as they slogged through the ever-present mud. They passed by clusters of graves with rough wooden crosses at their heads, a fresh image of the danger awaiting them.

The road was packed with military troops and gun wagons going in both directions. As they walked, the men of G Company began to hear the bark of rifle fire and burst of machine guns. Occasional stray bullets sailed past them, German bullets missing the parapet and penetrating to the rear. They had never been under fire before and the sensation prompted a murmur of nervousness in the ranks. "They're only strays," an officer said, realizing that the bullets, having traveled all the way from a German rifle across the trenches, would be nearly spent. "They can't hurt you. Don't pay 'em any mind." That advice was wasted on those of the men who knew a bullet was a bullet, stray or not.

As they got closer to the trenches and the bullets came over faster and more frequently, some of the men began to duck. "It's no use ducking," one of them called out. "You never hear the one that gets you." The men of the 82nd formally relieved the soldiers of the 26th Division in the Montsec Sector and took their places in the line, facing the forested hills where in a few hours the sun would rise.

Chapter Eight

The Shadow of Death

The 328th stayed in the Montsec Sector at Rambucourt until July 4. This was a relatively quiet sector where new troops got their first taste of battle before moving ahead into No Man's Land. York was placed in charge of an automatic rifle squad armed with Chauchats. These French machine guns, known as "show-shows" to the American ranks, were wildly inaccurate, much despised, heavy, bipod-mounted monsters. York led his men on frequent patrols but they never encountered enemy troops. The only small arms fire came from snipers, whose bullets humming by reminded York of hornets or bumblebees when he'd robbed their nests back in Pall Mall. A lot of artillery fire surrounded them, most of it ineffective but unnerving nevertheless, and an occasional canister of poison gas was thrown their way. In the hot weather, gas masks were unpopular at first, until the burning skin and searing throat caused by their absence convinced the men that being hot wasn't so bad after all.

Throughout the summer, the 328th rotated in and out of quiet sectors of the front lines without engaging in any action. The men were at fever pitch, straining for a chance at the Boche. They were tired of waiting and wanted to get the job done and go home. York sensed the soldiers in G Company wanted "to go out on top of the trenches and start something." He wrote, "Those Greeks and Italians and the New York Jews, ho ho, they didn't want to lie around and do nothing. They were always ready to go over the top, almost too anxious." This eagerness could be deadly if the men outran their flanking support or artillery protection and such eager troops frequently had to be persuaded to wait for their instructions.

A desire to leave the trenches was understandable. They were cold, filthy, and constantly oozing mud. A sturdy grid of wood planks allowed for solid footing in some areas. Miserable though the men were, they were more fortunate than soldiers elsewhere, where the front was stalled for months and troops lived underground for weeks on end. As one machine gunner grimly summarized, "Lice, rats, barbed wire, fleas, shells, bombs, underground caves, corpses, blood, liquor, mice, cats, artillery, filth, bullets, mortar, fire, steel: That is what war is."

Private York made brief, one-line notes in his diary as his unit moved in and out of action. Beginning July 4, he enjoyed a rest in Cormeville; July 17, back in the lines at Rambucourt; July 25, rest; August 2, in the lines at Mandres; August 8, rest; August 16, the lines at Pont-à-Mousson; August 24, rest in Liverdun; September 1, back to the front at Pont-à-Mousson. By that time his little red book was full and he began writing in a black French one, packing the worn and dog-eared red volume carefully away in his kit.

As he went about his duties, York continued his musings over a Christian soldier's position as both a defender of the faith and killer of his fellowman. He was no longer worried about his own safety on the battlefield or about his soul. But what a Christian soldier should worry about, the private wrote in his diary, was all the men who "passed out into the Deep of an unknown world and has left no testimony as to the welfare of their souls."

The diary entry went on: "There is no use of worrying a bout Shells, for you cant keep them from busting in your trench nor you cant Stop the rain or prevent a light from going up jes as you are half way over the parapet—So what is the use of worrying if you can't alter things just ask God to help you and accept them and make the best of them by the help of God; yet some men do worry, and By Doing So they effectually destroy their peace of Mind without doing any one any good."

Private York often thought about these matters, carrying a New Testament with him always, and reading from it in foxholes, trenches, and on the front lines.

Aside from his faith, the other constant in York's life was his love for Gracie. He thought about her continually and sent letters and postcards from France whenever he had the chance, always with a return address placed prominently on the page and always with entreaties to write him back soon. Battlefield conditions didn't allow him to write long letters but he'd had more time while he was still in America. In his last letter before boarding ship, York opened his heart to his beloved mountain girl. Who knew whether there would ever be another chance, even if he felt God would protect him?

A slow writer who could spend several minutes on a single sentence, he labored over his work. The handwriting was not neat but was very carefully rendered in precise horizontal lines. He imagined how her blue eyes must have shone when Pastor Pile handed the thick envelope to her at the post office and thought of her sitting at the table at home, holding the very sheets of paper he had held in her delicate white hands.

Co. G 328th Inf.
Camp Upton, L.I., New York
April 23, 1918
411 2nd St.

Miss Gracie Williams
My Dearest Darling

I will try to write you a few lines to night as I have just got in camp and got my bed fixed and It is now a bout 930 o clock…. And say, Miss Gracie please answer as soon as you get this letter for I want to hear from you once more before I sail, ho ho. For I love you. So will only say I mean by the Grace of God to come back to you some day. And say darling, I am so glad to know that you have promised to be True to me until I come back. I sure will be true to you darling, and if I should never get back to you darling, you can say that your best Lover and your Truest Sweetheart is gone. But please remember if you meet me there you will have to git right with God.

I am longing to see you. But I will sail for france in a bout ten days I guess at the longest, and I sure want to hear from you before I go. For its you I love. Oh yes Gracie there is not a day nor a night but what you are on my mind. Oh I never had so great love for no one as I have for you.

Oh say darling we come through 11 states to get where we are…. We come across a lake area at Baltimore, Maryland and you couldn't see anything hardly but water. We come through Philadelphia City and New York City and Washington, D.C., Newark, N.J., and Richmond, Va…. Oh say darling if I just knowed what to do to please you and make you happy until I get back to you…. I feel that I shall be rewarded with a sweet kiss when next we meet. Don't you think so, ho ho…. But if I get killed you can say that I died that you might stay free. Oh say darling I wish that you and me had married when I was at home. Then I would have knowed that you would have been taken good care of and you would have plenty of money to have got you eney thing that you wanted. And say dear then if I never got back you would have got $10,000.00 Thousand Dollars and that would have done you as long as you live and then you could have eney thing you wanted…; and listen darling if I don't never git back will you go and stay with Mother? That is my request, for Mother will have plenty of money and she sure will take care of you and you wont have to work, only just help Mother in the house. Oh say darling I can't never be satisfied as long as you are talking to the other boys so please promise me that you will not go with one while I am in france….

[T]he first time I left you in November you know where we were at…. [Y]ou were crying and I asked you not to let eney other boys kiss you and asked you to promise me that and you said you would not let eney one kiss you. So I hope you will hold your promise and be true.

So I will close. But you know darling its hard to say good-bye sweetheart. But just think that I am coming back if the Lord permits and I hope he will.... So I will write you darling if I go to France. So dont think I will forgit you. So good-bye from your loving sweetheart, with a kiss.

Alvin C. York.

On July 19, York received his first letter from Gracie in France. Once two-way communication was established, he felt reconnected with his faraway homeplace. He wrote asking about who got married, how church services were going, the weather and the crops, and he always reaffirmed his love for her. At the battlefront he wrote short notes and postcards; from the rear he wrote long letters weaving in descriptions of what he saw and heard with questions about home and repeated professions of love and faith.

From Cormeville July 5:

I wonder what you are thinking of just now? Well darling I have bin in the front line trenches and I have just now come out for a few days rest. But when I was in the front lines I thought of you and what you said in regard to religion. You promised me to git right with God; and I offtimes wonder if you have made the change. . . . I have stayed in the trenches at the front when the German shells were bursting and bullets were a singing a round my head. Yet I stayed there Day and Night and I just trusted the Lord and I never got hurt. So if you will always trust the Lord he will always take you through safe.

He wrote Gracie from the trenches at Rambucourt on July 20, celebrating the receipt of his first letter from her following its thirty-day trip from Pile's store. After only a paragraph, he broke off with a short explanation. "Well I haven't got any paper out here in the trenches and I want to write Mother a letter so I will have to close with all my best wishes for you." Later the same day he continued, "I had to quit writing you for a few minutes. Just now the Germans was sending some shells

over there was 15 shells struck within a few yards of me but I never got
hurt. I am still O.K. So I close. Good bye."

August 18, from the trenches at Pont-à-Mousson:

> *I would just give eney thing to see you. Oh say dear there is
> plenty of girls over here but there is no girl over here for me. So
> you know what I promised you before I left. That promise will
> stand true until the end.*

Two days later he wrote of a dream he had about her being saved
at church and holding a prayer meeting. York, who once lagged so far
behind Gracie in spiritual development, now worried about her salvation, and recoiled from the thought of spending eternity without her.

> *Say dear I have bin praying that you may be a Christian
> when I come back. So I dreamed that when I come back you
> were a Christian and holding a meeting so hope that dream
> will be true, ho ho.*
> *Yes say dear you are on my mind every day and almost
> every hour. No matter how hot the battle gets I never forget my
> little Gracie. I wonder if you think of me that way. I guess you
> do. well darling I would give almost eney thing to see you. I
> am sure that we could have a fine time together. But say dear I
> hope the time is not far off when we can meet and be together
> as long as life shall last. Oh say dear wont that be a gloryest
> time when we can meet to be to gether once more? Oh say dear
> if I should not get back to you I want you to meet me where we
> can live in peace and where no more tears will be shed and no
> more good byes to be sed. But where all is Peace and Happiness
> and Joy and when parting comes no more. Oh say darling what
> a wonderful time that will be? Will you meet me there? If we
> don't meet in this wonderful world eney more. But I hope to
> meet you by Thanksgiving Day or by Xmas eney way should
> I live and I am trusting in the Lord and I know he is able to
> carry me through and I believe with all my heart that I am
> coming. So you may look for me, ho ho.*

These were Private York's thoughts as he alternated time on the front with time of rest in the calm villages to the rear. He also spent time attentively observing his fellow soldiers and how they handled the day-to-day challenges of military life. His previous life, he realized more than ever, was so isolated and unstudied. Even in such unfamiliar and unnatural surroundings, York found himself wanting to learn everything.

He marveled at the story of four men in Company G who were detailed to take chow to the front line outposts one night. They were given the necessary passwords and sent forward. On the way back, one soldier got separated from the rest, and even worse, forgot the password. At best he would be disciplined; at worst, shot. He hit upon an idea and waited half an hour until another soldier came along. He halted the man as a sentry would do, demanded the password, let the soldier pass, and returned to the lines with the password fresh in his mind. "He was a Greek and he spoke very little English," York observed, "but that didn't stop him nohow. I'm a-telling you that's soldiering for you. That's using your head!"

Arriving at Pont-à-Mousson on August 16, Private York looked around to see an earthly paradise. After weeks spent hiking across muddy roads from one muddy trench to another, the town seemed marvelously clean and fresh. It was harvest time, with grapes hanging heavily on the vines and apple branches drooping like willows with ripe fruit ready to pick. The Moselle River wound its way through town with a gentle rush. To York and the others, it was suddenly hard to imagine there was a war going on so close by. The verdant scene reminded York of another beautiful valley many miles away.

Private York saw the city "wasn't mussed up at all. It hadn't been shelled nohow." There was evidently some agreement between the French and the Germans to leave this idyllic town alone and it was untouched by four years of war. Food, fresh water, hot baths, and gentle sunshine were in plentiful supply, as were the attentions of the local French girls, inevitably attracted to the healthy young American men, and the men to them. Alvin York wrote to Gracie, "those French girls stood there talking and I couldnt understand a word they said. I didnt understand what they wanted until they showed me, ho ho."

Private York and his company reported back to the front at Liver-dun on August 24, then returned to Pont-à-Mousson for a break on September 1. To their astonishment, the city was completely deserted. It was emptied in minutes by an advance warning that the battle for the surrounding countryside was about to begin. Residents took only what they could carry. Beds were neatly made, tables set for lunch, and food still simmered on the stoves. Some of the Americans helped themselves to the best meals they tasted for many months.

Shortly after the 328th arrived, Germans began shelling the city, with the first hits landing in the orchards York so admired, ripping jagged holes in the earth, destroying trees, grapevines, fences, and store-houses. A little while later, York heard an explosion so loud he thought it was an ammunition dump blowing up. The sound came from huge naval guns the Allies brought into position. To York, these guns were "much bigger than tractors and most awful long." Each round shook the ground as it was fired, then emitted a high-pitched whine across the sky on its way to Metz, fifteen miles away. As the barrage grew in intensity, the noise was so loud the men couldn't even hear them-selves shout. Allied airplanes buzzed overhead, adding to the excitement and cacophony, diving and circling in dogfights as the ground troops watched in horrified wonder. One wary observer professed he would never fly, promising, "The only way I'll ever be killed in an airplane crash is if it hits me when it falls." Others nodded in agreement.

After a few days of being camped on a hillside on the banks of the Moselle, just outside town, York and his division were on the move again. The 328th was heading for real action at last.

The Germans, during their early sweep across France in the summer of 1914, punched a southwesterly salient—a V-shaped bulge in their line of advance—fifteen miles or so into French territory. At the tip of the V was the medieval town of St. Mihiel, which the Germans occu-pied on September 28 of that year and had held more or less quietly ever since. Now the Germans were preparing to fall back. The salient was important to them because the land it surrounded was a source of precious iron ore vital for manufacturing the implements of war. But four years of fighting, along with the arrival of fresh, well-supplied American troops, made the German commanders realize they no longer had the manpower to hold all their ground. This was one piece they could give up.

The Allies were inconvenienced for years by the interruption the salient caused in rail traffic between Paris and the Lorraine region. Now they could put that inconvenience behind them, while also tidying up the battle line in preparation for a final massive assault under the direction of the French commander, Marshal Ferdinand Foch. General Pershing, leader of the American Expeditionary Force in Europe, assumed responsibility for taking the town at the point of the salient, then moving into the Meuse-Argonne Sector for the final push against the enemy.

The American First Army, positioned on one side of the salient point, and the 2nd French Colonial Corps, on the other, would be dependent on British and French armor and artillery. Earlier in the war the Europeans pleaded for soldiers and small arms, which the Americans sent by the shipload instead of field pieces, artillery ordinance, or other possible Atlantic cargo. As a result, there were more soldiers ready to take on the Germans than there were American support units to cover the offensive. Most of the three thousand guns sent to take the salient were French. Along the front, American pilot Billy Mitchell commanded an Allied air force of nearly fifteen hundred aircraft, less than half of which were American. The rest were supplied by French, British, Italian, and Portuguese forces.

On September 11, 1918, the Germans quietly began dismantling their defenses at St. Mihiel, with the hope of preserving their troops and supplies for more urgent business. But Pershing was ready to fight. His army waited in the trenches for a day as the covering artillery did its work. An hour after midnight, on the morning of September 12, the big guns began to roar in earnest as the offensive barrage began. At daybreak the First Army attacked.

York was promoted to private first class on July 8. He received a second promotion to corporal a few weeks later and was made a squad leader in Company G. To him that meant he should be in the lead as his men marched, serving as point guard and drawing first fire. But no matter how fast he moved forward, the men in his eager squad kept moving faster. They wanted to get to those Germans. Battalion officers had the same problem. As the 328th advanced on the town of Norroy against stiff resistance from German rifle and machine gun units, a number of American soldiers were hit because they insisted on advancing too rapidly. They bolted ahead of the line of advance and were easily picked off by the experienced German marksmen.

Despite these early casualties, the St. Mihiel assault proceeded with surprisingly little resistance. Corporal York and his company moved through Norroy to a hilltop on the other side of town, where at first they found themselves too far ahead of their flank, with Germans enfilading them on the right and shooting at them from the rear. American eagerness and firepower quickly subdued the defenders, even though to York his squad seemed to shoot a lot more bullets at the ground and sky than at the enemy.

The Germans rolled back to the east, having already decided to abandon the salient and hoping to retain as many soldiers and as much equipment as possible, firing shells of poison gas as they went. York and the others donned gas masks and kept going. Once the town was secure, the Allies went from house to house, looking for stragglers to capture. There were no enemy soldiers left, but some of the men did find a cache of wine aging in barrels. Declaring these prisoners of war were old enough, they knocked the bungs out of the barrels and caught the wine in buckets, their hands, and directly in their mouths as it cascaded out. Thus refreshed, they resolved to head immediately for Berlin.

York's squad came upon a big house, locked and shuttered. They suspected it served as the German headquarters. Surrounding the building, they stormed it, only to be met by a whole company of rabbits. The troops captured a storehouse filled with Belgian hares.

The little town provided an array of bounty on the hoof. Heading back to camp that night, one of the soldiers was leading a goat down the road. An officer stopped the man and asked what he was doing with the animal. "Sir, I'm just going back to put a little cream in my coffee."

From their position on the hillside beyond Norroy, York and his men could see a vineyard, still perfectly neat and unscarred by the fighting, filled with inviting bunches of grapes ripened to their peak. A few of the hungry soldiers, mouths watering in anticipation, made their way across to the vines and helped themselves to the cool, refreshing fruit. A German observation balloon spotted the soldiers and directed artillery fire to their position with disastrous results. Several Americans were wounded, and the men were ordered not to go back to the vineyard.

Sitting in camp that night, Corporal York found himself thinking for once not of Gracie but of food. Disobeying the directive passed down the chain of command through Captain Danforth, York decided to sneak over under cover of darkness and have more grapes. As he walked quietly along, far over to the side of the road to avoid detection by his own sentries, a shell exploded nearby. Startled by the blast, York turned and ran—into another running soldier. The corporal recovered his balance and braced himself for hand-to-hand combat before recognizing, by the light of flashing ordinance, the face of Captain Danforth. It seemed the captain was fond of grapes himself.

"Captain!"

"Corporal York! There are orders in effect forbidding troops in this area."

"Yes, sir, Captain."

"I would say also, corporal, that these grapes taste mighty good."

"Yes, sir."

Side by side, the two soldiers raced back to their hillside encampment.

The battle was decided by the evening of September 13, and by the 16th the St. Mihiel salient was securely in Allied hands. It was an easy victory compared to most, but it still had its visions of death and carnage. These were the first large-scale casualties the 328th encountered. For the first time Corporal York saw his fellow soldiers killed by rifle and artillery fire and tortured by poison gas. He later recalled, "There is no tongue or human being who can ever tell the feeling of a man during this time. But I never doubted in the thickest of the battle but what God would bring me through safe. I had the assurance, and I have always been taught that all of God's promises are true."

The 328th could have continued its penetration to the northeast through occupied territory and on to the German border. But Pershing was committed to an offensive in the Meuse-Argonne region, up the line of battle to the northwest, where the First Army would continue to drive the Germans north and east, pushing the front more and more into a north-south line. Anchored in Alsace, the eastern point of the front was the hinge of a great gate. The western edge of the gate started in Belgium and forced its way down all the way to the Marne River during the first months of the war. The Allies had slowly pushed it back open since then and by September of 1918, they didn't have far to go.

Marshal Foch originally planned to press the Germans hard to secure a favorable field position as the weather worsened, then hold his forces in place until the spring of 1919, when they could execute a massive assault to win the war. But the successes of the past few months persuaded him that perhaps the war could be won before the winter of 1918 after all. His strategy was to throw a massive force of 160 Allied divisions at the Germans, with different sectors beginning their offensives on different days, thus frustrating the Germans' attempts to put scarce reserves in the right places. Foch knew allowing an orderly withdrawal would permit the Germans to destroy railways, bridges, and communication lines; burn fields and villages; and carry their war matériel safely back behind pre-war German borders.

The 328th enjoyed a week's rest in St. Mihiel and then began preparations to take their part in the American offensive. Their objectives, Mézières and Sedan, were sixty-five miles to the northwest. The first part of the trip would be easy, moving parallel to the front. But beyond Verdun and the Meuse River, the front took a turn to the west, falling directly across their path as it ran through a huge, thick, heavily fortified forest.

The Germans could thank the Argonne Forest in part for their successful defense of the Meuse-Argonne sector so far. It was densely forested and beneath the trees grew a thick tangle of underbrush. Unlike some wooded areas of the front, the Argonne had seen little action, so its trees still crowded and jostled each other, rather than being thinned and splintered by gunfire.

Moving toward their rendezvous with 600,000 other American troops and 220,000 Frenchmen preparing to attack Mézières and Sedan ("Everyone in the fight!" Foch had said), the 328th left St. Mihiel on September 24. They boarded a narrow-gauge railroad without being told where they were going. When the train stopped, the troops were herded onto a fleet of old white French buses. The drivers were French colonials from Indochina and the sight of them fascinated Corporal York, who "done never seen a Chinaman before." The sense of novelty was evidently mutual, as the drivers persistently pestered the Americans for souvenirs.

The ride was harrowing. The colonials had only the skimpiest training before being pressed into service and were erratic drivers at best. Moreover, they were in a hurry. The end of the St. Mihiel campaign marked the beginning of the final offensive as far as Pershing was concerned. Foch had waited until September 3, to make his decision and there was much to do. The American general wanted his men in position, the faster the better. When Corporal York mused the drivers "must have sort of had the idea they had to get us there before they even started," he was more right than he could have known.

Two trucks overturned en route but no one was hurt. Once he accustomed himself to the jostling and racket, York slipped into a reflective mood. Even in the trenches with German shells crashing around him, he was able to write letters to Gracie and to his mother. That same sort of calm enveloped him as his bus sped through the French countryside. War, he decided, produced a strange combination of emotions. It turned men into fighting animals but at the same time it brought out a tenderness from knowing each other as well as the men in Company G did after fighting together; sleeping under the same blanket; seeing the same charred and dismembered bodies; and trusting each other with their lives.

York loved the men in his company as Christian brothers. He thought their shooting ability was terrible and he disdained their drinking and carousing, but in his heart he forgave them. If they cussed, it was because that was how they expressed themselves. If it didn't interfere with him, Corporal York decided what they did was none of his business; he had no right to pass judgment on them. Maybe they thought they would be killed in the trenches, so they might as well enjoy things while they had the chance.

As he rode, Corporal York thought of the men he lived and fought with over the past year. There were some real characters in the bunch. His platoon sergeant was an actor from Brooklyn named Harry Parsons.

Parsons was a natural at commanding the variety of personalities in the All-American Division. He was a big, husky man who kept his platoon's spirits up after a long day with songs and stories from his theater routines. They would all laugh and join in with him and nearly forget how afraid they were or how much their feet hurt. The sergeant was relatively quiet and unassuming until he was riled. Then he struck an incredible stance, teeth clenched and chin raised, swinging with both fists at the same time. Somebody usually went down but it was never Sergeant Parsons.

Corporal Early was another scrapper. Bernard Early, a naturalized Irishman, was a bartender in New Haven before the war. He was a master at drinking and cussing and raised the act of going AWOL to a fine art. Early was once a sergeant but was demoted for missing one roll call too many. If there was a fight going on, whether in the trenches or in the bar, Early was satisfied. He was also, York saw, a very brave and very good soldier.

Early's best friend was Corporal William S. Cutting, an ex-iceman from a Polish neighborhood in Boston. He could drink and cuss on a par with Early and was hard as nails. York heard him say that if the Boche ever threw bombs at him, he'd "just eat them for breakfast."

Then there were several privates York got to know: Saccina, Konotski, Sok, Swanson, Muzzi, Beardsley, Johnson, and a few others. He saw them as rough-minded, rough-living men who were at the same time tireless fighters and tough soldiers. "Most of them were always causing a lot of trouble," he reflected, "but they bothered the Germans a heap more than they bothered anybody else."

Chapter Nine

Paris and Home

By 5:00 p.m. October 8, 1918, some of Corporal York's friends were wounded, and some lay dead at the foot of Hill 223 in the Argonne Forest. The 328th Infantry took the Decauville Railroad that day, largely because the punishing defensive machine gunfire on the left side of the line had been effectively neutralized. Unaware of the flanking maneuver Sergeant Parsons had sent acting Sergeant Early to execute early in the morning, Captain Danforth was busy taking advantage of the slackened fire, moving Company G ahead across the plain toward the railroad tracks.

Around noon the captain, accompanied only by a messenger, returned to bring up his support platoons. As the two reached the edge of the woods on their flank, they ran into a group of forty-four Germans, who surrendered without firing a shot. More than three hundred prisoners were taken during the day. These and other duties kept questions about the fate of acting Sergeant Early's detail from the captain's thoughts.

At about ten o'clock the next morning, October 9, Corporal York and seven privates reported to Captain Danforth at his new position on the railroad. Danforth asked the men where they had been. Corporal York replied they were part of the detachment sent around the left flank against the machine gun positions the day before. He further explained how all the noncommissioned officers were killed or wounded and how he took command, knocked out the machine guns, and later marched a large contingent of prisoners far to the rear.

York received permission to return with stretcher bearers to see if any wounded were left alive at the battle scene. Seeing none, the men yelled into the underbrush, hoping some hidden wounded might still be alive. There was no answer. A salvage detail was already at work, packing up scattered weapons and other hardware. The six dead Americans were buried where they fell, beside the small stream they jumped just before surprising the Germans at breakfast. York noted how the undergrowth around where he stood, a little to the left of where the prisoners and the other Americans took cover, was completely shot to pieces, the ground chopped and churned beneath. A canteen nearby had eighteen bullet holes in it.

The American salvage detail had also already buried the German dead. Captain Bertrand Cox, commanding F Company, was the first officer on the scene after York's battle. He reported seeing "between 20 and 25 dead Germans on the scene of the fight." Another report counted "a dozen dead Germans and ten or twelve more pairs of legs sticking out of the bushes." One soldier saw thirty-five abandoned machine guns; a second counted twenty-eight; a third report noted "more than thirty."

Corporal York said a prayer for his buddies who died, Gentile and Jew alike. He prayed for the Germans too. They were all his brothers. Maybe their religion was different but he reckoned they all believed in the same God. He then led the detail back to company headquarters.

The 328th continued fighting its way through the Argonne Forest, reaching Fleaville on October 10, and Sommerance two days later. At both places army officials visited Corporal York to question him further about his part in the advance against the Decauville Railroad. Word circulated up the chain of command about how this big fellow from Tennessee captured 132 Boche and killed twenty or more all by himself. York had never spoken to anyone other than Captain Danforth and his other superiors about the events of October 8.

His capture of the Germans was not foremost in his mind at present. Looking ahead rather than to the past, York was worried about the effect the Argonne offensive was having on the 328th. He and his company were in the thick of it now and all day he heard the shouting of orders, the pleas of the wounded, and the agony of the dying on both sides, out of sight beyond the trees. The artillery and poison gas kept coming and the line was now advancing so fast the Americans weren't even stopping to bury their dead. At night, lying on the ground trying to sleep, York looked out over the carnage, the ghastly faces of the dead illuminated by German shells.

In Sommerance, Corporal York came closest to getting killed. He and some others were in an apple orchard when a German barrage began. The Americans were ordered to dig in. After months at the front, York felt he could tell from the sound what size shell was headed toward him and where it would land. The hits were not close enough to scare him at first and he dug only to follow orders, not to protect himself. As the firing continued, however, its accuracy improved. And the closer the shells got the faster York dug.

Digging was a constant in his life, on farms, in gardens, and on the Dixie Short Route back home. But he never dug like he was digging now. Dirt was flying furiously from the big corporal's spade when—BANG—there was a bright white burst followed by an ear-splitting report. A shell landed right in front of him, its concussive force sending him flying through the air and down again. He gathered himself up on his hands and knees, shook his head, and rose to his feet unhurt.

On October 31, the 328th emerged victorious from the Argonne Forest. The next day the brigade was taken out of the lines and spent the night at an abandoned German rest camp. Based on field reports and interviews regarding York's heroism in the battle of October 8, the corporal was promoted to sergeant on November 1.

Sergeant York got a ten-day furlough. On November 7, he took the train to Aix-Les-Bains, where he enjoyed the fine scenery, a motorboat ride on the lake, and a tour of the ruins of the ancient Roman baths after which the city is named. Since there were no military quarters nearby, he took a room at the Hôtel d'Albion. It was there on November 11 he heard the news the Armistice had been signed.

York described the celebration. "They sure was a time in that city that day and night. It was awful noisy. All the French were drunk, whooping and hollering. The Americans were drinking with them, all of them. I never did anything much, just went to church and wrote home and read a little. I did not go out that night. I was all tired. I was glad the Armistice was signed, glad it was all over. There had been enough fighting and killing. And my feelings were like most all of the American boys. It was all over, and we were ready to go home."

He sent a postcard of the local scenery back to Pall Mall. He wrote nothing home of his Argonne exploit and it was not something he thought much about. The card arrived at Pile's store around Christmas, its large November 14 postmark obliterating some of the short message, which read in part, "Hello. I'm OK. Sending you a postcard view of a little of this country along the coast. It's a nice scene. Well, that's all."

Headed back to Company G on the last day of his furlough, November 17, Sergeant York stopped in Champlitte, where he wrote in his diary, "The French had a dance there that night and they had to go by my bed to where they was dancing, and the girls would pull my feet until I couldn't sleep."

Along with thousands of other Allied troops, the 328th Infantry was scheduled to march in a Christmas Day review before President and Mrs. Wilson. To York's surprise, divisional orders came down for him to be a color bearer in the parade.

A huge crowd turned out in the city of Langres, braving a biting December wind, to see the American president and his wife. York passed in review before them as part of the color guard, "straight as an Indian," though not with such military exactness he couldn't sneak a sidelong look at the guests of honor. Mrs. Wilson cut a "very pleasing" figure in a sealskin coat with fox collar, matching toque with bright red rose trimming on one side, and "a little bunch of holly at her throat." The president wore a silk high hat, light gray fur coat, and beamed a wide smile to the soldiers. The president and Mrs. Wilson addressed the crowd, sending waves of cheers roaring up into the sharp winter air. York's only disappointment was that his duties kept him from Christmas dinner.

By January of 1919, Sergeant York was being observed closely as he performed his daily routine. He still had never written anyone at home about his capture of the Germans two months before and never talked about it unless asked directly. In one sense it was almost as if it never happened. And yet, the more evidence the division and brigade leadership gathered about York's skirmish, the more probable it seemed it was the truth.

Beginning in January battalion headquarters called in the privates who were with York in the Argonne offensive to make sworn affidavits about the events of October 8. Privates Percy Beardsley and Michael Saccina gave their testimonies on January 26, affirming York fired on the German machine gunners while other soldiers guarded the first batch of prisoners or ran for cover. Private George Wills stated he heard but could not see Corporal York shouting to the Germans to surrender. Private Patrick Donohue said he was busy guarding prisoners and only fired one shot before Corporal Cutting called to cease fire; Donohue made no mention of York.

On February 3, Brigadier General Lindsey, Major Buxton, and other officers went back to the Argonne Forest. They asked Sergeant York to retrace his actions of October 8 down the hillside and across the plain, now covered with snow. He stood on the spot where he surprised the Germans eating breakfast, as near as he could tell, and had his photograph taken. He told his story again as General Lindsey and the others, listening eagerly, following him through the shallow trench, down the hillside to the little stream, now crusted with ice, then back around what had been the southern flank of the conflict.

"How could you possibly have done this, sergeant?" Lindsey asked with a disbelieving edge to his voice.

"Sir, it was not man power," York answered simply. "It was divine power that saved me. Before I went to war I prayed to God, and He gave me my assurance that so long as I believed in Him, not one hair of my head would be harmed. Even in front of them machine guns, He knowed I believed in Him."

His skepticism and military crustiness both subdued, the general put his arm around the sergeant's shoulders and said quietly, "York, you are right."

On February 6, Private Joseph Konotski swore an affidavit at battalion headquarters that Sergeant York "performed in action deeds of most distinguished personal bravery and self-sacrifice. . . . Encountering a large machine-gun nest, all but seven men of his platoon were killed and all non-commissioned officers, except Sergeant York, who was at that time a corporal. His comrades had lost hope but Sergeant York kept his usual balance and self-control. He rallied his men and closed in on the enemy, using his rifle as long as he could conveniently reach his ammunition. Then he resorted to his pistol, with which he killed and wounded no less than fifteen of the enemy." Beneath Konotski's X, Privates Donohue, Sok, and Saccina, being duly sworn, subscribed their names in agreement, Donohue and Saccina thereby revising their earlier statements.

At Prauthoy on February 11, Sergeant Alvin C. York received the Distinguished Service Cross, pinned to his uniform during a special division review by Blackjack Pershing. Attaching the medal, Pershing addressed the assembly, describing the beaming sergeant as "the greatest civilian soldier of the war."

On February 15, Adjutant General F. L. Whitley, writing on Pershing's behalf, requested "additional information and testimony" be collected by General Duncan, commander of the 82nd Division, regarding York's actions "with view of reconsidering this case for the award of the Medal of Honor." Though the Distinguished Service Cross had already been awarded, Pershing agreed the corporal's actions might be deserving of even more.

Another affidavit was prepared on February 21, by Private Beardsley, also signed by Private Wills, affirming, "the German battalion commander surrendered to Corporal York. . . . A considerable number of German prisoners were taken on our way back over the hill. Corporal York made them surrender by having the German battalion commander call to give themselves up."

In York—quiet, well-mannered, and plain-spoken—military authorities saw a valuable tool for building morale among the troops as they waited to be demobilized and sent home. Sergeant York was ordered to Prauthoy to assess his interest in and potential for touring some of the American camps in France to share his story and keep up the spirits of the men as they impatiently counted the days until they could get back across the Atlantic.

York was agreeable to the plan because it gave him an opportunity to tell others how he prepared for war and how he came through. It allowed him to share the faith in God that so comforted and protected him. With Prauthoy as his base, Sergeant York began traveling around France meeting other soldiers. His frequent traveling companion was the division chaplain, Reverend Tyler from Milwaukee, "a nice man and a powerful preacher."

Word of Sergeant York's heroism was beginning to spread throughout the Allied units. When he and the chaplain arrived at a battalion headquarters or at a local YMCA, troops would come out by the hundreds to meet York, hear a sermon from Chaplain Tyler, and share their opinions, thoughts, and concerns. York had a big, friendly smile, and his self-effacing personality put everyone instantly at ease.

York and Tyler usually went out in the morning by car or motorcycle (which York had no taste for—"It was asking too much of God, traveling like that"), sometimes making it back in the evening, at other times going directly to their next scheduled stop. Though York had never spoken to such large gatherings, his easy manner, honed over three years in front of church congregations in Pall Mall, made him an effective speaker. To his audiences he was a real war hero and everything he said was interesting to them, whether it involved war against the Boche or war against the devil. As his celebrity grew, York even sat to have his portrait done, at General Duncan's insistence, by a painter from America who came mostly to paint generals and presidents for news magazines back home.

York's speaking trips were interrupted by a week of heavy snow and freezing rain. He held an occasional service at Prauthoy, two a day on Sundays. Typically his audience was large and enthusiastic. Not only did they appreciate a break from the boredom of waiting to go home, they heard this fellow was a hero who'd been recommended for the Medal of Honor. He was a gifted natural speaker with a quaint country accent and he obviously believed what he was saying about how God will protect people in battle or anywhere else if they'll just believe in Him.

On February 24, York made a return visit to Champlitte, where the playful French girls had robbed him of shut-eye by playing with his feet. His service was scheduled for seven o'clock, but when he arrived, a dance was in full swing. He had to wait half an hour for the revelers to clear the room. York then started his presentation by leading a hymn, followed by a prayer, and moving afterward to his "little talk."

The bad weather continued as York left for Bordeaux on the afternoon of February 27. He rode with other soldiers through a violent snowstorm in unheated boxcars, but to York it was at least better than "sleeping in those old French barnes where the cows sleep in the parlor and the chickens in the dining room, ho! ho!"

They arrived in Bordeaux the night of February 28, and stayed huddled in the icy boxcars until the next morning, when the men were allowed to go into town, and York found himself a nice hotel room. The following day, Sunday, York went to church at the local YMCA. Early Monday evening a Bible study was held, after which York was invited to speak. Again he led hymns, offered prayers, and then spoke to a large and attentive crowd. Speaking requests came in regularly and York found himself in front of a group almost every day somewhere in Bordeaux. He shared his story willingly. He also liked the work because it kept his mind off Gracie and his mother, and how badly he ached to be home again.

Even during the punishing winter weather, York and the others endured occasional drilling, marching, and reviews. Any sort of activity was welcome because it crowded out his otherwise constant thoughts of Pall Mall: a small cabin, a roaring fire, and his mother quietly carding wool by lamplight in her old rocking chair.

The sergeant did run across some excitement once in a while. One night in Bordeaux the officers decided to hold an officers-only dance at the YMCA. The idea didn't sit well at all with a group of private soldiers, bored by inactivity and emboldened by generous samplings of French cognac. Arriving uninvited, they helped themselves to a place on the dance floor, and to the prettiest girls in the room. Sergeant York, on duty at the time, was ordered by the furious captains and lieutenants to call out the guard and get the enlisted interlopers off the floor. The privates hung on tightly to their girls, dancing vigorously, while the officers began ordering them away. York quickly realized the task "was a harder job than busting the Hindenburg Line," and any serious enforcement of the officers' orders would ignite a real melee.

York arranged his own armistice. Clearing a path, he ran a rope down the middle of the dance floor, stationing guards along it at intervals. The officers danced in their exclusive area on one side, and the privates and their partners enjoyed their share of fun on the other.

Having spent two months traveling and speaking, Sergeant York rejoined Company G at St. Silva on March 14. On the 25th he left St. Silva and went back through Bordeaux on his way to a five-day furlough in Paris. On March 26, the tall Tennessean, born and raised in a valley without electricity, stepped off the train and into the City of Lights.

For centuries the French capital set the world standard for elegance and style. Now it was shaking off the brooding grayness of four years of war, ecstatic at the return of freedom and prominence. York took in the sights; he was impressed but not overawed. He visited Napoleon's tomb, the Tomb of the Unknown Soldier, so recently dedicated (he didn't stay long because it made him sad; he didn't want to be sad in Paris), and Versailles. "I liked Paris all right," he wrote in his diary on March 27. "It was a right smart place. The Eiffel Tower was not running at the time. I went to see it but I didn't climb it. It was tolerably high."

York also gave opera a try. He had never heard of it before but when his friends explained what it was—"music with a lot of them stringed instruments playing together"—he made his way to the high baroque masterpiece of an opera house in the heart of the city. He was incredulous at the ticket price: four dollars!—eight days' work at the forge. He bought a ticket nevertheless. "I sat through it all right. I liked the orchestra, but I don't think I'd ever again spend four dollars to see another opera like it."

While his companions forgot their war memories temporarily with the help of vin rouge and friendly mademoiselles, York continued touring the city and thinking of home. He saw his first Ferris wheel (which he called "Paris wheel") and the sight of one intrigued him enough to go for a ride. His interest turned to discomfort once he was on board and the contraption started revolving "and the sky and the ground got all mixed up. I not only forgot the war I done forgot everything."

One afternoon the sergeant found himself lost in the middle of
town. The city was filled with traffic circles, street signs he couldn't
understand, and probably more people than the whole state of Tennessee. The more he walked, the more disoriented he became. He tried
to find his direction by the sun but he couldn't see it. He tried to spot
buildings he passed earlier but they were all so big and looked so much
alike, he couldn't identify them. At last he approached a young woman
and asked her, in English, if she could help him get to his hotel. The
woman recognized the hotel name and walked York to a streetcar stop.
When the streetcar arrived, she told the attractive girl at the controls
where to let the American off, and the sergeant soon found himself
safely in front of his lodging. He thought it was funny that, while he
never took any pretty girls home in France, one of them had now taken
him home.

When his furlough ended, Sergeant York spent only a week back
in St. Silva before returning to Paris. He was chosen as the noncommissioned officer representative from his division to attend the organizational meeting of a new military veterans group called the American
Legion. Its purpose was to help rehabilitate U.S. soldiers injured in the
line of duty and to assist the families of all veterans with insurance,
compensation, and other related matters. York arrived in Paris at 8:30
on the morning of April 7, leaving him only two hours to find his
way to the Hôtel Gabriel. The meeting of officers and men from every
American military outfit in France lasted all day. When the proceedings
were adjourned about 5:30 that afternoon, the American Legion was
founded, with Sergeant Alvin C. York listed as a charter member.

On April 8, York attended the formal signing of the peace treaty
ending the Great War, held amidst the classical splendor of the Palace
of Versailles. Sergeant York was presented to Premier Clemenceau and
Marshal Foch, whom he spoke with through an interpreter. York also
spoke with General Pershing and reflected later on what he saw as a
common bond between the French and American leaders. "It is significant that their two great leaders and General Pershing, too, are all
religious men who believe in prayer."

That afternoon York joined some of his friends at the railroad station to get their first glimpse of royalty. One of the men read that the

queen of Romania was arriving in Paris and they all decided to walk down to the platform and wait for her. The train glided in and the queen alighted with regal bearing, her face covered with a stylish black veil. She peered up at the waving gaggle of doughboys, smiled, and waved her hand. To York she was "a very good-looking lady."

The next day Sergeant York visited Lafayette's grave. It was still decorated with remnants of the wreath Pershing placed there the previous July 4th when he proclaimed, "Lafayette, we are here." Two days after the Armistice, President Wilson added his own flowers, which were still there as well.

Hero or not, Alvin York was still in the U.S. Army. Back at St. Silva he fell in with full pack for a review on April 12, then spent twenty-four hours as sergeant of the guard beginning at 4:00 p.m. that afternoon. The next few days were filled with the routines of soldiering. Americans were grateful to see the harsh European winter weather finally breaking and they went about their duties knowing it couldn't be long before they would be going home.

In every idle moment York's thoughts turned toward his valley. In a letter from Bordeaux to his brother Joe, the sergeant wrote not of war and victory but of the comforting cycle of the seasons. "I guess that you are about ready to plant now, aren't you? I hope that you will have good luck and I hope the boys will also have good luck with their crops. I think I will leave France sometime in April for the States. Well, say, how is Mama and all the folks? And how is my G. W.? By now, fine I hope. Tell them all good bye from your only soldier brother."

April 18, 1919, was Good Friday. The 82nd Division held a review at St. Silva. There on the parade ground, Sergeant Alvin C. York was awarded the Medal of Honor by the division commander, Major General George B. Duncan. The accompanying citation, authorized by Congress and dated April 11, read: "For conspicuous gallantry and intrepidity above and beyond the call of duty in action with the enemy near Châtel-Chéhéry, France, October 8, 1918. After his platoon had suffered heavy casualties and three other noncommissioned officers had become casualties, Corporal York assumed command. Fearlessly leading 7 men, he charged, with great daring, a machine-gun nest which was pouring deadly and incessant fire upon his platoon. In this heroic feat the machine-gun nest was taken, together with 4 officers and 128 men and several guns."

In bestowing the award, General Duncan said, "The commanding general takes particular pride in announcing to the command this fine example of courage and self-sacrifice. Such deeds are evidence of that spirit and heroism which is innate in the highest type of American soldier and responds unfailingly to the call of duty wherever or whenever it may come."

York spent a quiet Easter, attending church and enjoying a fine Easter dinner at the invitation of a local family. By Thursday the twenty-fourth, he was back on the parade ground, this time reprising his first official military duty—picking up cigarette butts. The Allied commander, Marshal Foch, was coming, and everything had to look sharp. Foch might have been surprised to think that hours before he stood before this burly, redheaded sergeant to present him with his country's Croix de Guerre with palm, York was scratching up the grass on the parade ground for bits of paper that might mar the military precision of the moment.

That afternoon Marshal Foch approached Sergeant York on the reviewing stand, kissed him on both cheeks, and pinned the Croix de Guerre above his left breast pocket next to the Congressional Medal of Honor. He said to York and to the assembled troops and visitors, "What you did was the greatest thing ever accomplished by any soldier of any of the armies of Europe."

A translation of the French medal citation read: "All the noncommissioned officers of his platoon having been disabled, he took command of it, and with 7 men succeeded in silencing a nest of enemy machine guns, capturing several machine guns and 132 prisoners, including 4 officers."

Alvin York now held the highest honors two continents could bestow. Yet, outside military and political circles or beyond the geographic bounds where his heroic act was spread by word of mouth, no one had heard of him. The previous October, he had salvaged an advance, captured 132 Germans, and killed twenty-odd of them. Eyewitnesses said he did it essentially alone. York hadn't written a word about it in his frequent letters home to Gracie, Mother York, and others in Fentress County. There was no specific news coverage of the Decauville advance outside the region. Other than historians and career military men, few of the soldiers and civilians who saw Sergeant York receive his Medal of Honor could have named a single other recipient over the forty-seven-year history of the award. They weren't likely to remember this one either, other than to say they were present when it was handed out to some sergeant.

York still failed to recognize any real benefit to killing two dozen strangers who were his "brothers in Christ." He had done what he had to do and appreciated the attention it garnered him from Pershing and Foch, two men he admired as Christian leaders. That part of his life was over now.

With the rest of the 328th, York waited in Bordeaux for the ship that would take them home. His homesickness was reaching a zenith. As the days became weeks, each passing hour seemed longer than the last, and rainy weather made the gloomy atmosphere even more unbearable. As the second interminable week of May began, the *Sierra* arrived at the wharf. The elated soldiers reported dockside to be shipped aboard their transport. After the vessel had been loading for some time, the line of men crossing the gangway stopped. To his dismay, Sergeant York heard the word there wasn't room for everyone. Sure enough, the gangway was hoisted, the rail secured, and the ship disappeared into the afternoon sun, leaving sixty-six members of the 328th behind.

That night was the longest of the men's lives. But the next day, May 10, the USS *Ohioan* made fast at the wharf and loaded York and the remaining troops aboard. At 2:26 p.m. the lines were loosed and at long last Alvin York was heading back to his dear Gracie.

The first five days brought heavy seas. York alternated his time between gulping for fresh air on deck and lying on the berth below, vainly trying to keep his stomach under control. He didn't feel like talking "or doing anything but lying down and being left tolerable alone. I would have got out and walked if I could have."

Conditions improved later in the trip and from May 16 on the weather was fair, except for a single patch of rain on the nineteenth. May 18 was Sunday and York attended church services, seeking both spiritual and physical anchorage as he joined in the singing of "Jesus, Savior, Pilot Me."

On the morning of May 22, Sergeant York joined a crowd at the bow to watch the Statue of Liberty rise majestically on the horizon, followed by the New York skyline. The buildings, shimmering blue-gray in the distance, reminded him of mountains. Oh, he was homesick! He turned to follow Lady Liberty as she passed by to port. Meeting her serene gaze, his own blue eyes dancing in the midday sun, he nodded in silent agreement at a comment from a shipmate along the rail. "Take a good look at me, Old Girl. Because if you ever want to see me again, you'll have to turn around."

Chapter Ten

News from Alvin

About the time the 328th Infantry emerged victorious from the Argonne Forest on October 31, 1918, Joseph Cummings Chase, duly authorized by the War Department, arrived in Paris. Chase was a portrait painter on assignment for *World's Work* magazine, which, along with *The Illustrated War News* and many other publications, competed feverishly to feed the American public's insatiable appetite for news from the front. Readers wanted maps to put with troop movement reports and faces to put with stories of action, tactics, and heroism.

To satisfy both his public and his editors, Chase followed the American army after the Armistice, interviewing and painting portraits of generals and other luminaries along the front and inside occupied Germany. Over the rest of that fall and winter, Chase traveled to dozens of cities, zigzagging from one to the next in search of subjects. He mined local leads, sometimes getting recommendations on whom to paint next from the person sitting before him. His studio was a château one week, a hut the next. He painted in a castle on the Rhine and in a dugout.

World's Work was satisfied with the pictures and published them to enthusiastic response. Chase painted General Pershing twice, once in November at Chaumont and again in January at the Ogden Mills

House, the general's headquarters in Paris. The artist was pleased to have a second chance at Pershing. His November sitting produced the image of a serious, dignified, preoccupied leader. By January the great burden of war had been lifted with visible effect. Chase characterized Pershing at their second meeting as "altogether easy and gay." Jo Davidson, a sculptor, was also present at Ogden Mills House, sculpting a bust of the general as Chase worked before his canvas.

Another subject was General Douglas MacArthur, a brigadier at thirty-seven, whom Chase described as "one of the most picturesque men in the Army." MacArthur met his portraitist at a country house in Sinzig, built on the foundation of a nunnery where Charlemagne once lived. As always, Chase worked swiftly, the mood heightened by the fact he painted by candlelight.

In Major General George B. Duncan, the artist's eye observed "a powerful man, mentally and physically, while the Celtic wistfulness of his eyes and the large mobile mouth together give him the look of captivating whimsy." As the commander of the 82nd Division sat, Chase engaged him in conversation, as he customarily did his subjects. Chase noted with interest the general turned time and time again to the story of a corporal in his command who was drafted as a conscientious objector but nevertheless captured 132 officers and men while also "bagging" twenty-four Boche. Chase wrote in his notes, "It was only by accident that the story came to his own commander, from the adjacent battalion some time later. The facts were then verified."

General Duncan insisted Chase paint a portrait of York and summoned the Tennessean later in the evening to have it done on the spot. York sat obediently in the chair, saying little. Having written copious notes on his conversations with Pershing, MacArthur, and more than a hundred others, Chase only recorded one exchange with the unassuming sergeant that night in the town of Bar-Sur-Aube.

"Are you married, York?"

"No, I was always a kind of a mommer's boy."

The portrait, quickly executed but reasonably true, showed a handsome, ruddy-faced redhead with a trim moustache, hair blowing slightly in the wind, gazing resolutely off in three-quarter right profile. His double-breasted greatcoat was buttoned to the collar and the collar turned up in back. The magazine caption prepared to go with the image identified Corporal Alvin C. York as a "'conscientious objector' from the Tennessee Mountains who recovered from his pacifism sufficiently to kill with his rifle a machine gun nest of twenty-four Germans and capture 132. . . . This General Duncan pronounced the 'greatest single exploit of the war.'"

On one of his trips back and forth across France and Germany, Joseph Cummings Chase found himself sharing a ride with a reporter for *The Saturday Evening Post* named George Pattullo. Like Chase, Pattullo was in Europe in search of stories to satisfy the American hunger for war news. Though Canadian by birth, Pattullo worked for newspapers in both Canada and the States and served a stint in London as well. Striking up a conversation with the reporter as they bounced along in the back of a truck, Chase mentioned the story General Duncan told him about this Tennessee corporal who "killed a machine-gun nest full of Germans and captured more than a hundred, all single-handed."

Pattullo's interest was instantly aroused. He was in fact on his way to the Argonne and when he arrived at battalion headquarters, he immediately sought out Major Buxton. The Rhode Islander confirmed Chase's story and arranged for Pattullo to meet York. An investigation was underway at the time to confirm the details of York's exploit, and affidavits were taken from the privates in York's detail in preparation for recommending that Congress award him the Medal of Honor. On February 3, Pattullo accompanied York and others to the scene of his battle at the base of Hill 223, stepping off the action with them and listening attentively as York recounted his story.

After three days of interviews and investigation on his own, George Pattullo decided he had the makings of a phenomenal story. Furthermore, no newspapers anywhere seemed to have gotten wind of it yet. Four months after it happened, there was still no word of York's miraculous achievement in the European or American press. Yet all the elements of a truth-stranger-than-fiction saga were here: A backwoods mountain boy from Tennessee who didn't believe in war was drafted. He was an elder in the church, convinced that killing was against God's teachings. He was persuaded to change his mind, came to France, and not only served his country but became a hero and Medal of Honor recipient. Pattullo couldn't imagine any other story so clearly distilling the principles Americans fought and died for, while at the same time proving the strength and courage of American soldiers.

Great as the opportunity seemed, Pattullo had one serious barrier to overcome. Publishing his narrative in *The Saturday Evening Post* would require a six-week lead time. In six weeks anybody might discover the story and put it on the wire service, stealing his thunder and demoting his report to "background follow-up" status. There was also the chance other reporters might overhear him talking with York or someone else about the events of October 8, or otherwise get word of the scoop somehow. Pattullo respected his competitors' ability to smell a story and wondered how he could keep it under wraps with so many other reporters crisscrossing the continent.

Most of all he worried about leaks in the censorship network. Reporters were known to pump censors for tidbits from the dispatches they processed and a well-placed bribe could render all of Pattullo's work and secrecy practically worthless. He went to General Nolan who was at the top of the censorship chain of command and explained his position. He was willing to invest the time to write a story that could be both a morale booster and a public relations bonanza for the army, he told the general, but he wanted assurance no one would leak his work to other reporters.

Pattullo asked if Nolan would be willing to take up the matter with General Pershing. Nolan replied it wasn't necessary. He could handle the matter himself. Censors, the general explained, could not prevent other reporters from discovering the story on their own, nor could they prevent another reporter's version from being released ahead of Pattullo's. What Nolan could guarantee however was, assuming others did not come up with the story, there would be no leak through the censors.

That was the assurance the reporter needed. He assembled notes from his meetings with York and others and the scribblings he wrote as he followed York down Hill 223 and through a shallow trench at the edge of the Argonne. The finished article was titled "The Second Elder

Gives Battle," and the first few lines of Pattullo's final draft set the stage
for quite a saga.

> *Alvin C. York comes from Pall Mall, Fentress County,*
> *Tennessee, and is second elder in the Church of Christ in*
> *Christian Union. The sect is opposed to any form of fighting;*
> *they are conscientious objectors. But York refused to seek*
> *exemption, went to war, and as Corporal York of Company*
> *G, 328th Infantry, killed twenty Germans on October eighth,*
> *captured one hundred and thirty-two prisoners, including a*
> *major and three lieutenants, put thirty-five machine guns out*
> *of business, and thereby broke up an entire battalion which was*
> *about to counterattack against the Americans on Hill 223 in*
> *the Argonne sector near Châtel-Chéhéry.*
>
> *He outfought the machine-gun battalion with his rifle*
> *and automatic pistol. There were seven other Americans present*
> *at the fight, but it was York's battle and only York's. But for*
> *him not a man of them would have come out alive except*
> *as prisoners. In my estimation it stands out as the greatest*
> *individual feat of the war, not only because of the amazing*
> *things he did that day but because of the man's deep religious*
> *convictions and scruples. . . .*

The reporter asked York what Pastor Pile would say when he heard
what had happened. "What can he say?" answered the sergeant earnestly.
"What can any of them say? 'Blessed is the peacemaker,' isn't he? Well
there was sure some stir-up in this country!"

Pattullo described an impromptu demonstration of the Tennessean's shooting skill during the interview. Drawing his automatic pistol,
York emptied it into a penny matchbox at forty paces without a miss.

The story quoted York as he described the German bayonet charge
at the height of the action.

"'I had my automatic out by then, and let them have it. Got the
lieutenant right through the stomach and he dropped and screamed a

lot. All the boches who were hit squealed just like pigs.' 'You killed the whole bunch?' 'Yes, sir. At that distance I couldn't miss.'"

The account concluded:

> *There on the scene of the fight at the foot of York's Hill are six graves where our dead lie buried. Simple wooden crosses mark them, and at the head repose the helmets, rifles and belts of the soldiers who gave their lives. Close beside their last resting place purls a tiny stream, and over the wooded hills broods a cathedral hush.*
>
> *We stood beside the graves in silence. At last I said: "I cannot understand, even now, how any of you came out alive."*
>
> *York replied, simply but earnestly: "We know there were miracles, don't we? Well, this was one. I was taken care of—it's the only way I can figure it."*
>
> *The last I saw of the big fellow he had only one worry— that he might be late getting home for the April meeting. They have a week of revival every spring in Pall Mall and he wants to be on hand; but he was gassed and greatly fears that his voice will be ragged for singing.*

Spring brought warm weather and clear skies to the Valley of the Three Forks of the Wolf. Since receiving the first word from her son after he left for the war, Mary York delighted in hearing about his travels to New York and overseas. He was an observant boy who turned his letters to her into exotic travelogues. She had never traveled any farther than Jamestown—she drove a yoke of oxen there once and went back a few times since—and never thought much about what might be out beyond the walls of the cabin where she raised eleven children and lived more than half her life. She could scarcely envision his descriptions of the tall buildings of New York or the rolling sea that took two weeks to sail across.

As any mother would, she feared constantly for her son's safety and took relief in receiving each letter, not only because of the news it brought, but because it told her Alvin was still alive and well. She never learned to read or even to write her name. So when a letter came she put her carding or spinning aside and listen with rapt attention as Pastor Pile, Gracie, or one of the neighbors read it to her. Frequently she asked them to read it again, and still again, committing line after line to memory. Once she heard it enough, she put it face up on the corner of the mantle, where it remained until the next letter arrived. After a new letter came and was read and reread to her satisfaction, Mother York put the old one carefully away and replaced it with the new one in the same spot on the mantel. That way the letter over the hearth, which visitors knew they were welcome to pick up and read, was always "the latest news from Alvin."

Toward the end of April 1919, according to form, Mother York was getting letters written about a month before. Alvin was looking forward to coming home soon, the most recent notes said, and was getting ready for his first furlough in Paris. He always asked about her health, about the farm, and sometimes requested an update on his prize possession, a pair of mules his brothers were supposed to be taking care of. And he never wrote without asking about Gracie.

Working beside the fire one afternoon, Mother York was startled by an animated knock at her cabin door and even more surprised to open it and see Will Wright, president of the Bank of Jamestown. He was uncharacteristically agitated; his arrival attracted a small cluster of York children and neighbors looking in to see if there was anything the matter. Herding them all inside around the fire, Wright held up a copy of *The Saturday Evening Post* for April 26, 1919. There, in a big photograph in the middle of the front page, dressed in a garrison cap and heavy overcoat, standing in underbrush dusted with snow, was Alvin C. York.

Wright began to read aloud, forming a semicircle with the others around Mother York. Her eager gaze was riveted on the banker and when he looked up after completing the lengthy story, tears were running unchecked down her face. As incredulous looks and comments slowly worked their way around the group, Mary York quietly asked Mr. Wright to read the story again—and five more times after that.

Chapter Eleven

Homecoming

"Where's York?" "We want York!" "Who knows where York is?" The reporters yelled at the top of their lungs, leaning over the railing of their chartered harbor tug as the USS *Ohioan* steamed slowly toward the Manhattan skyline. "Which one of you is York?" A group of wire service and newspaper men skittled out to meet Sergeant Alvin C. York before he docked, hoping to scoop the other reporters, photographers, and newsreel cameramen left fidgeting on the pier. They circled the transport as it eased along, waving to soldiers on deck and shouting above the din of marine engines and the water slapping against the hulls of the two vessels.

The buzz on deck quickly made its way to York. "You've got quite a welcoming committee out here," someone told him. It was true there were a lot of people in this boat circling and a lot more waiting where the ship was headed to dock. He heard the ship had received a cable asking if he was aboard, but surely this was just what every ship full of soldiers got upon returning home, and rightly so. He and his friends gave all they had in the cause of freedom and a little official thank-you would be appropriate. His shipmates must be mistaken. This couldn't be just for him.

The truth became clear, though, when the first line from the *Ohioan* was slipped over a davit on American soil at the Hoboken docks. There were bands and banners as far as the passengers could see and hundreds of people shouting, playing, singing, and waving. Twenty-seven thousand soldiers sailed in the convoy that day but the banners all had York's name on them. The crowd was screaming for him. As the gangway was placed, members of the Tennessee Society of New York and other dignitaries stepped forward to greet the world's most famous hero. Special arrangements were even made to forego the usual customs and immigration processing except for a quick disinfecting in the "decootie room."

The welcoming party waited, the band played, and the crowd strained for a first glimpse of the brave mountain warrior. Numerous false alarms—"There he is!" followed by a surge of bodies one way or another—served only to heighten the suspense. Ten minutes passed, then fifteen. But Sergeant York was nowhere in sight. Unfazed by German machine gunners or Parisian beauties, the hero of the Argonne barricaded himself in a cabin below decks at the sight of such commotion. Nothing had prepared him for a homecoming like this.

Yes, he did his duty. Yes, he was promoted to sergeant and received medals from Pershing and Foch. But here were people he had never seen, who couldn't possibly know him or the circumstances surrounding the battle of Hill 223. He was proud to do his duty and grateful to God for sparing him. That, he thought, would be the end of the story. This spectacle was more than he could absorb.

After twenty minutes Sergeant York unlocked the door and climbed up to the deck. As he appeared the crowd roared with all the pent-up energy the waiting produced. The sound started near the gangway, where the crowd could see him shaking hands with the dignitaries who boarded ship. Then it surged out along the pier in both directions, venting excitement and generating more excitement at the same time. The small group on deck posed for pictures, civilians replete with vests and watch chains, and York, half a head taller than the rest in his size 11½ boots, in uniform with the Congressional Medal of Honor over his left breast pocket, and beside it, the Croix de Guerre, pinned in place by Marshal Foch. The sergeant had gained thirty-five pounds since the day he weighed in at the draft board in Jamestown, but he looked trim and healthy. As prescribed by military tradition, the officers present saluted the Medal of Honor recipient; York snapped a salute in return.

At last the party disembarked, leading York down the gangway into the shouting, waving crowd. He blushed and waved in return, a wide smile beneath his red moustache. Members of the crowd jostled and shoved for the privilege of carrying York's few belongings to a waiting fleet of cars.

He was swamped by photographers, newsreel cameramen, and reporters. Was he really a conscientious objector? "I don't approve of taking human life unless it is necessary, but I considered it necessary." How did he kill all those Germans by himself? "It was the hand of God that guided us all and brought about the victory."

Encouraged to give his account of the battle, he remained silent. Pressed repeatedly, he finally replied only, "I kept my automatic in my right hand all the time, and my rifle in my left, and kept on firing."

It took half an hour for the group to reach the limousine waiting at the curb. At last York and his hosts climbed in and were immediately surrounded by a wave of people stepping forward for a closer look. Several more minutes passed before the car could move forward toward the great canyons of Manhattan.

As York and his party crossed the Hudson River by ferry, he saw people gathered at the landing on the Manhattan side. They waved to him, and he waved back. Paper streamers and confetti began falling from the windows of the buildings far overhead. It looked like a blizzard to the wide-eyed visitor. He still thought the celebration was for all the returning soldiers. When a fellow passenger in his car explained this was for him alone, York refused at first to believe it.

The entourage pulled up in front of the Waldorf-Astoria, where the Tennessee Society of New York booked rooms adjacent to the presidential suite for their guest of honor. Liveried bellboys fought each other on the sidewalk to carry Sergeant York's pack, blanket roll, and trench helmet into the ornate lobby. Inside, the desk clerk offered York the registration book but was waved off by the manager. "He can register in his suite," said Oscar of the Waldorf, leading York and his party through Peacock Alley to the gilded elevator cage. The manager held the elevator door until everyone was squeezed into the car, accompanied them upstairs, then clapped his hands imperially as a signal for the waiting maids to unlock the doors of Sergeant York's suite. Heads of state were shown less hospitality by the renowned Oscar Tschirkey.

As the double doors swung open, York walked in and took a look. The suite was filled with richly-upholstered furniture, its brocaded walls hung with elegant pictures. The picture catching York's attention immediately, however, was a small framed photograph of his mother, peering out through wire-rimmed spectacles from beneath her black sunbonnet, which the Tennessee Society had his family send up from Pall Mall. York took off his cap and, finding no nail to hang it on, set it down on the edge of a divan.

"That's the first picture I've seen of my mother in several days," he joked. He did without pictures of his family at the front for some eighteen months, saying he'd rather leave them at home than in the trenches.

The society had another taste of home for the sergeant. Its members arranged for York to speak with his mother by telephone from his suite. Mother York made her way from her cabin down to Pile's store, where, among the cracker barrels, salt blocks, and cans of axle grease, Pastor Pile was trying to help operators along the line complete the connection. At the other end of the wire, ensconced in rococo splendor while thousands longed for a glimpse of him, Alvin waited patiently at the phone on his drawing room desk. As his mother's voice came through and the conversation began, Tennessee Congressman Cordell Hull, a member of the welcoming committee, gently but firmly shooed all the "top hats and gold braid" out into the hall for the duration of the fifteen-minute conversation.

(News of the phone call started a rumor in Pall Mall that Alvin was back from France and would be home the next day. Well before noon the following morning, friends and neighbors began assembling at the head of Wright Hollow, where they could intercept him as soon as he started down into the valley. They waited until dark, then walked back to their cabins, figuring he was delayed somehow and would be home as soon as he could.)

The night of the twenty-second, a banquet was held at the Waldorf in Sergeant York's honor. York was seated at the speaker's table between his division commander, Major General Duncan, and Vice Admiral Albert Gleaves, a fellow Tennessean in charge of the cruiser and transport fleet that had carried York to war and back. Someone read a telegram from Secretary of War Baker, sending his "very sincerest regards" to the distinguished soldier.

Unaccustomed as he was to such opulence, York was nonetheless at ease throughout the meal. His dinner table at home was set with the simplest dishes and utensils; here there was half a drawerful of big and little knives, forks with three prongs and four, spoons to the right and spoons above, serving chargers, and a cupboard's worth of glassware short and tall. York watched carefully but circumspectly as the person seated across from him ate and used the same silverware he did.

The questions were endless. What will you do now? "I'm thinking about the ministry." What about your farm in Tennessee? "I haven't had time to think about it, really." How do you feel about all the cheers and celebrations here in New York? "They plumb scare me to death." As the meal progressed, the sergeant found his mind wandering to thoughts of his mother and Gracie, his brothers and sisters, and his old coon hounds, now so tantalizingly close. There was nothing in New York for him.

As everyone in the room stood, a toast was drunk to President Wilson, then to Sergeant York, and finally to General Duncan. One after the other, the celebrants rose to heap praise on their guest. York was mentioned so many times the toastmaster, upon beginning his introduction of Duncan, presented him to the assembly as "Sergeant—er, that is—Major General Duncan."

Duncan spoke of York's achievement in the Argonne as "the most outstanding act of gallantry, not only that this world war has ever produced, but that I have ever heard of," and said that he was proud to be seated next to him. Joseph Cummings Chase, who painted the two of them on the same day in France, told the others at his table it was indeed a pleasure to see the two of them together again.

When it was his turn to speak, York's remarks were characteristically brief and humble. "I guess you all understand that I'm just a soldier and not a speaker. I'm just a soldier, but I want to thank the society and General Duncan, and I want you all to know that what you all have done for me is highly appreciated and I never shall forget it. Thank you very much."

Exhausted after twelve days at sea and an afternoon and evening packed with celebrating, the sergeant finally retired to his suite high above the city streets hours after bedtime. The room had twin beds. York had never seen a bedroom with two beds for one person before and wasn't quite sure what to do at first. By and by, he tried them both.

At the request of the Tennessee Society, Sergeant York received a special five-day furlough from the adjutant general, and the society was going to make sure he made the most of every minute. The next morning York was off on a sightseeing tour, planned by the society's Help York See New York Committee, covering the whole of Manhattan. Crowds cheered him everywhere he went and the newspapers had a field day. York observed that by the time his stories made it into print, he had "whipped the whole German army single-handed."

There was some snipping from a few soldiers on the homecoming York received while they got nothing. On May 22, the day of York's arrival, the *New York Times* published an interview with George Edward Buxton, now a lieutenant colonel, who docked the day before on the *Sierra*. He was asked if York's heroic story was true. Colonel Buxton told reporters that in investigating the events of October 8, after York was recommended for the Distinguished Service Cross, the results were such that he was recommended for the Medal of Honor as well. "The more we investigated the exploit," Buxton's quote in the *Times* ran, "the more remarkable it appeared. He is one of the bravest of men and entitled to all the honor that may be given to him."

A reporter asked Sergeant York what he thought about the complaints from his fellow soldiers. He had heard nothing of the matter and when he asked for details learned the complaints were from some of the men he lead in battle. "Sure 'nough?" he replied. "Well, those men whose names you mentioned all made affidavits with other soldiers to Lieutenant Colonel Buxton that I had done all the things claimed." Whether his old squad members were tired, bored, jealous, or had a change of heart, York did not stop to consider.

The night of May 23, York left for Washington by train at the invitation of Congressman Hull, whose district included Fentress County.

Arriving at Union Station the next morning at six o'clock, York was escorted by Hull to the visitor's gallery of the House chamber, where members and visitors alike fractured the hushed decorum of the room by leaping to their feet and cheering wildly upon seeing the famous soldier. York returned their greeting with a simple salute.

As York and Hull walked through the Capitol, everyone from senators to office boys crowded around to shake the sergeant's hand. The visitors called on the Secretary of the Senate, James Marion Baker, who congratulated York heartily in front of an assembly of onlookers. Then the Tennesseans rode to the White House. President Wilson was out, but his private secretary, Joseph P. Tumulty, greeted them and invited them to sit and talk. Tumulty and Hull did the talking, it turned out, while York sat listening quietly in a corner. After a while the trio adjourned to the White House lawn, where they posed for newsreel cameramen.

Time and again the reporters asked York to recount something of his adventure in the Argonne but he would say nothing. One of them asked what he, the great hero of the world war, wanted to do most of all. "I'd like to go home and see my little mother," he answered.

On May 25, York returned to New York, this time to Long Island, where he attended a banquet and occupied the president's suite at the Garden City Hotel. His host there, a transplanted Tennessean named Malcom Meacham, told the assembled press, "I would not be surprised if York would be the next governor of Tennessee. He can have anything he wants down there."

The next morning, after a turn around Nassau County, York motored back to Manhattan, where he was met by a delegation at the Queensborough Bridge to escort him to yet another celebration at the Waldorf. Earlier in the week his hosts asked him what he wanted to see and do. What he really wanted to do was to go home, but he kept the depth of his homesickness to himself and insisted he was happy looking at whatever they wanted to show him.

To satiate their curiosity and satisfy some of his own, he finally told them one sight he would truly enjoy was the subway. While he was away in Washington, the Tennessee Society and local city officials arranged a special tour of the Interboro Rapid Transit subway line. Accompanied by the IRT superintendent, treasurer, and a full load of other dignitaries, he toured the entire system aboard the *Mineola*, the private car of IRT president Theodore P. Shonts.

Hoping for a tidbit of a war story from the sergeant, a reporter asked him as he emerged from the subway if it was anything like the trenches. "Not much," were his only words.

York drove through Central Park, down Riverside Drive, and paid a short visit to Grant's Tomb. When he entered the Stock Exchange, bidding halted spontaneously as traders stopped their work to applaud; some reports insisted York was hoisted onto the shoulders of the excited throng. Crowds cheered him everywhere, and his handsome features received regular notice in the papers. When he spent part of the day in the company of Miss Elaine Peters, daughter of the president of the Long Island Railroad, the front-page headline back in Nashville read "York Sees Subway and Tours City With Belle."

More banquets were held, as well as a party at the Winter Garden Theater in Times Square. Throughout his stay, York was bombarded with offers of wealth and riches in exchange for the use of his name. Public relations men knew a sure thing when they saw it, and Alvin York, handsome, unsullied, and a hero by any standard, was as sure as it got.

In the five days after he docked at Hoboken, York received an offer of ten thousand dollars to let a magazine ghostwrite his autobiography; thirty thousand dollars for thirty days on the vaudeville stage talking about his exploits; fifty thousand dollars for six weeks from another vaudeville producer; and there was talk of a motion picture deal. Florenz Ziegfeld and Lee Shubert, two of Broadway's most successful showmen, were rumored to have made overtures. He deferred any sort of discussion of these opportunities, insisting his first priority was to see his family. (There was even a story going around, which no one was willing to put to York for confirmation or denial, that a wealthy New York socialite offered him a mansion, a Cadillac, and a stipend for life to father her child.)

Finally his furlough was over, and Alvin York could go home. He reported to Camp Merritt on Long Island for orders and transportation to Camp Oglethorpe, Georgia, where he would receive his official discharge. He left Camp Merritt before receiving a message from the adjutant general in Washington offering a commission as a second lieutenant in the inactive reserve. There is little chance it would have interested him.

Others were also trying to catch York on his way out the door. Governor Albert H. Roberts of Tennessee left word for him at Camp Oglethorpe and even announced plans to visit him there, in hopes he could convince York to allow the citizens of Nashville to welcome him with a special celebration. Roberts was thinking ahead to July 4, a natural date for a statewide celebration in honor of America's greatest hero. The governor also wanted to appoint York as an honorary colonel on his staff and was eager to announce the sergeant's acceptance.

In Chattanooga York was met by Brigadier General W. S. Scott, commander of Fort Oglethorpe, and his staff. As the sergeant and brigadier shook hands on the platform, doughboys from the 82nd who were on a departing train yelled greetings at York. He unconsciously let go of the general's hand to wave, then walked on the commander's right to the platform shed where a crowd of ladies was waiting for husbands, fathers, and brothers returning from the war. The general, overlooking this breach of military decorum, fell back as York continued along the line of women, who showered him with roses. When he left the station, the sergeant's arms were loaded with flowers.

The general escorted York to his hotel, where York declared he would appreciate the chance to get a haircut. News of his plans traveled faster than he could make his way downstairs. The manager of the hotel barbershop stood ready at the door to provide his expert assistance. As York settled himself in the chair, a pretty manicurist set to her work without waiting to be asked, rubbing and massaging the famous visitor's thick, calloused hands.

An attentive audience grew larger and larger, huddling around the chair and filling the shop where Sergeant York was held captive with hot towels, lather, razor, and strop. Two ministers invited him to speak in church on July 4. One woman, whose son was in his division, wondered hopefully if York was born in Alabama. Another bystander asked him about the Tennessee Society. They talked as long as he sat there.

After shaving his distinguished customer, then cutting and singeing his hair, the barber began a massage and shampoo. Halfway through the shampoo, York interrupted the man to ask him what he was doing. He had turned down something called a "shampoo" in New York, not knowing what it might involve.

The barber explained. From his horizontal position, York responded lightly, "That's the first one of them I've ever had. They are not so bad."

Completing his turn in the barber's chair, York walked to the mezzanine to speak to a group of ladies who asked to meet him. One of his hosts, Mayor Jesse M. Littleton of Chattanooga, noticed the public watching York from the floor below and led York to the rail, prompting people in the lobby to raise a mighty cheer.

York surprised the mayor, who knew of York's shyness and reticence to speak, by asking if he thought York should say something to the crowd below. "Go to it," the mayor responded with a grin.

In New York he had little to say, but here, back in Tennessee, Alvin York felt inspired in a way he had not at the Waldorf-Astoria or in the chambers of the Capitol. Here, this unlettered mountain man stood at the mezzanine rail and spoke from the heart, thanking his audience for the kindness Tennesseans showed him on his way home. He praised the American army in Europe, declaring that the loss of a generation of men in France, England, and Germany left America "the best Christianized nation in the world."

In closing he said, "In the war the hand of God was with us. It is impossible for anyone to go through with what we did and come out without the hand of God. We didn't want money; we didn't want land; we didn't want to lose our boys over there. But we had to go into it to give our boys and young ladies a chance for peace in the days to come.

"Those boys who fell have done a great deed and a deed that will never be forgotten by America. Thank you."

When he finished, the audience exploded in a frenzy of applause. The Tennessee hero had found his voice.

To the strains of "Dixie" coming from the dining room, York, General Scott, and the mayor went in to lunch. Inside, at a reception sponsored by the Chattanooga Rotary Club, York made further remarks on the fruits of sacrifice and the importance of faith "without the slightest

Above
William York and Mary Brooks York (in light blouse), with nine of their eleven children, c.1905–10. Alvin, standing at far right, was already an experienced blacksmith and expert marksman. (All photographs courtesy of the York family.)

Left
Mary York at her garden gate in Pall Mall, the week of Sergeant York's return from the war, June 1919.

Above left
York arriving at Hoboken, New Jersey, aboard the USS *Ohioan*, May 22, 1919. York had hidden below decks waiting for the crowd to leave but was finally persuaded to come out and acknowledge the cheers.

Above right
York in the Argonne Forest, February 3, 1919, as he walked officials through his movements of the previous October 8. He was unaware that authorities were considering a Congressional Medal of Honor recommendation. This picture accompanied the *Saturday Evening Post* article of April 26, 1919, the first public account of York's heroic feat.

Left
The painting of York by Joseph Cummings Chase. As York's brigade commander sat for the same artist, he had told Chase about York's bravery. Chase repeated the story to a reporter during a chance encounter. Otherwise, York's action might have remained buried in military records. (Reproduction courtesy of the Smithsonian Institution.)

York, Colonel Buxton (far right), and other dignitaries at the Hoboken docks preparing to leave for a ticker tape parade down Broadway in York's honor, May 22, 1919.

York and his hosts in his suite at the Waldorf Astoria. The photo of his mother was waiting in the room as a surprise. At far left, Tennessee congressman (later secretary of state) Cordell Hull; behind Mother York's photo, Dr. James King, president of the Tennessee Society of New York; seated right, Colonel Buxton.

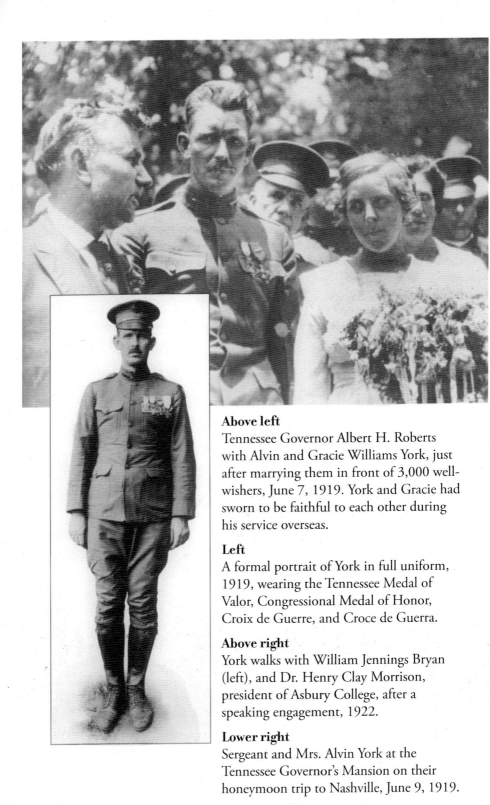

Above left
Tennessee Governor Albert H. Roberts
with Alvin and Gracie Williams York, just
after marrying them in front of 3,000 well-
wishers, June 7, 1919. York and Gracie had
sworn to be faithful to each other during
his service overseas.

Left
A formal portrait of York in full uniform,
1919, wearing the Tennessee Medal of
Valor, Congressional Medal of Honor,
Croix de Guerre, and Croce de Guerra.

Above right
York walks with William Jennings Bryan
(left), and Dr. Henry Clay Morrison,
president of Asbury College, after a
speaking engagement, 1922.

Lower right
Sergeant and Mrs. Alvin York at the
Tennessee Governor's Mansion on their
honeymoon trip to Nashville, June 9, 1919.

Right
Sergeant York in front of his home in the late 1920s, holding Woodrow Wilson York, with Alvin Jr. and George Edward Buxton York.

Above
The home built as a gift to York by the Nashville Rotary Club. York, Gracie, and Alvin Jr. moved in on Valentine's Day, 1922. The gift also included 400 acres of prime riverbottom farmland. At left, as the house appeared shortly after completion; at right, the house today. The large porch was added in 1961 to accommodate York's wheelchair.

Right
York was afraid of flying, despite the interest in aviation sweeping the country in the 1920s and 1930s. After a single demonstration flight over the Everglades in 1926, he never flew again, even when American Airlines offered him free transportation on speaking tours.

Left
In 1928–29, York traveled extensively to promote his book, *Sergeant York: His Own Life Story and War Diary*, to raise money for a school to benefit mountain children. During the ten years since returning from the war, he had become an experienced, compelling, and popular speaker, commanding fees up to $500 per night plus expenses, in addition to voluntary contributions from the audience.

Above
Studio portraits of
Alvin and Gracie,
c. 1930. Alvin was 43
that year; Gracie was
30. These photos still
hang today in the York
homestead in Pall Mall.

Right
This photo ran
in the June 10,
1939, issue of *Time*
magazine covering
York's appearance
at the Golden Gate
Exposition in San
Francisco. The
accompanying article
described the sergeant
as "fat, arthritic and
peace loving."

Left
Betty Smythe, York's agent for his speaking tours; Hollywood producer Jesse Lasky; York Institute principal P. D. Stephens; and York, during one of Lasky's first visits to Fentress County. Lasky was beginning research on the movie Sergeant York at last, after chasing the story for 20 years.

Right
Looking at home movies of a shooting match Lasky brought back to Hollywood from Pall Mall, director Howard Hawks was fascinated by York's habit of licking the front sight of his rifle to take the glare off before firing. Later, York hammed it up for photographers, and the move became part of Gary Cooper's screen portrayal.

Right
Sergeant York and Gary Cooper at the Hotel Astor on Times Square, July 2, 1941. The movie *Sergeant York* had its world premiere that night at the Astor Theater.

Left
York's objection to tobacco was well known on the set of *Sergeant York*. When York happened upon Gary Cooper smoking during a break, Cooper apologized and put out his cigarette. Later Coop sent York this photo of himself in costume, inscribed "To Sergeant York, This is you – from me, with apologies – and best regards. Gary Cooper 1941."

With his first royalty check from Hollywood, York began construction of the York Bible Institute on his farm in 1942. Of the $40,000 total cost, York provided $38,000. The shortage of both students and teachers during World War II hampered the school's early development. Only a few years later the building was abandoned. It sits today, derelict but still straight and solid.

Even after meeting with presidents and movie stars, York always settled comfortably back into the routine of farm life in Pall Mall. Throughout the 1940s, York became steadily more interested in cattle breeding than farming. Here he takes his brother Albert, nephew Oplis Wright, and sons Woodrow and Andrew for a ride in the cattle truck, c.1940.

Above
Sergeant York and Gracie were hospitable to a fault, regularly feeding 20 or more people several times a day, even when money was scarce. Two and three seatings per meal were commonplace, with friends, family, and perfect strangers receiving equal treatment. Clockwise from York in this 1951 scene: Gracie (on her customary corner to the sergeant's left), Alvin Jr.'s son Jimmy, Lela Dishman, and Doll Hatfield (hired girls who helped in the kitchen), Andrew Jackson York, Jimmy's brother Johnny (partly hidden), and Alvin Jr.'s wife, Bethel.

With his grandson Jimmy watching, York cleans his muzzle loading "hog rifle" in 1951. He usually used a lighter, more modern rifle or shotgun by this time, but still claimed none of them was as accurate at short distances.

Above
York and Pastor Rosier Pile on the porch of Pile's store in Pall Mall, where York registered for the draft in both world wars. The second story porch has recently been removed.

Left
Sergeant York and Gracie outside their home, July 1952. York had already had several small strokes but was still active in cattle breeding, farming, and mineral speculation.

Right
Even in later years, York was a captivating speaker who knew how to convey his feelings to an audience. This Memorial Day speech was in Tullahoma, Tennessee, in the early 1950s.

Below
York examines a toy tank with his grandson Johnny, c. 1953.

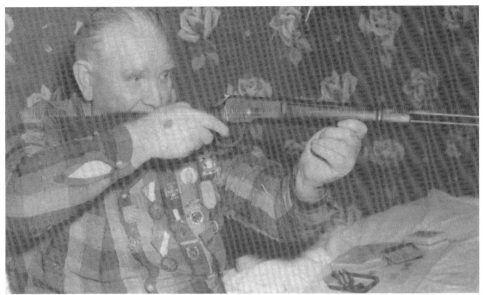

After a cerebral hemorrhage in 1954, York spent the rest of his life paralyzed from the waist down. Here he displays his medals and shooting form, probably for birthday visitors in the mid-1950s. The sergeant's birthday rivaled Christmas as the biggest annual celebration in the York home.

York posing with another Tennessee recipient of the Congressional Medal of Honor, 1961. Seven years after his hemorrhage, York was noticeably frail, but remained interested in visitors and current events. The Circ-O-Lectric hospital bed was a gift from the American Legion. York had attended the organizational meeting of the Legion in Paris in 1919.

Right
Gracie York and sculptor Felix de Weldon at the dedication of the Sergeant York statue on the Tennessee capitol grounds in Nashville, December 13, 1968. It would have been York's 81st birthday. Plans for a dedication on October 8, the 50th anniversary of York's heroic battle, had been cancelled because of a delay in shipping the statue from the foundry in Rome.

Below
Alvin C. York about 1940. "This is the way I remember him," says son Andrew. "He met all those famous people and everything, but he was just a farmer. He was just Daddy."

hesitance or words of embarrassment before the crowd," as the local newspaper reported.

At Fort Oglethorpe on the afternoon of May 29, 1919, the moment he waited so long for arrived at last. Serial No. 1910421 was mustered out and, officially, Sergeant York became a private citizen again. Practically and unofficially, though, it was still "Sergeant" York who pulled into Crossville, Tennessee, the next day on the Tennessee Central to find six automobiles—Jamestown's entire fleet—waiting to take him in triumph back to Fentress County. He hesitated briefly on the steps of the coach. "Which rig do you all want me to get into?" he asked with a laugh. Other passengers stuck their heads out of the windows to wave and cheer as York selected a car, climbed in, and rode away.

The motorcade reached Jamestown at about 7:00 p.m. Mother York was there waiting to greet her boy, along with friends from Pall Mall and every crossroad in between. Little passed between Mrs. York and her son.

"Hello, Ma," he said.

"Hello, Alvin," she replied quietly.

Sergeant York took a seat beside his mother in their farm wagon, two mules pulling the greatest hero of the war up and down the torturous path that "threaded its way through the mountains," wrote one weary traveler, "like a wounded snake."

Though it was getting late for country folk, everyone stayed up waiting for the first glimpse of Alvin and Mother York up the road. They all wanted to welcome him back. When he came into view, they started shooting off their .22s and hog rifles. One neighbor bought a new box of cartridges for the occasion and fired her pistol in the air until it got too hot to hold.

Friends called out to him. "Hello, Al." "Good to see you again, Al." "How you feelin'?"

"Oh, fair to middlin'. How's that corn lookin' this year?"

It was well after dark when the half-dozen rigs and a few men on horseback crested the ridge and looked down into the Valley of the Three Forks of the Wolf. Lamplight from the houses in Pall Mall splashed a warm golden glow into the night. The stars shown brilliant in the clear, black sky. Down the mountainside York and his mother rode across the flat, fertile plain, on to the other side of the valley and to the cabin where Alvin York and his ten brothers and sisters were born. Pastor Pile was there to greet him, accompanied by most everyone else in the valley. Sergeant York was home.

That night, after the crowd finally dispersed, Pastor Pile had a long talk with Alvin to see if the soldier's experiences had changed his spiritual foundations. The parson saw nothing to worry about. Though he tried to have Alvin declared a conscientious objector, Pile now saw nothing against scriptural teaching in what York did on the battlefield. "It's all in a man's own conscience what is right or wrong," Pile said. "The hand of God was on you, Alvin. The simplest teach the wise, we are told. I know it was not education nor money that made you what you are. It was the hand of God."

His mention of money brought up two other items Pile wanted to discuss. The first was the offer he heard York received to publish his autobiography for ten thousand dollars. "I reckon I'd have been a-getting busy writin' if it had been me," he said with a wink, secure in the knowledge York felt no temptation. The other news was from the Nashville Rotary Club, which announced it was organizing a national drive among the Rotary chapters in America to raise fifty thousand dollars for the purchase of a farm for Alvin.

"I don't know much about that," York replied, "'cepting what I've just heard some people say. I guess Maw and the rest of us can attend to that part of it." No one had approached York directly about the offer and that night was no time to try and figure it out or speculate on what might happen. He did think, though, whatever he did he would do it here in the Wolf River Valley. "It's where I've been all my life, and I reckon it's the best place for me," he said. "I reckon I have had chances to leave, but I ain't 'specially got a hankerin' for it."

A reporter who accompanied York all the way from Chattanooga asked about his and Miss Gracie's future plans. York mused in silence for a minute. "Well," he answered at last, "I reckon I might get married sometime. Anybody's likely to do that, you know."

Pressed for more details, the ex-infantryman threw back his head and roared with laughter. They'd all know the answers soon enough!

After Pastor Pile left, Alvin ran all the way to Gracie's house, then together they walked out under the stars. After so many months apart, so much uncertainty, and so much prayer, they were looking into each other's eyes again at last, holding hands and talking of the future. They renewed their vows of love for each other. And Gracie Williams, nineteen and beautiful in the starlight, agreed to marry Alvin York as soon as arrangements could be made.

Alvin's diary had been his constant companion in the trenches and on the battlefields of France for the most tumultuous months of his life. Now he felt the story was complete. In his final entry, York reflected on the first days of his homecoming:

> *My people from all over the mountains, thousands of them, were there to meet me. And my big redheaded brothers were there. And we all had a right smart time. And then I lit out for the old log cabin and the little old mother. And then I went to see Gracie—*
>
> *I didn't do any hunting for a few days. I'm telling you I went hunting Gracie first.*
>
> *And then, when it was all over and I had takened off the old uniform of the All American Division and got back into the overalls, I got out with the hounds and the old muzzle loader; and I got to thinking and wondering what it was all about.*
>
> *And I went back to the place on the mountain where I prayed before the war, and received my assurance from God that I would go and come back. And I just stayed out there and thanked that same God who had taken me through the war.*
>
> *The End*

Chapter Twelve

A Man Profited

The first of June was a Sunday and as always, members of the Church of Christ in Christian Union made their way across the valley to meet for the service. This particular morning, most of them set out early, and the ones who did not found themselves standing outside with the rest of the crowd in the late spring sunshine, listening to a familiar sound coming from the service within. It was the second elder back at his post, leading the singing in his strong tenor voice, unchanged by the horrors of war, German gas, or the highest praises the world could offer.

The congregation was swollen by the friends and neighbors who were there to see Alvin and welcome him home. They were joined by tourists and reporters who made it over the mountain from Jamestown in their automobiles to see this famous mountaineer.

Any doubt York might have had about his struggle with the sixth commandment was put to rest by the reception Pastor Pile and church members gave him. They held nothing against him for killing, considering the circumstances. "He did his duty as he saw it," Pile told a reporter.

Before and after the service, Sergeant York was besieged with requests from friends and strangers alike to "tell us what happened." He put them off at first. Then, seeing the reporters would not be denied a few official words from their hero, agreed to speak after the conclusion of the service.

After the closing prayer, the crowd began chatting noisily, the excitement heightened by the quiet required of them during the preaching. As York rose at the front of the church, the room was quickly wrapped in silence again, all eyes on the tall redhead standing on the plain puncheon floor before them, his cheeks flushed at the attention.

He said little for a man who had seen so much and none of it was about liberty or freedom or blasting Germans. "I've been offered all the fame and treasures of the world," he said to the congregation, while those outside strained to hear through the door and windows. "But your love means much more. I mean it enough to want to stay right here and work with you and serve with you. I served in the war and did what I did because it was what a man ought to do when he believes. I believed, and the hand of God was with me."

With a large following of reporters and visitors in tow, York walked down the road to the ramshackle building that had served as his school. His audience chuckled as he rose to his full six feet inside, where the low ceiling hemmed him in. "I remember when the teacher used to give us a larumping, why, when she swung the switch over her head it'd hit against the ceiling. That didn't stop it though." The sergeant laughed and everyone laughed along with him.

Word was out that York and Miss Gracie Williams were sure to be married soon, and this intelligence brought the young girl into the public spotlight for the first time. Reporters sought her out, eager to give the world all the details of the woman the most famous hero in the world had chosen for his wife. Gracie had never set foot out of Fentress County and maintained a mountaineer's reticence around strangers. That reticence, though, was balanced by a genuine friendliness and innocence the newspapers found almost too good to be true.

The newspapers described Gracie as a woman who "fulfills what popular romance expects of a great hero's love. She really is pretty and winsome, and she is fair, with the mountain sunrise in her cheeks and with lips that are red and smile most roguishly. Tourists who have looked in vain for the complete type of beauty which popular novelists are so fond of describing, and which popular sentimentality imagines, can find it all in Grace Williams . . ."

She was not a classic beauty like the long-necked courtesans who graced the pages of soap advertisements, nor like the very painted ladies of motion pictures and vaudeville. She was innocent and straightforward of character but wise and confident, with an assurance born of the absolute certainty of what was right in the world and what was wrong. She had radiant long hair wound in two braids on the sides of her head, and clear, creamy skin. She was the picture-perfect bride.

Reporters and strangers questioned her eagerly about her life in the valley and her plans for the future. Clearly and honestly, she answered them about Alvin's early years in the wilderness when "he always let on like he never wanted to go to church, but I told him he'd have to go if he wanted to go with me."

She had known, too, how to keep from encouraging him in his mischief. "I never paid any attention to the way he'd cut up, because that's liable to make a man show off." She also admitted her parents didn't think Alvin was a good match for her, that he was "worthless and wouldn't ever amount to anything. And so," she concluded, "I never promised him anything, one way or another, before he went away. I told him I'd let him know when he came back. And now he's come back." Whether or not they pledged their love before being separated was no reporter's business.

What, they pressed, did she tell him? "Wait and see," was all she would say.

Reporters also quizzed York about his plans. His refusal of all the offers to capitalize on his fame made national news and new proposals were still coming almost every day: seventy-five thousand dollars for a motion picture of his life, twenty thousand dollars to endorse a Browning machine gun. The deals came so quickly and unexpectedly York hadn't actually thought too much about them and couldn't even recall many of them specifically. He knew he wasn't interested in them at present but, he told the newsmen, he might consider some of the offers later, after he had the chance to rest for a while.

By the middle of the week, the rumors were confirmed: Alvin and Miss Gracie were going to be married on Saturday. When news of the announcement reached the capitol in Nashville, Governor Roberts swung into action. He had been denied his moment in the spotlight with York at Fort Oglethorpe when the sergeant was discharged; he missed again when York declined his invitation to speak in Nashville next July 4. Now he had a chance for an even greater triumph. He could perform the marriage ceremony in Pall Mall.

The Nashville newspapers reported, "a message was received Wednesday asking the Governor if he would consent to marry the young couple Saturday while he was attending the homecoming exercises at Pall Mall." To the sergeant's neighbors and kin, this news would have been unbelievable. Alvin and Gracie shied away from publicity and both felt deep admiration and respect for Pastor Pile. He was the obvious choice to marry them. But with a politician's instincts, Governor Roberts anticipated the national exposure Sergeant York's wedding would receive and was determined to share the stage. The arrangement was soon confirmed and Roberts scheduled his journey to the Valley of the Three Forks of the Wolf.

The question arose whether or not the governor had the authority to marry anyone. Roberts's office quickly pointed out that a legislative act passed in 1889 permitted him and the speaker of each house of the general assembly to perform marriages in Tennessee. With the matter settled, Roberts and his entourage of a dozen or so set off Friday morning on the two-day trip to Pall Mall.

On Saturday, June 7, 1919, the weather was clear and warm. By the time the sun topped the ridge above Wolf River braiding its three tributaries and heading west, people were already beginning to gather along a slope upriver and around to the north where the flat bottomland began its climb up the limestone hills. There was a beech grove there, with the biggest trees large enough that two men together could hardly reach around them. Beneath their canopy were some younger trees, walnut and hickory mostly, with occasional tulip poplars and evergreens mixed in. The ground was a carpet of ferns and moss grown thick on the mountain springs nourishing them here and there. At the top of the slope, near where the hill became too steep to climb, was a horizontal outcropping of rock, and just below it, a smaller rock. Below these rocks the long slope worked its way down to the valley bottom, where the York Spring flowed out beside Coonrod Pile's old cave. It was the rock where Alvin and Gracie sometimes met and where they had decided to be married.

All the buildings in Pall Mall combined would never hold the mass of people from Fentress County and beyond who wanted to see the wedding of Sergeant Alvin C. York. The beech grove formed a large, comfortable natural amphitheater, where there would be plenty of room for everybody. After the service, all would be invited over to the adjacent field for the marriage feast, which was already being prepared.

The guests came in their Sunday best, women in their bonnets, men in summer hats, clean and pressed overalls and freshly laundered shirts. Some wore suits if they happened to have them. The children were in their cotton and linsey finery, though those with shoes didn't seem to keep them on very long with so many creeks to wade and trees to climb. All through the morning the horses and farm wagons arrived, filled with animated celebrants and laden with pies, cakes, cornbread, biscuits, beans, peas, cob corn, okra, cucumbers, potatoes, tomatoes, onions, pickles, relishes, jelly, molasses, and every kind of meat smoked, salted, and on the hoof.

There weren't enough dinner tables in the valley to put it all on. In the field beside the beech grove, men made long, simple frames of lumber and sawhorses, and unwound whole rolls of wire fencing across them, tacking the wire in place with nails. Then they spread tablecloths and sheets over the wire, producing enormous, sturdy banquet tables.

Governor Roberts and his staff arrived at midday, tired and dusty but grateful to be at the end of their journey. After leaving Jamestown that morning, they had to push the cars several times and walked part of the way along the rocky, serpentine road up over the valley rim and back down. Their shoes were scuffed and their white dress shirts damp with sweat, but they had made it and would play their part in what some were calling the most important celebration in the state since the end of the Civil War.

In front of the York home, Roberts presented Sergeant York with the uniform of an honorary colonel on the governor's staff, eagles and all. The governor also talked privately with York and Pastor Pile about the photographers and newsreel cameramen who swarmed around the hillside. Roberts suggested the newsmen not be allowed to record the wedding service. It was a personal moment, and besides, overexposure could hurt York's chances to reap the benefits of his fame if he decided to do so later.

The sergeant's mother already had her say on the question of photography. Dressed in her customary black dress, black sunbonnet, and white apron, Mary York posed gamely for pictures in front of her cabin for a while but it seemed as though the photographers would never have all the pictures they wanted. Finally she announced the picture session was over. "I'm getting old now, and when a person gets old she don't look purty." Over a chorus of denials she continued, "I bet there's a lot of women are now saying, 'Wonder what that old woman wants to get her pictures in the papers so much for?' Bet they think I'm trying to show off."

Mother York consented to a few more shots. As the newsmen adjusted their cameras, they continued peppering her with questions, asking whether she thought her son did right by killing all those Germans. "Well," she answered, "I believe Al wouldn't have done it if it hadn't been right. I don't believe in fighting, but a man has got to fight for his mother and sisters, ain't he?" There was a note of mild irritation in her answer, as though she resented having to take a public stand on the matter. As far as she was concerned, it was all old business.

A wedding rehearsal was held inside Mother York's cabin. The large number of reporters milling around began to grate further on Governor Roberts's nerves. This ceremony, he admonished them, was not being staged for public amusement. York was one soldier who was not going to be found "prancing in the footlights," he said firmly. "He is not a boy who is going to be led around the country like an Italian with a monkey on a chain."

Nashville reporters estimated the crowd under the beech trees at twenty-five hundred. National wire service writers said it was three thousand and a member of Governor Roberts's staff was sure there were five thousand. By any count, it was the largest gathering the Wolf River Valley ever saw. On the flat rock outcropping at the top of the slope, two standards and a crossbar decorated with red, white, and blue crepe paper framed the scene. Off to one side, Sergeant York appeared in his army uniform, with the Medal of Honor and the Croix de Guerre above his left pocket. Miss Williams, standing beside him, wore a new dress of light pink silk, embroidered around the bottom with red and blue flowers. Two small front pockets were decorated with silk handkerchiefs embroidered with Allied flags Alvin had sent from France. The bride wore white gloves and carried a bouquet.

There was no music. Sergeant York and his bride walked forward accompanied only by the rustle of leaves in the wind. The rock surface was covered with rose petals and the couple, Governor Roberts, Pastor Pile, and the other participants stood on them as they took their places, framed by the colored paper. At the couple's request, Sergeant York and Miss Williams stood facing the thousands who came to see them. The governor's staff, bridesmaids (Miss Ida Wright and Miss Adelia Darwin), the groomsman (Sergeant Clay Brier, who was in charge of transporting drafted Fentress County men, including York, to their training posts), and Pastor Pile stood behind the couple, also facing out. The governor took his place on the smaller rock below and in front of them. He would perform the ceremony with his back to the wedding guests, but before he did so, he faced them and delivered a rousing address honoring York's bravery and his evident resistance to worldly temptations. After praising President Wilson and railing against Bolshevism, he praised the groom's selflessness and bravery.

"They say that we people of the mountains may not be as learned as some others and may not shine in the parlors," Roberts concluded, "but in the great crucible where men are tested and tried, did you ever hear of a Fentress County boy failing to do his duty? Oh, how much, how much, would Mississippi, Kentucky, Massachusetts, or New York, how many millions would they give if Alvin York had been born there instead of Pall Mall, Tennessee!"

As he finished his remarks to a thunderous ovation, the governor signaled to a sheriff, who mounted the rock pulpit and announced pictures of the wedding ceremony would not be allowed. Shouts of protest fell on deaf ears as the lawman said he was ordered to arrest anyone who took photographs during the service. Helpless, the cameramen capped their lenses to wait.

Their wait was a short one. Turning to the bride and groom, Governor Roberts spoke the vows for them to repeat. Alvin calmly recited his words. Miss Gracie then promised "to love, to honor, and to cherish Alvin Cullum York." (Omission of the promise to obey made front-page headlines the next day.) The couple stood serene and relaxed, framed by the festive bunting, sheltered and cooled by the ancient trees, as the governor pronounced them man and wife. Then as thousands cheered, Alvin and Gracie, filled with a love no time or distance or world war could diminish, tenderly savored their first kiss.

The celebration moved to the adjacent field where the enormous wire tables stood heaped with food. Cattle, sheep, goats, and hogs brought in that morning on the hoof were roasted and ready to serve from heaping platters. Gigantic chunks of fresh honeycomb formed mountain peaks here and there. Children ran squealing and chasing each other, crawling around on the automobiles parked under the trees. (Many of them had never seen a car before. Though Parson Pile and one or two others in Pall Mall owned cars, most of those who could afford one didn't think they were worth the trouble it took to coax them in and out of the valley.)

At the dinner, reporters continued to question Sergeant York about refusing the riches of celebrity. Some ventured the comment that it might be foolish or improper not to accept them on behalf of his wife, his family, and his church. He patiently replied that every man had to lead his own life. He belonged in these mountains and woods; they were all he knew. He would be happier here than anyplace else on earth and that was worth all the riches in the world. "We're simple people back here, and our wants are not many," he told them. "Maybe if I had lots of money I'd get into trouble and be unhappy like many rich people I've heard about."

"Wouldn't it be worth a try?" they insisted. York shot back quietly with a passage from the Gospel of Matthew. "'For what is a man profited, if he shall gain the whole world and lose his own soul?' I'll never give up my church and compromise myself with God for the sake of mere dollars."

As the crowd melted away toward sunset, Sergeant and Mrs. York opened their wedding presents. The Bank of Jamestown gave them three shares of its stock. The governor gave silver. The Rotary Club of Nashville sent Gracie a watch studded with diamonds. The Rotary was devising a plan to raise money to buy a farm for the new couple as well and had also arranged, along with the Chattanooga Rotary Club, to send the newlyweds on a honeymoon to Salt Lake City.

Governor Roberts persuaded York to come to Nashville as his guest for the first part of their honeymoon. He also hoped the sergeant would appear at the Own Your Own Home rally at the capitol. This program, sponsored by the Labor Department, was developed to help soldiers get resettled in society. General Pershing endorsed it and Roberts and others promoting the movement in Tennessee saw the handsome hero as a valuable drawing card for generating interest. Now that he was home, had seen his mother and married his sweetheart, York agreed to visit Nashville.

The next Monday afternoon, June 9, Sergeant and Mrs. Alvin York arrived at the passenger terminal in Crossville after a punishing fifty-mile ride. With them were Pastor Pile, Mother York, best man Sergeant Brier, York's friends W. L. Wright, Clay Conatser, and W. E. Mullinix, Mrs. Mullinix, and Gracie's two bridesmaids. For Mother York, Gracie, and most of the rest, this would be their first train ride. As the Tennessee Central No. 1 pulled to a stop, the party was motioned to a special coach at the end of the train, arranged by Major Rutledge Smith of the Council of National Defense for their comfort and convenience.

The train steamed out of Crossville, due in Nashville at 7:20 that evening. It was soon obvious the arrival would not be on time. Tennesseans wanted to see their famous native son, and York did not disappoint them. Along the hundred miles or so to Nashville, the 7:20 stopped fifteen times to let Sergeant York step out onto the platform, acknowledge the heartfelt cheers of the citizens, and say a few words.

More than an hour late, Train No. 1 eased to a stop at Nashville's Union Station. Thousands jammed the platform and the street outside to welcome the governor's guests. Excited cries of the large crowd were momentarily lost as, on cue, every locomotive and factory whistle in town let go a hair-raising blast, singing out in celebration. As York and his party made their way slowly to waiting automobiles, hundreds surrounded him to touch him and shake his hand. Once in his car, York was further delayed by hundreds more who blocked his path straining to see him, shake hands through the car window or shout a quick word of congratulation. It was an enthusiastic replay of the reception he received in New York two and a half weeks before.

The group arrived at the governor's mansion, then York, Mrs. York, Mother York, Pastor Pile, and Sergeant Brier continued to the Ryman Auditorium, where a restless crowd, packing the hall and spilling out onto the sidewalk and street, was kept at bay for two hours with patriotic sing-alongs.

Pastor Pile and Sergeant Brier entered the hall with the governor's staff. The audience, thinking it was York, began a great ovation which tapered off when it became clear the hero was yet to arrive. In a minute or two, a great surge of applause filtered in from the street as York, Gracie, Mother York, and the governor strode inside and up onto the stage.

The Ryman, built as a tabernacle by a repentant riverboat captain twenty-seven years earlier, shook with thunderous shouts and applause, its curved oaken pews creaking with the excitement. The smooth wooden floors, oiled to keep dust down, glistened in the brilliant electric light as York and the others took their seats.

Governor Roberts began by citing several Tennesseans who distinguished themselves in the Great War, including Admiral Gleaves, York's dinner partner in New York who was in charge of transporting soldiers to Europe and back safely. "And now," he continued, "we are gathered here to do honor to this young Christian hero who believed he was doing his duty before God. And he helped in making our victory able to be accomplished."

Pastor Pile spoke briefly, then Governor Roberts presented a specially struck medal from the state of Tennessee to Alvin C. York. The sergeant rose to accept the award and held up his hand for quiet. In an address that took less than a minute, he never mentioned France, the Germans, or the Argonne Forest.

Gentlemen, it is with pleasure that I can tell you how considerate Tennessee people are of me. I appreciate it highly. So highly that I cannot tell it as strongly as I feel it here. [He

pressed his hand to his heart.] I have never met Tennessee
people who are not proud of their soldier boys.

The American army in Europe has accomplished the
greatest victory known. They accomplished it with a will and
with a spirit. It is the greatest army in the world today.

Let's make this nation a more Christian nation than it is
now. And while we shall always want to better our cities and
our nations, it is more important to better ourselves. I thank
you.

After the long ovation began to subside, Governor Roberts prevailed upon Mother York to stand. "This," he said, "is the mother of the world's greatest hero." Mary York did not speak but calmly removed her sunbonnet and smiled in acknowledgment of the cheering crowd.

Tuesday was a whirlwind, beginning with a visit to the tailor to have his new colonel's uniform fitted. A reception at the governor's mansion was slated for nine o'clock but the late night kept York and the rest from their accustomed early rising. It was after ten when York and the governor returned from the tailor shop to find Mother York in the middle of a knot of a hundred people or more on the front porch of the governor's house. She was exhausted, but these people came to see her son and she felt obliged to entertain them as best she could until he could get back.

After an abbreviated reception, Sergeant York and Governor Roberts rode to the capitol where the Own Your Own Home rally was already in progress. As was his custom, York spoke only a few words during the meeting but every speaker there referred to the modest hero as an example of the kind of American family man who deserved the chance to own a home. They considered his presence among them endorsement enough.

An expectant crowd watched York emerge from the capitol and another was waiting for him when he arrived at the Hermitage, the elegant columned plantation home of Andrew Jackson a few miles east of Nashville. Newsreel cameras whirred as York stepped along the garden path beside the house and stopped before the refined classical tempietto marking the grave of the hero of the Battle of New Orleans. It was appropriate, the speaker for the Ladies' Hermitage Association noted, for the hero of 1918 to visit the home of the hero of 1815. It was also fortunate, an observer might have concluded, that these ladies, in searching for funds to restore the century-old house, happened upon such a handsome and popular figure. Like New York motion picture producers and Own Your Own Home advocates, they saw the drawing power true heroism bestowed.

Before leaving the Hermitage, York had a meeting with the Rotary Club committee set up to help him buy a farm. They wanted to know where he wanted to live and what kind of farm he would prefer. York continued to insist he wanted to stay in Pall Mall. He had never lived anywhere else and never saw anything that would change his mind. The committee told York the first fund-raising effort was planned for that afternoon at the local baseball field, where the Tennessee Volunteers had a game.

York arrived at the baseball park in Sulphur Dell just in time to catch a torrential downpour that cancelled the game. Disappointed fans were encouraged to come back the next day for a make-up double header and watch Sergeant York pitch to Governor Roberts.

Tuesday night a Rotary Club dinner honored Alvin York with songs, poems, more gifts, comedians, and politicians. Playing to his national audience, Governor Roberts challenged reports about York being a conscientious objector. He noted Northern newspapers were unkind in their depiction of Southerners in general. He insisted, "we are not ignoramuses," though his own remarks drew a peculiar comparison between learning and fighting: "We don't have much literature in our homes, and we think our children are none the worse for it. Our boys learn athletics early. A boy up there [in Pall Mall] considers himself disgraced if he cannot shoot and fight and swim. He is a born feudist. He fights for what he believes is the truth, and when he starts in, it is to come out victor."

After a humorist named Jeff McCarn proclaimed York—with a glance at Gracie—to be "the best 'dear'-hunter in Tennessee," Pastor Pile stood and spoke briefly. A "monster ovation" then greeted Sergeant York as he rose. Again York's remarks lasted only a minute or two. He had nothing to say about his battlefield victory in France, only thanks to God for his deliverance and to the people of Tennessee for their generous hospitality.

Wednesday, Sergeant York arrived at the baseball park in Sulphur Dell to throw out the first ball of the second game. York had never seen a baseball game and knew little about it. After a short lesson, the tall visitor walked out to the pitcher's mound with a new baseball and borrowed glove. Governor Roberts, in his customary three-piece suit, took up a position behind the plate. York let fly, and the baseball shot straight and true toward the governor, who found the delivery too hot to handle. The umpire called a passed ball as the fans applauded enthusiastically. Someone retrieved the ball for York, who autographed it and gave it to Gracie. Plans were to auction it off for the York Farm Fund.

A reporter approached Mother York in the stands and asked if she liked the game. "I think it's fine," she declared.

"Would you like to stay around and learn to be a fan?"

"What's a fan?"

"That's somebody who's always going to a ball game because they like it."

"No, I don't think I would. But I think it's fine."

That night a dinner party was held in York's honor at the Hermitage Hotel in Nashville, followed by a vaudeville show at the Princess Theater. The audience rose and applauded until York and his family were seated. The guests of honor had to be divided between the two front boxes, since there wasn't room for all of them on one side. They appeared to enjoy the dancing, singing, and other acts, and the sergeant and his bride both laughed long and hard when a woman singing "A Good Man Is Hard to Find" looked Gracie in the eye as she sang, "Give him plenty of love and treat him right!" After the show the York party adjourned to the Fifth Avenue Theater for a showing of a war picture titled *Home Town Girl*.

The newlyweds' honeymoon plans called for them to leave Nashville Wednesday for Salt Lake City. The first stop, arranged by the Rotary Club and including lunch with the mayor and other dignitaries, was supposed to be Louisville. York changed his mind about the trip after a talk with Pastor Pile, who advised against it as unnecessarily worldly and tempting. The two of them composed a telegram and sent it to their disappointed hosts in Kentucky, saying the trip to Salt Lake would be "merely a vainglorious call of the world and the devil," and York could "serve God best" by staying at home.

On Thursday morning Sergeant York and his companions boarded the Tennessee Central for Crossville and the ride overland to Pall Mall. Home at last with his beloved Gracie, his dear mother, his hounds, and his hog rifle, Alvin could take a little rest and figure out what to do next.

Chapter Thirteen

Shaping the Vision

Alvin and Gracie moved in with Mother York and Alvin's younger brothers and sisters. Work soon began on a house for the newlyweds sited end-to-end with the York cabin, built so close, in fact, it was possible to climb out of the cabin window and across into the house without touching the ground. York fell easily back into the routine of the valley, seeing to the hay and vegetable crops, tending the livestock, and escaping to the solace of the woods, sometimes with friends, sometimes alone, always with his hog rifle and his hounds.

Despite Alvin's lack of interest in publicity, the Own Your Own Home organizers, the Ladies' Hermitage Association, Governor Roberts, and other public figures were quick to recognize the power his hero status conferred. While they respected the veteran's humility and religious faith, they showed no hesitation in exploiting him for their own ends. York in turn felt no sense of exploitation. In his innocence, he saw only the attention, thanks, and offers of financial help.

He didn't stop to add it all up, but the total of the proposals he received after stepping off the *Ohioan* at Hoboken a month before amounted to something over a quarter of a million dollars. He made $1.60 a day as a laborer on the Dixie Short Route before the war.

Schoolteachers in Fentress County—professionals with a certain status attached to their calling—earned one hundred dollars a month or less. Twenty-five thousand dollars would have made Alvin York a rich man; ten times that could have set him and his family up for generations.

But, "For what is a man profited, if he shall gain the whole world and lose his own soul?" Alvin could never explain the tragedy of war or the deaths of other soldiers. He was ready to settle down in the valley of his ancestors with the woman he loved so long and won at last, and never look back.

The world, though, came looking for Alvin. Almost every day someone made the trip from Jamestown to call on Sergeant York. Strangers stopped in at Pile's store, where the pastor or one of his customers pointed the way across the valley to the York homestead. If York was in, he welcomed visitors politely and accepted their congratulations but he invariably declined every request to recount his adventures in the Argonne. If York was out in the field or hunting or fishing, Mother York or Gracie would invite callers to stay until he got back, pausing from their work to offer a refreshing glass of cool spring water.

Week after week the visitors came, some of them with still more offers. While York seemed content to let the opportunities lie, prominent men in New York and Nashville took it upon themselves to do otherwise. E. A. Kellogg, secretary of the Tennessee Society of New York, announced in mid-June he was serving as York's financial advisor and that York was planning to film a "historical picture" titled *The Divine Call.* Production would get underway soon with a fifty-thousand-dollar advance and profits would go to York to fund his education.

Less than two weeks later, the project was pulled from Kellogg and placed in the hands of George N. Welch, Tennessee State Railroad Commissioner and a close friend of Governor Roberts. Welch wrote that York "ran away from a New York shyster and asked a Tennessean whom he knew to assist him in his efforts." The more likely explanation was Roberts engineered the agreement between his friend Welch and York. It was the beginning of a tug-of-war between Tennessee and out-of-state interests to influence York's vision for the future.

The Wolf River Valley in the summer of 1919 was a place Old Coonrod Pile would have found very familiar, even though he would now encounter a handful of automobiles; one or two telephones; a kerosene or carbide gas generator for electric lights here and there; and some of the men trading their old hog rifles for breech-loaders. Other than those few twentieth-century intrusions, life was much the same as a hundred years before. Families cleared land and built houses and barns by hand with the help of their neighbors. They plowed with horses or mules; they lit their homes by kerosene; they got their water from springs; they warmed themselves with fireplaces and wood stoves.

Farmers worked by the signs—planting potatoes under a waning quarter moon made less vine, more potato; castrating hogs with the moon in Pisces kept them from bleeding to death. They passed down traditional home remedies—boiled chestnut leaves on a burn; a spider web or lamp black on a cut; a dose of rendered polecat fat for chest congestion. Entertainment centered around church services and socials, weddings and funerals, corn shuckings and other harvest events, and a few men thereabouts who could put down a hoe and pick up a guitar or fiddle.

The world outside, by contrast, was on the brink of unimaginable change. In May, a U.S. Navy seaplane made the first air crossing of the Atlantic Ocean, hopscotching from New York to Newfoundland, the Azores, and England in fifty-seven hours. Henry Ford was churning out Model Ts by the millions at prices working men could afford. Women were expecting to vote in their first presidential election soon. An experiment called radio was almost ready for commercial introduction. Movies were soaring in popularity. The heavy economic losses of the Great War shifted the world's financial balance of power from Europe to America for the first time. President Wilson's dream of a League of Nations pointed toward a future of peace and prosperity.

In Paris and New York, Alvin saw the new world and he found nothing in it for him. Pastor Pile had even dissuaded him from taking a honeymoon trip to Salt Lake City. York also knew Pile wrote to the newspapers after their return from Nashville, expressing regret for being seen attending a vaudeville show. "I am sure my friends meant well," he explained, "but that was no place for Pastor Pile. I am very sorry I was there and have deeply repented of same."

The world outside the valley had its pitfalls. Equally true, however, was the fact the world held valuable benefits. Alvin York saw great cities alive with clean electric lights, smooth, wide boulevards, and men and women who daily reaped the benefits of an education they took for granted. He saw the vast chasm between what he learned in his few winter weeks at school and what a man needed to make the most of his God-given abilities.

When he left Fentress County for training camp in Georgia, York's writing skills were poor, his speaking skills primitive. Through a year and a half of practice and keen observation, he improved them dramatically and saw the value of educating himself further. Few of his neighbors would ever have the chance to better themselves without a year-round school they could get to regularly, even when the creeks were high.

The mailman rode over from Jamestown every day on a roan horse, carrying mail in pouches hung across his mount like saddlebags. Until recently the load was light. These days the bags bulged with mail, swinging with the gait of the horse and flapping against its sides. Most of the correspondence was for Sergeant Alvin York, who had been accustomed to receiving a handful of letters in a year and was now getting a pouch full or more a day.

Many writers, assuming a man as famous as York must be fabulously rich, sent pathetic requests for money. Other letters came from prisoners and their families, requesting York's help in securing a pardon. He also received business proposals of every description and usually a marriage offer or two per week, typically including a detailed description of the writer's most admirable qualities. Overwhelmed after his initial efforts to answer every letter, York started keeping them in a big wooden box under his bed.

Alvin had promised to attend the Tennessee Independence Day festivities on July 4 with Governor Roberts. Since Gracie was under the weather, Alvin invited his sixteen-year-old brother George along as a traveling companion. They arrived in Nashville on the evening of the third and were received at the governor's mansion before going on to Commissioner Welch's home to spend the night. In stark contrast to his arrival the month before, there were no great crowds at the station, no hordes blocking the street. York and Welch discussed their moving picture project, and the two of them met with the Rotary Club committee appointed to buy York a farm. York traveled to the town of Gallatin for a celebration, then returned to the state fairgrounds in Nashville for a second appearance. That night, Alvin and George took the Tennessee Central back to Crossville. There was no special coach for them.

It appeared as though Tennessee was already losing interest in its native hero. Out of state, however, the crowds were as big as ever. York accepted an invitation to appear July 12, at the Methodist Centenary Exposition in Columbus, Ohio. Another guest there was Lieutenant Commander Albert C. Read, who, two months before, became the first man ever to fly across the Atlantic. York and Read were given separate receptions, York's first.

The coliseum in Columbus was packed to the doors with an enthusiastic audience. In response to his welcome, York replied: "I wish I could make a fine speech to you, but I am not a speaker. I'm just a plain mountain boy from Tennessee. All I have to say about the war in France is in honor of God, for without His help we would not have won. I live and practice a full salvation and I believe in continual prayer. While I was in France I prayed continually to God that I might come home without a scratch from the Germans, and I did."

Commander Read spoke about the frustrating lack of interest in flying in America, compared with the far-reaching government and public support it was receiving in Europe. Read and York met at lunch and received medals struck in their honor by the Exposition. In the afternoon the two guests toured the exhibits together, crowded every foot of the way by thousands who wanted to see and speak to them, protected from the crush by a cordon of soldiers.

Back home in Pall Mall, offers continued arriving in the mail pouches every day—endorsements, magazine features, biographies, moving pictures, religious causes. In Fentress County, York neither expected nor received any special treatment as a hero. If anything, there were people in the county who resented all the attention lavished on York and stiffened at the thought of the Rotary Club's plan to give him a farm for nothing. In Nashville and the rest of the state, by contrast, York had the sympathetic ear of every politician and public official. And in Columbus, Ohio, and other points outside Tennessee, York was still hailed as an American hero. The further from Pall Mall a traveler went, the greater was the stature of its most famous native son.

As corn grew tall in the summer sun, Alvin sorted through the piles of mail and thought about what he should do. He refused to profit from the blood of others—on that point the decision was clear and unshakable. But what was the right thing to do with all the choices being laid at his feet? With the stroke of a pen on an endorsement contract, he could live in unimaginable luxury for the rest of his life; a hero savoring his just reward.

York never claimed to be a hero. When he and the rest of his squad surprised the German infantry at breakfast at the foot of Hill 223, there was no time to consider one course of action over another. Corporal York was brave, resourceful, cool-headed, and an incredible shot with his Eddystone and his Colt .45. Through it all, though, there was never time to make a hero's choice. It was a soldier's conditioned, visceral response: kill or be killed.

God protected him in battle and brought him back home safely. The battle made him famous; fame gave him power. If he didn't care anything about power for himself, what should he do with it? Let it wane like it was already starting to do in Tennessee (if his Independence Day trip to Nashville was any indication)? Cash in on his war experiences after all to raise money for his family and his community?

There was no reason to choose a hard life over an easy one. Except that to Alvin York, an easy life bought with soldiers' blood was as unimaginable as it would have been to stand in the Argonne Forest with his rifle at his side and let the Germans shoot him.

Sometime over the next eight weeks, York made a hero's choice, dramatically altering not only his own life, but the lives of thousands for generations to come. He resolved to use the fame and power God's protection in battle gave him to help a precious constituency who could never help themselves: the children who were growing up in his beautiful, isolated valley with almost no chance of getting an education.

Alvin York began to shape the vision of a free, year-round school for children of the valleys and mountains of Tennessee. Its buildings would be sturdy and warm, so if a girl or boy didn't have a coat or shoes, they could still come to class. It would have the books, facilities, and money to attract good teachers. Most important of all, it would be built where the children of his valley could get to it or give them free transportation out of the valley and back. Students could even board there during the week.

The school would be dedicated to helping boys and girls grow up to take their place in the world with confidence and teach them trades that would provide them with a secure livelihood. All the students would learn to read and write, along with basic arithmetic, history, and science. The boys would learn farming techniques, animal husbandry, and carpentry. The girls would learn spinning, weaving, and home economics. All students of every age would receive courses in religion, sharing the Christian message Alvin felt guided him so safely and securely through life.

The country wanted to see and hear Sergeant Alvin York. Now he had something to talk to them about.

The idea of raising money for a school appealed to Welch. Along with officers of the Nashville Rotary Club, he and York made plans for an ambitious speaking tour to solicit construction funds. Before August was over, an itinerary was set tracing a four-pronged route over the entire eastern half of the country: southeastward to Chattanooga, west to San Antonio, north to Detroit, and finally up through New England to New York and Boston. Civic leaders and organizations jumped at the chance to host a reception or dinner in honor of America's greatest hero and Rotary Clubs in major cities took the lead in securing lodging and arranging logistics.

York remained firm in his view that it was wrong for him to talk to a paying audience about killing Germans. This presented a dilemma for Welch, who knew York's war remembrances were what attracted the crowds. The two men reached a compromise, agreeing someone would travel with the sergeant and tell of his Argonne adventures by way of introduction, then York would talk about his dream of educating the mountain children of Tennessee.

Welch helped York assemble a troupe to make the trip with him. The sergeant and Gracie would be accompanied by Pastor Pile and York's Fentress County friend and best man, Clay Brier. Welch also recruited his friend Dr. Gus Dyer, a professor at Vanderbilt University in Nashville, and invited Edgar Foster, whose *Nashville Banner* was working with the Rotary to raise money for the York Farm Fund, to send his son Stratton along as a personal assistant to York. Foster was flattered at the opportunity offered his son but worried the arrangement might look too much like nepotism. He asked his son to choose a friend of his to accompany York instead, and Stratton selected his Vanderbilt fraternity brother Lipscomb Davis to make the trip in his place.

The group met at the passenger depot in Crossville and took a southbound train to Chattanooga, where York made his first speech as a private citizen on the day of his discharge. The audience of well-wishers in the hotel lobby then were warm and enthusiastic in their response to his impromptu remarks from the mezzanine that afternoon. Shortly he would see whether they were still interested in what he had to say. And he would taste—whether sweet or sour—the first fruits of a hero's choice.

Chapter Fourteen

Onward Christian Soldier

The Chattanooga newspaper considered it a "fair-sized crowd" in attendance September 9, at the Bijou Theater. "The crowd was not large, not much more than half the lower floor being filled." A modest attendance seemed to have no effect on the big-boned mountaineer as he mounted the stage dressed in a new suit, vest, and bow tie, his thick red hair freshly combed, moustache neatly trimmed. He stood still, hands behind his back, speaking more in the earnest tones of a sermon than the inciting, fiery way of a storyteller or a man appealing to strangers for money. As Gracie, Professor Dyer, and local luminaries watched from the sides of the stage, York spoke simply and from the heart about the mountain children who had no schools, no teachers, no roads, and no hope.

Speaking in "a silvery accent of pleasing resonance" using "words which have always been distinctly Tennessean, and which give added interest to his audience," York explained how he hoped to raise $150,000 for a series of schools throughout the mountains of central Tennessee. He emphasized repeatedly that any money he collected would be used for that purpose and no other. "Just after returning I was offered $1,000 a night," he told the audience, "and just by signing a contract it was $50,000 for me. That's not such bad wages . . . when you'd been working before the war for 50 and 75 cents a day. But even so, what does it profit a man to gain the whole world, and lose his own soul?"

The sergeant spoke only briefly. Professor Dyer then took the podium and went on at length about York's adventures in the Argonne Forest, his selflessness, and the need for schools, in a manner the local newspaper found "impressive, interesting, and convincing."

The group returned to Pall Mall filled with optimism. The audience was receptive, and the sergeant made a profit on the trip. Welch helped York set up the Alvin C. York Foundation to manage the funds and keep a careful public accounting.

After a few days' rest, York, Gracie, Professor Dyer, and Lipscomb Davis, who was now serving as secretary of the York Foundation, began an ambitious journey that quickly made "fair-sized" crowds a thing of the past. With York detailing his vision for a school and Dyer describing York's battlefield adventures, Tennessee cities rekindled their interest in their native son. Notices in Knoxville proclaimed, "Alvin C. York, The World's Greatest Hero, and TENNESSEE'S OWN, Will Deliver An Address Monday Evening, Sept. 15th"; "Sergt. Alvin York, the pride of Tennessee and the whole world. . . ." Unlike his Chattanooga appearance, this one was written up ahead of time in some detail by the local press, touching on his hope of raising money for mountain schools, and promising he would "tell Knoxvillians the story of his wonderful fete in France."

Those who paid the dollar for a reserved seat in expectation of war stories heard instead of eager, promising boys and girls who had no educational opportunities and little chance of getting them. In introducing York, Judge Hugh M. Tate put the soldier on the spot by suggesting in front of the audience that he tell them all of his great war victory. The crowd murmured in anticipation, but York was not one to be backed into a corner, even on stage in front of hundreds of listeners. After speaking about the schools he dreamed of building, York said he appreciated the interest of the people in the war. But, he went on, he hoped the audience would realize recalling that autumn day in France also reminded him of times when the soldiers he learned to love as brothers were falling so thick and fast by his side that at times he was walking "literally in their blood."

The next stop, two days later, was Birmingham, for their first engagement outside Tennessee. The reception was promising. "Greatest Hero of World War Speaks Here Tonight" proclaimed the local papers, adding breathlessly, "Today Birmingham is to have what movie magnates and vaudeville kings have offered fortunes for and yet have failed to get . . . [we] will get Alvin C. York and will hear from him the story of how he became the greatest hero of the world war."

Even though his train arrived at 4:30 in the morning, a crowd awaited him on the platform. Rotary Club members and a local contingent from York's 82nd Division, headed by Colonel Crampton Harris, were also on hand, but the officials had to scramble for space with reporters, photographers, and ordinary people jostling and crowding to see this redheaded hero and the shy, charming wife who clutched his arm tightly, staring silently and wide-eyed at the commotion.

When Sergeant York and Gracie stepped from the train, they were immediately engulfed by the waiting crowd. They made their way to their hotel and reappeared for a late breakfast about five hours later, walking off the elevator into a wall of photographers and well-wishers. Moving at the center of a large and growing cluster of onlookers, they finally seated themselves at the table amidst a sea of whispers: "That's him. That's Sergeant York!"

It was ten o'clock by then, hours after York's accustomed breakfast time, and he tucked into his meal with unashamed eagerness, only to be interrupted by a reporter with questions about the war. "Let's lay off the war," the sergeant replied with polite firmness. "I prefer to think of other things. The school for instance." He launched into a short but detailed description of the educational system he had in mind. "We plan to make it possible for students to attend the school whether they have any money or not. They'll learn academic subjects part of the day and get practical instruction in agriculture the rest. There'll be a shop so they can learn trades if they want to."

After breakfast the sergeant and Gracie took a tour of the city and then returned to the hotel for a Rotary Club luncheon. Members and guests packed the dining room. When York was introduced, the storm of applause required him to wait several minutes before he began to speak. As before, he talked briefly but sincerely about his vision for a school and sat down with the barest mention of having "been overseas."

"Now about the war—" a questioner began. York raised his hand. "Don't mention that. I left that over there, and don't want to think about it."

York took a tour of the steel mills at nearby Ensley, then went with Gracie to the Jefferson Theater for his public speaking engagement. Patrons were assured the theater would "make a heroic effort to afford room for every person possible." The building was packed to the rafters. The presentation opened with the introduction of Professor Dyer, who recounted the events of the previous October 8. He told of York's rural upbringing and of his dream of providing schools for mountain children. In closing, he quoted York, saying, "The best stock in our country has been locked up in the mountains and we can't afford to leave them there."

Captain W. F. Enneking, regimental adjutant of the 82nd Division, then introduced Sergeant York. As York rose, a thunderous ovation filled the theater, and the audience stood as one to pay tribute to America's greatest war hero. Relaxed and easy on his feet in spite of the noise, York waited for quiet and then delivered the speech he would make, with few changes, on many subsequent occasions. A newspaper reporter took the whole five-minute presentation in shorthand. The transcription took less than half a column in the next day's edition:

> *My purpose in coming here tonight is not to talk about myself. The men who were in France and in the fighting do not like to talk about it, as you have probably found out. They want to forget it. I am here to tell you how when I came back, I suddenly saw the need of education for the boys and girls of our mountainous country. I have learned as a result of my own lack of it just how much they will be handicapped when they grow up without it.*
>
> *Everyone should be anxious to raise the standard in this country and there is just one way to do it: by religion and education. America is a diamond in the rough. No other country in the world has a generation of young men such as we*

have today. And we've got to lend a helping hand to see that they and the coming generations are not held back by a lack of education. In my county there are boys and girls who haven't had an opportunity to go to school for more than two years, and the same is true in many other sections in the South.

And it is to change that situation that I am here. I see the need of a school for those boys and girls.

Since I came home I have been offered a thousand dollars a day, but I remembered those lines in the little book that I always carry with me. "What shall a man profit if he gain the whole world and lose his own soul?" And I felt that if I accepted that offer, that if I forgot those boys and girls in Fentress County, I would be losing my own soul. So instead, I'm giving my time to help them. I'd rather see them totter to and from a good school every day than to have half a million dollars in the bank.

I am here tonight in the course of a lecture tour, the purpose of which is to raise funds to give them that school. I am not begging. I am simply pointing out the need of those people in the mountains of Tennessee and giving you a chance to subscribe what you will to its endowment fund.

Nine days into the tour, contributions and pledges were exceeding a thousand dollars a day—a year and a half's average wages in Fentress County.

The Yorks, Lipscomb Davis, and Professor Dyer met with similar success in Huntsville and Montgomery. Theaters were packed at a dollar a head, with all money going to the foundation. "This great American Soldier should be seen and heard by all patriotic red-blooded Americans" trumpeted the announcements in Huntsville, where all the school children got a half-holiday. In Montgomery York gamely granted an interview to "'Jimmy' The Boy Reporter" among many others.

Each welcome was more dazzling than the past. By the time they reached New Orleans on the morning of September 19, their arrival sparked a major extravaganza. Never hesitant to host a party, citizens of the Crescent City began gathering at the Louisville and Nashville station more than an hour before the train was due. By the time it chuffed into view, a thousand people had pushed and squeezed their way onto the platform. Various official greeters from the New Orleans Advertising Club and the Rotarians, sporting colored arm bands, struggled against the crowd. Police were finally called in for fear someone would be pushed off the platform in front of the engine.

York's train slowly approached. Every time a member of the crowd spotted a uniform through the window of a car, the cry would go up, "There he is! There he is!" After a moment there was a mad scramble at one spot where forewarned Rotarians gathered and down the steps came York, dressed in a green suit and hat, with Gracie holding tightly to his arm. The Rotarians formed a human shield around the party as they were welcomed by the mayor and the Ad Club and presented a key to the city by a couple dressed in antebellum Creole finery identified as Mr. and Mrs. New Orleans.

As the sergeant and Gracie turned to leave the platform, the crowd surged in the same direction. Burly seamen from the naval station were brought into service to clear a path. The Yorks worked their way through to the street, where a coach drawn by four white horses waited to take them, along with Mayor Behrman, to a reception at the Grunwald Hotel. The resplendent coach-and-four eased away from the curb to join a parade, which by then included two dozen mounted policemen, a platoon of policemen on foot, the police band, several rows of Rotarians, an honor guard of soldiers, sailors, and marines, Ad Club members, and automobiles filled with ladies from the reception committee.

Eager Rotarians who followed York through the hotel lobby and up the elevator to his room found him a man of few words. Pumping his hand and peppering him with questions, they were answered with a gesture toward a large gift basket on a nearby table. "We sure do like fruit," he said.

York spoke that night at the Sydney Lanier High School auditorium, then at a large public hall, The Athenaeum, the next day. The New Orleans press compared his heroism with the deeds of Beowulf, Charlemagne, Lancelot, and Richard the Lionhearted, yet observed, "You would take him for the sewing machine salesman who rides around town in a buggy with a machine strapped in the back, looking for whom he may interest on the installment plan. . . . It's a comforting thought . . . that a man who has done what York has done should look like anybody else. And the comfort is increased by his acting like anybody else —only moreso." On Sunday York and Gracie attended church twice, once at St. Charles Avenue Baptist Church, then at St. Charles Avenue Christian Church. Between the two services, York addressed an Advertising Club convention at Tulane.

The next stop was Houston, where, before a large crowd at the City Auditorium, he finally agreed to say something about his war experiences, "in the language of the mountaineer, here and there rather ungrammatical, but withal picturesque," according to one account. In a few sentences he sketched out the barest statistics of the Argonne battle. "But I didn't come here to talk about the war," he then said, and began afresh the story of his mountain children and his dream. Following York's remarks, one person on the platform declared, "Had the sergeant possessed the education which he is seeking to give to others, he might have stood in Pershing's place." Contributions that night alone totaled $2,659.

After the southern tour Sergeant York and the others ventured northward through Lexington, Kentucky, and then to Louisville, where York listened with amazement to an explanation of union locals and closed shops. "If I had men working for me and they told me that I couldn't hire anyone but the man they said, why, I'd tell them all to go," he said. "And I'd get men who were willing to work with the men I'd select. The men who never heard of any other union except the union of democracy."

The group continued northward toward the Great Lakes: Grand Rapids, Detroit, Kalamazoo, and Flint. An observer in Saginaw said of him, "There is something Lincolnesque about this character; simple, steadfast, self-sacrificing in its manifestations towards helping others. Such men, such character, form a mighty influence for national good; prove how sound at the core the great heart of the people is."

Northern reporters scarcely knew how or whether to try to reproduce York's unfamiliar mountain drawl in print. Some wrote what they knew he meant. Others left in the unconventional grammar that, for example, used "seen," "seed," "had seen," and "had seed" to mean one and the same. Still others made an attempt to record his accent with phonetic accuracy. Reporter Eleanor Stinchcomb quoted him thus: "I am shorely eager to get learnin' fo' these child'en in the mountains. And the reason is because I know I need one so. And the mo' I travels, the mo' I know I needs one. Me and my brothahs used to study at home evenin's, and ouah fathah was good, and would help us with what we didn't undastand."

Women reporters being rare, she also managed to charm a couple of opinions out of him on issues of the day. On prohibition: "I certainly believe that law foh prohibition is a mighty good law, for drink nevah did me any good, and no good has been done by any man in drink." On women's suffrage, which would become law within the year: "I do not believe the ladies should vote, at least not for several yeahs, till they have got used to the idea. They have been goin' along, nevah thinkin' 'bout politics, an' they will many a lady vote wrong. They is enough ignorant men voters."

After triumphant appearances in Chicago and St. Louis, the group returned to Pall Mall for Christmas. York's brother took charge of fall planting for him while he was away, but, true to his consistently stated future plans to "be a farmer," the sergeant was anxious to see about his fields and fences in person. In three months, he figured he had raised about forty thousand dollars and had pledges for fifty thousand more, which he considered "a good start" for the children of Fentress County who had gone without a school far too long.

With the new year, York and Lipscomb Davis left for New England. Professor Dyer remained in Nashville. Awaiting the birth of her first child, Gracie stayed at Mother York's. As required by the decorum of the day, the official explanation of Gracie's absence was she had the flu. She was, in fact, miserably ill all winter due to the effects of her pregnancy.

York and Davis arrived in Baltimore on January 21, 1920. York followed the pattern of their earlier successes, speaking little if any about the war and a great deal about education. In Gracie's absence, questioners were freer with their inquiries concerning York's opinion of French women. "I don't care to talk about French women," he answered plainly, and would comment only that their skirts were "very short" and the necks cut "very low."

York continued on to Portland, Worcester, Boston, and Providence. The cold and deep snow were hard on a Tennessee mountain man, even one who spent the previous winter riding around in unheated French boxcars. His tour of Portland, Maine, in a new Moon automobile was curtailed by snow-packed city streets. Always hale, York felt himself growing tired and uncomfortable, and by January 28, he was confined to bed. Doctors were summoned and could not agree on whether he was suffering from exhaustion or appendicitis. At last the appendix was identified as the culprit, though the case was a mild one.

Arriving in Worcester, he slept until 1:15 in the afternoon while a capacity crowd of nine hundred Rotarians and guests waited in the hotel ballroom below. Unwilling to disappoint his listeners or miss out on a solicitation opportunity, he rose from his sickbed and entered the ballroom to tremendous applause from "one of the largest noonday luncheons ever at the Bancroft."

He stepped down from the podium after his usual five minutes while the meeting continued, as they customarily did, with a discussion of local affairs (this day's topic: the metric system), local causes, and the inevitable sing-alongs. Patriotic tunes like "God Bless America" were favorites, as were popular songs such as "The Old Oaken Bucket," "Wait 'Til the Sun Shines, Nellie," and "I'm Forever Blowing Bubbles." These were followed by the special fraternal songs of whichever Rotarians, Ad Club, or Temple served as host at the festivities: "The Brotherhood," "Dear to My Heart," "Rotary Forever." The songs would usually be sung by a glee club or quartet, often accompanied by a lively and enthusiastic piano player of local renown.

A thousand miles from Boston and Worcester that same day, Gracie York sat at home in Pall Mall, writing an answer to the most recent letter from Alvin. In the six months of their marriage, this was the longest they had been apart. The sergeant wrote faithfully to his beloved Miss Gracie from the road and mentioned her frequently in his talks and interviews.

She missed him terribly. Her own house next door was unfinished and she was still living with her mother-in-law and a houseful of Alvin's brothers and sisters, helping Mother York with the chores. She was sick, lonesome, and worried about her husband's welfare. Gracie was holding up remarkably well under the circumstances, but she wanted her Alvin home.

Taking a sheet of the sergeant's own newly-purchased stationery with "Alvin C. York/Pall Mall, Tenn." engraved in blue at the top, she wrote in pencil with a firm, angular hand.

> *Sgt Alvin C. York, My Darling Husband*
>
> *I will this morning try and ans[wer] your most kind and loving letter which I rec[eived] and was more than glad to hear from you. Well darling I was very very sorry to hear that you were dated up untill the 26 of Feb. I no if time seems as long to you as it does to me that you could not stay away from your darling so long.*

In public and even in front of family members, their expressions of affection took the form of a look or a smile or Gracie's firm hold on the sergeant's burly arm; nothing more. It was only in their letters that they revealed a glimpse of the passionate devotion that defined their lives.

> *Sure wish you were hear so I could get some of those sweet kisses of those roses cheeks of yours. . . . I would give the world and all that is in it if I could only get to see you this morning and put my arms around your neck and kiss you and call you my darling Husband. Every body is getting along allright seems like but me and I haft to worry and cry all the time nearly seems like. Maby you can come back sooner than March darling. I never will stay at home again unless I haft to for it would not of hurt me as bad to of went as it did to stay at home. . . . Oh how happy I would be this morning to see my darling come in at the door.*

She wrote about daily affairs too. The new barn still wasn't started. The ground was too muddy to plow. But the constant undercurrent, bubbling to the surface in almost every line, was that home wasn't home if the sergeant was away.

> *Well this is all I guess. Remember your darling wife prays for you everyday.*

> *Your darling loving wife Gracie York.*
> *1,000 kisses XXX to my darling.*
> *I will have the stove set up soon as possible.*

Chapter Fifteen

World Affairs

W hile York was out raising money for Tennessee school children, his friends were raising money for him with far less success. The Nashville Rotary Club mounted an energetic fund-raising campaign on the sergeant's behalf and secured the deed to three separate but adjoining plots of land—four hundred acres in all—from the Wright family in Pall Mall. The land once belonged to Old Coonrod and was some of the richest, levelest land in the valley, bordered on the north by the Wolf River and on the west by the main north-south roadway. It was land Alvin often looked down upon from his mother's seventy-five acres along the eastern foothills. Now it was his.

Actually, it was his only in part. The Rotary Club took title to the property on November 18, 1919, by paying less than half the purchase price of twenty-five thousand dollars and taking out three promissory notes totaling $12,062.50 plus interest. Despite the club's best efforts, the fund-raising drive did not go as planned. The club even distributed George Pattullo's glowing account from *The Saturday Evening Post* in pamphlet form, but the story hadn't brought the response they expected. The people had clamored for a chance to honor Alvin York. For whatever reason, they were not now taking advantage of the opportunity.

The enormous debt incurred on his behalf worried York a great deal. He never considered using any of the thousands he was raising for a school to help pay off the farm, accepting only enough to cover travel expenses. Everything else went into the York Foundation fund. He had lived all his life in a barter economy. People didn't have much money and seemed to get along all right without it. Now he was somehow connected with a king's ransom in promissory notes and was helpless to do anything much about it.

Farming and livestock would not pay such debts for many years. York's cash flow was further restricted by the fact that since he quit smoking in 1915, he refused to grow tobacco, the most lucrative cash crop in the region. There was money from endorsements to be made on every hand, but it wasn't the kind of money Sergeant York was willing to take. "I told 'em all that this uniform of Uncle Sam's ain't for sale," he said often.

York's personal income once came from farming his mother's land, blacksmithing, and working on the Dixie Short Route. Now he had no time for any of those. He was away in Boston or San Antonio raising money for a mountain school, sometimes collecting thousands of dollars in a single night, instead of plowing or harvesting or shoeing a mule. The more he was away, the less time he could spend earning a living. He had a new wife, a baby on the way, and a mother and siblings who increasingly looked to him for support. And now there was a farm with a twelve-thousand-dollar debt. Even though the debt wasn't officially his, he felt responsible for it. Many of his neighbors in Pall Mall assumed York had money to spare when he actually had barely enough to live on.

In Washington, Representative Cordell Hull sent up a trial balloon on behalf of his famous but financially strapped constituent. He inquired among members of the House Committee on Military Affairs, including fellow Tennessean Hubert F. Fisher, whether they would entertain a proposal to allow Sergeant York some financial relief. Sensing, if not enthusiastic endorsement, at least a murmur of interest, Hull appeared before the committee on October 22, recounting York's historic actions of the previous year and reading his military citations and most of Pattullo's *Post* story into the record. There the matter stood as

York worked his way through the bitter November weather in Kalama-zoo, Flint, and Chicago, soliciting funds for schools in a place his comfortably fur-wrapped audiences could scarcely imagine.

As Sergeant York's business advisor, George Welch grew weary of the moving picture business. He and York heard nothing from the New York producers to convince them York's story would be told the way York wanted it to be. The picture companies smacked of worldliness and excess. Their stock in trade was money, not morals, and the various proposals they discussed back and forth offered little encouragement that a film project would proceed.

Welch then turned to the idea of a book. It wouldn't be a war book, since that was the part of his life Alvin cared least about, though the Argonne victory would play a justly prominent part. It would be a book about a proud mountain people, their history and traditions, and their need for modern schools and roads. This was an entertainment medium and a story York could approve even as second elder. Welch selected a New York writer named Sam K. Cowan to write the book. Cowan was well known within book and magazine publishing circles. His connections were seen as a valuable asset in getting the book before as large an audience as possible.

For his trouble in arranging a deal with Cowan, Commissioner Welch took a considerable drubbing at the hands of his political opponents. They wondered aloud in the Nashville and New York press what sort of contract Welch had with York and why Welch deserved the 50 percent of York's proceeds he was rumored to have taken. Dr. James J. King, a physician from Columbia, Tennessee, and president of the Tennessee Society of New York, not only took Welch to task but laid blame on Governor Roberts as well for denying the brave war hero the full measure of whatever his memoir was worth. He wrote to Welch on January 20, 1920, suggesting the way to clear the air was to send the Society photographs of every contract between the commissioner and Sergeant York. "All we want," said King, "is to see that York gets a square deal."

When Roberts and Welch declined to answer, Dr. King retaliated by denying the governor an invitation to an event he had been looking forward to with boyish enthusiasm for almost a year. Roberts was the guest of the Society the previous April when the battleship *Tennessee* was launched and expected to be invited back in the spring of 1920 for her commissioning. When friends in New York suggested the Society host the governor's return, there was an "emphatic refusal on the part of the Tennesseans to entertain or have anything to do with the Tennessee executive." Alvin York was now a hot political issue.

While Welch and his opponents argued the propriety of a contract with Cowan, Alvin agreed to another business proposal on his own. Among dozens of letters in the Pall Mall mail pouch one day was an inquiry from the Chattanooga Medicine Company, asking for permission to use the sergeant's and Mother York's names and pictures in an endorsement for the health tonics they produced.

Their products were popular all-purpose cures of the sort typically containing peppermint oil, alcohol (a vital ingredient during Prohibition), petroleum, vanilla extract, and numerous secret ingredients. The resulting liquid often looked like motor oil, smelled like minty tar, and tasted terrible, but was aggressively marketed as a cure for arthritis, hysteria, neuralgia, dyspepsia, skin rashes, dandruff, and a raft of feminine complaints.

Chattanooga Medicine Company produced two tonics, Wine of Cardui and Thedford's Black-Draught. For years their successful advertising campaign was based on endorsements by renown citizens, doctors, and men of letters who sang their praises. Prominent on each ad was the statement that these spokesmen were not paid for their comments. Implied was the idea that this wonderful news was something they willingly shared for the benefit of other sufferers.

The clear indication that no payment was involved may have appealed to Alvin and his mother, or perhaps it was an interest in helping a business from the mountains of Tennessee. Whatever the reason, the two of them, after declining so many offers, agreed to appear in what the company called its "birthday almanac." On October 28, 1919, between his San Antonio and Chicago trips, Alvin met with a company representative in Pall Mall and signed a statement for his mother declaring Black-Draught was "splendid for torpid liver, sour stomach, head aches and such." She also praised Wine of Cardui as an aid to coping with the stress of change of life. "I was so nervous I couldn't stand any thing. . . . I used a number of bottles and got well."

On the third day of the new year, 1920, the Chattanooga Medicine Company representative was back in Pall Mall for an endorsement from the famous soldier. York obliged by signing a handwritten statement, witnessed by the company representative, affirming, "My mother doesn't think she could get along without it, and we, when children, dared not complain unless we wanted to be dosed with Thedford's Black-Draught. You may publish this also with any picture as you wish."

Whatever he was expecting, the full-page advertisement appearing a few months later confused, disappointed, and angered Alvin York. His name was set in headline type all the way across the top, exceeded in size only by the huge white-on-black legend at the bottom: "Thedford's Black-Draught For the Liver." His photo—Congressional Medal of Honor on his chest—took up a fourth of the ad or more. His signed statement was there, along with a paragraph in smaller type summarizing his heroic day in France. His mother was not mentioned.

Another full-page ad pictured York in the top center, with smaller photos of Gracie and Mother York, the three of them surrounded by wings, a star-encrusted shield, and silhouettes of doughboys with rifles raised, charging a line of barbed wire. They were, trumpeted the headline, "A Black-Draught Family."

In its March 13, 1920, edition, *The Stars and Stripes* noted York's evident change of heart about accepting endorsement offers but did its best to give him the benefit of the doubt. "Maybe this is no fault of Sergt. York's. The testimonial sharks operate by strange and devious methods, and York is essentially a plain man of simple and direct purposes. When he started out to kill Germans he operated with wonderful efficiency, but that is no sign that some slick, persistent patent medicine booster may not have talked a testimonial out of him."

It was almost May before York knew anything of the controversy. He was preoccupied with an agenda growing more frantic by the day. There were consultations with Commissioner Welch in Nashville about the waning prospects for a motion picture on suitable terms and whether to turn their attention to a book by Mr. Cowan. The new house next to Mother York's cabin was finished, and Alvin and Gracie moved in. Down beside the river, York's picturesque four hundred acres, bought but not paid for, had to be cleared of its liens somehow, and the land put to use. His mother's farm needed attention and Alvin's brothers were not inclined to take care of it without his supervision.

Most worrisome was the fact Gracie's baby was due at any time and she was not well. During one of the sergeant's trips in April, Gracie wrote two or three times a week, full of professions of love, yet not hiding her fears about their future. Clearly she was worried about money, as well as the health of her unborn child.

> [April 9:] *Say darling I no that I have got the prettiest and best Husband in the World or ever will be and if you was to get hurt or killed I would go crazy. I hope you will soon have our farm paid for and that we won't haft to pay any attension to no one.*

> [April 15:] *I got to feeling funny when I was a Ironing today. I have been pretty bad today. I guess it was me working and carrying water. The boys haven't harrowed your ground yet neither have they turned theirs yet they haven't worked but one day a piece sence you have been gone for you. [You] asked me what I wanted. I would rather see you tonight as for to have New York and all there is between here and there.* [She enclosed a handful of wildflowers.]

> [April 17:] *Oh how happy I would be for to be in our house tonight so I could sit in my honeys lap and lay my arms around your neck and oh darling how I love you I would rather for that to happen tonight than to have this house full of gold.*

When York finally saw the new Black-Draught ads, his liver was anything but torpid. He had worked honestly and selflessly for months, traveling thousands of miles at all hours in all weather, to establish himself as a man unmoved by wealth, concerned only with the well-being

of Tennessee children. Now with a single stroke, the Chattanooga
Medicine Company undid everything. If his audiences thought he was
interested in money after all, they would stop donating to the school
fund. Contributions would slow to a trickle and his dream would die
on the vine.

He cut short a tour to Washington, New York, and Philadelphia,
and returned to Pall Mall, stating his position in a brief but firm letter
to Chattanooga Medicine Company on May 1.

> *Now I never gave you any right or permit to do this and*
> *you have damaged me already $50,000 and I am going to see*
> *a lawyer and see if I cant make you stop sending out your cards*
> *with my photo on them and also pay the damages.*

An officer of the company answered York's letter promptly on May
4, incredulous that York could be upset, considering the signed and
witnessed statement on file in his office. York, in his plain spoken sim-
plicity, was yet a powerful man, and the company wanted to do right by
him. He wrote York the company was "disposed to comply with your
wishes as to the use of the picture, but we cannot permit you to assume
that we are subject to criticism for anything we have done. Kindly let
us hear from you, giving us your reason why you have apparently so
completely changed your mind."

York fired back another salvo, believing he was approached to
appear in an almanac entry, not an ad campaign. No one, York wrote,
"has any thing that I have written or signed that will cover the things
which you have advertised and you have already damaged me $50,000
in my work and I would not of had you to do what you have done for
$50,000 for thousands of people now believe that I sold out to the
patent medicine co."

The company contacted Mrs. Hattie Lee Grimm, the representative who took the Yorks' statements, showed her copies of the sergeant's
letters, and asked her to clarify his position and smooth the matter over
with another visit.

York received Mrs. Grimm cordially on May 19. Grimm and her
daughter Caroline spent the previous night in Jamestown and left for

Pall Mall in their Model T at 6:30 a.m. The steep grades and rugged rocks stranded them; they walked the last four miles.

When they arrived at the York home, the sergeant was out fishing. Mother York and Gracie came in from the garden to greet their guests and they all exchanged pleasantries for an hour and a half until Alvin returned with four big fish on his string. Mrs. Grimm explained she was there to address his concerns about the Black-Draught ads. York responded that nothing he said or agreed to covered such displays. He faced tough questions from reporters in New York and Philadelphia who saw his endorsements and wondered if he had sold out. York abandoned his tour to come back and deal with the controversy and felt Chattanooga Medicine Company should make up the money he would have raised had he completed the tour.

Mrs. Grimm diplomatically insisted her company wanted to do what was right and would be willing to make a contribution to his school project. But she also showed the sergeant copies of the statement he signed, even pointing out where in the room he sat to sign them.

Finally York agreed that if the company would publish a statement saying he received no money for his endorsement, he would be satisfied. Hattie Lee wrote out a statement and read it aloud:

"The question had arisen as to the money received by Sgt. Alvin C. York for the Black-Draught testimonial published by the Chattanooga Medicine Co. Sgt. York did not receive any money or recompense for this testimonial. This being a remedy used in his mother's and his family, he gladly said so."

York signed the sheet with Mrs. Grimm and Caroline signing as witnesses. Grimm also invited the sergeant and his mother to review the almanac page proof she brought along. Centered in the page was a line drawing of Mother York in an oval frame. Above and below were roughly equal blocks of type; the top one retold Alvin's war story, and the bottom contained Mary York's testimonials for Black-Draught and Cardui.

Invited to comment, Mother York said, "It's nothin' agin me." Mrs. Grimm asked her to sign the page and Alvin stepped forward and signed for her. This layout was much closer to what he had in mind in the first place and he was hopeful his statement would counteract the bad publicity of the others.

They all had a cup of coffee together and York showed Mrs. Grimm and Caroline the pistol he confiscated from Lieutenant Vollmer that morning beyond the foot of Hill 223. The Grimm ladies began their walk back to their abandoned Model T and reached Jamestown just after dark.

The Chattanooga Medicine Company delayed publication of Sergeant York's statement, producing another exchange of letters. York, with his next tour six weeks away, was concerned about going on the road again "until the question of his selling out died down." The company suggested a meeting face-to-face and offered to pay York's way to Chattanooga. York insisted his statement be published immediately. The company offered to meet York in Nashville with Mr. Welch for more discussion. York then let the issue drop. His mind and heart were suddenly on other matters.

Gracie and Alvin were in their new house next to the York cabin only a few weeks when the time came for their child to be born. Even though it was her first baby, Gracie felt something was strange and wrong. She was sick throughout her pregnancy and often "didn't feel right."

Her maternal premonitions were correct. On June 5, 1920, a son was delivered. When Gracie saw him for the first time, her feelings of relief and delight at his birth were shot through with raw pangs of despair. The boy had hydrocephalous—the mountain people called it "watery head." Excess spinal fluid trapped in the brain made the baby's head overlarge, the skin pliable to the touch. The slight pressure of a finger left an impression like a sponge.

They planned to name him Alvin Jr., but it was clear this frail boy would not live to carry his father's legacy. There was no treatment possible, nothing anyone could do except treasure whatever time the child would be with them. Alvin, Gracie, and Mother York took turns holding the tiny infant, rocking him in the living room of the new white house and swaddling him in the bed beside Gracie at night. The second elder sang hymns to his son, particularly his own favorite, "Onward, Christian Soldiers." They offered prayers of thanksgiving for the precious new life and prayed for a miracle of healing. They prayed too for understanding to accept God's will whatever it was.

News of the birth traveled quickly through the valley. A steady stream of visitors came by with food, a word of encouragement, and their own prayers of hope.

The boy lived four days, died peacefully, and was buried in the cemetery by the Methodist church, only a few yards from the grave of Old Coonrod Pile.

Alvin and Gracie had little to say after the simple funeral. Like many mountain people, they accepted death without question, as a part of God's natural order. Their mourning was quiet, brief, and private.

Within a month Gracie was expecting again, and Alvin was dividing his time between planning for the future and coping with the present. The speaking tours were going well, with large and responsive audiences. York was encouraged, despite the fact pledges far outpaced the amount of cash actually deposited in the York Foundation's Nashville bank account.

Alvin was a quick study on the stump. His trial by fire in the year after his return from Europe molded him into a dynamic, articulate speaker with great persuasive power. He still shied away from discussing the war; sometimes the person introducing him would do that, knowing the crowd was eager for the story. His message was unchanged from earlier speeches in Birmingham and New Orleans. But he learned to take better advantage of the aura generated by his fame and rugged good looks to capture his listeners and move them to action.

While the future seemed promising, the present continued to frustrate York and the friends who were trying to help him. He and Gracie needed money. One of the three promissory notes on his farm was up for payment in November and no one knew where the funds would come from. Alvin had high hopes of helping retire the debt with income from the book Sam Cowan was writing about him—York and Welch agreed the money could be used for that—but any proceeds from that project were obviously a long way off. Farming continued to be a struggle, since York was traveling so much and had trouble getting others to keep his place up properly for him.

In Nashville, Commissioner Welch was besieged not by crop cycles and lazy siblings but by political opponents. He was running for another term as railroad commissioner and his challenger, Luke Lea, was having a field day. Welch's agreement with author Sam Cowan was for Welch to get nothing beyond repayment of what he advanced Cowan to get the book underway. Whatever the book earned over and above the advance, Welch affirmed, should go to the York farm fund.

Those facts did not prevent Lea from questioning Welch's motives in his newspaper, the *Tennessean*. According to the contract in question, claimed Lea, "Sergt. York was to receive 50 percent of the proceeds for editing the book—a legitimate percentage—and Mr. Welch 40 percent, though there is no evidence to show what services Welch & Co. were to render." Someone at the Tennessee New York Society compared it to a "Baltimore prizefighter's" contract, "by which the manager, for merely signing up his man, gets half of the money."

Welch steadfastly insisted the agreement among York, Cowan, and himself was their business alone, and if the three of them were satisfied, it was no one else's concern. In an open letter to the *Tennessean*, carried in newspapers statewide, he called Lea's bluff.

> *Since you have demonstrated an interest in Sergt. York, I propose to you that if acceptable we go down to the Rotary Club and personally donate $1,000 each to be applied to this worthy undertaking. I am making this proposition in order to be a good fellow and to retain, if possible, your respect with the hope that you may keep out of my personal affairs.*
>
> *I further propose, if satisfactory to Sergt. York, and if it is your wish, to turn over to you whatever contracts I might have with him, upon your reimbursing me for the amount which I have advanced, which will enable you to assist him in his undertaking.*

At least in published reports, Luke Lea made no response.

Sam K. Cowan spent six weeks in Pall Mall taking in the scenery, absorbing the pace of mountain life, and talking with Alvin, his family, and friends. He collected tales about Old Coonrod Pile, went to husking parties, attended church, and joined the men with their dogs in the field. Returning to New York with six hundred dollars in advance money, he began writing what he thought could either be a magazine serial or a book, or both. Serials were immensely popular, and top fiction writers like F. Scott Fitzgerald earned far more from magazine stories than from novels. Cowan knew the press idolized York and thought at first he would have more choices and a better bargaining position with a serial.

As he settled in to write, however, he saw the project would take far longer than he anticipated. It would not be finished in time to ride the crest of euphoria following the end of the Great War. His personal finances grew tight as Cowan declined a six-month project paying five thousand dollars and another job paying twenty-five hundred to keep working on Alvin York's story, hoping for a jackpot. The writer continued taking only what newspaper assignments he could without interrupting progress on the book and moved his wife and two boys into a smaller apartment in order to get by on a reduced income.

He thought about asking Welch for more money but decided against it. In addition to his advance, Cowan's agreement gave him 20 percent of whatever Sergeant York realized from the project. A bigger advance from Welch would probably mean giving up some of his percentage, and though his piece of the pie was small, Cowan expected it to be a very big pie.

Between writing sessions Cowan began making the rounds of publishers, pitching his story in the spring of 1921. Newspaper syndicates and magazine editors turned him down cold. They were convinced the public was sick of war stories. The *New York Herald*, eager to syndicate the York saga only months before, rejected it now as old news. *The Saturday Evening Post*, source of the feature article most responsible for York's fame, returned the manuscript unopened, saying it had already done its story on the subject. Others made a similar response, all the way down to the bottom of Cowan's list—*Harper's, Scribner's*, and one or two other magazines so "notoriousy cheap" he didn't even send them manuscripts.

Through an agent Cowan and Welch hired, the story was submitted to book publishers who took a nibble here and there. The John C.

Winston Co. kept the manuscript for months, as did Revell, yielding various offers to co-publish with another house or to publish it as "a set of fancy little books." Cowan finally decided to take the bull by the horns, retrieving the manuscript and targeting the best book publishers in New York to call on himself.

Funk & Wagnalls was interested. The response was a tonic to Cowan, who reported enthusiastically to York, "to have Funk & Wagnalls say they think they can make a 'classic' out of it, is some pay for the blood I have oozed." The publisher's attention came at least partly because Sergeant York was back in the national news. With the birth of a healthy son, Alvin Junior, on March 18, 1921, Sergeant York became a family man who needed his financial affairs settled and secured. In July the *New York Times* reported York "worked enough to kill a dozen ordinary men, but the season has been against him. His hay was practically burned up and other crops failed, and Alvin was left in the hole." The article also mentioned the unpaid balance on the farm.

Congressman Hull's proposal in the House to award York a retired lieutenant's pension had led nowhere, and on August 5, Tennessee Senator Kenneth McKellar introduced a bill in the Senate Military Committee giving York the rank of captain with retired pay. Opposition in the committee quickly derailed the bill. The same summer York was offered two thousand dollars to test fire a new rifle. He agreed to do so until he saw his visitors unpacking camera equipment. He would fire it, he said, but not as an endorsement. The company wanted only one shot and one photo, but York would have none of it. The visitors packed their camera gear and left.

On October 5, the Tennessee Society of New York announced it would subscribe funds to help pay a five-thousand-dollar note due November 18, on the York farm. If this note was satisfied, the rest of the balance could be refinanced for another year at least. Back in Pall Mall, Alvin York scrambled to do what he could. On November 16 he executed an oil and gas lease on Mother York's farm, signing his name along with the rest of his brothers and sisters under her X in exchange for one-eighth of the proceeds and fifty dollars a year. In the end York kept his land, and the story of his financial difficulties was detailed by the *New York World* the first week in December.

All this activity prompted Funk & Wagnalls both to make an offer and to insist on a speedy response. Cowan wrote separate letters to York and Welch on December 9, and sent them copies of a contract already signed by Funk & Wagnalls with a proposal expiring December 20. The author was flustered at York's repeated questions about royalty and payment arrangements and wounded by what he considered insensitivity on Welch's part to the sacrifices Cowan had made to get the project finished. But for now all was forgiven as Cowan underlined the terms offered.

The publisher would pay a royalty of 10 percent of the retail price, rising to 12.5 percent for sales beyond fifteen thousand copies. At two dollars a copy, that yielded twenty cents, rising to twenty-five cents. By their previous agreement, York would get 80 percent of the royalty amount, Cowan 20 percent.

Cowan specifically pointed out two other points. One was that the contract explicitly excluded magazine and newspaper serial rights, and movie or theatrical rights, meaning they could provide additional income later on. The other was an explicit identification of who held the copyright. "All copyright privileges accruing to the author under this contract are hereby assigned to Sergeant Alvin C. York, of Pall Mall, Tenn."

"Could anything be clearer?" concluded Cowan. "Could anything be fairer?"

These arrangements were fine, but a couple of other issues troubled York regarding the finances. Other publishers talked about giving a larger royalty than 10 percent. Cowan replied that although the royalty was smaller, the splash a prestigious publisher like Funk & Wagnalls would make insured far more books being sold, netting more money in the long run. His book would have first-class advertising and the promotional push wouldn't stop at the first hint of falling sales, as it often did with smaller publishers.

The other matter was a cash advance. York felt burdened constantly by the unpaid lien on his land. Moreover, a fine new house for him, Gracie, and Alvin Jr., was going up on the property. Others were planning to pay for it, but York wanted to fund at least a portion and have money for furniture and incidentals. Cowan explained how royalties were paid twice a year with the first payment coming six months after the release of the book. Even so, Cowan was able to secure a promise from the publisher that, upon written request from Sergeant York, York would be sent a payment the first quarter the book was out, then that amount would be deducted from his first regular royalty check.

The final version of the contract, signed December 28, granted a royalty of 15 percent. Cowan was to get two-fifths, and York, three-fifths. The writer had improved both their slices of the pie, his own somewhat more than the sergeant's.

On April 20, 1922, Funk & Wagnalls Company, of New York and London, published *Sergeant York and His People*, by Sam K. Cowan. As befitting a major release, the company mounted an impressive marketing campaign: review copies to the 150 largest newspapers in the country, plus special mailings to 300 more; a four-column newspaper ad also promoting the Funk & Wagnalls publication *Literary Digest* in 156 major newspapers; an ad on the table of contents page inside *Literary Digest*, with a circulation of 1.3 million; and advertising to the trade in *Publisher's Weekly* and elsewhere.

For all the efforts, initial response was disappointing, with advance orders for only three hundred copies. Booksellers were putting war books on the bargain tables at twenty-five cents on the dollar, and despite the sylvan tone of Cowan's title, retailers insisted on seeing some demand for the book before they would stock it. From a slow start, sales climbed steadily, and Cowan enjoyed getting letters from readers with questions about specific issues in the book. One wondered if a man could really hear a cow bell in Pall Mall all the way from Overton County, seventy miles away. Another wanted the location of a tree described as having a message carved in it by Daniel Boone.

York inquired again as to how soon he might see his first check from New York. He hoped to have his new house paid for quickly, but Cowan warned him not to count on royalties so soon.

Redoubling their efforts, the Nashville Rotary Club, with assistance from the *Nashville Banner*, collected all the money required to pay off the two remaining notes on the four hundred acres purchased two and a half years before. Presentation of the deed to York was delayed so Club trustees could include the text of York's Medal of Honor citation, the affidavits of the privates who stood beside him in the Argonne, quotations from General Pershing and Marshal Foch upon presenting the sergeant with his decorations, and other evidence of the heroism deserving of such a lavish gift.

The document was grandly titled "Warranty Deed From Trustees on behalf of the Rotary Club of Nashville to Sergeant Alvin Cullom [sic] York, A gift from the people of America to the greatest hero of the World War" and executed on May 18, 1922. The American people made good on their promise; Sergeant York was once again owner of the land of his ancestors.

The previous Valentine's Day, Sergeant York and his family had moved into a fine new house in the most prominent corner of the property, where the main road crossed the Wolf River on the only bridge in the valley. The house had two full stories plus dormers, with stone chimneys on both ends and a side porch on the south. The front door and small classical porch faced west, the back opened to the yard and the fields beyond, and the north end was a few dozen paces from the bank of the Wolf.

Inside on the ground floor was a library to the north of the entry and a living room to the south with a big fireplace at the end. Along the east side of the house were the Yorks' bedroom, a large dining room, and a kitchen with another big fireplace. Upstairs were six more comfortably large bedrooms, each with its own closet, for family, visitors, and children yet to come.

The home boasted a telephone—one of only two or three in the valley—and a carbide gas generator producing enough gas to power a light fixture in every room. It was a palace worthy of America's greatest hero.

Chapter Sixteen

Larnin'

With his family provided for at last, Alvin York turned all his attention and energy to building his school. His original plan called for a network of small, self-contained satellites scattered across the county so there would be classes close enough for every child who wanted to attend. It soon became apparent the logistics of such a proposal were too complicated.

Consulting with his business advisors and school administrators in Jamestown and Nashville, the sergeant came up with a more economical and manageable alternate scheme. There would be a single campus with a main administration and classroom building, a dormitory for boys and another for girls, a stock and dairy barn, agricultural department, woodworking shop, and dressmaking shop. The cost estimate for the main building was $100,000, with the rest of the buildings and facilities adding another $150,000. Equipment and furnishings, salaries, and a proposed endowment fund brought the total price tag to an even $2 million.

The architectural firm of Manley, Young, & Meyer in Knoxville produced a striking design for the main administration hall, which would be the first structure built. Its brick walls were trimmed in limestone, and its styling borrowed heavily from the Gothic splendor of Oxford and Cambridge. The most prominent features were large symmetrical wings fronted with lancet windows and a magnificent tower rising sixty-five feet above the center entrance. Inside were administrative offices, twenty or more classrooms, and a gymnasium.

The Alvin C. York Foundation was reorganized as a non-profit educational corporation to "found and maintain a school or schools in the mountain sections" and boasted a distinguished board of trustees that included Methodist Episcopal Bishop James Atkins, Cordell Hull (by this time chairman of the National Democratic Committee), former Treasury Secretary William G. McAdoo, Joel O. Cheek (whose Maxwell House Coffee, named after a Nashville hotel, soon brought him fame and fortune), and familiar friends such as Professor Dyer, Pastor Pile, Edgar Foster, former Governor Roberts, and others.

Net of expenses, York deposited more than ten thousand dollars in the Bank of Jamestown by the spring of 1925 as a result of his speaking tours. He had promotional brochures printed describing the school he envisioned, with quotes from various newspapers about his foundation. He had, as always, far more speaking offers than he could accept, often providing a fee plus the opportunity to solicit contributions. In spite of his popularity, however, it was clear York would never reach his $2-million goal without help.

Through his travels across the eastern half of the country, York continued to maintain a high public profile and his stock in the Tennessee legislature was very strong. The *Fentress Countian* of April 3, 1925, reported how lawmakers decreed Federal Aid Road No. 28, the part of the Dixie Short Route passing through Fentress County, should be named in honor of Sergeant Alvin York, "this great American Soldier, of whom Tennessee is exceedingly proud, and for whom the people of the State maintain a very high degree of admiration and appreciation" and officially designated it the York Highway.

A more significant honor was bestowed a few days later when R. I. Hutchings, a schoolteacher in Fentress County and member of the state legislature, proposed the state put up fifty thousand dollars toward the completion of the Alvin York Agricultural Institute. The legislature was notorious for its economic stinginess and there were some who felt

Hutchings was wasting his time. Besides, the state had never funded a high school before, leaving that chore to the local school boards.

Hutchings's impassioned oratory caught his audience unprepared. He argued for a school that would benefit "the poor, barefoot mountain children" who had no chance for an education and no lobbyists or any other access to the powers in the halls of state. His remarks left the penurious lawmakers weeping openly. A vote was taken and the motion passed sixty-one to twenty.

On April 13, legislation was approved establishing the Alvin C. York Agricultural Institute, with curriculum and teacher salaries to be controlled by the state board of education. A separate board of trust was appointed to manage the money York raised and to accept a donation of land for the school from W. L. Wright, president of the Bank of Jamestown. A fifty-thousand-dollar state appropriation was authorized for the project, on the condition Fentress County issue and place seventy-five thousand dollars' worth of bonds, two-thirds of which would go to match the state's contribution, and the rest for a new elementary school in Jamestown to be operated by the county school board.

The institute's organization was the torturous result of the many egos involved. The state had its oversight, but the trustees for the Agricultural Institute (not the York Foundation trustees) would now control the money from York's lecture tours. The county government had its say by issuing the bonds, and the Fentress County school board retained a piece of the action by virtue of its management of the new elementary school. Founder York was head of both the institute and foundation boards and was agreeable to any accord, however confusing, if the result produced the school he was after.

Such a tinderbox of compromise soon attracted a spark. The seven members of the newly-appointed Alvin C. York Agricultural Institute Board of Trust were all Fentress County men and some of them had no use for the bishops and coffee millionaires on the board of the Alvin C. York Foundation. A number of local leaders in Jamestown wondered why the community should even issue bonds to fund a project the state would have control over. There was almost immediate confusion and disagreement over who was in charge of what.

The first big sticking point became the question of where the school would be located. Charged with making the choice, the seven-member institute board quickly deadlocked four to three. Members W. L. Wright, J. T. Wheeler, O. O. Frogge, and J. S. Linder wanted the new school at or near the location of the existing high school in Jamestown, where the development would suit their business interests. The others, W. M. Johnson, Max Colditz, and York, preferred a site north of town, along the York Highway (now a graded all-weather road, but not yet paved) on the way to Pall Mall.

Those in favor of the Jamestown site pointed out it was the more accessible spot, and already public property. The minority faction believed regardless of practicality Sergeant York ought to have the school anywhere he pleased. It was after all his idea, built in his honor, with money he raised. York preferred the northern site because it was closer to Pall Mall and it provided plenty of land for a school demonstration farm and other projects he had in mind.

The county bond election passed handily on May 23, with 1,136 in favor and 140 opposed. In the third precinct, which included Jamestown, the vote was 452 to 2. "Of the two votes cast against the issue at Jamestown," reported the local press, "one was cast by a woman and the other by mistake."

Through the summer of 1925, those on each side of the location question solicited support and gifts individually for their site and the board met periodically to report on contributions, assess progress, and try to come to some sort of resolution. As chairman Sergeant York presided over these meetings at first in a spirit of friendship. When it became clear some board members were firm in opposing his location choice and had no inclination to be persuaded, he grew first impatient, then angry. He had expended his time, energy, and reputation on a school for mountain children, only to have its progress hamstrung by petty bickering.

Not counting the $25,000 earmarked for the elementary school, the institute now had control of $50,000 from the state, the same amount from the county, and more than $10,000 held in trust by the York Foundation. This total of more than $110,000 was more than enough to fund the administration building if only the location could be settled.

Exasperated, York held a public meeting at the county courthouse to air his opinions and frustrations. To a large audience of friends, many of whom had known him all his life, York laid the blame for delay in building his school squarely on the board of the institute. He "came out flat-footed in no unquestionable terms," reported one listener in saying the delay was selfish and unacceptable. Furthermore, if the people of Jamestown weren't willing to give him any more support than provided so far, he would build his school somewhere else or resign from the institute board.

Offers of land and money were tendered on the spot. A lumber company offered one thousand acres. The nearby town of Allardt offered six hundred acres and $10,000 to have the school built there. York had played his ace and won the hand. On November 30 the institute trustees informed the state funding board they were agreed on a site north of Jamestown and, with the help of the American Legion, they would be preparing a nationwide campaign to raise $2 million.

Alvin York watched all this with mixed emotions. While he was happy the conflict was resolved, men he considered his friends had fought against him in building a school from which they stood to benefit. During this time lecture tours and meetings of the institute board kept him from his farm duties, which reduced his personal income, and he was further distracted by recurring bouts of abdominal pain since his illness in New England in 1920.

Settling into the fine new house beside the river, the York family continued to grow. A second healthy son was born in the summer of 1923, whom Alvin named George Edward Buxton York after the battalion commander he so admired. By the time the institute board agreed on a site for the school, a third York boy had joined the household. The sergeant suggested Gracie name him, since York named the other two. She chose William Jennings Bryan York, after the great orator with whom York shared the speaker's platform at Asbury College in Kentucky three years before. The sergeant thought honoring Bryan was a fine idea but little Alvin, whom they called Junior, didn't care for the name and suggested Woodrow Wilson York instead. Woodrow Wilson it was.

The summer of 1925 also brought Sergeant York the acquaintance of a man who would become his friend, secretary, confidant, and closest ally. At first glance the two could hardly be any different. One was an unschooled, rawboned mountaineer, the other a Brooklyn-born college graduate. But together they fashioned a unique and effective partnership, combining York's energy and vision with his friend's eloquence and administrative skills.

By the time Arthur Samuel Bushing came to work at the Bank of Jamestown, he was a seasoned financial administrator with experience in Washington state and Chicago. Because he was a New Yorker, some of the locals wondered whether he was Jewish—which he wasn't (he was Presbyterian)—but no one evidently suspected him of being German, which he was, one generation removed. He was born Otto Samuel Busching in 1876, to parents who came to Brooklyn from Germany about twenty years before. Though his father died when he was three, Otto was able to attend college in Kentucky through the generosity of a benefactor who recognized his potential. He changed his name in 1915, after being denied a request to travel to Europe as assistant secretary of the Brooklyn YMCA because of his German ancestry.

At Sue Bennett College in London, Kentucky, Bushing met and married a Pickett County girl named Arza Story. They eventually settled in Jamestown, where Bushing was impressed by Sergeant York's ambitious plans for a school. His work at the bank made Bushing familiar with the agricultural institute's affairs and he soon offered his services as secretary to the institute. From then on, York's frequent response to a letter was to thrust it into Bushing's hand and say, "Here, Bushin'. You know how to handle this."

York's independent streak began to assert itself as he considered the vast amount of time wasted on squabbling by small-thinking people who enjoyed the limelight but did not ultimately share his vision. Determined to move forward with or without the support of his own board of directors, Sergeant York planned a trip to Florida to meet with American Legion officials there about setting up a formal fund-raising program. The Legion in Knoxville boldly set its city goal at $25,000 and the state's goal was set at $100,000 on the way to the $2 million total.

From Florida, where an unprecedented land boom was churning out new millionaires in record numbers, York got word of potential donors who might come through on a grand scale. Most intriguing of all was an indirect assurance that financier John D. Rockefeller was interested in his school. If, a source suggested, York could get the first buildings built without "becoming entangled with the state" or involving another wealthy individual (who might, perhaps, steal some of Rockefeller's expensive thunder), Rockefeller would "endow the school handsomely at the proper time."

Alvin York saw two pathways ahead of him. One was lined with friends and acquaintances who at first joined his educational crusade then turned against him. The other led to independence, apparent financial stability, and the freedom to do whatever he thought was best for the "poor, barefoot mountain children." To fund his Florida trip and keep development of the institute administration building on schedule without the money still held hostage by arguing factions, York had to have ready cash of his own.

Three weeks before Christmas, Alvin and Gracie York traveled to the city square in Jamestown. At the courthouse they signed an eleven-thousand-dollar mortgage, with options for more, on the four hundred acres the Rotary Club gave them on behalf of the American people. If building the York Institute on his terms required him to go his own way and let the institute board go theirs, he was ready to sacrifice one dream for the other.

After Christmas York huddled with his friends and advisors in Nashville, quietly testing the waters without revealing his plans regarding an independent movement. He met with Professor Dyer, Lipscomb Davis, Edgar Foster, and others. In an address before the First Presbyterian Church Men's Club on January 11, 1926, York underscored the importance of support from his native state, saying other states would be looking at how Tennessee responded to his appeal in assessing their own involvement. State chapters of the American Legion, he explained, would spearhead the effort, and he was "confident of getting" the $2 million required. His own lack of education, he continued, made him see how the mountain boys and girls needed a good school in their community to satisfy their need and desire for "book larnin'."

York knew by now to anticipate his audience's desire to hear the story of his Argonne fight from his own lips. He had always refused to talk about it in the past but this day was different. If York were to walk away from the institute foundation and the state and start raising money himself, he would have to use all the persuasive power he could muster. If the big draw was the war, perhaps telling about it wasn't so bad after all, as long as his priorities were clearly understood.

York succinctly recounted the whole story: the charge, the repulse, his gathering the remains of his devastated squads and capturing wave after wave of Germans, the surrender of the enemy "major," and all the rest. It was the only thing he could have done under the circumstances, he continued, and it was only the Lord's will that brought him through safely.

Then he moved on to a description of his plans for the institute, affirming, "Educating the boys and girls of the mountain districts and telling the gospel of Jesus Christ are far more important to me than reciting my experiences in France."

After sharing his vision of classrooms and programs that would give his neighbors chances to succeed such as the sergeant never had, York closed with stirring words: "When I die, I had rather it be said about me that I gave my life toward aiding my fellow man than for it to be said that I became a millionaire through capitalizing on my fame as a fighter. I do not care to be remembered as a warrior but as one who helped others to Christ."

In February York traveled to Miami to meet with American Legion officials who could organize his fundraising there and with prominent prospective contributors who could prime the pump. Florida real estate was soaring in value and the newly rich and York were eager to meet each other, he for the support, they for the press and prestige. York flew over the Everglades in an open cockpit airplane and made the rounds of meetings and receptions. He reported proudly how the Tennessee legislature contributed $50,000 and the school, when completed, could take care of more than eight hundred students a year. Of the $2 million required, $800,000 would take care of all construction.

He fielded questions about his religious beliefs and drew comparisons between his school and one in Dayton, Florida, named for William Jennings Bryan. "If this school is a center of learning, it will be well," said York of Bryan Memorial School, "But if it is a place where religious hatred is encouraged, it will be more than useless." In Fentress County, he told his audience, "Most of us stand with Mr. Bryan and the Bible, but we let the other fellow believe what he wants. We don't want to stir up a fuss."

Carl G. Fisher, one of Miami's most successful developers, pledged $10,000, and others followed suit with smaller sums. Interested as they were, some of them found their attention divided between the proposal of the famous redheaded Tennessean and simultaneous local efforts to raise money for the University of Miami. The chairman of the university campaign committee proposed an ambitious plan requiring a total of $10 million. And they were still $2 million short.

The members of the American Legion in Florida wanted to know specifically what kind of support their counterparts in Tennessee would lend to the York Institute. Sergeant York returned to Nashville the last weekend in February to find out. Speaking at a Legion banquet in the Hermitage Hotel, York explained that the mountains of Tennessee were the stronghold of the purest strains of the Anglo-Saxon race, and that to educate the children there would be to produce men and women who would go forward to "form the moral and spiritual cornerstones of the great American ideal—democracy."

The sergeant then told his audience of the promising reception the Florida Legionnaires gave him and how the whole country would be taking the cue from Tennessee's response. A resolution was passed on the spot pledging the local organization's cooperation and support, and a committee was appointed to draft a telegram informing the Miami Legion of the action.

While cooperation and support wouldn't pay carpenters and bricklayers, the sentiments at the banquet indicated a high-profile national organization was firmly behind York and his efforts. Rockefeller, Fisher, and other wealthy men across the eastern half of the country looked favorably upon the idea. York had raised upward of sixteen thousand dollars on his own by then and had access to twenty-five thousand more (including options) through the mortgage on his farm. The only impediment to the whole process seemed to be four members of the Board of Trust of the Alvin C. York Agricultural Institute in Jamestown, Tennessee, who continued to drag their feet at every opportunity.

On March 16, 1926, Alvin York played another ace. "As chairman of the Alvin C. York Agricultural Institute board of trust, it is with deep regret that I tender my resignation," he wrote in a letter to the board published in newspapers across the state. Bushing's editorial skills behind the scene were evident as the letter continued. "Hampered by the inaction of the majority of my committee and failing thereby to obtain that cooperation which is necessary in any high and altruistic endeavor, and in view of the pressing need of the boys and girls of this section to whom I am pledged to obtain for them a better chance, I cannot in justice to the cause be further enmeshed and held back in the performance of my duty, so clear and unmistakable."

He went on to praise the state for its appropriation to the cause and to thank his fellow Tennesseans for their donations, while claiming the school project would move ahead "as well if not even better" as a private venture than under public oversight "in view of all the circumstances."

"Provisions can be made and promises already given me which makes possible the early erection of an initial building as a foundation upon which to establish a great institution, and with God's blessing and the sympathy and support of the purposeful citizens of America, the children of the mountains of Tennessee are going to have the opportunity too long denied them.

"To this enterprise and in the rendering of such service I have dedicated my life. And with divine help it cannot fail."

A letter to York's friend Edgar Foster at the *Nashville Banner* revealed far more of the true degree of turmoil among the factions in Fentress County than Bushing's elegant words. The controversy over location was irritating enough yet only part of the story. County school bonds, approved by a wide margin of voters, had been printed and prepared in denominations of five hundred dollars as required by law. The law also required the county judge to sign the bonds, but Judge J. Noble Wright, stung at not being appointed to the institute board of trust, refused. His term ended a month later, after a contested election, and the new judge signed the bonds.

By that time, however, the local banks that had agreed to purchase the bonds (including the Bank of Jamestown, whose president, W. L. Wright, was an anti-York member of the institute board) were having second thoughts and requested the county readvertise them. The county dutifully wrote up the required public notices, which then had to be signed by institute trustees. The trustees refused, thus blocking the sale of their own bonds.

Alvin York imagined he was leaving this hornet's nest of local politics for good when, on March 26, he signed the charter of incorporation for The Alvin C. York Industrial Institute. "Industrial," he and his advisors thought, would have broader appeal for fund-raising purposes than "agricultural," and the change would also limit confusion of the old regime with the new. Board members besides York were Pastor Pile, a respected local attorney named W. A. Garrett, and a handful of other close friends York could depend on. Arthur Bushing served as secretary. The nonprofit corporation they headed was founded to build and operate a school as "a monument and tribute" to the great war hero Sergeant York.

Determined to learn from his experience, York included minutely detailed requirements for the industrial institute board of directors. Members, declared the new charter, "shall be comprised of men and women whose character, achievements, patriotism, high ideals and good judgment prove their ability to help direct the affairs of said corporation so as to make it the greatest possible factor in promoting good citizenship. Recognizing that the basis of Christian citizenship and character is a profound belief in the Bible as the inspired Word of God, the Board of Directors of said Corporation shall be chosen from among those whose faith in God and man, whose love of country, obedience to the laws of the land and moral code are such as to be a beneficent influence to those whom they govern."

Fentress County suddenly found itself on the verge of losing the whole show. Jolted into action, the community rallied in support of its most famous son. A deed of gift, unique as far as anyone in the county could determine, deeded the county poor farm to York for his school "in order to lend him a helping hand, and to bid him God's Speed in his noble and most worthy undertaking." The deed was signed by Judge E. J. Wright, who earlier signed the school bonds after his predecessor refused.

The poor farm was 135 acres of good, flat land adjacent to the twelve hundred or so acres already donated along the York Highway north of Jamestown at the site York wanted. Even better than acreage, the property included a large, sturdy, two-story frame building where poor-house inmates, the caretaker, and the caretaker's family lived. The county bought another farm and moved the poor farm residents—the handful of homeless, helpless or otherwise unfortunate citizens who were wards of the county—onto it.

"The great moving spirit in this development will be nobody but Sgt. Alvin York," bubbled the *Fentress Countian* at the news of York's resignation and the county's gift, "and whether we agree with him in every particular or not we are all bound to admit that he can bring home the 'berries.'

"So if he chooses to hook up with some of us and unhorse the rest we will just have to get up on our hind legs and holler 'Hooray' for Sgt. York."

York would have his school after all, and apparently on his own terms, after seven years of fighting. The Germans, by comparison, took a little more than three hours to dispatch.

May 8, 1926, was clear and mild; early morning held the promise of a perfect spring day ahead. By daylight Fentress Countians were arriving at the courthouse square in Jamestown, preparing to march to a picturesque rise on the west side of York Highway, a mile north of town. The low hill there was thickly forested with pine, the deep green needles of a thousand trees whistling in the breeze that carried their fragrance across the road toward the poor house, now standing empty and expectant.

The pine forest once belonged to Bruno Gernt, an immigrant who made his way from Germany to Cincinnati and on to Fentress County to found the nearby town of Allardt. His family was the largest land-holder and largest taxpayer in the county. Teutonic roots notwithstanding, the Gernts donated 235 acres to the York school, reserving timber rights, and York accepted with thanks. It was on the Gernt plot, out of more than fourteen hundred acres now at his disposal, where Alvin York decided to build the administrative headquarters for his industrial institute.

The crowd came by car, wagon, and on foot, the farm wives carrying squirming children and bulging picnic baskets, everyone milling in and out of the stores and businesses around the square, meeting friends, savoring the excitement. The Tennessee Secretary of State, Ernest N. Hanson, was there, as was a contingent of professors from the University of Tennessee in Knoxville. Distinguished as these guests were, they were outshone on the square by the University of Tennessee marching band, whose members mingled with the crowd in their regal uniforms, with drums and trumpets glinting in the morning sun.

At ten o'clock the festivities got underway. With the band in the lead, the crowd of twenty-five hundred or more headed north on York Highway. After the musicians came the children. Following them were cars carrying the adult dignitaries and after them everyone else came running, walking, and astride horses and mules.

By the time the last stragglers left the square in Jamestown, the drum major was already executing a left face off the road toward bleachers built in the pine woods a mile from the courthouse. Once the crowd regrouped, rousing speeches were delivered by Secretary Haston and others, followed by a welcome hour-and-a-half break allowing the celebrants to savor the contents of their picnic baskets.

After lunch and an invocation by Pastor Pile, a speech was given by Boston writer and editor Joe Mitchell Chapple, an admirer of York's, who retraced the soldier's war exploits and his tireless efforts to improve the education of mountain children. Chapple recalled the story (ever popular in this old Union stronghold) of Abraham Lincoln's struggle to overcome his lack of schooling and the "pinnacle of fame and immortality" he reached as a result.

There was more speaking and more music. Then Sergeant York rose from his seat and after a few brief remarks, stepped off the platform and walked to a designated spot in front of the assembled crowd. With the familiarity of a man accustomed to long days on the farm, he thrust a shovel into the ground, planting it firmly with the sole of his size 11½ brogan. The crowd exploded in cheers. The construction of the Alvin C. York Industrial Institute was underway.

For all the celebration, the institute was still shackled by confusion and controversy. The state's fifty-thousand-dollar appropriation had not been spent and authorization for it was coming up for renewal. The funding was offered to an organization from which York subsequently resigned. Arthur Bushing had written a gracious letter on the sergeant's behalf, encouraging the legislature to go ahead with a state-supported school for the region on its own. At the local level, the disastrous county bond issue had, in addition to the York project, funded an elementary school whose aims and management were uncontested. The school board was anxious to get at least one building for all its trouble and wondered how to hive off part of the money to get it done.

York saw encouraging signs as he considered his next step. He had significant pledges from Florida businessmen, $16,000 in the bank from his speaking engagements, and available cash from his mortgage (though he borrowed twice against his property during the year and would do so twice more before year's end). Henry Ford sent two tractors to help with construction of the school. York even collected $729 in cash at the groundbreaking ceremonies. There had to be some way to close the chasm between the money he had and the million he needed. (Deferring the endowment for the time being, he lowered his goal from $2 million to $1 million.)

Sensing the inevitable, the county school board decided to make a separate peace with York and his new corporation. On September 3, the school board approved a contract consolidating Fentress County High School with the Alvin C. York Industrial Institute. Classes were to be held in the old poor farm building on institute property until the new building was completed. The county agreed to pay teachers' salaries and all expenses, with any institute tuition, if charged, being turned over to the school board. The old high school, built in 1908, would be demolished and the site used for the new elementary school. The institute reserved the right "at any time it deems proper and necessary" to employ its own superintendent and teachers.

Three days later, September 6, 1926, the Alvin C. York Industrial Institute welcomed its first students to classes in the poor house, and the four teachers hired by the county settled down to their tasks, teaching agriculture, mathematics, economics, history, home economics, and English. Some of the children walked as far as three miles, then rode fourteen more, sitting on benches along the sides of a bus, boys facing girls across a center aisle. Plain as the transportation was, it was an improvement over the farm truck which, fitted with plank seats, had hauled children to the old high school mornings and afternoons and hay and livestock across the county the rest of the day.

On the other side of York Highway, in the pine forest where the band had played and Sergeant York turned his shovel of dirt to the roar of the crowd, men began clearing a building site, and the Gernt family began hauling off their logs. On up the highway in Pall Mall, in his fine white house by the road, York pondered how he would avoid foreclosure on his farm and where he might come up with nine-hundred-odd thousand dollars for the school bearing his name.

Chapter Seventeen

A Private War

Financier Carl Fisher had generously pledged ten thousand dollars to the York school the previous February, and in the summer of 1926, Arthur Bushing wrote asking when the donation might be forthcoming. Fisher replied he wouldn't be able to send the money at the moment but would supply three one-year notes totaling ten thousand dollars, plus interest at 6 percent. "It is necessary for me to conserve my cash at this time for development work at Montauk. . . . If I have a lot of luck in the next couple of years I will dig up a complete dormitory for you." He closed by suggesting the notes and collateral be held by a local Fentress County bank.

After several more weeks, Bushing inquired about the promised notes and collateral. He received a curt note from Fisher's representative informing him Mr. Fisher's personal and business interests were comingled to the extent that providing collateral would require board meetings and other "red tape." Furthermore, "Mr. Fisher nor any of his interests have been in the habit of giving collateral notes and his unsecured note should be ample security for any loan especially of such a small amount." The letter concluded saying the notes would be held by a Miami Beach bank.

After another delay Bushing requested an update and documentation on the note. He was advised this time, "The failure of the chain banks has worked a hardship on all of the Florida banks, and they have been compelled to tighten up on their loans considerably. . . . The name of Carl G. Fisher is well known throughout the country and there should be no difficulty in handling this paper through some of the banks in your vicinity that are interested in your enterprise." Farmer's Bank of Jamestown had no trouble "handling the paper."

The week of Columbus Day, Sergeant York traveled to Philadelphia as a delegate to the American Legion convention. Several noteworthy issues needed to be discussed, including whether, as some had suggested, next year's meeting should be held in Paris where the Legion was founded, and whether or not General Pershing would accept their offer to be the national commander of the organization.

York sat in the lobby of the Spruce Hotel talking with Major J. G. Sims, a boyhood friend serving as secretary to Tennessee Senator L. D. Tyson. Recognized by other delegates, York soon attracted a crowd of Legion members and reporters. From his perch on the couch, he took advantage of the impromptu audience to talk about the school he was building. "It is the only hope of the boys and girls in the mountains thereabouts to obtain an education," he said. The administration building was underway and he was working to raise a hundred thousand dollars for its completion. (He did not mention the fact that if he had the support and respect in Fentress County he evidently enjoyed in Philadelphia, the school would be built and open.)

A reporter in the group interrupted York. "What about the time you captured all those German prisoners and guns?"

As though he neither saw nor heard his questioner, the sergeant continued without pause. "Oh yes, I forgot to tell you. The school is one mile from the square at Jamestown, on York Highway."

Again the reporter broke in. "But Sergeant York, what about all those Germans? I'm sure we'd all like to hear something about that."

York continued as before. "There isn't another school like it within a radius of fifty miles." He went on to tell about the curriculum, the facilities, and his plans for the future.

At that moment a large contingent of Tennessee delegates entered the lobby. They and the sergeant greeted each other with cheers, smiles, and handshakes. Reporters could see further pursuit of their quarry was hopeless for the moment. Major Sims, who was born within fifteen miles of the York cabin, told a reporter sitting beside him, "All Alvin wants to talk about is that school. He works night and day for it." Trying to draw him out on the war was a waste of time.

As the Tennesseans walked from the hotel to the convention hall, they were encircled once more by reporters who continued with questions and comments in hopes of prying loose a war quote for the evening editions.

"Well it was some stunt capturing four hundred machine guns."

"Who told you that?" the sergeant asked. "It was only thirty-five."

"Well it was no cinch to capture four hundred German prisoners in one day."

Still walking, York patiently if somewhat wearily helped the man get his facts straightened out, then disappeared with his friends into the convention hall.

In Nashville the next month, York chaired a meeting to develop an advertising and publicity plan for the institute. His friends Dr. Dyer and Arthur Bushing were there, along with businessmen from Chicago, Boston, and Florida. The sergeant reported the school was doing well, its four teachers and seventy-five to eighty students comfortable in the old poor house building. Attendance was good in recent weeks despite the bad weather.

The group then got down to a discussion of how to raise the money to build the institute using only private funds. The men enthusiastically agreed York should keep lecturing to try and improve the visibility of the school. Surely if people only knew about the institute's mission, they would support it financially. The group also planned a new brochure with an architectural rendering of the administration building and endorsements for the school from General Pershing and other luminaries.

They also talked about *Sergeant York and His People*. The book had not produced either the exposure or the contributions York hoped for.

The institute was shipping boxes of books to York's speaking venues, offering a copy as a gift to anyone who donated six dollars or more. In rich and elegant prose, Sam Cowan told the story of York's life in the backwoods, his victory in the Argonne, and his return to Pall Mall, where he hung up his uniform and put on his overalls. Of course the book included war stories, but the people, relationships, and noble history of the Valley of the Three Forks of the Wolf played key roles. For every reader who wanted this version of York's life, many more, like the reporter back in Philadelphia, must have wanted to know, "What about those Germans?"

The Nashville meeting bore ample fruit over the next few months. On December 16, three days after his thirty-ninth birthday, York addressed a dinner gathering of the University Club of Boston. In the club lounge, paneled in hand-carved walnut and hung with expensive chandeliers, York sat through his introduction, then rose and faced his expectant audience. His six-foot frame carried 230 pounds, sixty pounds more than the day he reported to the draft board in Jamestown, and his bright red hair was gray at the temples. (He often responded to comments about his unruly red shock with, "You may find a redheaded man in a penitentiary, but you'll never find one in an insane asylum.") His round, fleshy face had the incipient jowls of a successful merchant in early middle age. But the smile under the luxurious red moustache was as wide and genuine as ever and his blue eyes shown with a sparkle undimmed by years of struggle and frustration.

The soldier-turned-teacher impressed University Club members with his sincerity and single-mindedness. He spoke of the work accomplished on the school so far and what he hoped to do. He would, he said, help keep costs down by raising food for the school on his own farm. The *Boston Traveler* noted of York, "Like knights of old, he goes forth with high ideals. His message is one of inspiration and love of his mountain people. And once hearing him, no listener could doubt the high purpose which leads him onward in his mission."

Targeting specific audiences he hoped would be inclined to make donations, he also addressed a Boston meeting of the Military Order of the World War. He told his story of the advance down Hill 223 then turned to the reason for his visit. "There are no roads where I live," he told the assembly of veterans. "There are no railroads, but some of the beautifulest boys and girls that ever were. There's where I got my beautiful wife. But a third of them can't read nor write by the time they're sixteen. There's only one chance for a high school education there. That's the establishment of this school."

He described the flavor of life in Fentress County, covering everything from marksmanship to moonshine, which, he admitted, was still much in evidence. Returning to his main theme, his voice rose in intensity as he bid his listeners farewell. "By the grace of God, if I hold my strength, I know the American people are not going to refuse me." As the roar of applause reverberated through the room, the cheeks of more than one member of the Military Order of the World War glistened with tears.

The institute had its brochure printed, studded with endorsements from famous figures. General Pershing wrote in part, "One of the greatest bars to the progress of the mountain districts is the lack of educational facilities. The accomplishment of your aims would do much to overcome this handicap." Cordell Hull wrote, "I cannot commend to others in terms too strong the merits of your school movement, nor invoke too earnestly their aid." Senator McKellar wrote, "This project must go through. It is little enough for a grateful people to do for your community." Quotes from Governor Austin Peay, General Sir Douglas Haig, and other luminaries were also included.

Over Christmas and a fund-raising trip to Kansas and Missouri the following month, York took stock once again of his position. Public crowds in the prairie states were large and supportive. On January 18, 1927, he even enjoyed the novelty of having his address at the University of Missouri in Columbia broadcast over the radio. (He winced at the news but showed "only a slight nervousness" once the speech began.)

Still, after subtracting travel expenses, those appearances did not net large contributions. He began seeking out educational venues and business clubs in hopes of listeners who were predisposed and capable of significant gifts. The results were little different from earlier trips: great acclaim and excellent press coverage (and now radio) but not much in the bank once the smoke cleared.

York's personal finances continued to suffer. He wasn't home to manage his farm and couldn't rely on any of his family to do it for him. On the contrary, York became a meal ticket of sorts in the Wolf River Valley, though he could by no means afford it. York had his own wife and children to support, plus Mother York, and Gracie's sister Kansas. When Alvin and Gracie moved into their big house by the river, one of Alvin's brothers moved his family into the two-year-old house the sergeant vacated. Friends and relatives assumed York was flush with cash, as famous as he was. They knew nothing of the mortgage on the farm and increasingly came to him for money, loans, bank collateral, and other financial support. He never discussed his financial straits and never turned anyone down.

One midwinter night, an errant spark caused York still more financial distress. He awoke to the sound of cattle terrified by a fire in the barn. As the animals thrashed around inside, desperate to escape the flames, York ran across the barnyard from the house to unlock the barn doors, release the stock, and put out the blaze. Gracie, wrapped in a robe against the bitter cold, ran down the kitchen stairs to the dinner bell, mounted on a pole in the back yard. She rang it furiously, awaking the neighbors, who came as fast as they could, bringing buckets and washtubs to carry water from the York Spring and the Wolf River nearby.

When York and his exhausted neighbors beat out the last of the fire after daylight, the family tallied their losses: barn destroyed, a season's hay burned, tools ruined, all but two of the cattle killed. Such tragedy would have strained any farmer's finances; York's precarious position made the loss all the more difficult.

The sergeant's single-minded devotion to his school was unaffected by the fire. As he began rebuilding his barn, York's mind frequently drifted to the fine brick and stone structure he envisioned building on his pine knoll outside Jamestown.

At the groundbreaking ceremonies the previous spring, York had optimistically announced the building begun that day would be finished on October 8, the anniversary of his famous battle. When the construction contract was let on July 1, he revised the opening date to

January 1, 1927. January was upon him now and he still had no building and no money to build one.

What he kept coming back to time and again was the hundred thousand dollars—fifty each from the state and county—still lying on the table. That money was appropriated in his honor, for his school. There had to be a way to get to it around all the egos, politics, and spheres of influence.

On January 26 York made a decisive move. In a joint session of the Tennessee General Assembly, he held legislators spellbound as he quietly and calmly reviewed the events transpiring since the formation of York Institute's first board of trust almost two years before. He then asked the assembly to nullify the special act of April 13, 1925, which appropriated state money for the Alvin C. York Agricultural Institute and impaneled its board. Instead he wanted a new board, with himself as head, that would finish the school according to his wishes with money intended for the purpose.

He alluded to Judge Wright's refusal to sign the school bonds the legislature approved and county voters passed—news to most of the lawmakers in the chamber. York wanted control of what the state wanted to give him and that required wiping the slate clean with a new board of trust.

The next day House Bill No. 296 was introduced on the floor, "To amend the laws relative to the distribution of the funds for the building of the Alvin C. York Agricultural Institute and the appointment of a new board of trust." George Stockton, representing Fentress County, rose to speak. Allied with the anti-York faction in Jamestown, he moved the bill be tabled but did so without challenging the popular hero directly. This was a local issue, he said, and state politics had no place in it. His voice rising, he declared that if everybody would simply leave the present building committee alone, "they would build a monument to Alvin C. York and Fentress County that all would be proud of."

Mr. Gleaves, one of three sponsors of the bill, replied that a state appropriation of fifty thousand dollars made it the state's business and public donations were made on the strength of York's notoriety. Donors expected York to run the school. Gleaves furthermore requested the bill

not be tabled but sent to committee and "thrashed out" like any other
bill.

Stockton responded that such action would subject the local officials in Fentress County to an embarrassing public airing of their political laundry. (The anti-York faction could ill afford to have its tactics
publicly displayed.) Stockton also told the session he thought Sergeant
York had the best of intentions but was influenced and manipulated
by "outside interests, notably from New York." They took advantage of
York's lack of business acumen, Stockton claimed, and used the hero's
fame to line their own pockets.

Others joined in the debate, one claiming the reason the building
committee had not been more successful was, "Sgt. York is the committee chairman and he hasn't called a meeting for a year." That was true;
York was busy with his new nonprofit corporation and private fund
raising.

Another representative, Robert Beck of Memphis, affirmed the sergeant's heart was in the right place but that he had no understanding
of business practices. Beck claimed York raised seventy-five thousand
dollars for his school but spent sixty-four thousand dollars on travel
and other expenses.

Mr. Stockton called his motion and the bill was tabled by a vote of
forty-eight to twenty-four. York was defeated.

Before returning to Pall Mall, York made a statement to the newspapers that remarks in the legislature questioning the integrity of the
institute were "without foundation" and accusations he was swayed by
New York interests were "absolutely unfounded and cannot be maintained by truth or intelligence." He also insisted on an opportunity to
clear his name. "In view of several statements by Representative Stockton on the floor of the House, I welcome and insist that a thorough
investigation be made before this matter is dismissed from the present
general assembly."

On February 2 the bill was brought up a second time and was again
the center of a spirited discussion. After rehashing the arguments of the
previous week, the bill was voted down again, forty-nine to thirty-nine.
The one bright spot in the process was a resolution passed to appoint a
committee of inquiry into the management of the York Institute. The

sergeant was satisfied that even if his school was still in limbo, he would at least have a chance to clear his name.

Endorsements and contributions continued to reach York: American Legion posts sent their collections, as did the American Federation of Labor and the International Printing Pressmen and Assistants Union (either unaware of York's anti-union sentiments or unaffected by them). Newspaper appeals encouraged contributors to send $1.32, a penny for every German captured by York; or, if they could afford it, a dime or a dollar per prisoner.

As preparations for spring planting got underway in the Wolf River Valley, the Alvin C. York Industrial Institute proceeded with its classes at the poor farm building, funded as promised by the county. York divided his time between his office in Jamestown and his seat behind two big light-gray Percherons pulling a plow across his rich, black bottomland. The legislative pot in Nashville continued to simmer on through February and March. Finally, on April Fool's Day, 1927, York received his vindication.

That day the members of the Tennessee legislature abolished the board of trust they created at York's request almost two years before, substituting in its place a board consisting of York and the members of the state board of education. The new private act completely unraveled the old one, conveying all money, land, and power to the new regime. The Fentress County burghers who, in York's eyes, were nothing but trouble, found themselves suddenly powerless to impede him any longer.

A happy and relaxed Alvin York attended graduation services for the Alvin C. York Industrial Institute Class of '27 on Friday night, May 27. Since there was not enough room for the ceremony at the poor house, it was held at the First Methodist Church in Jamestown, where the baccalaureate service had been celebrated two nights before. Valedictorian Allen Dayhuff presented his address, then the fifteen graduating seniors, five boys and ten girls, received their diplomas from a beaming Sergeant York.

The poor farm property was recorded as a deed of gift to the new Sergeant York Industrial Institute, even though some reports claimed York exchanged it for the deed to sixty-five acres and fifteen hundred dollars cash. Whatever the specifics, York soon found his ownership of the property challenged by the old Sergeant York Agricultural Institute. The county had in fact given the property away twice by mistake. The agricultural institute received its deed first, but the industrial institute had already registered its deed before the duplication was noticed.

As he understood his agreement with the county, Sergeant York owned the poor house property, and the school board paid for operation of the school. When the question of ownership arose, York declared the property was rightfully his and he wouldn't renew his operational partnership with the county for the next school year.

Ocie Oswald Frogge, superintendent of the county school board and an anti-York member of the agricultural institute board, insisted the building belonged to the original York group and not to the sergeant's new renegade band. York clarified his position in a note to the county board, informing its members that if all county school property in the poor house was not removed within two days, "we will proceed to remove same off our said premises and you will be charged with the cost of removing same."

The sergeant was true to his word. Promptly at nine o'clock on Monday, July 11, he and a crew of men and boys arrived at the poor house and, as one witness said, "proceeded to eject the desks, stoves, hardware, domestic science equipment, and other furniture and place it along the right of way of the highway." Having made his point clearly and publicly, the sergeant then proposed the consolidation of the industrial institute and the state board of education, cutting the county and the old agricultural institute out of the picture entirely.

As he savored his continued progress with the Institute, York considered plans for a new book he hoped would succeed where *Sergeant York and His People* failed. Despite his attitude about discussing the war, he offered to sell his war diary in the hope it would bring in money for the school, and pay off the mortgage on his farm. (The prospect of renewing the mortgage was a long shot at best; the bank president's family once owned the York land and were the ones to sell it to the Rotary Club. They would be only too happy to buy it back at a bargain price in bankruptcy court.)

Unfortunately publishers that once clamored for Sergeant York's story no longer seemed interested. Once they looked at the two worn, slender notebooks, they turned him down, claiming as historical and interesting his story was, it did not contain enough material for a book. This shortcoming was soon resolved by an unexpected visitor from New York.

Tom Skeyhill, a dashing Australian writer and a veteran wounded at Gallipoli, came in search of York during a drive through Tennessee in the spring of 1927. After negotiating roads he described as "primitive and barbarous" that "did everything a decent, civilized road should not do," Skeyhill made his way to Jamestown. He did not like what he saw. "It is an unkempt, straggly town," he wrote later, "with no sense of style or even comfort. Cows browse in the side streets, and so do pigs. Debris is never swept away except by the wind. It is an old town, and it looks its age."

Adding to his displeasure was news that the sergeant had just left for Florida. One of the locals directed Skeyhill to the York Institute offices, which consisted of a room up the back steps of the bank building. Arthur Bushing greeted the writer, apologized for the sergeant's absence, and offered to give whatever information he could. The two men drove out to the site where the administration building would be. Sitting under a pine tree, Bushing told Skeyhill the story of York's Argonne battle and the long-running effort to build his school.

After an exchange of letters over the next several months, Skeyhill embarked again for Fentress County, this time to meet York and to learn his story firsthand. Progress had brought the railroad much closer to Pall Mall than Crossville and Oneida, where mountain residents drove for so many years to pick up their guests. A new logging train ran from Oneida to the village of Louvaine, only seven miles from Pall Mall. As passengers were few and logs plentiful, the train consisted entirely of flatcars and boxcars. The few passengers boarding the train rode in the caboose with the brakeman and the mail.

The dapper New Yorker found himself in the company of lumberjacks, surveyors, local residents, and stacks of parcel post. Warming to the adventure, he spent his time asking fellow passengers, and those who came to meet them at the various stops, about Sergeant York. All of them spoke of him "with an esteem that bordered on reverence."

Bushing met Skeyhill at Louvaine and drove him to Pall Mall. It was Sunday, so the two went on to the local Church of Christ in Christian Union, known as York Chapel in honor of its most famous member. They parked Bushing's car among the mules, horses, buggies, and other autos and went inside. On benches arranged in a semicircle around the stove, sat a crowd of boys and girls in their Sunday best, rapt with attention. In the middle of the circle, reading aloud from the Bible, was Sergeant York, his large frame appearing enormous among the children. After he finished reading, York walked around the circle, bending low over each child and whispering a passage from the morning lesson. Then, back in the center, he called on them one at a time to read the passage aloud. When they stumbled, he responded with a gentle smile and a word of help.

Bushing and Skeyhill quietly took seats in the rear, but York saw them enter. With a grin, he introduced the two newcomers to the class, then asked if either of them would kindly recite a certain passage from Isaiah. A pause followed. After the sergeant repeated his invitation, Bushing gamely took a try. Skeyhill, who by his own admission "had not peeped into the words of this ancient Hebrew prophet for a long time," stammered and bluffed under the sergeant's steady gaze. With a hearty laugh, York waved them into the circle where they joined him and the children in a rousing chorus of hymns.

After the lesson the class walked outside toward the road, with York carrying one child and holding another by the hand, the rest following merrily behind. Gesturing at his young charges, York said, "There's not much I can do for older people who are set in their ways and beliefs. But it's not too late to help these boys and girls toward a brighter future."

Skeyhill was invited to Sunday dinner at Pastor Pile's, and after a short tour to the old cave where Coonrod Pile once lived, sat down to "a sumptuous meal of beef, pork, chicken, beets, sweet potatoes, turnips, lettuce, homemade pie, and freshly drawn spring water." After the meal he arrived to spend the balance of the afternoon at York's house on the bank of the Wolf River.

The house was full, as it always was on Sunday. Mother York, in her long calico dress, bonnet, and gingham apron, sat in her customary place beside the living room fireplace. She greeted Skeyhill shyly but answered his polite questions with simple directness. "I ain't had much larnin'," Skeyhill later quoted her, trying to mimic the sounds so strange to Eastern ears, "but I raised up a family of eight boys and three girls in a one-room log cabin and they's all eleven living. And that teaches you something about life."

Eight of York's brothers and sisters were there that day and greeted the stranger with "Howdy" and little else. Try as he would, he could not engage them in conversation much beyond "I reckon." York's four boys, including the newest addition, Sam Houston York, scampered in and out as Gracie came in from the kitchen to sit with her guest. Skeyhill was taken with Gracie's innocent mountain beauty. "Though she had given birth to four children, she had not lost her girlish glow or even her girlish ways," he observed.

Skeyhill spent the winter of 1927–28 in Pall Mall and Jamestown, with board and lodging provided gratis by Mr. and Mrs. Bushing. Their war experiences gave the writer and his subject a common bond. They met at Suva's Restaurant over beef and cornbread, at the farm between chores, and in the small institute office behind the bank. Skeyhill sat by the fire as York read the Bible to his family at night, he joined in the conversations at the Raines store in Pall Mall and at Pile's, and he talked with York's family, friends, and the many men and women in the county who knew and loved the sergeant.

Skeyhill also accompanied York and his friends on hunting trips and excursions to the shooting match ground on its ledge above York Spring. Skeyhill typically turned out for a day in the woods dressed in coat and tie, vest, and a snappy fedora. Businessmen from Jamestown would all be expected to wear similar "work clothes" on the hunt— three piece suit, watch and chain, and a hat or cap. York sometimes wore a tie as he ran to the baying of his beloved red hounds. When visitors joined them, he would occasionally sport a bow tie and snap brim cap as the group followed the dogs after coons, squirrels, possums, and other game.

Skeyhill proposed a book on York's life, which he considered fascinating and potentially lucrative. York told the writer how he turned down ten thousand dollars for his biography in 1919 and had no interest in commercializing his war record. He told Skeyhill of the war diary and the publishers' rejection of it. Skeyhill eagerly asked to see the diary. York had put the two notebooks in the vault of the bank in Jamestown and since then took them out only twice for reporters, on the condition they would not publish any of what they read. Both journalists broke their promises and York was determined to keep the diary in the vault until his death, then leave it to his children. Even Arthur Bushing had never seen it.

Skeyhill had almost given up hope when, one day, York asked him if he still wanted to see the notebooks. His manner was "so jovial" Skeyhill "wondered if he was in earnest." York produced the notebooks and Skeyhill devoured their contents, determined more than ever that this man's life should be documented both as a war story and a story of the "life and culture and struggles and hopes" of York and his mountain forebearers.

Skeyhill knew York was in financial distress. His school was on uncertain financial footing, he was giving regular financial assistance to numerous neighbors and family members, and his barn had recently burned. For all that, money would not sway the mountaineer. Skeyhill appealed instead to his sense of patriotism, insisting the American public had the right to know about York's inspiring life.

York agreed to the book idea. Skeyhill studied the diary and the few pages York wrote of an autobiographical sketch. They met almost daily, going over the diary page by page. Skeyhill asked for clarification and elaboration on all the entries, while a stenographer took down York's answers. The author wrote to the War Department for official records and to the men who served with York in the 82nd Division to confirm their versions of the facts.

Not only was York allowing his diary to be published, he changed his mind about telling the story of his war experiences. He was willing to give the public what it wanted, if it also gave him the chance to raise money for the institute. Trapped by political infighting in Jamestown and Nashville, he was a hero in New York, where the previous summer he signed a contract with the Famous Speakers bureau. The contract, dated August 11, guaranteed him $500 per week net for a minimum of ten weeks. He was to receive $250 per speech, or $350 for two speeches the same day. He could take up free will contributions from his audiences in addition to his fee and would not "on any occasion or at any time have his picture upon the screen in any moving picture show."

Famous Speakers earned their stripes. On February 6, 1928, York was authorized a $10,000 advance for the publication of his book, half of which he gave to Skeyhill. Two weeks later, serialization rights were sold to *Liberty* magazine for $30,000. Famous Speakers received $15,000 of the magazine total, York $10,000, and Skeyhill $5,000.

York's financial windfall came just in time. His mortgage note had come due and Suza Williams, a wealthy widow in the community who supported York's work, loaned him the money to pay off the bank. When York signed his contract with *Liberty*, Betty Smythe, York's agent, in turn loaned him the Famous Speakers portion on top of his own so he could pay Williams back.

Where *Sergeant York and His People* was focused and literary—if somewhat wide of the truth in places—Tom Skeyhill's writing had the romantic passion of Shelley or Scott. The style was far from York's simple ways of expression: stirring, soaring, visceral. In *Sergeant York: His Own Life Story and War Diary*, Skeyhill introduced his hero thus: "Broad-shouldered, stout-chested, deep-dugged, thewed and muscled like an ox—a mountain of a man, York of Tennessee. And like the mountain he has his feet on the earth and his head in the stars."

Much of the diary was there, along with York's additional remarks, his autobiographical sketch, and Skeyhill's own commentary, more than three hundred pages in all. This was an Alvin York the public had never seen. Now the question was whether the public wanted to see him.

Chapter Eighteen

Gain and Loss

As the 1927 school year approached, York discovered his victory in the state legislature the previous spring, complete as it seemed, was still not the end of the battle for control of the institute. The county school board was not accustomed to losing so publicly. Those with Republican leanings in particular were spoiling to settle the score with York, a stalwart and vocal Democrat, for besting them in front of their friends and constituents. The state board of education had moved to strip the Fentress County men of their power. But the legislature in Nashville was a long way off, and because the county bonds also funded the new elementary school, the county board managed to hold on to enough influence to make Alvin York miserable.

One of York's opponents, C. P. Garrett, insisted York made a shambles of the school but that negative publicity was withheld because of the sergeant's war record. In an editorial response to his accusation, Arthur Bushing blasted Garrett, claiming he was practicing as a lawyer though he was not trained as one. Furthermore, "2. He does not tell the truth. 3. His statement is mischievous. 4. His painful and labored presentation of alleged facts is on its face palpably fictitious."

Two months later York filed a $750,000 lawsuit against the Bank of Jamestown, W. L. Wright, O. O. Frogge, and others on behalf of "all school children of Fentress County and the Alvin C. York Industrial Institute." His goal in doing so was to continue rallying public support and prove to his adversaries in Jamestown he had no intention of giving up, whether or not they released the public money for his school.

Before the legislature the previous February, York refused to discuss personal conflicts publicly. "I am not going to say what is the matter with the board, and I am not going to engage in personalities. I am not even asking that I be retained on the board," he told the assembly.

He later changed his mind about engaging in personalities. In an indication of the height to which arguments escalated, York filed a lawsuit in circuit court charging J. D. Frogge with slander—an extremely rare action in a place where everybody knew everybody else. York charged that on December 1, 1927, Frogge slandered him on the public sidewalk in Jamestown. The exact nature of the comment was left to the public's imagination; it was never entered in the records of the court. J. D. Frogge denied all charges and the suit was enjoined.

Through seven years of work, Sergeant York had overcome every obstacle between him and a school for the mountain children. Even so, a public slur was more than he was willing to tolerate. Though he had felt his name cheapened by the tactics of the Black-Draught ads, this was worse. At about the same time, as his sparring with the school board continued, York decided to withdraw his support again from the poor house partnership. He demanded his name be taken off the school and declared he would have nothing more to do with it.

The Fentress County School Board was only too happy to oblige. The building going up in the pine forest would still be York's, but the school in session across the street in the poor house was renamed Fentress County High.

Commencement that next spring was held not at the Methodist church but at the courthouse. Instead of accepting their diplomas along with a firm handshake and wide smile from Sgt. York, the eight graduating seniors received their certificates and a word of congratulations from Superintendent Ocie O. Frogge.

Alvin York still had a school to build. With the publication of Tom Skeyhill's book by Doubleday, Doran, & Company in 1928, the sergeant planned a speaking tour to encourage sales and promote the institute. York prepared a speech that ran just over an hour, made up of readings from his war diary, an account of the events of October 8, 1918, and closing with an appeal for his school. His lengthy introduction was filled with mountain history, his own pioneer heritage, and tall tales, including one illustrating the value of a good bottle of moonshine on a cold night.

> *An old-timer strolled down to the sawmill where the half-frozen lumberjacks were cussing as they endeavored to thaw out their machinery and get it a-going.*
>
> *"Mornin', Dad," said one of the lumberjacks.*
>
> *"Mornin'."*
>
> *"Purty cold last night."*
>
> *"Yep. A little grain?" He offered the jug.*
>
> *The son shook his head. "You didn't come all the way over from home this mornin', surely?"*
>
> *"Nope. Slep in the woods."*
>
> *"How'd you keep from freezin'?"*
>
> *"Built up a far again' a holler tree. Hit heped some."*
>
> *"All alone?"*
>
> *"Nope. Hed m' dog with me."*
>
> *"Where is he?"*
>
> *"He's up thar. Froze to death."*

After delivering his written remarks, York left five minutes at the end of his speech for ad lib comments about the current progress on his school and what remained to be done. Leading up to that point, he talked of God's calling him to use his fame in the cause of education. Traveling in France showed him how the same mountains isolating him and his people from the temptations of the world also isolated them from good things. "And so I am dedicating my life to building a school down there in the mountains and giving the mountain boys and girls the chance I never had."

He referred only obliquely to his struggles back in Jamestown.

*For years I have been planning and fighting to build
the school. And it has been a terrible fight. A much more
terrible fight than the one I fought in the Argonne. Most
all the mountain people are for me and can scarcely wait
to see our school open. But a few powerful people down our
way have been trying to block it. And so I had to go into the
front line and fight another fight. And I couldn't use the old
rifle or the Colt automatic this time. And it has been a long
hard fight. And I'm kinda tired. But it's coming. We won
the fight. And the school is going up at this moment. And
soon those mountain boys and girls, and the grown folks too,
if they like, will have the chance to get a sensible American
education.*

*And that is why I am here tonight, ladies and gentlemen.
Not to show you a lot of medals and other decorations. Not to
brag about my war experiences, but to tell you how I was called
and came through it all to see the light; and how that light is
guiding me to build a school in the mountains.*

*If we want to avoid future wars, and we do; if we want
to remove the threat of destructive radicalism and anarchy; if
we want to prepare our great country for her world leadership;
then we must learn the lesson of the fundamental truths of life.
We must believe in God and His Holy Word; we must always
be willing to fight, and better still, to live, for our country. And
we must bring up the younger generations to be worthy citizens
of this republic. And we can best begin that by affording them
a decent education.*

Back in Jamestown the political pendulum had swung the other
way again. Removing York's name from his school inflamed public
opinion to the point where O. O. Frogge and his confederates had no
choice but to reconsider their position. On April 12, York dropped his
$750,000 lawsuit. By the time school started in August, Alvin York
was back in charge and reclaimed the original name for the school, the
Alvin C. York Agricultural Institute. There was only one institute again,
so the prospect of confusing the original "agricultural institute" with its

replacement "industrial institute" was no longer a problem. York also decided the agricultural description suited his project better after all.

The modern brick elementary school, approved by county bond voters at the same time as the Institute, was finished and open as the community watched the York administration building rise on its knoll among the pines. A third year began for the high school in the poor house, with enrollment of more than one hundred and a senior class of fourteen. The faculty grew to five members from four the first year, though not one member of the original group remained; unsure of whether they would have a school to teach in from one year to the next, they all moved on to more stable situations.

Other than the larger attendance, conditions were the same as in years past. There were textbooks and desks for all the students. Each classroom was furnished with a blackboard, a box of chalk, two erasers, a water bucket, and a broom.

Both enrollment projections and financial considerations prompted changes in the new institute's building design. The central section was being completed much as planned. The Gothic stone entrance tower and side wings were omitted to save money, leaving an elegant two-story brick building with a stone pediment over the central door. There were administrative offices, an auditorium, and twelve classrooms, each flooded with light from large, multi-pane windows. A drive was cut through the forest from York Highway straight to the front door. Standing on the porch of the poor house at recess, students could watch the bricklayers at work across the street and imagine what it was going to be like to have class in such a place.

Between seeing to construction details and working on his farm, York was continuing his lecture tour at a frantic pace, remaining on the road for weeks at a time, arranging engagements in geographic clusters for efficiency. The serialized version of *His Own Life Story and War Diary*, which ran in *Liberty* magazine over four weeks beginning July 14, was a sensation. York spoke at athletic clubs, advertising clubs, fraternal organizations, and also accepted occasional invitations to preach.

York prided himself in the fact he had never been sick since he got pneumonia while stringing fence wire in the rain in 1906 (evidently his stomach trouble during a 1920 New England trip wasn't serious enough to count). As he neared his forty-first birthday, the years of stress, a diet of "plain country cooking," and the resulting weight of 245 pounds were taking their toll. On September 28, 1928, York had his gall bladder removed, spending the tenth anniversary of his Argonne victory in a Nashville hospital bed. The surgery went well and York returned home to recover, taking the faulty gall bladder, packed in a bottle of formaldehyde, as a souvenir. Less than a month after returning home, he was on the road again.

Crowds were large, enthusiastic, and generous. From Boston on November 5, York wrote to the editor of the *Fentress County News* how listeners were eager to visit the school and see it for themselves. "If people a thousand miles away are interested enough to come to the mountains to see this school, looks like to me that all of the little petty malice that has bin between the two party's would B laid down and all of us join hands for a better and bigger York school."

A week later, from his room at the Waldorf, York wrote to Bushing. "Having some big meetings. Cant find sitting room for the crowds hundreds are turned away from my lexture. Cant get in buildings." Cigar boxes passed through the audience came back stuffed with voluntary contributions, which went to York in addition to his fee of $250 per speech.

Back in Jamestown that money became the bricks and mortar and stone that continued to build Sergeant York's ten-year dream. At last, on the morning of February 11, 1929, all 108 students and five teachers of the Alvin C. York Agricultural Institute strode proudly through the door and into the entry hall of their new building. Modern steam radiators hissed softly, warming the air without smoke or cinders. Municipal electric power was not available, but the school had its own generating plant, and electric lights shone in every room. Beyond the front hall was an auditorium, the only one in the county. The building also had a remarkable feature many of the students heard about but had never seen: indoor plumbing.

Plans for the gymnasium were temporarily shelved, but a barn on the property served the purpose well. Since the generator supplied only the main building, power for the five lightbulbs in the gym came from a truck whose back axle was propped up and one of the rear wheels connected by a belt to a second small generator.

York paused from his northern tour long enough to take part in the opening day festivities but was soon on the road again. He found himself on a treadmill of sorts, forced to tour in order to raise the money to keep his school going. Yet when he was away, O. O. Frogge and other adversaries worked to chip away at his control of the institute. The school needed him home too: now that the building was finished and he was in charge as president, he was responsible for day-to-day decisions others couldn't or wouldn't make. The farm was a steady drain as well, losing money more often than showing a profit.

Except for the farm, York's affairs when he was away were managed by Arthur Bushing, whose energy, resourcefulness, and tact continued to serve the sergeant and his causes with distinction. He was officially the secretary of the institute but served unofficially as publicist, ghostwriter, troubleshooter, and peacemaker among the various factions still roiling around the school.

To keep the farm going when he was traveling, York depended on several of his brothers, particularly Sam and Joe. The rich acreage on the river bottom yielded crops of hay, wheat, corn, and vegetables, but without York's attention, there never seemed to be any extra income to put in the bank.

York came up with other ways to improve his household finances while he was away, with mixed success. Since 1921 he had leased various parcels of land for oil and gas exploration, usually for fifty dollars or one hundred dollars per well per year, plus one-eighth of the proceeds. The demand for petroleum was exploding as America bought cars and built roads at an unprecedented pace and even the somewhat marginal geology of Fentress County attracted the attention of energy companies nationwide. As the value of land and mineral rights rose throughout the decade, York and Bushing invested in property and in various speculative partnerships.

Some oil and gas production took place on the York land but there were no significant strikes. Occasional discord between the sergeant and his leaseholders also arose. In 1926 York was sued by

Standard Oil Company of Louisiana, claiming its right of exclusivity
to the property was violated. A compromise settlement that July cost
York $288.65 in damages, plus court costs.

Another moneymaking venture was a store the sergeant opened
just across York Highway from his house in 1925. His invoices identified the business owner as "Sgt. Alvin C. York, Dealer in General Merchandise and County Produce." York built a comfortable, single-story
wooden building with a porch running all the way across the front
and a lean-to addition on the north side containing a small mill wheel.
When his speaking schedule allowed, he spent many happy hours at
the store visiting with customers, talking with friends on the porch, and
welcoming a steady stream of strangers who came over the mountains
on the recently-paved York Highway to meet him.

The store's record as an income producer, though, was marginal.
York was occasionally sued by his suppliers when insufficient cash flow
kept him from meeting his obligations. He in turn filed lawsuits against
customers who hadn't paid their bills. Before one such filing, which
he ultimately won, he wrote to the account holder without results:
"We can pay our store bill only as promptly as our customers pay us.
Our reputation is in your hands. Your cooperation is appreciated. Your
account is $102.14 past due and unpaid with interest for six months."

With the school building open and tour bookings strong, York and
the institute began to feel a little more comfortable, more certain their
enterprise would succeed. The Institute's financial statement for March
12, 1929, showed assets of $27,031.14, including more than $11,000
in cash, and no liabilities. Even the practically-minded Arthur Bushing
bought himself a new red Chevrolet roadster. In the following months,
Alvin and Gracie learned another child was on the way, making the fifth
in nine years. Gracie and Mother York began making preparations to
welcome the new arrival as York again hit the lecture circuit.

Another project for the year was a new book. With one volume
about the famous sergeant under his belt, Tom Skeyhill thought he
could retailor the book for the juvenile market and began rewriting the
York story as a frontier adventure for boys called *Sergeant York: Last of
the Long Hunters.*

Outmaneuvered by York and the state legislature, a group of prominent Jamestown locals still seethed at their loss of power. On August 6,
nine men, including O. O. Frogge, bank president W. L. Wright, sheriff
C. A. Norman, the county tax assessor, court clerk, coroner, and others,
filed a resolution with the state board of education demanding York be
relieved of his responsibilities. They claimed the board of the institute,
with York as chairman, was acting beyond its authority, especially in
the matter of promoting religious instruction at the school. The county
provided money for the school upon the assurance that the state board
of education "would manage and control and operate said School as a
State School free from the influence of any religious sect or church."

They protested therefore "against the request and demand of Sgt.
Alvin C. York that he be elected or employed by you as the head or in
any way in the control or management of said institution, believing
that to do so would greatly injure the school, impede its progress, and
be against the best interest of the people."

As the date for the start of the 1929–30 school year came and went,
the state board of education batted the issue of control back and forth.
Students excited about being the first to start their year in the new
building waited two weeks for classes to begin, then four, with no end
to the hostilities in sight. Dewey S. Hunter, the principal, took a job
elsewhere, and several seniors, fearful of not graduating on time, transferred to schools out of town. Those who remained busied themselves
with workshops, seminars, FFA events, and other pursuits to keep their
interest up and hopes alive. A group even presented a student production of *Flapper Grandmother* in the new auditorium.

Amidst all the uncertainty, Alvin York received an invitation from
Washington. The army was celebrating the eleventh anniversary of his
world-famous fight in the Argonne by staging a full-scale reenactment
of the battle. He was invited to be the guest of honor. York took a break
from his protracted conflict with Frogge and company to commemo-
rate a much easier and more decisive victory as the guest of a grateful
nation.

Corporal Cutting, Sergeant Parsons, and Acting Sergeant Early
accepted airplane rides at government expense to the War College in

Washington for the event. York declined to fly. As the veterans of Company G arrived and renewed their acquaintance, they joined tens of thousands of spectators who gathered to watch American soldiers, some costumed as Germans, play out the events of the charge down Hill 223. The men ran through the woods, hunkered through trenches, and rolled in and out of foxholes to the cheers of the delighted onlookers. As the soldier portraying York marched his prisoners to the rear, roars of applause echoed through the countryside in the crisp autumn air.

A few days later Alvin York reprised his visit eleven years before to the House of Representatives. As in 1919, he was given a standing ovation, one of only a handful of private citizens ever accorded such a double honor. He then boarded his train at the elegant beaux arts Union Station a short distance from the mall and headed back to Fentress County to see if he could get his school started before the year was too far gone. In the capital he was a national hero; in his home community, he was still thwarted in trying to realize the dream he sacrificed a hero's reward to build.

Tragedy awaited him in Pall Mall. Little Sam Houston York, nineteen months old, fell ill. Sam's fever climbed and he began having convulsions, arching his back in his mother's arms, eyes rolling back into his head. Stretching his neck made his knees bend involuntarily. The boy was diagnosed with meningitis, an inflammation of membranes around the brain and spinal cord. No treatment was available.

Gracie's first boy had lived only four days. Sam Houston had time to build a treasury of memories even in so short a time. For over a year and a half, he took his place in the family and had his part in the daily routine, his pallet on his mother's bed. After a violent but mercifully short illness, Sam fell into a coma and died.

The other children were quarantined and not allowed out of the house to attend the funeral. They watched from the window, tears streaming down their faces, as the funeral procession moved slowly past the house, following their brother's tiny glass-topped coffin from York Chapel to the cemetery. With tears welling in his own eyes, Alvin confided later to Tom Skeyhill, "Gracie will never recover from it."

Putting his grief behind him, York resumed his battle with the board of education. During his absence the board was unable to pass a resolution demanding his ouster. Thus the school year at the York Agricultural Institute finally began on December 2, with York remaining as head of the institute board of trust. The vacancy in the principal's office was filled, and all but two of the seniors who started class elsewhere returned, making a graduating class of seventeen. The school added a second bus and began carrying boys on one bus, girls on the other.

York was soon back on tour with his "Sergeant York's Own Story" lecture. The Famous Speakers agency supplied newspaper ads, window cards, circulars, photographs, and other promotional material at its expense, as York continued to draw large crowds. In spite of the cash flow, York still frequently found himself short of money. Though the state board of education was theoretically paying for the operation of the institute, it always seemed to need something, and York spent all the money he had. He wrote to Famous Speakers regularly, inquiring about advances and expense checks. His checks were mailed from New York to Pall Mall, where Arthur Bushing would send them on to wherever York was at the time, but never seemingly fast enough.

York drew a modest salary, less than a thousand dollars a year, as head of the institute. He had other small income sources in his farm, store, and mineral leases. With a family, including three children living and another on the way, plus various friends and relatives who received stipends, loans, gifts, or jobs from him, York's personal financial health remained precarious, even as the institute ledger grew fat with donations.

At least some of the trouble was that York was supposed to submit expense reports in order to be reimbursed for his travel costs. This requirement revealed the sergeant to be an inattentive bookkeeper at best. He would jot down "$27.00 ticket, $8.63 Pullman, $1.45 supper" on the back of an envelope and shove it in his coat pocket, where it would stay for weeks. Famous Speakers went out of its way to accommodate their star lecturer, doing its best to apply his sketchy information to their accounting system. The organization also occasionally advanced his expenses before receiving an expense report, and, when he was in danger of running out of cash on the road (when he didn't have expense money because he hadn't turned in his last report), the agency offered to wire the next venue to request direct cash payment to

York instead of payment by check to Famous Speakers. Betty Smythe knew she would eventually get her money. Alvin York was meticulously honest, if decidedly poor at paperwork.

The touring continued with plans for a swing up the east coast to North Carolina, Washington, New York, then west to Illinois and back to New York. On April 14, 1930, another son, Andrew Jackson York, joined the sergeant's household. Six days later Andrew's father was speaking at the American Legion in Ellsworth, Kansas.

As he tirelessly promoted his school and *Sergeant York: His Own Life Story and War Diary*, York corresponded with Tom Skeyhill on *Last of the Long Hunters*. Rather than make another trip to Tennessee, Skeyhill did most of the work this time from his home in Great Neck, New York. Other than a little news about the institute building opening and the eleventh anniversary festivities in Washington, there was not much fresh information, just a more adventurous flavor to capture his younger target audience. Skeyhill signed a contract on April 23, 1930, with the John C. Winston Company in Philadelphia, one of many publishers who passed up Sam Cowan's book eight years before. Skeyhill split his advance fifty-fifty with York, who was delighted at the revenue but concerned when he learned he would have to wait until June for the money. Skeyhill was listed as editor on the previous book. This time he got full credit as "Official Biographer of Sergeant Alvin C. York."

Last of the Long Hunters was short on facts and long on swashbuckling adventure. The title came in part from the claim York's first Wolf River Valley ancestor, Old Coonrod Pile, was one of a band of explorers in the Cumberland Mountains called long hunters. These men were hunters and trappers who earned their name by spending months at a time away from home on far-ranging "long hunts." There was evidence a group of these hearty pioneers came through the valley some time around 1770, when the area was still part of the American Colony of North Carolina.

There was also somewhat stronger evidence, in the form of a tombstone in the Wolf River Cemetery, that Coonrod Pile was born in 1766. The image of a four-year-old boy trapping beavers and fighting Indians was obviously the stuff of fantasy, but Skeyhill ignored the problem, and York let it pass.

Other assertions were equally romantic. For example, the book boasted of General Sam Houston's connection with the Wolf River Valley. The fact was Houston lived for a time in Overton County and when Fentress County was formed, Fentress absorbed a section of adjacent Overton. The land changing hands, however, was not where Houston lived.

Still other claims were almost certainly untrue but impossible to prove or disprove. Skeyhill claimed Daniel Boone recorded killing a bear in the county, carving "D. Boon CillED A. BAR in thE yEAr 1760" on a tree nearby. Boone, a Pennsylvania native, was a notoriously bad speller but there is no evidence he was ever any closer to the Wolf River than the Cumberland Gap, seventy miles to the east, through which he passed in 1769 on his way from North Carolina to Kentucky.

Last of the Long Hunters had not only photos but paintings of York as well: embracing his mother on the night of his conversion, praying at Bible Rock, shooting Germans. The war hero "with one foot on the fire ledge and his head under the parapet" in the predawn darkness of October 8, 1918, is described as "a tall, redheaded, raw-boned Tennessee mountaineer. Back home in the mountains he is known as the greatest shot that ever squinted down the long barrel of a muzzle loader and 'busted' a turkey's head. The purest Anglo-Saxon blood in the world flows in his veins, and his dialect is similar to the language which Chaucer and Shakespeare used hundreds of years ago. . . . This morning he is destined to fight probably the greatest individual fight in the annals of modern or legendary warfare. He is going over in the second wave."

These passages from the opening paragraphs typified the combination of fact and fiction in the book. In fact, York was the best shot in a community of superior marksmen. In fact, the bloodlines and speech patterns of the mountain folk were unusually pure, owing to their isolation. (Few people who spent their lives exclaiming, "My stars and garters!" ever heard of the royal awards bearing those forms. Fewer still would have recognized the aural similarity between "Summer is a-comin'" and the Middle English of Chaucer's day: "Summer is y-comen.")

The fiction was in the imagery of the trenches, already fixed in the public recollection of York's battle, even though there were no American trenches on Hill 223. Company G went "over the top" of a hill, not a trench.

Along with fighting the Germans, characters in the new book did plenty of fighting against the Indians. Daniel Boone, Andrew Jackson, and other luminaries led the charge against savages who scalped and tortured their way through page after page.

Introducing the book was a facsimile of a letter to York as President of his Agricultural Institute, from President Hoover. Dated May 28, 1930, it read:

> *My dear Sergeant York:*
>
> *The work you are doing to carry the light of knowledge to boys and girls is part of a movement for universal education that has been an undenied passion of our country and therefore cannot fail to attract the warmest sympathy of all our people. I wish you full success in your endeavors.*
>
> *Yours faithfully,*
> *Herbert Hoover*

Surely an endorsement from the president was good for business, though York had little use for the Republican's government policies. Gracie believed she had a firsthand look at the results of the Hoover administration when a hobo came to the kitchen door asking for something to eat. She fed him on the porch as the boys, who had never seen a hobo before, stared at his scraggly face and asked about the pole across his shoulder with a few items tied in a bandanna at the end. Observing their fascination, the hobo said, "Before we get through with this Hoover administration, you'll see more people than me in this shape walking down the road."

Chapter Nineteen

Hard Times

Sergeant York was a faithful correspondent on the road, continuing a habit begun with his first letters from Camp Gordon. He wrote to Gracie almost every morning, since speeches, dinners, and radio broadcasts often kept him out past midnight. York asked about everybody's health and about day-to-day matters on the farm. He told her about the weather and reported on the crowds at his lectures and sermons, which were invariably large and friendly. He would also sometimes include special greetings for the children, signing his name after each one.

> *Hellow Alvin C. York Jr. How are you?*
> *Sgt. York*
>
> *Hellow George E. B. York How are you?*
> *Sgt. York* [and on down the line]

Early in December of 1930, the sergeant wrote to advise Gracie on plans for his forty-third birthday celebration. In particular, he wanted to be sure all the guests had plenty to eat.

Have the boys to kill a hog so you can have fresh meat.
And be sure to cook a nough to have plenty for every body. You
could buy you a turkey if you want to and have it instead of a
chicken. Just suit your self.

Gracie needed no instruction on how to feed a crowd. Mealtime at
the York home evolved into a day-long production. Like all farm families, the Yorks were up before sunrise and Gracie, after seeing to the children, headed straight from the ground floor bedroom she shared with
her husband, through the dining room, to the kitchen. With the help
of at least one hired girl and sometimes as many as three, she stoked the
fire, carried in stove wood, and brought water from the spring across
York Highway in front of the house.

Breakfast was as close as they came to a family meal, with the sergeant, the four boys, Mother York, Gracie's sister Kansas, Gracie, the
kitchen help, and the field hands enjoying an early morning feast of
eggs, fried ham, chicken, coffee, buttermilk, and more. As the sun rose
through the dining room windows, platter after platter of Gracie's fresh
biscuits appeared and disappeared. She made them by the dozens every
day, measuring the ingredients by eye, rolling out the dough, then cutting them out with the rim of a glass.

Lunch was a far bigger production. As midday approached, one of
the children or hired girls rang the dinner bell off the kitchen porch.
Another usually walked across York Highway to the York store in the
unlikely event anybody missed the signal. The family and hired hands
who came in to the table were often outnumbered by other guests. Any
customers in the store at lunch time were invited in to eat, and usually
accepted. Politicians and businessmen from Jamestown, Nashville, or
anywhere else who were at the house or the store talking with the sergeant were also invited. Tourists and strangers who drove to Pall Mall
to meet York were welcomed as well and eagerly joined the crowd. The
children's friends came, too, and the friends of friends if they happened
to be around. Twenty or twenty-five for lunch was commonplace,
friends and strangers, farm hands, and legislators sitting without regard
to station or dress. A man sweat-stained and dirty from pulling stumps
was as welcome as a preacher in his best white shirt.

Meals always began with a prayer of thanksgiving from the sergeant, then organized themselves into the two or three seatings required to give everyone a place. York sat at the head of the table, with Miss Gracie on the corner to his left. By the time the meal was over, Gracie and the girls had only a little while before they had to start getting supper on. Supper brought a different set of faces to the table but was otherwise about the same as lunch.

York clearly had as much regard for his friends and hired hands as he did for the powerful New York movers and shakers who came to see him from time to time. He talked easily and completely unselfconsciously with everyone, regardless of background or station.

York's perspective on relationships was well illustrated one Saturday. The table was packed with dinner and diners as always, with others waiting their turn in the living room. There was a knock at the door and in came Leo Hatfield, a young man who, until recently, worked as a field hand on the York farm for fifty cents a day. With Hatfield was his new bride, whom Hatfield wanted to introduce to his famous boss. Hatfield didn't realize, however, it was York's birthday, and the house would be packed with the usual crowd plus invited guests. The young man made his way through the living room to the sergeant, seated at the head of the dining table, thinking he would introduce his bride, wish York a happy birthday, and leave.

When York saw the newcomers, he greeted Hatfield with a hearty handshake. Upon hearing their news, he not only insisted they stay to eat but that they sit beside him as his guests of honor. Explaining the situation, York asked the men on his left and right, prominent politicians who came to consult with York on state affairs, to give up their seats. With a nod of assent and a word of congratulation to the newlyweds, the two gathered up their plates and went to finish their meal in the kitchen.

It was impossible to avoid the financial strain of feeding so many people but everyone expected it of him now, and the sergeant would not disappoint them. He bought his kitchen groceries from the same wholesaler who supplied his store. That helped him some. The farm helped too, yielding a steady stream of vegetables and meat for the hungry hordes.

York family hospitality went beyond the table. Just as anyone within earshot was welcome at meals, one and all were invited to participate in the evening family devotional. In fact, attendance was expected. Every night when the sergeant was at home, family and any houseguests present gathered in the living room around the fireplace. York read from the Bible, frequently adding his own thoughts in the form of a short homily. Then all got down on their knees and the sergeant led them in prayer. After prayers it was bedtime.

Kansas and the older children went upstairs to bed. York and Gracie retired to separate double beds in their room; Gracie took the baby to bed with her, moving each child in turn to a bed upstairs whenever a new arrival came along. Though one of the six second-floor bedrooms could have been hers, Mother York preferred a pallet in front of the living room fire.

The Depression was beginning to affect Fentress County, though with less severity than in the cities. There was still a market for the timber the county produced and the arrival of paved roads made it possible to carry livestock and tobacco out for sale as well. The thought of twelve million Americans unemployed made the four-hundred-dollar annual salary of a teacher at York Institute seem a plum prize. In 1931 York's friend, best man, and onetime lecture tour companion, Clay Brier, became principal of the institute, giving the sergeant hope the future of the school would be less contentious than the past.

Yet his detractors kept up the pressure. In their resolution before the state board of education in 1929, O. O. Frogge and others had complained about York's insistence on teaching religion at the institute. They continued to hammer at the state authorities and at York about the matter. The state took no action for the time being. York's position was clear and immovable: everything about children's lives was affected by their understanding of God. No facts in any book were as important as knowing and understanding Christian morality. Without a bedrock foundation in what was right, further information was useless.

After more than three years of continuances and delays, the slander suit York filed against J. D. Frogge came to trial. On April 14, 1931, the jury found in favor of York, awarding him $500 in damages and assessing court costs of $139.96. Anticipating this development, Frogge previously disposed of a most impoundable asset, two parcels of land, by recording the sale of them to his wife for $1,000. York claimed the deeds to the two tracts should be nullified and the land sold to pay his judgment.

Instead, the court ordered ten shares of stock Frogge had in the Bank of Jamestown, valued at one hundred dollars a share, be sold to pay the judgment. Frogge claimed the shares actually belonged to his wife and she received the dividends. He did concede, however, "by accident or mistake the Cashier of said Bank of Jamestown, in issuing said stock certificates, failed to put the abbreviation 'Mrs.' before the name J. D. Frogge and so said certificate and record thereof does appear in the name of said J. D. Frogge." Somehow this mistake went unnoticed for nine years.

As the Depression deepened, York saw the agricultural institute continue to grow modestly, even as his own fortunes began a more rapid downward spiral. After the stock market crash in October 1929, the Tennessee legislature tried to shift financial responsibility for administration of the institute to Fentress County. The county sued, claiming the special arrangement the sergeant negotiated to keep his school out of the county school board's control required the state to provide funds. The courts sided with the county, forcing the state to apportion part of its shrinking revenue to the school.

This victory emboldened the county to insist on not having to pay for bus service to the institute either, an expense the county assumed after the legislative compromise of 1927. During the 1931 school year, the county stopped running school buses, and the state refused to assume responsibility. Sergeant York paid to operate the buses out of his own pocket until the impasse was resolved and the state began paying for them.

Sergeant York's crowds in 1931 were different from those of two or three years before, when they clamored for his stories of heroism and "barefoot mountain children" at $250 a night and stuffed cigar boxes with money. Other urgent business preoccupied them now. Financial survival was more important than aging stories of the Great War. Listeners could imagine their own children being barefoot as easily as they could some Tennessee hillbilly. (Asked about his opinion of the National Recovery Act, York said he preferred his own 3-F Plan: "Put your Ford in the garage, your family in the field, and your faith in God.")

York was in Dallas when he received word that American Airways, Inc., would offer him a complimentary ride back to Nashville in exchange for the publicity such a prominent passenger would bring. York reacted warily, asking how experienced American pilots were and whether he could be assured of having a seasoned captain on his trip. American replied that all their pilots had at least four thousand flying hours and good pilots were in the airline's best interest as well as that of the passengers, noting, "an experienced and able pilot is the best insurance for a $75,000 ship."

Betty Smythe, York's agent in New York, wrote to him, encouraging him to take the offer. She was trying to put the financing together on a motion picture about the sergeant, but her contacts were not convinced Sergeant York was a popular enough figure to risk the investment. Smythe suggested accepting the ride "may help us with the promotion work of our moving picture project here, showing the importance of your place in country's estimation. You know these hard boiled New York business men . . . who have to BE SOLD on the higher up's place of identification." York refused the ride.

In honor of Memorial Day in 1932, World War veterans assembled in Washington to remind the government of its promise to pay bonuses based on days overseas and wounds sustained. Most career soldiers had long since received their money but few draftees had gotten anything. York stood to benefit if the so-called Bonus March was successful.

Veteran doughboys, now middle-aged or older, set up tent camps amidst the capital's marble monuments. President Hoover ordered General Douglas MacArthur (who sat for the same portrait painter as York in France) to clear the "bums" out, claiming they were not veterans at all but a bunch of Communist agitators. That the men were indeed veterans and mostly unarmed was a factor in Hoover's defeat later in the year by the man who was Secretary of the Navy when York was in uniform, Franklin D. Roosevelt.

A week before Roosevelt's inauguration on March 4, 1933 (the last to be held on that month and day), Alvin and Gracie celebrated the arrival of their first daughter. In keeping with the tradition of naming children after American patriots, they christened her Betsy Ross York.

No pension was awarded to York or any other soldier as a result of the Bonus March. Two attempts over the years by his friends in Congress to grant York retired pay, first as a lieutenant, then as a captain, failed. His speaking schedule remained full, but the schools and clubs booking him no longer routinely paid $250 for an appearance. Betty Smythe accepted engagements for $150 and was relieved to get them.

The years of effort by York to earn a living and build support for his school were affecting his health. Traveling day and night even in the worst weather, he kept up a grueling schedule of appearances. When he was in Fentress County, he was besieged by favor-seekers, embroiled in conflict at the institute, and working his crops whenever he had the time. Exhaustion, continued abdominal complaints, and arthritis confined York to his bed in the spring of 1933. As before, when the lecturing stopped, the income stream stopped. Though his school was being operated with public funds, York still had to pay institute staff and supply all other financial support for the board of trust. He also continued to envision the dormitories, workshops, and other additions that were part of his original plans.

The members of the county board of education continued to attack York. They insisted to the state legislature the sergeant was incompetent in managing the school's affairs, forced his religion upon the student body, hired unqualified friends and relatives, and should be removed from his position. They further declared it was "manifestly unfair for the state of Tennessee to support a school for one county and not all counties." The board suggested the York Institute become a vocational school open to any Tennessean who passed the eighth grade.

Members of the state board of education were convinced that without Sergeant York's energy and notoriety, the school would fail. Seeking some ground for compromise, the state ordered an audit of the school's books to assess the charges of mismanagement.

Arthur Bushing's meticulous records showed, as of December 3, 1932, assets of $20,503.03, including more than $9,000 in cash and a half-acre lot on Long Island donated by Carl Fisher and appraised at $1,000. The institute had no liabilities. Sergeant York insisted through this audit his administrative abilities spoke for themselves. His institute was financially sound in spite of the fact the state deprived him of operating funds and the county gave him no support whatsoever. Besides, "if there's any money being wasted," York concluded, "it's my own."

Governor Hill McAlister, hesitant to move against the famous Tennessean, suggested a compromise for the next school year. The governor and the state board of education would establish closer oversight of the school, moving beyond the "advisory" status given them in the 1927 legislation. York and his institute directors would remain in charge.

A letter from the Anti-Saloon League in Washington underscored the increasing difficulty York had maintaining his income on the road. Not only were fees shrinking; they were going unpaid. The league wrote to York, stating its members were "very sorry that it is not possible for us to send you at least a hundred dollars in further payment for your New York and Missouri work. The states are apparently entirely unable at this time to raise the money and are absolutely unable at present to do more than keep going from day to day. . . . You are wanted in Minnesota for a convention address [plus several other engagements] for $75 a day, $50 a day and expenses in cash, with the rest when we can raise it . . . I can't tell you how much I regret being compelled to write you as I have about money due for past work and to suggest more speeches for less money per day. . . ." Betty Smythe warned him that henceforth he should get a certified check for his fee before going on the platform.

York found himself sinking deeper and deeper in debt through 1933 and 1934, with no promising solution in sight. He spent freely on family members and gave several of them jobs on the farm, at the store, and at the institute. He also was an easy touch for someone who needed a cosigner for a loan. As he stood on the sidewalk in Jamestown one day, York saw a newsboy come by without any shoes. "Where are you shoes, son?" the sergeant asked. "I don't have any," replied the boy. Taking the youngster by the shoulder, York marched him into the nearest store and bought him a pair on the spot.

York continued getting more involved with mineral companies, selling rights for oil and gas, as well as for a more recent discovery, barite. First mined in the county in 1915, barite was processed for use in industries as varied as sugar refining and the manufacture of vacuum tubes. The real barite boom came with the oil boom. Barite was a crucial component in drilling mud, a humble-looking but meticulously formulated sludge used in oil wells to keep drilling bits cool and flush rock debris to the surface.

York became a major local speculator and deal-maker, buying additional land outside Fentress County in order to lease out the barite and coal rights. He also leased the mineral rights on other tracts, some covering a thousand acres or more, and then subleased them to companies from Texas and Louisiana on better terms.

Just before the 1934 school year, York was informed that because of economies forced by the state board of education, the York Institute would not have enough buses to pick up children in the Wolf River Valley. Those boys and girls were absent on the first day of school, September 11, because they couldn't walk the twelve to fifteen miles each way. Alvin York had come up with a bus in 1926 and he came up with another one now, providing his neighbors' children a ride to school, and going still deeper into debt.

His financial troubles never affected the sergeant's personality. Even to his adversaries, with very rare exceptions, York was friendly, hospitable, and generous. His big smile and distinctive laugh were lavished on any and all who cared to enjoy them.

Because he traveled so widely and spoke so frequently—sometimes townspeople heard his nationwide NBC broadcasts from Washington or elsewhere on the network's Nashville affiliate, WSM—and because he entertained so freely, most people, including many of his neighbors, continued to assume he made a fortune. He wore fine clothes when he came to town, had a store, owned an office building on the square in Jamestown, the best farm on the Wolf River, leased thousands of surrounding acres, and donated lavishly to the institute he founded. They knew nothing about the growing list of chattel mortgages on file at the county courthouse and the increasing difficulty with which he took on new debts in order to pay off old ones.

In good times or bad, nothing was a better tonic for York than hunting. Following in his father's footsteps, there were many days when he went out to where his hands were working the fields, declared the day's work at an end, and invited them to get their guns and join him in the woods. They would go in search of squirrels, raccoons, possums, and more, but Alvin's favorite was always fox hunting.

York and his friends would pick a spot in the woods and build a campfire, then let their dogs loose on the scent. It was a matter of great pride whose dogs picked up the trail first and one of York's half dozen red-faced hounds was often the first one to let out a howl. Though everyone recognized the baying of his own dogs, a lively discussion typically followed the first sound from the pack as to whose dog was first and whose merely picked up the cry. Following their sound as the sun set over the valley rim, the men picked up their pace once the change in the dogs' wails indicated they had their prey treed or cornered. When they caught up with the pack, the fox was dispatched, and men and dogs returned to the campfire for a rest and another round of conversation. The companionship and the joy of the hunt could take York's mind off of even the most pressing problems.

Though now in middle age, the sergeant was still a fine shot. He and his friends enjoyed the sport of shooting squirrels with a .22 instead of a shotgun. It was more of a challenge that way and cheaper besides. A box of fifty .22 shells cost twenty cents, while shotgun shells cost three cents apiece.

As they walked beside a neighbor's barn lot one day, York pointed out a rooster to his friend Leo Hatfield. "See if you can shoot a hole in his comb with that .22 of yours. Otherwise we'll have chicken and dumplings for supper." Hatfield aimed and fired, leaving a neat hole in the comb and not another mark on the bird.

Hatfield was also with the sergeant one of the few times other than speeches when anyone ever heard him mention the battle of the Argonne. The two of them were on a cliff above a rock quarry, looking down into the Wolf River Valley just after sunrise. The valley was filled with rolling fog. "That reminds me of the Argonne Forest," the sergeant said quietly. "That's like it was when we went into battle, with trees and brush all around and you couldn't hardly see nowhere. Then afterwards there wasn't anything standing. The brush was all shot down." He paused. Both men stood motionless, looking down at the fog. York spoke again. "There was a higher power with me, Leo. Otherwise I wouldn't have made it."

With the election of Roosevelt, York's old friend Cordell Hull was appointed Secretary of State in 1933, and early in 1935 congressional legislation was once again introduced to give the famous sergeant a pension. As York prepared for a speaking tour to New York in February, the Senate considered a bill to appoint him an army major and retire him at $2,250 a year.

York's travel plans reflected the new economies he and Mrs. Smythe at Famous Speakers were putting into effect. More and more he was staying in private homes to save on expenses. He was accepting luncheon events for fifty dollars each, and Mrs. Smythe sent him detailed instructions on train fares in order to take advantage of weekend and round-trip discounts.

York repeatedly frustrated his agent by backing out of commitments she made in order to speak in Tennessee or handle some sort of local business. His agreement with Famous Speakers gave him the right to book his own appearances in Tennessee, but he was supposed to coordinate with Mrs. Smythe and was at least theoretically responsible for reimbursing the agency for missing dates unless doing so was "unavoidable."

Mrs. Smythe vented her frustration in a letter to York on February 4, 1935. She had to reschedule an appearance in Binghamton, New York, and cancel others; there were two dates she could not cancel because he asked for, and she agreed to, a fifty-dollar advance in addition to expenses for these trips.

> *Alvin York! Why do you treat me so badly? WHY?* ———
> *I've been trying since early December to get this business for*
> *you—and now you let me down like that. I cannot afford*
> *to throw away this money even if you can make more down*
> *there. Besides when you wait so late to make such decisions, it*
> *involves expensive telegraphic expenses to change dates, etc.*

By the time he arrived to speak in Troy, New York, on February 15, the House Military Affairs Committee was on its way to denying York his major's pension, noting the sergeant's military exploits were already "fittingly rewarded with the highest honor the government can bestow."

Some even publicly questioned the propriety of York's "highest honors." The Connecticut American Legion challenged the story York could have captured and killed so many of the enemy all alone. The Legion's surprise attack on one of its most illustrious charter members was led by York's old platoon mate, Bernard Early. York's frequent trips north were thoroughly reported in the local press, and Early, tending bar as he had before the war, was tired of seeing his comrade in arms get so much attention when Early got so little.

In *His Own Life and War Diary*, York described Corporal Early as friendly and brave but also as a wild Irishman who loved a fight and who could put away an "amazing" amount of liquor. Pressed by the national news media to comment on the accusations he wasn't the war hero he was supposed to be, York's only response was, "I don't care to make a statement."

In an affidavit prepared for Tom Skeyhill on April 11, 1928, while he was at work on *His Own Life and War Diary*, Early confirmed York led the remains of the three flanking squads from Company G after Early and Corporal Cutting were wounded. Early now modified his story to say he himself was actually in charge through the main part of the battle and York was only responsible for marching the prisoners back to Allied lines at the close of the skirmish. As evidence of his claim, he said the "German major" surrendered his pistol to Early, acknowledging him to be the leader. York assumed command only after Early was wounded.

On August 12, the *New York Times* published an interview with Captain Danforth, now a lieutenant colonel, who called Early's claim "unwarranted," saying Early was wounded and out of action before "the real fight started," and "credit was given where credit was due." Reporters, spoiling for a fight, continued to agitate York for a newsworthy rejoinder. York stood firm and would not make a statement.

The controversy and the challenge to his pension request in Congress from the Military Affairs Committee revived debate on the question of why York labored so long and hard for money on one hand and refused it so stalwartly on the other. Editorials suggested York should have accepted the fortune the moviemakers offered early on, telling them the money would be used only to help his school. That would have made him an even more popular star than he already was back when "the public was so keen on him."

One writer figured York "could have made enough money in two years to have had his buildings all completed. Modesty is an appreciated trait as it is a rare one. But when a man is filled with an urge to benefit others, he should not be confused as to what is the personal equation and what is the best for his enterprise." Commentators were welcome to their opinions; York saw the matter differently. No success, even the institute, was worth compromising his standards. Uncle Sam's uniform still wasn't for sale.

Mail trucks on the smooth black asphalt of the York Highway replaced the postman on horseback in bringing sacks of mail to the sergeant. Along with the press, the mail bags, too, contained advice on how he should make his money while he could. Most of the letters echoed the advice of a preacher from Sweetwater, Tennessee, whose admonition York had kept in a drawer ever since receiving it in 1922.

> *I have noticed in the papers that you have refused offers of large sums of money to connect with the entertainment world. I believe you are making a terrible mistake in turning down these opportunities to get big & easy money. You owe it to yourself & family to get all the money you can. Let your light shine. The Good Lord has given you the opportunity to get ahead. . . .*
>
> *You would be doing a good work in giving good clean entertainment to the people. Let men see your good works. Go out & entertain them & get all the money you can.*
>
> *If you don't get the money while you can you will be needy in your old age. See how much good you can do with plenty of money. It will be too late bye & bye.*

As the 1936 elections approached, Alvin York, like other Democrats, saw an easy reelection victory ahead for Roosevelt. The president calmed the fears of a nation stranded in the worst financial doldrums in its history, setting up the federal insurance of bank accounts, establishing the Social Security Administration, and proposing a minimum wage, which was on the verge of becoming law.

To his surprise York found himself proposed as a candidate for the opposition. The Prohibition Party, meeting in Niagara Falls, nominated Dr. D. Leigh Colvin for president and Sgt. Alvin C. York for vice president.

Established in 1867, the Prohibition Party fielded its first presidential candidate in 1872 on a platform of a constitutional ban on alcohol, regulation of public utilities, and "equal voting rights for women and Negroes." Despite such populist appeals, the party's national influence peaked in 1892 with its presidential ticket receiving 270,000 votes—2.5 percent of the total. The Eighteenth Amendment, long the party's dream, abolished the sale of alcoholic beverages and, ironically, almost put the party out of business. With the repeal of prohibition near the end of 1933, the Prohibition Party once more had a cause to promote.

In his keynote address, Dr. Colvin encouraged the 172 national delegates and other listeners that their party and "all the moral forces of the country proceeded upon the theory that the Eighteenth Amendment is still rightfully a part of the Constitution, temporarily in eclipse, but to be reinstated."

The two major national parties, he said, were conspiring to solve the problems of paying for Social Security by encouraging old people to drink themselves to death. "The sober judgment characterizing the Prohibition Party is a better insurance of the right solutions."

York's name was placed in nomination on May 7, 1936. That night wire service reporters called him at home in Pall Mall. "This is the first I've heard of it," the sergeant told them. When asked if he would accept the candidacy, he replied, "No. I won't accept. I'm not running for anything." He went on to explain that, though he supported the party's stance on alcohol and its overtly Christian approach to public policy, he was not willing to run against a fine man and fellow Democrat like President Roosevelt.

Had he been so inclined, Sergeant York could have provided the reporters with a much more interesting scoop. He was preparing to resign from the Alvin C. York Agricultural Institute.

The latest battle involving the school began the previous summer when York insisted the principal, his old friend Henry Clay Brier, be fired. Brier had the misfortune to be principal at a school that also had

a chairman in the person of Alvin York. Brier represented the county
school board in handling the institute's daily affairs and the county
board opposed York at every turn. Brier and York, childhood friends,
were thus set against each other by virtue of the positions they held.
York continued to insist he should be able to run the school as he saw
fit. Any attempt by Brier to assert a principal's authority was seen by
York as thankless meddling by the county board in an enterprise the
board continued to oppose.

There were also whispers of improper behavior on Brier's part, to
the point where Brier's friends secured an affidavit from a man who
gave Brier and a female teacher rides to school, swearing, "at no time
did any one in [my] car sit in any other's lap or do anything which
resembled any such action."

The last straw came when Brier decided to fire the sergeant's brother
Jim, who worked as the school janitor. York told the state board of education it was time to decide "who should make recommendations, me
or the principal."

Old battle lines were reinscribed and old grudges rekindled. The
school was outgrowing its original twelve classrooms and except for
the old barn being used as a gym, there were still no other buildings
on campus. Neither York's speaking engagements nor state appropriations ever netted enough money to add the dormitories, shops, and
other buildings that were part of the original $2-million campaign.
Plans were proposed to build a principal's residence and a new gym, but
the money was never allotted. York, the county decided, just couldn't
follow through and make things happen.

The new round of open conflict caught the attention of state legislators eager to trim costs wherever they could. Claiming the dissension
would lead to wasteful spending of taxpayer money, they withheld a
third of the school's appropriation, which they agreed to release when
the disagreement was settled.

One solution for adding more space caused particular friction
between York and others and may have been the reason Brier wanted
to fire Jim York. The National Youth Administration, a New Deal program to help young adults between the ages of eighteen and twenty-five
learn a trade and get a job, made a group of its workers available to help

build a new gym. They would learn the crafts of carpentry, stonework, plumbing, glazing, and the rest, and receive a small stipend, and the institute would get its building. To take advantage of this windfall, the school had to have a place for the NYA workers to live.

The old poor house building, unused by the school since the new building opened across the street, was the only option. York opposed billeting NYA workers there because Jim York and his family lived there. If space was required for NYA workers, Principal Brier's solution was to fire the janitor and hire another one with no expectation of lodging for his family at public expense.

On May 8, 1936, Alvin York resigned his position as chairman of the institute board in front of the state board of education in Nashville, expecting once again to restructure the school's support mechanism and head a newly-formed board. Criticism of his performance, York said earlier, revealed "more of a tendency at fault-finding than at fact-finding." The state withheld approved funds from the school, harped on minor points (such as cluttered storage rooms), and exhibited "a total lack of understanding of the conditions and the difficulties attending" the operation of the institute.

"It's my school," he declared. "I founded it and built it. I am going to expect the next legislature to take it out of the hands of the state board and turn it over to me, the man who founded it and fostered it without a penny of salary." He had, he said, turned down an offer of fifteen thousand dollars a year to be president of another school.

This time York lost. The state board accepted his resignation, along with Brier's as principal. Paul B. Stephens was appointed in Brier's place. After ousting the sergeant from the institution he founded and built, the board twisted the knife by changing the qualifications for the job of president of the school. Henceforth, all presidents would have to have a college degree. With his formal education equivalent to the third grade, York could no longer qualify for the post.

Jim York and his wife, Zonia, moved out of the poor house but continued to work at the institute, he as janitor, she as cook for the twenty-five or so NYA students who moved in behind them. The institute board approved the sale of a hundred acres of timber on school property for money to buy materials for the gym. An appeal was made for donations to finish out the work, to which Sergeant York made a generous contribution.

Arthur Bushing prepared a final accounting of the institute's affairs for the state board of education. Between the first day of 1926 and September 1, 1935, the institute posted income of more than $76,000, with a cash balance of $1,331.97. Sergeant York took out $6,576.41 in "salary and expenses" in those eight years and nine months and raised over $38,000 on the school's behalf, not counting $3,400 he left behind for the original agricultural institute.

The closing accounting also noted three loans to Bushing totaling $4,200, which were repaid; one loan of $3,000 to York, which was also repaid; and two loans to R. C. Pile—Pastor Pile—totaling $8,355.47 including interest, which had not been repaid.

After ten years of serving Sergeant York in various capacities, Arthur Bushing found himself without a job. His official duties as secretary and bookkeeper represented only a portion of the time and attention he devoted to the sergeant and his enterprises. Bushing gave Tom Skeyhill free room and board for months when the writer was working on his book about York; he covered York's overdrafts with his own money when the sergeant's expense reimbursements were late; he even loaned Joe York money, which went unpaid.

York considered reviving the old industrial institute to fight for control of the school and asked Bushing to volunteer his services. Bushing in turn requested a modest salary, which York could not pay. Forced to seek more fruitful employment elsewhere, he explained his position in a letter to York on December 10, 1935: "To my way of thinking there is a certain responsibility devolving upon one as secretary and trustee, and since in your judgment the conserving of these Industrial funds . . . does not merit the small sum which I was willing to take in sharing this responsibility with you, I think someone else, more willing and able to assume the responsibility and to donate their time, should be selected in my place." Bushing had asked for $12.50 a month. York didn't have it.

Chapter Twenty

Slings and Arrows

York did not brood over losing control of the institute. He stayed
busy with his farm, the store, mineral leases, speaking trips, an
unflagging stream of visitors, and the arrival of a second daughter, Mary
Alice (named after both grandmothers), in 1935. Another son, Thomas
Jefferson, early in 1938, brought the household to seven children plus
the sergeant, Gracie, Mother York, and Kansas.

Furthermore, Alvin York had a new cause. From the ashes of defeat
in the Great War, Germany had rebuilt itself into the most potent political and military force in Europe. The German momentum concerned
York, particularly since so many public figures in America insisted a
conflict across the Atlantic was none of America's business. All around
him, as he read of Germany's push into Alsace, the Sudetenland, and
Austria, York saw complacency, laziness, and inattention. Japan, said
the sergeant, was fighting an undeclared war in China, "and after it
conquers that country it is going to come over here. I'd just as soon we
got into it now as later."

He noticed particularly the public pronouncements of Colonel
Charles Lindbergh, whose 1927 ticker tape parade in New York was
the first to eclipse his own for size and spectacle. York did not begrudge

the transatlantic aviator his popularity. But the flyer was an outspoken noninterventionist, an attitude in which York saw the danger of decline and defeat.

In his speeches, York began mentioning the sinking of the USS *Panay*, an American registered patrol ship on the Yangtze River bombed by the Japanese a month and a day after York's prediction that the island nation would "come over here" soon. Filled mostly with reporters and embassy employees fleeing the Japanese attack on Nanking, the ship had huge American flags painted on the awnings of her upper deck, floodlit at night, identifying her as a neutral craft. The *Panay* was sunk by Japanese bombers the afternoon of December 12, 1937.

In the sergeant's view, the stronger and more prepared America was to fight, the less likely it was she would have to do so. He recommended a larger army, navy, and air force, more airplanes, and a well-trained civilian militia. He saw great potential for reserve training in the Civilian Conservation Corps. The CCC was a New Deal program to provide jobs and training to the unemployed and also to furnish parks and recreation areas across the country with gates, walls, picnic pavilions, lodges, cabins, roads, and other improvements. York thought the men participating in the CCC should have military training as part of their daily routine. This would increase the number of trained and ready soldiers by tens of thousands at almost no cost to the government.

As Thanksgiving approached in 1938, York distilled his thoughts into a lengthy telegram to the New York *Journal American*:

> *There is a state of unrest encircling the entire globe today which seems to have brought about great fear of another world war. The answer to this fear is millions of soldiers being armed with the very latest and best equipment. It seems to me the best plan for keeping us out of the war would be to build up a much stronger national defense on all lines, and put at least two hours per day military training in all our CCC camps. Did the United States gain anything from the last war? Yes, it gained much—it gained great prestige with all nations and was respected by all nations up to the time of the bombing of the*
> *Panay by Japan. And then we failed to get Japan to understand*

by meeting her face to face with armed forces, that our human
rights and our property rights were the base of our liberty and
freedom. Then we lost to some extent that prestige. . . . We
should not surrender any of the prestige or rights we now hold
to any nation of dictators, because to do so would betray the
faith of our forefathers who so bravely fought for our freedom
and liberty, which we hold so sacred today. If Germany and
Italy attack France and England, should the United States help
either side? I don't see how we could keep out of war unless we
surrendered our human rights and our property rights in the
whole European country and bottled ourselves up in the United
States. We should build up our army and navy to ten times its
present strength. And we should fortify every foot of coastline we
have, and fortify it strong. And we should start our factories to
making airplanes and build up our air forces to fifty thousand
fighting planes, twenty thousand bombing planes, and five
thousand scout planes . . . For in my opinion, the better we
are prepared to fight, the less trouble we will have with other
powers.

This stance was a far cry from York's public pronouncements in earlier years. Asked by a *New York Times* reporter if America should get involved in Germany's affairs when Hitler first came to power, York said, "I believe in letting those fellows fight their own battles, and we'll fight ours when the time comes. I think we ought to quit meddling in their family fusses over there. The United States should fight a defensive war only."

York's most immediate battle was not with Germany and Japan, but with his creditors. Like many of his neighbors in Fentress County, the sergeant became a familiar figure at the Cookeville Production Credit Association, where he took out various short-term loans using crops and livestock as collateral. One note pledged "35 head of steers and heifers now being fattened" in exchange for a $775 loan. Another listed "50 tons of hay, 800 bushels of corn on hand, 97 ewes, 92 head of Hereford and black angus cattle, and a few rams and lambs," for a loan of $2,000.

The sergeant had become quite a cattle farmer. By the mid 1930s, he accepted the fact that, for whatever reason, he could not turn a profit on his crops. The land, he figured, was about farmed out. (His travel schedule, preoccupation with the school, and the lack of assistance from neighbors and family also played a part in his continuing yearly shortfalls.) Livestock was the way to make land pay, but local breeds weren't adequate for the job.

After studying the subject, Sergeant York decided the best cattle for the Wolf River Valley were white-faced Herefords from Texas. He could scrape together enough money to buy some breeding stock but didn't have the extra cash for his own train ticket. He was able to hitch a ride with someone to Texas, bought his Herefords, and rode back to Pall Mall in the cab of the cattle truck. The cattle thrived, giving the York farm a badly needed financial boost. Following the sergeant's lead, other landowners in the valley began raising Herefords too.

Times being what they were, hitching a ride was a common way to travel all over the country. The sergeant and Gracie never passed a traveler walking along the road in Fentress County without offering a lift. One day Alvin slowed down as they passed a stranger walking on the shoulder, dirty, disheveled, his feet caked with mud. "Are you going to let that man put his muddy feet in your nice clean car?" inquired Miss Gracie. "I surely am," affirmed the sergeant, in keeping with his frequently repeated admonition: You don't have to look up to anybody no matter how much they're worth, and don't ever look down on anybody no matter how little they have. A muddy stranger was plenty good enough to ride in his car.

The J. D. Frogge slander case continued to bob to the surface occasionally and by the fall of 1938 it had taken several strange turns. After Frogge tried to hide his assets by transferring them to his wife, York sued to invalidate the transactions. York's lawyer, W. A. Garrett, eventually convinced the court Mrs. Frogge couldn't have had the money to buy the fifty-five acres she "bought" from her husband.

The land was ordered sold at public auction, and York, on Garrett's advice, attended the sale and bought the land on November 24, 1935. By the fall of 1938, he still hadn't paid for it, and the court ordered it sold again to pay interest, fees, and liens now totaling $1,042. J. D.

Frogge died in the meantime and since no one had yet paid her for it, his widow was selling timber off the land even though it supposedly belonged to York.

York had thought he was bidding jointly with Garrett for the property and that the lawyer would then take his fee—half of whatever settlement was finally paid—in land rather than cash. Demanding his payment, Garrett pointed out the deed was in York's name and there was no joint ownership. York had yet to receive the five hundred dollars awarded to him in 1931, owed more than a thousand dollars on the land, and had no cash to pay Garrett. Garrett sued his client to recover costs, and York suddenly found himself in opposition to his former counsel. York hired a new attorney, John Hale, and mounted a defense against Garrett. The case eventually worked its way to the state supreme court. York and Hale lost, and York had to pay a judgment in Garrett's favor, plus court costs. The court agreed to let the sergeant pay in installments.

Hale assisted York on another case in the summer of 1938. York was sued by Barium Ore Company of New Orleans for sixty thousand dollars. Barium Ore claimed York was obliged to grant the company exclusive mineral rights to a plot of land in Pickett County and instead sold minerals to a competitor. Though his oversight was a result of disorganization rather than dishonesty, losing the case would have ruined York. Fortunately for him, the prosecution could not build a compelling case, and the sergeant was acquitted.

October 8, 1938, was the twentieth anniversary of the battle in the Argonne Forest. A reporter drove from Nashville to Pall Mall in hopes of interviewing York for the wire services. He arrived at the York farm to find the sergeant high up on a scaffolding behind the barn, building a silo out of rock. Seeing the visitor pull in, York climbed down from his work to greet him.

"Do you know what today is, Sergeant York?" asked the reporter.

"Yes, I do," York answered.

"Well, do you still think about that battle?"

"That happened a long time ago," the sergeant replied. "I don't have anything to say about it now."

The reporter persisted. York eyed his questioner for a moment. Then, without malice or rudeness, he said quietly, "If you'll excuse me, I've got a silo to build," and headed back toward the barn.

Speaking engagements continued to come in through his New York agents, sometimes keeping York away from home for extended periods. He was out of town one bitterly cold January night in 1939, when Mother York was roused from her pallet on the living room floor by flames licking up from beneath the hearth. Sparks had fallen under the bricks somehow and started a fire down in the subflooring. She was more than seventy, and her eyesight was fading but Mother York recognized the danger and bolted into Gracie's bedroom where she was asleep with baby Thomas.

Gracie roused the rest of the house, sending Edward and Woodrow to get water from the river and dispatching Junior to the back stoop to ring the dinner bell for help. Throwing on coats and shoes, the two boys raced with buckets through knee-high snow to the river, only to find it frozen solid. Then they ran across to the spring. It was also frozen. In desperation they filled their buckets with snow and bolted for the door. Out back Junior was having no better luck with the dinner bell. In his excitement he yanked on the rope so that the clapper went around and around the inside of the bell in frantic, silent circles.

Lacking air under the hearth and drenched with melting snow, the fire soon went out with no damage to the house or injury to the family.

Another minor crisis had longer lasting effect. The York home's original carbide gas generator was later replaced by a kerosene system. Wires ran from the generator to a pole near the kitchen door. One cool afternoon the boys were all playing basketball in the yard between the house and the barn. After a few minutes, several of them shed their jackets, tossing them on the grass or across the nearby clothesline. One jacket made its way to the generator, where a stray sleeve flopped over the exhaust manifold.

The coat started a fire, which the boys easily put out, but it ruined the generator. Sergeant York had recently written to Governor Prentice Cooper in Nashville, asking when electricity from the Tennessee Valley Authority would make its way over the mountain to Pall Mall. The hydroelectric generators at Norris Dam had been up and running for more than two years and York expected to see his people taken care of. The governor told York power transmission lines were working their way to the Wolf River Valley and it shouldn't be long before he and his friends had electricity.

That being the case, and money being scarce, York left the broken generator alone and went back to kerosene lamps. Where there had been a ceiling bulb in every room, the warm golden glow of firelight now shone from table lamps and fireplaces all through the big white house by the highway—a glow that revived memories of late twilight on the hillside more than twenty years ago, when a young mountain man, strong, hale, and very much in love, watched a beautiful honey-haired maiden walk down to the valley floor toward a cabin whose windows shown with just such light.

Sergeant York was recommended once again for a military pension and once again it was denied. The secretary of war, Harry H. Woodring, believed the sergeant's heroic service to his country was "properly recognized by the means provided by law in the award to him of the Congressional Medal of Honor." The military retirement system, the secretary continued, was for the purpose of "vitalizing the active list" by removing old or unfit officers from the field to make room for fresh career military men. "The utilization of the retired list as a means of benefiting an individual who never held a commission in the military forces of the United States would be in violation of the fundamental purposes of the retirement system." Because he wasn't an officer, York did not qualify for help.

In the spring of 1939, York prepared for his first trip to California. He had several appearances lined up there over the summer, including the Golden Gate International Exposition in San Francisco and the state fair in Sacramento. For all the planning he had to do, he still found time to fire off a letter to Governor Cooper to "most earnestly request" the dismissal of P. B. Stephens as principal of the York Institute. Even after the sergeant resigned as head of the institute board, he remained intensely interested in the affairs of the school and accepted invitations to hand out diplomas the three years since his ouster. The institute board eagerly rid themselves of York as an administrator but highly valued his figurehead presence as a boon to publicity. If York felt any slight in this arrangement, he never mentioned it.

The sergeant claimed Stephens used state gasoline in his car, bought hogs for himself with state money, and skimmed funds from the NYA checks sent to girls working at the institute. The governor promised to look into the matter.

Stephens, who by all accounts was an excellent and effective president, was cleared by the inquiry. The state gasoline was to reimburse Stephens for fill-ups he paid for in town; the hogs were purchased by Stephens's twelve-year-old son, who made $1.50 a week tending milk cows for the school and bought hogs with his York Institute paycheck; the "skimmed funds" were to reimburse the school for books the NYA girls bought on credit.

New buildings were under construction at the institute, enrollment was strong, and the administration had excellent relations with the state and county boards of education. A comparison with the sergeant's years in control showed York to have been a visionary and a tireless promoter for the school, but simply did not have the administrative training and experience to manage day-to-day operations. The school would never have existed without him; yet it could not have continued growing had he stayed in charge. Stephens' management acumen and spirit of compromise won friends and funds from the legislature where York inspired factional infighting and delay.

York departed for his trip west. In its June 10, 1939, issue, *Time* magazine noted the sergeant's appearance at the Golden Gate celebration, held on Treasure Island in San Francisco Bay, in the magnificent shadow of the world's longest suspension bridge, only two years old. The brief article described the sergeant as "fat, arthritic, and peace-loving," and the accompanying photo did little to alter the perception. He was stuffed like a sausage into his war uniform, buttons straining, his chest covered with medals. "I don't know what the last war was about," the magazine quoted York as saying, a far cry from the "prestige" and "respect" York identified as the fruits of the war in his message to the *Journal American* a few months before.

On the other side of the country, the New York World's Fair was in full swing, its Trylon needle towering 610 feet above the crowds in Flushing Meadow on the site of a former ash pit. York was invited there with Governor Cooper and other dignitaries to celebrate Tennessee Day on July 22. Though the theme of the fair was "The World of Tomorrow" and visitors stared in awe at television, nylon, and other modern miracles, York's speech looked back to the noble and exciting history of the long hunters. Governor Cooper offered to lend the sergeant his speechwriter in New York for the occasion but York declined with thanks, saying he "probably couldn't read somebody else's speech anyway." York made reference to Daniel Boone and identified Old Coonrod as a long hunter, following the story line in *Last of the Long Hunters*. He described the pioneers settling in the Wolf River Valley where they "faced the tomahawk and the scalping knife, and a soil that had never been caressed with a plow."

Of course this was all romance and adventure rather than fact but York knew the crowds loved it and was not adverse to a little Tennessee storytelling. He was sorry Arthur Bushing was not there to enjoy it with him. "I've got a Jim Dandy speech on the last of the Long Hunters," he wrote to Bushing from New York. "I want you here so you can hear me spread some bull."

He may have looked fat and arthritic to the reporters in San Francisco but the man on the podium in the Court of States addressing thousands of spectators and a network radio audience that Saturday afternoon in New York was strong and graceful. His graying hair was still thick and full; his mannerisms confident and controlled after twenty years of public speaking; his robust tenor voice strong and commanding; his admittedly overweight frame stylishly camouflaged by a well-tailored three-piece summer suit. This masterful orator was in sharp contrast to the unlettered rube some of the sophisticated international visitors might have expected.

"We want the world to know that we are Americans," he said of his fellow mountaineers. "The spiritual environment and our religious life in the mountains have made our spirit wholly American, and that true American pioneer spirit still exists in the Tennessee mountains. Today with all the clamor of the world and its evil attractions, you still find in the little humble log cabin houses that old fashioned family altar of prayer which is the true pioneer spirit—that of the long hunters." His own prayer, he concluded, was "God save America and strengthen our arms. And lift up the hands that hold up our flag, Old Glory, that she, the Stars and Stripes, wave over the land of the free and the home of the brave."

As she had done so faithfully through the years, Gracie wrote Alvin almost every day while he was at the World's Fair. As he walked around the grounds trailing a large cluster of admirers, lunched with Governor Cooper and fair officials at the Waldorf, and returned for exhibits on electricity, railroads, and Democracity, the enormous signature exhibit inside the 180-foot Perisphere, Gracie wrote long letters touching on local news, family matters, and her struggle to manage the household on less and less money.

> I am afraid you are working too hard and I don't like that part. Say Dear I had rather do most any way that is right and not have much to wear or eat and keep you home with me. . . . Never have any body wanting to buy wheat yet. You have two notes hear from Bank to renew. I can't do anything about them until you come home . . . I know quite a bit that needs doing but money is scarce and it don't haft to be done and I thought I would try to get by on as little as I could. Some times I don't know what to do hardly. . . . Your newspaper picture makes you look so slim. Hope you don't fall off any more. You looked so tired.

She also mentioned how Clay Brier, hearing P. B. Stephens was out of favor as principal of York Institute, wondered if there was a chance York would help him get his old job back.

Sergeant York wrote regularly as well, with most of his comments concentrated on the institute. He was determined to remove P. B. Stephens from his position as principal and used his time with Governor Cooper at the fair to lobby for his dismissal. York also kept up with the latest school bus crisis. The state stopped funding institute buses again. This time the new county school superintendent, Wilma Reagan, who was a member of the first graduating class in 1927, came up with county funds to keep buses running. Though this should have pleased the sergeant, years of conflict with the county made him resentful even of this assistance; he was worried about Reagan having too much influence over institute matters. (Reagan replaced O. O. Frogge, who was anticipating his seventh two-year term as superintendent. When it looked as though Reagan would win the appointment over him, Frogge had a friend in the state legislature pass a bill requiring superintendents be popularly elected. The bill passed; Reagan won the popular vote by a comfortable margin.)

Back in Pall Mall late the following week, York followed through with a plan he had simmered over for a long time. As he had said in New York and in hundreds of speeches before, he believed the linchpin holding America's freedom and prosperity in place was Christian worship in the home. One of York's original goals for the agricultural institute was religious instruction. But the sergeant's insistence on teaching religion became a point of contention with the school's various ruling bodies and was one of the levers his opponents finally used to pry him out of office.

The institution York dreamed of and struggled for so long was up and running. What it lacked was a suitable foundation in Christian education. York decided to start another school, not to compete with his first one, but to complement it. The institute taught English, crop rotation, and seamstressing. His new school would teach the mountain boys and girls about Jesus.

On July 31, 1939, York, Gracie, Pastor Pile, York's lawyer John Hale, and his friend and pastor R. D. Brown registered a charter of incorporation for the Alvin C. York Bible School, in order to "give instruction in the Holy Bible and to teach the fundamental Christian religion as contained therein," along with literature, the arts, music, and other subjects to "prepare its pupils and students to live and practice a full Christian life." The charter further declared no theory of evolution could ever be taught at the school and no one could be a member of the corporation or the board "who does not profess to believe in the divine origin of man and that the Holy Bible is the inspired word of God." With legalities out of the way, they sat down to discuss how they might raise some money.

Alvin York took three steps that summer in hopes of improving his family's chronic financial difficulties. First, he applied for old age assistance on behalf of his mother. Mary York's mind was still sharp, but at seventy-three, she walked with difficulty, and was almost completely blind. Second, he filed a request for veteran's benefits for himself. Then, for the first time in his life, he applied for a job. There was an opening for project superintendent at Cumberland Homesteads State Park, the Civilian Conservation Corps camp in Crossville. York wrote to his fellow Democrat and farmer, Senator Albert Gore, in hope of getting the position.

The news on Mother York's welfare application was not good. She was denied, said the form letter addressed to her, because "your children are able and willing to provide you with the necessities of life. Due to our limited funds for this program we have to expect children to care for their parents when they are able to do so."

The application for veteran's benefits stalled in limbo, with the Veterans Administration requesting an affidavit showing York's annual income, and York not responding to their requests. With all his bank loans, crop loans, payments to the court on the J. D. Frogge matter, travel, and business expenses on one side; his speaking, farming, and store income on the other; and the legal status of his contributions to York Institute unclearly in the middle, York had no idea what his total net income was and no way to find out.

The good tidings came from the National Park Service, which was in charge of the Civilian Conservation Corps. A letter informed Sergeant York he was under consideration for the job he requested. The Park Service would have to interview him for the job and suggested a date. At the appointed hour, the interviewer appeared at the institute, where York had once more taken an office but Jim York informed him the sergeant was out of town and would be back in a week and a half. A week and a half later, York still hadn't contacted the Park Service, so the Park Service sent him a telegram asking him to call "at the earliest possible date."

At last the interview was held, and York got the job. He began as temporary superintendent on October 6 and was permanently appointed on October 24. His salary was twenty-three hundred dollars per year, fifty dollars less than the major's pension he was almost awarded four years before.

The job was a good fit for York. He spent a lot of time outdoors, where a lifetime of farming made him comfortable. He supervised a cadre of healthy young men, eager to learn and delighted to have any sort of job, as they built cabins, roads, and picnic shelters in the park. The sergeant was also in a position to grant favors and help the men who helped him over the years. Knowing his inclination to serve others, the favor-seekers descended like locusts.

Project superintendent York wrote to Senator McKellar asking for a friend's appointment as a referee in bankruptcy. He sympathized with his workers' creditors when they wrote York seeking restitution and talked to the men about paying up. He solicited an appointment as custodian of his park for the son of a friend. Even his old Fentress County nemesis, Ocie O. Frogge, asked York to help him get a job with the welfare department. In response York wrote to Welfare Commissioner Paul Savage, "there is no man in my county that could come to you with a better endorsement of Democrats and business men than has Mr. Frogge."

Superintendent York mentioned Frogge again when he wrote the authorities to straighten out delayed welfare payments for a neighbor who made a living for herself and two children doing washing for fifty cents a load. "Now Paul," he wrote to Commissioner Savage, "this is just another case where the investigators have not visited this poor home and have failed to do their duty. This woman lives something like three miles from the highway in mountains, and these little girl investigators with their high heel shoes fail to visit these poor homes. . . . I must still insist on the appointment of Mr. O. O. Frogge. He will go out into the hills and see these poor families. . . ."

York's persuasive skills fell short. In his reply Commissioner Savage observed, "We have had so many protests against the appointment of Mr. Frogge that we feel that it would possibly not be wise to place him in the welfare program when he is objectionable to so many people."

Superintendent York's idea of fair employment was to see Tennessee Democrats award jobs to other Tennessee Democrats. To Bain Stewart, CCC director of personnel, he wrote:

Now Bain, you know there is entirely too many Tennessee
jobs taken away from our good old Tennesseans and given to
out of state men who never pay a tax in Tennessee and who
never vote in this state.

To Senator McKellar, upon hearing the Crossville Camp might be
closed rather than those at Pickett Forest and Pikeville:

You no doubt know that J. O. Hazard, State Forester,
is a Yankee and he has his Yankee school mate in as Project
Superintendent at Pickett Forest. Senator, these are the boys I
would like to see trimmed up and put out of their jobs.

To Yankee Robert Maxwell, at the Division of State Parks:

. . . I feel that if I had a native Tennessean in your place
who would be interested in having the State Parks finished
as soon as possible in order to save the taxpayers money
and not just interested in a nice salary, I could get better
cooperation. . . . We old time Democrats, taxpayers and voters
are just living in hope that our good friend Prentice Cooper,
Governor, will soon find a native Tennessean to play your part
in this Park Service, someone that is interested in his own state
and in our good work in the Conservation Department. If
there is no native Tennessean and taxpayer that is capable of
filling your place, then we suggest that your office be abolished.

York scarcely settled into a routine in Crossville before he became
restless. He chafed at spending his days so far from Pall Mall. He found
himself scratching for funds supposedly already appropriated for his
projects. When someone told him he would have $114 to buy flagstone,
he took him at his word and ordered the flagstone. When the money
was held up, York was confused and frustrated. The lack of cooperation
and the political posturing galled him. Playing politics in Jamestown
and Nashville, he was playing with people he knew and understood.
These foreigners in the Park Service were nothing but an irritation.

On December 11, Superintendent York wrote a one-sentence letter to General Frank T. Hinds at the Bureau of Veteran's Affairs in Washington.

My Dear Mr. Hinds,

I would like very much to have a job with the new Veterans Hospital at Murfreesboro, Tennessee, if salary was satisfactory, Thanks.

While waiting for an answer from Veteran's Affairs, York pondered a discreet request from a large contingent of people from the fourth congressional district of Tennessee. They wanted him to run for senator against his friend and benefactor Albert Gore, who wrote York upon his appointment at Crossville, "I think it is a fine thing to have the outstanding hero of the World War as Superintendent of one of our camps, and I am especially delighted that it is happening to one of the camps in my district." The sergeant indicated some interest in the prospect but had not campaigned publicly for the office.

The Parks Department scheduled the Crossville camp to close on March 31, 1940, but changed the plans and decided to leave York's site open. Therefore, York's letter of resignation, to be effective April 15, took the department by surprise, especially since he lobbied so hard for the job in the first place, then fought equally hard to keep the camp open.

What the Parks Department and the rest of the world would soon discover was that Superintendent York had received a better offer. Once again, as happened so many times over the years, Hollywood came knocking. This time, at long last, the hero of the Argonne opened the door.

Chapter Twenty-One

Hollywood Intrigue

On May 22, 1919, as Sergeant Alvin C. York paraded up Fifth Avenue beneath a fluttering cloud of ticker tape, one spectator looked out upon the scene and saw the ingredients of a great motion picture. From his eighth-floor window at the corner of Fifth and Forty-first, Jesse Lasky gazed down at the ruddy, handsome soldier riding in an open car and surveyed the sidewalks and office windows jammed with admirers. Lasky had spent his whole career in the entertainment business and he could see the story of this brave and humble mountain man had the potential to make them both a fortune.

Lasky was a heavyset, lantern-jawed man of thirty-seven, graying at the temples and balding on top, with a few long hairs in front combed straight back over his thinning scalp. He was gregarious and energetic and was well on his way to building a reputation as a movie producer matching the one he once enjoyed as a Broadway showman.

While young Alvin York had been watching his father swing a blacksmith's hammer in Pall Mall, Jesse Lasky was swinging a pickax in the Yukon gold rush, hoping to strike it rich. When his money ran out, he took a job playing the cornet in Alaskan honky-tonks. Back home in San Francisco he and his sister Blanche formed a cornet duo and began performing in vaudeville houses to support themselves and their widowed mother.

One day another act on the bill asked if Lasky would be interested in managing his business affairs for him. Lasky agreed and found he preferred to work away from the footlights rather than in front of them. Soon he was representing the biggest stars in show business, including Al Jolson and Mary Pickford. By 1911, when his Folies Bergère Theatre opened on Broadway, the press was comparing him with the illustrious Florenz Ziegfeld as one of the country's greatest theatrical producers.

He sailed to Europe, returning with entire troupes of performers from London, Paris, and Berlin. The shows were a smash hit, but their extravagant production costs soon bankrupted the company. Three years later, Lasky and Blanche's husband, Samuel Goldfish, a wealthy glove merchant, formed a motion picture company with Adolph Zukor and Cecil B. DeMille. They decided to name it Paramount Pictures, after the apartment building where the agreement was signed.

Paramount produced *The Squaw Man*, the first feature film ever shot in Hollywood, in 1914. DeMille originally planned to set up a studio in Flagstaff, Arizona. When the train pulled in he got off, took one look at the seemingly featureless landscape, and got back on. The train went on to California, from where he sent a telegram to Lasky in New York: "Have proceeded to California. Want authority to rent barn in place called Hollywood for seventy-five dollars a month."

Lasky believed successful movies began with a good story. Going against a trend calling for lots of action, lots of stars, and little plot, Lasky paid top dollar for rights to stories from Sir James Barrie, David Belasco, and Zane Grey. (Barrie, the creator of Peter Pan, accepted a fee of $100,000 and 50 percent of the profits from movies based on his work.) In the story of Alvin York, the producer saw a triumph for Paramount.

Summoning an assistant to his window perch, Lasky told the man to visit York at the Waldorf, offer him any amount of money he wanted, and come back with a deal. Along with a gaggle of others, Lasky's emissary made his proposition in vain to the sergeant. "Uncle Sam's uniform ain't for sale," was the answer, regardless of price.

Through the years Lasky continued to contact York from time to time, always with the same results. He was working at RKO Studios in 1939 when a studio executive there rekindled his interest by suggesting, in light of the world situation—with Austria and Poland overrun, the English Channel threatened by German attacks from the North Sea, and Hitler marching relentlessly toward Paris—York's story would make a popular movie. Lasky read stories in the national press of York's interest in helping the allies and of his disdain for isolationists, especially Colonel Lindbergh. He thought perhaps he could convince York that making a movie was the best way to present a patriotic, pro-Allied message to the country.

Another reason for his renewed interest was Jesse Lasky desperately needed a hit. While his brother-in-law's career soared, Lasky's traveled an unsteady course. Lasky forced Samuel Goldfish to accept a nine-hundred-thousand-dollar buyout and leave Paramount in 1916. Goldfish went into business with another group including two brothers named Selwyn. They named the new company by combining "Goldfish" and "Selwyn:" Goldwyn Studios. When Goldwyn prospered, Goldfish capitalized on the publicity by changing his own name to that of the studio. Samuel Goldwyn went on to establish a Hollywood production company, sell it to Louis B. Mayer, then form Samuel Goldwyn Studios, one of the most successful independent studios in Hollywood.

Paramount meanwhile prospered throughout the 1920s. In 1930 the studio turned a profit of $18 million. In 1932, with the Depression slashing revenues and Lasky continuing to spend, the studio lost $16 million. Lasky was forced out. He worked for Twentieth Century Fox, then for United Artists, always walking in the shadow of his former glories. He produced a radio show for CBS in Hollywood called "Gateway to Hollywood." This show scoured the country for fresh new talent, then brought winners of local competitions to California for auditions with the major studios. The show launched the careers of several young stars, including Linda Darnell, and a girl from Houston named Josephine Cottle, who by the end of the competition took the stage name Gale Storm. "Gateway to Hollywood" went off the air in 1939, leaving Lasky searching for a new project. A Sergeant York movie could salvage his career.

Lasky assigned a screenwriter named Harry Chandlee to dig up whatever material was available on York at the public library. The more the producer learned, the more excited he became. Though he had tried numerous times over the previous twenty years without success to get York's attention, Lasky decided to approach the famous soldier again. He wrote a letter to York in Pall Mall but received no reply. He followed with a telegram, asking the sergeant to meet him at his convenience to discuss "a historical document of vital importance to the country in these troubled times."

In Crossville, taking a break from his duties at the Civilian Conservation Corp camp, York read the telegram forwarded to him there. He had resisted any overtures from the movie companies because he felt it was wrong to profit from death and the horrors of war and, as he so often said, it seemed a selling out and cheapening of the patriotism and faith he cherished.

This proposal was different. Lasky mounted a persuasive sales pitch, pleading with York to let his story be told for the benefit it would bring to the country. The story of his life would rouse America to a patriotic stance against Hitler, promoting the cause of York and like-minded citizens who refused to sit by and let the Nazis devour Europe. It would show the value of faith in war and the role of home and family in spurring soldiers on to victory thousands of miles away.

The chance to make money was also appealing. His personal finances were strained as always. Moreover, the sergeant was eager to begin construction of his Bible school and already preparing a beautiful hillside meadow on the farm for it, between his big white house and the site of the cabin where he was born. The school would have classrooms and a meeting hall made of flagstone, surrounded with an arched colonnade. The movie would make it all possible. Plans were also underway at York Institute for a manual arts building, dormitory, and other expansions a Hollywood windfall could support.

York wrote back to Lasky that he would be willing to talk. Shocked and elated, the producer flew from Los Angeles to Nashville, arriving early on the morning of March 9, 1940. Having flown in as close as possible, he took a taxi more than a hundred miles further east to the Crossville hotel York suggested. Though the men had corresponded for years, they had never met. The hotel desk clerk introduced Lasky to the Tennessean in the lobby. Members of the press, probably tipped off by Lasky, were waiting in Crossville as the meeting took place. The sergeant came straight from overseeing CCC work at a nearby rock quarry, dressed in rough trousers and a worn leather jacket. When he entered the hotel amidst the popping of news photographers' flashbulbs, he protested, "I don't have my Sunday clothes on," gesturing toward Lasky's impeccably tailored suit.

The two ate lunch at the hotel, then drove to Jamestown to visit the York Institute. Lasky also produced a copy of *His Own Life Story and War Diary* and asked York to autograph it.

On March 12, the men met again, this time at the Mark Twain Hotel in Jamestown. York was accompanied by a quiet woman with big blue eyes whom he addressed as "Miss Gracie." He didn't introduce her at first and when the two left the room for a minute, Lasky asked the hotel clerk who she was. "That's his wife," the clerk replied with a grin.

Later, in Lasky's room overlooking the Fentress County Courthouse, Miss Gracie sat on the only chair, and the men sat side by side on the bed to discuss the prospects of a business relationship. York told Lasky he was thinking about running for senator against Albert Gore but couldn't campaign as long as he was on the government payroll as a CCC superintendent. York considered quitting his job to campaign for office and it looked as though his camp might be closed anyway. He liked Lasky's movie idea but wasn't firmly decided on his next move.

The three of them drove to Pall Mall, where York entertained Lasky at his home and showed him the site of the Bible school a few hundred yards east of the house. York's obvious passion for the new school made his well-dressed visitor think he could be persuaded to make a picture at last.

The same day an Associated Press item datelined "Hollywood" announced Lasky had "completed arrangements" to film the life story of the famous Sergeant York. No deal was made but the news sent reporters scurrying to their telephones that evening for a comment from the war hero. Their calls to Pall Mall were answered by Gracie, who informed them the sergeant was already in bed. Could she wake him up? No, she didn't see she could. Did she have any comment on the announcement? She'd prefer to let the sergeant do the talking tomorrow.

At 11:00 a.m. on Thursday, March 14, York and Lasky met again, this time at the Hermitage Hotel in Nashville, with their attorneys in tow. Lasky had already announced to the press the picture would be made, York would serve as technical advisor, and production would take about a year. Rumors circulated about Lasky offering York twenty-five thousand dollars for his participation but that the sergeant "held out" for twice that amount.

Lasky scheduled a flight back to Los Angeles before dawn the next morning. When it became obvious they wouldn't reach a final agreement by then, he postponed his trip a day. The producer opened Thursday's session by handing York a contract. "That's not for me," York said, handing it to his Jamestown attorney and friend, John Hale. With a glance at the document, Hale placed it calmly aside, saying this was not the kind of agreement York would sign. "What we want," he explained, "is a plain old Tennessee contract that simply says what you shall do and what the sergeant shall do."

The negotiations continued the next day, Friday, and again Lasky changed his travel plans. "It's exactly the kind of movie I'd want," said York during a break to reporters milling about in the hotel lobby. The contract details, he continued, were less important than that he and Lasky understood each other as men. "You know, there isn't a great deal of difference between trading for a mule or a movie contract. What really counts is the trader."

Lasky and his attorney expected an easy time of it from their two backwoods counterparts. But by the end of the day Friday, they still didn't have a deal. As much as York wanted the movie to be made, he would only consent if he could get enough money from the enterprise to build his Bible school and help with the improvements at York Institute.

Tired and frustrated at failing to achieve his twenty-year goal after coming so close, Lasky left Nashville at 3:50 Sunday morning for the twelve-hour trip by air back to California. Speaking to reporters on the ground in Los Angeles, Lasky said he was confident an agreement was still possible and that the only snag was "a technical one about distribution."

In less than a week Lasky, York, and their lawyers were back at the Hermitage trying once more to put the final touches on an agreement. "It's your patriotic duty to let your life serve as an example and the greatest lesson to American youth that could be told," Lasky declared. York agreed but there were certain conditions he would not budge on. By Friday, March 22, the last major impasse was on the matter of which state's laws would govern the contract. Since Lasky was a California resident, RKO was a California company, and the movie would be made there, the Hollywood team insisted the contract be under the laws of California. Because York and Hale were familiar with Tennessee law and on first-name terms with its most important lawmakers, they were equally determined the contract should be filed in Tennessee.

Every once in a while, York stood up and left the negotiations without a word, returning a few minutes later. When one of these mysterious disappearances lasted longer than usual, Lasky got up to see what was going on. He walked to York's room two doors down and knocked softly. Hearing no answer, he gently opened the door to find the burly sergeant on his knees praying beside the bed. Lasky closed the door and returned to the negotiating table to wait. After a short time York returned and the conversation resumed.

By noon on Saturday the sides seemed hopelessly deadlocked. Staring out the window at the Tennessee capitol building a block away, Lasky had an idea. The producer had called on Governor Prentice Cooper before his first meeting with York and the governor gave his hearty endorsement to the movie idea. Lasky now went down to the hotel lobby and called the governor's office. He told Cooper the deal was made and asked if the governor would like to witness the signing of the contract. Cooper immediately offered to have them sign in his office. They should come right over, he suggested, as he was leaving town for the weekend.

Before going upstairs, Lasky tipped a bellboy to come to his room in five minutes and say he had a call from the governor. The message was delivered as promised and Lasky left the room, pretending to take the call in the hotel manager's office. When he returned, Lasky announced Governor Cooper knew they were ending their negotiations and invited them to the capitol to sign their contract.

John Hale insisted his side was not ready to sign. Lasky observed it would be unwise to keep the governor waiting. "We don't have to sign the real contract," Lasky explained. "We can let him witness a dummy contract. Then if we don't come to an agreement before we leave tonight, there's no harm done. But if we do sign while the governor is away for the weekend, we'll still have a picture of him as a witness. That would please him, and incidentally, it would be very good publicity for the picture and your state."

"We could tear up the photograph if we don't sign the contract," York thought aloud. Then, after a moment, "The governor's a good man. Let's don't keep him waiting."

A horde of photographers milled about in the next room as the group assembled in the governor's office. When Lasky explained they weren't actually ready to sign, the governor opened his desk drawer and pulled an impressive, official-looking document. "Then you might as well sign this bill that I can't get through the legislature," he said. "I'd like to see some use made of it."

On a signal from Governor Cooper, the elegant padded leather door to the reception room opened, disgorging a tripping, shoving horde of photographers. The signers took their poses, the cameras clicked, and the negotiators walked the block back to their hotel to talk some more.

Late in the afternoon, through the open windows of their room, the men heard newsboys on the street. "Extra! Extra! Contract signed for Sergeant York movie!"

"I guess we'll have to sign it now," York said with a combination of resignation and relief. He still didn't seem completely at ease but agreed to sign.

Under the terms of the contract, dated March 23, 1940, York was to receive twenty-five thousand dollars on the spot, plus an equal amount the day after the picture was released, or by October 1941, even if the picture was not completed. He would also receive a salary of five hundred dollars for every week he served as a technical consultant. After the movie grossed $3 million, he would get 4 percent of everything above that figure. The higher the sales, the larger his percentage, topping out at 8 percent of everything over $9 million.

York deleted and initialed two places in the final document. He scratched "actor" and "producer" from the services he agreed to render to Lasky if asked (leaving in "writer, collaborator, director or technical advisor"). He also scratched Sam Cowan's book, *Sergeant York and His People*, from the list of books available to Lasky for use in developing the script. The others were *His Own Life Story and War Diary* and *Last of the Long Hunters* by Skeyhill. York was comfortable that he owned Skeyhill's books free and clear, but there was some question about Cowan's. They would go ahead without it.

The tortured compromise on the issue of which state had jurisdiction over the agreement was recorded in Paragraph XV. ". . . It is a fact that this contract is executed in the State of Tennessee. It is agreed, however, that the interpretation, construction and enforcement of this agreement shall be governed by the laws of the State of California, provided, however, that if anything in the applicable California law would impair or invalidate the rights to compensation granted to York by the terms of this agreement, and the applicable provisions of the Tennessee law would not impair or invalidate the same, then, and to that extent the Tennessee law shall govern."

Hollywood columnists were already speculating on who would play the lead in the movie, which Lasky gave the working title, *Argonne Forest*. Spencer Tracy, arguably the most popular actor on the screen, was definitely a contender. Raymond Massey was a possibility, even though he was a Canadian, following his success as the title character in *Abraham Lincoln in Illinois*. Henry Fonda and James Cagney were also mentioned.

Lasky would only say the star he had in mind was one of the top ranking actors in Hollywood, an outdoorsman, hunter, and gun fancier in real life, who was about the height and weight York was in France. Seeing the value of letting the speculation mill run on, he refused to say more, even though in his own mind the question was settled. One of the few points York and Lasky agreed on early in the negotiations was the only actor for the part was Gary Cooper. "Coop," as his friends called him, was York's choice from the beginning, and Lasky thought the lanky star had the ideal combination of grit and tenderness to make a smash hit.

Lasky had felt him out enough already to know Cooper was not keen on the idea. For one thing, he was interested in appearing in the upcoming movie production of *For Whom the Bell Tolls* written by his friend and hunting buddy Ernest Hemingway. But the biggest drawback for Cooper was knowing York was a hero who was still alive. Though he played Marco Polo and Wild Bill Hickock with confidence, Cooper was afraid of not living up to the real Sergeant York.

On his way home the day the contract with York was signed, Lasky sent a telegram to Gary Cooper from the Nashville airport. "I have just agreed to let the motion picture producer Jesse L. Lasky film the story of my life, subject to my approval of the star. I have great admiration for you as an actor and as a man, and I would be honored, sir, to see you on the screen as myself. Sergeant Alvin C. York."

As he turned away from the Western Union counter, Lasky was stopped by a stranger. "Pardon me, Sergeant York, but I heard you dictating that telegram. Could I have your autograph so my kids will believe I really saw you?" Lasky signed Sergeant York's name, shook the stranger's hand, and continued through the airport lobby.

The morning after arriving in California, the producer went to the bank and borrowed twenty-five thousand dollars on his life insurance. The check he gave York on Saturday would have been worthless otherwise.

Lasky began making the rounds of the studios, looking for a place to make his film. Though he was working at RKO, Lasky's contract with York was with Lasky personally, not the studio. RKO turned the proposal down even though one of RKO's executives suggested the idea. His old colleagues at Paramount did likewise. Nobody had made a successful war picture in years, they said, and despite Lasky's insistence this was not a war picture, no one was interested in a movie about Sergeant Alvin York.

He called an old Paramount friend named Charles Einfeld, now head of advertising and publicity at Warner Bros., to see if that company might be interested. Einfeld suggested that if Lasky could appeal to Harry Warner's sense of patriotism, he might have a shot. Lasky presented the idea to Warner at his weekend home. When he finished, Harry got his brother Jack on the phone, and they agreed to begin the picture immediately.

Lasky moved into his new office at Warner Bros. on April 8, with a contract that produced an impressive return on his twenty-five-thousand-dollar investment in Sergeant York to date. As producer, he got forty-thousand dollars in exchange for assigning all his rights with York over to Warner Bros.; a salary of fifteen hundred dollars per week with forty weeks guaranteed; and 20 percent of the gross above $1.6 million moving to 25 percent of gross after $2.5 million.

Lasky started working with screenwriter Gene Fowler on a treatment of the movie plot, but other commitments prevented Fowler from accepting the script assignment. Lasky signed on Harry Chandlee instead, who did the original research on the story and who had just completed the screen adaptation of Thornton Wilder's Pulitzer Prize–winning play, Our Town. Chandlee, Lasky, cowriter Julian Josephson (who wrote movies starring Spencer Tracy and Tyrone Power, among others), and Lasky's nineteen-year-old son, Billy, traveled to Pall Mall the week of April 22 to interview York's family and friends and get a taste of mountain life.

One of their first surprises was that no one in Fentress County much cared that they were from Hollywood. They got no more attention than any other stranger, an odd sensation for men accustomed to trailing autograph seekers and aspiring actors everywhere they went. Lasky and Chandlee found the mountain people shy and reticent until the conversation turned to Sergeant York. Then the locals couldn't say enough about what he did for the community and how he was the same man now as before he went off to France.

The troupe brought a still photographer from Nashville, and Billy Lasky took 16 mm movies for reference back at the studio. At Lasky's request, Sergeant York and his friends staged a typical turkey shoot, which the California visitors observed intently, taking pictures and jotting notes. (One characteristic they noted in particular was Sergeant York's habit of licking the front sight of his rifle before shouldering it, which reduced the glare.)

The group also hired the same Nashville stenographer Tom Skeyhill used twelve years before when researching his first book. Her memories of whom the author interviewed and where they lived proved a valuable resource for tracking down details. Many interview sessions produced only the affirmation that Alvin was a "fine man" or some such general statement; specific details of the Yorks' private life were scarce and illusive.

Lasky was still mum about who would play York in the movie. "I know the star I want, if we can get him," he told reporters. "He is under contract to another studio and it is a question whether he will be available. If we can't get him, there are many others who can fit the role."

For the part of Miss Gracie, a delegation from Clarksville, Tennessee, visited Lasky in Pall Mall to promote Helen Wood, a local actress whose father was killed in the Argonne. Lasky interviewed the young woman and agreed she was a good actress but said he would be inclined to cast a better-known star in the part.

Back in Hollywood Lasky began looking for the most promising plan of attack for securing Gary Cooper. Though he and Coop had little in common personally, they lived across the street from each other in Brentwood and were social acquaintances. Lasky felt he could persuade the actor to overcome his fears of playing a living hero; the greater challenge was getting him away from Lasky's ex-partner and ex-brother-in-law, Samuel Goldwyn. Cooper was under contract to Goldwyn Studios, and Warner Bros. would have to work out a deal.

Lasky decided on a straight approach, meeting with Goldwyn to request the loan of Cooper for the film, now tentatively titled *The Life of Sergeant York*. With uncharacteristic calm, Goldwyn said he would be pleased to work out a deal. Lasky rushed to share the news with Jack Warner, who was immediately suspicious of such a friendly gesture from a normally ruthless and hard-bargaining competitor.

As Lasky watched, Warner called Sam Goldwyn to thank him for such courtesy. Warner's smile soured when he learned what Goldwyn expected in return. "You're kidding!" he shouted into the receiver. "Bette Davis is our biggest star! I can't do it!" He slammed down the phone and glared silently at Lasky. To get Cooper, he would have to trade his most famous, most profitable property. All of a sudden it wasn't such a good deal after all.

Negotiations for some sort of Gary Cooper-Bette Davis trade began as Sergeant York made his first trip west to meet with writers, and also, Lasky hoped, to meet with his neighbor Coop. The sergeant, accompanied by John Hale, arrived in Hollywood via Chicago and the Santa Fe *Chief* on August 22, 1940. The Warner Bros. publicity department arranged a grand reception at the Los Angeles train station, including a committee from the Veterans of Foreign Wars, local Congressional Medal of Honor winners, the police band, a drum and bugle corps, color guard, and the American Legion accordion ensemble. York and Hale were escorted to the steps of city hall for a formal welcome and then to the Hotel Roosevelt in Hollywood, where they spent the rest of their visit in quiet luxury only a short distance from the Warner Bros. lot in Burbank.

The studio sales staff was briefed on the movie and the sergeant's arrival. Lasky wanted to give all the senior sales executives an autographed copy of *Sergeant York: His Own War Story and War Diary* but couldn't find the fifty copies he needed. The book was out of print, and in 1938 Doubleday had made a standing offer to York to buy the plates for $150. At York's request, Arthur Bushing, who was working as a clerk for a county judge but still helped the sergeant with his affairs, sent for the plates, then shipped them to California so Warner Bros. could print copies. Warners also printed York's signature in them.

What Lasky wanted to do most of all during the visit was to introduce Alvin York to Gary Cooper. He thought meeting the real hero would make Coop feel less uncomfortable about playing him. The day after York arrived, Lasky invited him to his enormous house, where the maid served Lasky scotch to accompany his cigar, and York drank tea. Then they walked across the street to Coop's spread, even more grand, and rang the doorbell. Coop answered the door, padding down the hall in his socks. Lasky introduced the two men and they shook hands, York's huge, thick, calloused fingers grasping Coop's tanned hand, which looked small and almost delicate by comparison.

It didn't take Lasky long to realize, as he recalled later, he "introduced two of the three most uncommunicative men I've ever met in my life. Had Calvin Coolidge been there, it would have been a three-ring wake." Try as he might, the producer could not get a conversation going. Every effort "was greeted with huge blobs of dead silence." Finally he remembered his neighbor's collection of Luger pistols and other guns. "By the way, Sergeant, Coop has a fine collection of firearms," he volunteered. Cooper led them to the gun cases in his trophy room, where he and Sergeant York talked about guns and hunting for a solid half hour, while Lasky stood quietly in a corner.

As soon as they returned from Pall Mall, Harry Chandlee and Julian Josephson began organizing the facts of York's life into a screenplay, submitting their first report on May 8. It wasn't a script or treatment, but simply a digest of their research and some of the pitfalls they could expect to encounter as the script took shape.

From the beginning they were determined, as York was, not to make a "war picture." The story, they said, would focus on York's life and the lives of his fellow mountaineers, "rather than to aggrandize war or even heroism." They saw York's religious beliefs as a potential liability if not handled properly. "There is great danger of his appearing to be merely a religious fanatic and thus lose heavily in audience understanding and sympathy. We feel especially, if it is even suggested that York believes he has Divine assurance that he will not be killed, his heroism will be greatly lessened." (York would have found their comments incredulous.)

Another issue was the often repeated quote, "Uncle Sam's uniform isn't for sale," which could be misinterpreted as pro-war propaganda in light of world conditions. Their objective, they reported, was not to "wave any flags" in the movie, "but when the picture is over to have made the audience wave flags."

There was also the question of dozens of living characters who would have to be portrayed in the film, from York's Fentress County neighbors to Cordell Hull and General Pershing. They had to grant their permission to be portrayed and would be sensitive to the facts recounted and to their own subjective views of events. The contract with York obliged Lasky, and now Warner Bros., to stick strictly to the truth regarding the Argonne battle. Anything relating to the advance on the Decauville Railroad had to be taken directly from the Congressional Record, which would require gaining permission from Captain Danforth, Major Buxton, and all the survivors in York's squad. In other parts of the movie, "deviation from exact fact . . . and the inclusion of fictional scenes" for dramatic or practical purposes were allowed.

The studio prepared permission releases and sent them to every-one the writers were considering putting in the film. General Pershing returned his with pleasure, his patrician signature large, elegant, and precise at the bottom. Secretary of State Cordell Hull also gave per-mission, as well as Major Buxton (retired from the army and a textile executive in Atlanta), Miss Gracie, Alvin's brother George, Pastor Pile, Mother York, and others. The job of running down York's old squad was given to a member of the location department named Bill Guthrie. He usually went looking for the perfect mountain range or the place where the ocean hit the rocks just right as the sun came up. This time he went looking for people.

And not a moment too soon. Lasky received a letter dated June 12 from one Otis B. Merrithew of Brookline, Massachusetts. He wrote that he enlisted under the name William B. Cutting so his mother would not know he went to war if his name was published on a casualty list. Cutting, like York, was a squad leader on the left flanking maneu-ver at the base of Hill 223, and his affidavit of what happened that day was among the evidence submitted with York's Medal of Honor recommendation.

Like Acting Sergeant Early, who stirred up trouble through his American Legion post in Connecticut ten years before, Merrithew chafed at the attention given to York over the years. Now it appeared there was some big Hollywood money to be made and Merrithew thought he deserved some of it. "I have contacted all of York's and my former 'buddies,'" he wrote, "and they claim that they did not sign any affidavits and if they signed any papers in France they thought that they were signing a 'supply slip' for a suit of underwear or some such thing." He made this claim despite the official record stating the affidavits were read back to each soldier before signing.

Merrithew continued, "These same men *will* sign an affidavit and forward it to the United Press, if you proceed to go through with any battle scenes without consulting us six survivors."

By itself Merrithew's carping was not a problem, but Warner Bros. realized it could grow into one. If Merrithew stirred a pot of dissension among York's squad members, it could make obtaining releases from them a touchy matter. And because the studio was contractually obligated to York to recount the Argonne Forest battle accurately, the whole squad couldn't simply be written out of the picture.

Challenges also came from another quarter, in the form of a cautionary letter from attorneys in San Francisco representing Sam Cowan. York and Lasky carefully excluded *Sergeant York and His People* from the list of books the script would be based on. Even so, Cowan's lawyers pointed out that Cowan's contract with Funk & Wagnalls expressly excepted "all movie and dramatic rights," and that he, Cowan, was the sole owner of such rights. Until his contract with Lasky, Alvin York was always specific, consistent, and absolutely unyielding on the issue: no one had any rights of any kind to make a motion picture about his life. Cowan and his lawyers thought otherwise.

The Warner Bros. attorneys wrote to John Hale in Jamestown, hoping he could produce a contract between York and Cowan or some other definitive documentation of their agreement. The California lawyers found the copyrights involving the York picture "in rather a befuddled condition." York had nothing in writing and couldn't remember the specifics of conversations almost twenty years before. The clause in the Funk & Wagnalls contract Hale suggested might settle the matter was the one Cowan added, boasting in his letter to York, "Could anything be clearer? Could anything be fairer?" The clause stated, "All copyright privileges accruing to the author under this contract are hereby assigned to Sergeant Alvin C. York, Pall Mall, Tennessee." The question then was whether or not "all copyright privileges" included the movie and theatrical rights specifically excepted from the agreement.

On another negotiating front, Samuel Goldwyn and Jack and Harry Warner were still sparring over the trade for Gary Cooper. Goldwyn wanted Bette Davis for the film version of Lillian Hellman's hit play *The Little Foxes* and was holding out for her in exchange for Cooper. Goldwyn had been talking about borrowing Davis since January, and now that the Warners had some added incentive, he hoped to make the deal soon.

Aside from all the egos involved, there were two stumbling blocks. One was Coop: he was still not convinced he was right for the part and was still interested in *For Whom the Bell Tolls*. Another was that, thinking he might not be able to get Davis after all, Goldwyn had extended his loan of another actress from Warners, Miriam Hopkins, for the part instead. With the prospect of a Cooper-Davis exchange growing closer, Goldwyn now wanted Warner Bros. to take Hopkins back so Goldwyn wouldn't have to pay her fifty-thousand-dollar salary while he figured out what to do with her.

Harry Warner considered Goldwyn's move regarding Hopkins an effort to change the deal at the last minute. On August 16, he wrote a one-sentence letter to Goldwyn vice president Reeves Espy in response to Espy's attempt to explain Goldwyn's position:

> *I have not the time to investigate the matters you explain in your letter, but if that is the case just advise Mr. Goldwyn to forget the deal entirely.*

Tracking down York's old squad, Bill Guthrie from the location department learned the years were kinder to some soldiers than others. His first meeting was with Captain Danforth, York's Company G commander, later promoted to major. Danforth was enthusiastic about the movie project and flattered to be included. When the talk turned to money, Danforth wanted fifteen hundred dollars to sign his release. This was considerably more than Guthrie and the studio expected to pay but they wanted Danforth's cooperation, and they paid what he asked, hoping to fare better with other survivors.

Guthrie visited Otis Merrithew in Brookline to secure his signature on a release. Merrithew, a truck driver with a wife and three daughters, was still unhappy about the attention lavished on York since the war. But he signed for $250, saying it would pay for his oldest girl's first year at college, a dream she had almost given up.

Percy Beardsley was still a bachelor, living on a farm in Roxbury, Connecticut, with his father. As with Danforth and Merrithew, Guthrie explained what the studio wanted, then produced a one-page form and asked him to sign. The amount paid was left blank on the printed contract and Guthrie filled it in each time, based on whatever the negotiated fee was. Beardsley wanted fifty dollars and Guthrie quickly assented.

Guthrie covered ten thousand miles during the fall and winter of 1940 finding York's old comrades and getting their releases. Joe Konotski was a millworker and father of six in Holyoke, Massachusetts; Bernard Early tended bar in Hamden, Connecticut; Mario Muzzi lived three flights up on New York's East Side and worked as the night watchman in a paper mill; Patrick Donohue was unemployed and spent his days in a Massachusetts bar; Feodor Sok worked at a CCC camp in Buffalo, New York; Thomas Johnson lived as a recluse in Denison, Texas, where Guthrie passed him the contract under a cloth partition and never saw him; George Wills lived next to the Philadelphia dump and salvaged aluminum and brass.

Except for Danforth and Merrithew, the men had little interest in Guthrie's project and no hint of the value of their signatures. Most settled for twenty dollars and were glad to get it. One or two got ten dollars; Patrick Donohue signed for five dollars.

Lasky originally announced production on the York film would start in September, but by then he still had no script and no cast. He added Abem Finkel to his writing team, and Lasky was writing some as well. True to his word, Lasky was not writing a war picture. The script was developing into the story of a man who wanted a girl, but to get her, he had to satisfy her parents by getting a farm. Heroics on the battlefield enabled him to get the farm, which got him the girl. This plot line gave the writers the freedom to develop characters and incidents any way they wanted but still fit the historical facts of the Argonne battle into the action. It also made the war battles a means to an end— the farm and Gracie—and not the main focus of the story.

In the early days at Paramount, Lasky had given a cub writer named Howard Hawks his first job in the movie business, writing title cards for silent films. Now Lasky wanted Hawks to direct Cooper in the Sergeant York film. Hawks had just started shooting *The Outlaw* for Howard Hughes but he felt a debt of gratitude to his old boss and knew Lasky was getting desperate for a hit. Hawks and Lasky met in Lasky's office at Warner Bros. Lasky was hungover and unshaven, wondering whether his movie would ever start production and thinking ahead to the second $25,000 payment he would owe York in October of 1941 under the terms of the contract, even if no film was ever made.

Hawks read through the screenplay and listened as Lasky told York's real life story, which was far different from the script as it stood. The truth, not the script, electrified Hawks. "Jesse," he said, "I'll make the picture if it's OK with you that I do just the story you told me." Jesse happily agreed.

"Now what we need is Cooper," said Hawks. "You can't get him," Lasky replied. "I've tried to." Hawks returned to his office at Hughes' RKO Studio and got Gary Cooper on the phone.

"I just talked to Lasky," he told the actor. "Didn't he give you your first job?" Coop admitted, yes, Lasky gave him his start in the business. (Lasky gave the former Montana cowboy his first noteworthy acting job in the silent 1925 hit, *Wings*. Though on screen for barely two minutes, Cooper received thousands of letters from theatergoers enamored with the brave young soldier who snapped his men into shape, took a bite of a chocolate bar, and went resolutely out to his death.)

"Well," said Hawks, "he's broke, he's got the shakes, he needs a shave, and he's got a story that I don't think would hurt either one of us to do." Hawks went to Cooper's home to talk matters over. Coop kept delaying discussion of the movie with talk about guns. Finally Hawks said, "Look, Coop, we have to talk about this." To which the actor replied, "What is there to talk about? You know we're gonna do it."

Together they went to see Hal Wallis, the executive producer at Warner Bros. who would oversee the project on the studio's behalf. Hawks prepped his friend beforehand: "If I say, 'Isn't that right, Mr. Cooper,' you say, 'Yup.'" After exchanging pleasantries, Hawks cut to the businesses at hand. "We'll do the picture if you stay out of our way and don't interfere at all. Isn't that right, Mr. Cooper?"

"Yup."

"We're gonna change the plot, the story, around. Isn't that right, Mr. Cooper?"

"Yup."

Hawks also got Wallis to approve the addition of John Huston to the script-writing team. Huston was the son of the famous actor Walter Huston and a successful writer and actor with his own ambitions to direct some day. Ten days into shooting *The Outlaw*, Hawks told Howard Hughes he was leaving to start another movie. "You've always

wanted to direct, haven't you, Howard?" he asked his boss. Hughes said
yes. "Well here's your chance."

"Do you really think I can do it?" Hughes asked.

"I'll tell you when it's done," replied Hawks.

Hawks gave the York project new life and all the disparate elements
began coming together at last. Chandlee, Finkel, Huston, and writer
Howard Koch, whose credits included *Gone with the Wind*, continued
hammering out the scenes for a picture now called *The Amazing Story of
Sergeant York*. On September 8 Lasky announced the movie would star
Cooper and would premiere in Nashville around the first of February.

The trade for Bette Davis was finally approved by everyone but
Davis and she was powerless to stop it. She would go to Goldwyn for
The Little Foxes, and Cooper would go to Warners for *The Amazing Story
of Sergeant York*. Each star would be paid $150,000 for twelve weeks'
work, plus $12,500 for every additional week required. Goldwyn
dropped his insistence that Warners take Miriam Hopkins and agreed
to loan Walter Brennan to the York production as well as Cooper. Brennan, a three-time Oscar winner as supporting actor, would play the part
of Pastor Pile at $2,312.50 per week, with ten weeks guaranteed.

Other members of the cast included Howard da Silva, Noah Beery
Jr., and Ward Bond. Fifteen-year-old June Lockhart was cast as York's
sister Rosie. Veteran character actress Margaret Wycherley was signed as
Mother York at $850 per week with four weeks guaranteed.

The problem came with casting Gracie. The real Miss Gracie was
shy, circumspect, chaste, modest, and traditional. Typical Hollywood
heroines were bold, sexy, exciting, effervescent, and clever. The script of
The Amazing Story of Sergeant York and the actress who played Gracie
had to find a middle ground satisfying both images. On his visit to
Warner Bros. in the summer of 1940, York specifically asked that the
actress who played Miss Gracie be a woman who didn't smoke. One
ingenue available for the part was a contract player named Joan Leslie,
whose beauty was one more of innocence than sex appeal. She had a
fetching manner without being sultry. And she didn't smoke; she was
only fifteen.

On October 3, 1940, Joan Leslie did a screen test for the part of
Gracie, playing opposite handsome young George Reeves, who enjoyed

a few minutes on screen as one of the Tarleton twins in the previous year's blockbuster hit at Selznick Studios, *Gone with the Wind*.

Lasky kept looking, wanting a stronger, more desirable woman to play the role. Paulette Goddard was mentioned but neither she nor another actress who was Lasky's first choice ever even tested for the part. Lasky kept pulling Gracie's character away from discreet country maiden and toward hot-blooded mountain lover. His ideal for the role was a gorgeous, young full-figured brunette named Jane Russell, and Lasky thought she would be dynamite in the film. Fearing the explosion surely to follow from York, Wallis and Hawks vetoed the idea.

Still simmering from his loss of Bette Davis to Goldwyn—and the complaints from his sales department that followed—Jack Warner continued looking for a way to get his Sergeant York picture made without loosening his hold on his most popular actress. On November 14 he sent a letter to the head of the Warner Bros. legal department on the dark blue letterhead reserved for only the most personal and sensitive messages. "Very confidentially, if we get a break at all with an actor with whom we are dealing for SERGEANT YORK and which we will know in the next few days, what legal steps must we undertake to get out of the Bette Davis commitment with Goldwyn?"

The next day a dark-haired B-picture leading man reported for a screen test as Sergeant York. He was finishing his third year as a Warner Bros. contract player and it had been a good year for him. In January he married a promising young actress named Jane Wyman and soon thereafter landed a featured role opposite Pat O'Brien in *Knute Rockne— All-American* to glowing reviews. Audiences remembered the moment in the film when he lay in the hospital bed encouraging his teammates to go out there and "win one for the Gipper."

Ronald Reagan, Jack Warner thought, might let him have his Sergeant York picture and still keep Bette Davis from Sam Goldwyn. Reagan tested in four different scenes, seventeen takes in all. He was good, and he looked the part. But he wasn't what the real Sergeant York or the moviegoing public wanted. He wasn't Gary Cooper.

The Hollywood columnists continued their running commentary of the Davis-Cooper story. Rumors surfaced that once he finished his current work on *Meet John Doe* with Frank Capra, Cooper would go to Paramount to begin *For Whom the Bell Tolls*. Goldwyn responded by saying he would never loan Cooper to Paramount. Paramount fired back that Cooper was never requested.

On December 4, 1940, a headline in the *Hollywood Reporter* announced, "Gary Cooper Finally Okays 'York' at WB." The director and star were in place, the script was almost finished, the public was excited, and Jesse Lasky prepared to start shooting the picture that would put him back on top in Hollywood.

Chapter Twenty-Two

Coop and Hawks

The original start date for the picture, January 2, 1941, had to be postponed a month because Cooper's contract guaranteed him a vacation between projects. While Warner Bros. waited on him, the company continued looking for an actress to play Gracie and labored day after day on the script. For ideas on tone and descriptions, the writers looked at reference footage a studio film crew shot in Pall Mall the previous October.

Hawks and Lasky made screen tests of Linda Hayes and Susan Carnahan for the part of Gracie on January 16. They also tested Helen Wood, the Clarksville, Tennessee, actress whose supporters lobbied Lasky in Pall Mall. Nashville had its own local star, too, a singer and model named Gay Parkes. Lasky received a petition signed by Governor Cooper, former governor Roberts, city councilmen, and hundreds of residents who wanted Lasky to give Parkes a test. This far into the production, the busy producer was not interested in auditioning another hometown girl.

There was considerable dissension among the writers. Hawks thought John Huston's additions and changes made the script come alive, but other writers, Abem Finkel in particular, were worried that the plot was too far from what York approved in September. Finkel thought

the motivations for York's drinking in earlier drafts of the script—the
desire for a bottomland farm and his longing for Gracie—were gone.
"Therefore," he wrote in a barb-filled memo to Hal Wallis on January 9,
"York is drinking because he's just a 'stew bum.' York'll love that!!"

Finkel also took exception to the way the love story in the film was
shaping up. "At the slightest hint that Gracie gave York the 'come on' . . .
[the real] York would reach for his rifle gun and come a-shootin'. You
must remember that York knocked off 35 German machine gunners
and he wasn't even sore at them. Can you imagine if he really got mad?"

The depiction of Pastor Pile was also a problem. The revised plot
indicated Pile didn't know any better than York did whether York
should go to war as a conscientious objector. "This definitely implies
that either Pile hasn't the courage of his religious convictions or he is
not sincere in his religious beliefs. The record of his whole life proves
that he had both."

Finkel concluded, "If York should be shown a picture containing
material he never approved, and which shames him, insults his wife,
and ridicules his friends and neighbors, you could scarcely blame him
if he got good and sore."

The writers were also struggling to work around the fact that Miss
Gracie's father, Asbury Williams, absolutely refused to allow his name
to be associated with a motion picture. He had nothing against Alvin,
he said, but it would be a sin to be associated with movies, and he
would not do it under any circumstances.

Since the plot of the movie revolved around Gracie's father not
wanting her to marry York until he could afford a farm, the script was
in trouble without Williams. Four rich and successful Hollywood writers found themselves boxed in a corner by a frail, bedridden old dirt
farmer who never saw a movie and never would. Eventually they solved
their problem by rewriting the character as a fictitious uncle.

Lawyers from Burbank and Jamestown were still trying to sort out
the claims made by Sam Cowan that he should be paid part of York's
portion of the "adaptation" of his book. Another character by the name
of Marie Adels also entered the ownership drama. Adels claimed to
be Tom Skeyhill's common law wife and on behalf of herself and her
twelve-year-old daughter, Joyce, wrote to Warner Bros. of her interest in

the movie and her expectation she would be properly compensated for her late husband's work. Skeyhill had died, insolvent, in a 1932 plane crash that also injured Adels's brother.

The Warner Bros. legal department wrote John Hale again, who wrote Sergeant York again, asking what sort of arrangement York had in writing with Skeyhill. As expected, the sergeant had nothing in writing. The particular question revolved around the magazine version of *His Own Life Story and War Diary*, serialized beginning in the July 14, 1928, issue of *Liberty* magazine. The articles, argued Adels, had been jointly copyrighted in the names of Skeyhill and York, separately from the book. Based on her late husband's half interest in the magazine story Warner Bros. was filming, she demanded half of whatever York would earn.

Another flap appeared over the money paid to York's old squad members. Tipped off by a comment on radio's "Fred Waring Show," newspaper wire services reported that men who served with Sergeant Alvin York in the war were being paid $250 each for permission to use their names in the movie. This was the first any of them knew about what others were paid. George Wills, the Philadelphia junk man who signed for $20, was quick to contact the newspapers, on January 10, and say no one offered him $250.

The widow of a Captain Tillman, who replaced Major Buxton in the field upon the latter's promotion shortly before the charge down Hill 223 (and whom Buxton insisted be contacted by the studio), wrote Warner Bros. to say her husband signed his release for nothing. "True Mr. Tillman did not make Mr. Guthrie sign a contract for any certain amount, but had he only known he was to be called so soon, he certainly would have for the sake of his family."

As the assorted protests gathered steam, other survivors of York's squad called their own newspapers or their local American Legion posts. Warner Bros. had asked the Legion to help find York's fellow soldiers and the veterans now wondered whether the Legion deceived them. Warners' publicity department tried for a preemptive strike, releasing a statement on January 9 that Sergeant York "asked that his comrades receive credit for their share in putting an entire German machine gun battalion out of action." But what the men wanted mostly was a little more recognition and cash, in light of all that was lavished on their famous colleague.

The light-blue interoffice WarnerGrams were flying thick and fast through the offices in Burbank as Lasky and company weighed their options. They already had the signatures they needed, but the prospect of bad publicity was worth rethinking. To bring all the people in question up to the $250 mark would cost another $1,835. They could, they decided, make the payments through the American Legion posts, giving that organization a publicity boost and allowing Warners to avoid the appearance the company knuckled under pressure or did anything wrong to begin with.

The studio sent the checks with cover letters to the American Legion posts nearest each man. The $1,835 was a bargain in the end, far less an expense than the $2,691 in the movie's budget for hairdressers.

Two key provisions of Gary Cooper's contract were: the director of the Sergeant York film had to be a top-level talent making at least $3,000 per week, and Cooper would be consulted on the casting of his costar. Cooper was delighted to be working with Hawks, who had a great record of success in Hollywood and shared Coop's love of firearms and hunting. The star was less certain about Joan Leslie in the part of Gracie. She got the news she would play opposite Gary Cooper in the York picture at a studio party celebrating her sixteenth birthday. Cooper was thirty-nine and felt unsettled about the prospect of love scenes with a girl barely old enough to drive. Nevertheless, he made no formal objection. The script wasn't finished and the legal tangles were still unresolved but the cast and crew were set, and the studio gave its approval to begin.

Warner Bros. production #350, now simply titled *Sergeant York*, started shooting Monday, February 3, 1941, on Sound Stage 6 at the Burbank studio. Cooper was half an hour late for his 9:00 a.m. call, which surprised no one, but otherwise the first day went well. The first scene shot was set in a blind tiger on the Kentucky border. The company worked until 12:50 in the afternoon, took an hour for lunch, then worked again until 5:45. As was his custom, Hawks also had tea and cakes on the set for his staff.

The crew of twenty-five included Hawks and his assistants, three men operating the camera, four for sound recording, prop men, electricians, hair, makeup, and wardrobe supervisors, and a still photographer for publicity shots. On the set with Cooper were nine other members of the cast and Coop's stand-in, Slim Talbot. Slim, costumed and made up exactly like Cooper, took the star's place for light checks, setting camera positions, run-throughs, and other such situations so the actor could rest; Coop appeared on the set only when Hawks was ready to roll film. Rounding out the ensemble were two horses, a mule, and their handlers.

The company shot ten different setups that day, five of them in a single take each. Even though the script remained incomplete, Hawks was working on a forty-eight-day shooting schedule established by the studio. The first day running so smoothly was a good sign.

The actors did their homework and their efforts were paying promising dividends. Joan Leslie wrote Miss Gracie, asking her for a picture, which Gracie sent. She carried it throughout the shooting for inspiration and good luck. Alvin and Gracie sent recordings of their voices for Cooper and Leslie to use in getting their mountain accent right. Sergeant York even lent Cooper one of his hats to wear in the film.

Some of the cast members had firsthand experience that served them well. Walter Brennan was in the Great War, served on four fronts, and was wounded and gassed. Charles Trowbridge, who portrayed Cordell Hull, came from a family of diplomats. Even the bit player appearing as Marshal Foch had received the Médaille Militaire from Marshal Petain at Verdun.

With production underway, the studio persuaded York to take part in a special NBC Network broadcast on February 20, promoting *Sergeant York*. The sergeant traveled to Chicago to speak in honor of the Veterans of Foreign Wars and Cooper, Brennan, and others in the film played scenes from the movie, broadcasting from Hollywood. The resulting positive publicity put an end to the residue of commentary regarding York's squad members and their $250.

Though he continued to be uncharacteristically nervous at playing a living hero, Cooper worked professionally and well with Joan Leslie.

Their first day on the set together, February 13, someone said, "Coop, here's your wife." Looking down at the young girl dressed in flat shoes and a gingham dress, Coop joked, "I can see how I'm gonna really feel like a hillbilly with a child bride." Throughout the production he continued to comment with a chuckle that he felt like a criminal or a cradle robber whenever he and Leslie embraced.

The company had fallen five days behind schedule by mid-February and Hawks still didn't have a completed script to shoot from. Lasky, Huston, and other writers were adding and changing pages on the set. Eric Stacey, the production manager, didn't know whether to dismantle sets or let bit players go at the end of a day because he didn't know what would be needed next as the script continued to change.

When scenes involved Leslie or June Lockhart, Hawks had to stop shooting at 5:00 p.m. since, as minors, the girls could only work eight hours a day. That made it more difficult to make up shooting days. Some days, though, were marathons of efficiency. On February 8, Cooper, four supporting cast members, one mule, twelve chickens, and three dogs completed fourteen setups, thirty-two takes in all, and shot three days' work in nine hours.

To add authenticity to the picture, York sent Cooper his own 125-year-old muzzle loader. The studio wanted a second one and sent $250 to John Caldwell at the Tennessee Department of Conservation with a request to buy one for them. He sent back four and a check for $50. Collectors said the guns were virtually priceless.

As they toiled only days ahead of the shooting, writers kept the studio research department busy with requests for barnyard photos, details about the habits of horses and mules, the definition of hybrid corn, and other mysteries. They also sent numerous requests for information about the Bible. "Which Commandment is the one that says 'Thou Shalt Not Kill?'" "What is Luke 22:36?" "What was 'the writing on the wall?'" Finally Huston and Hawks had the research department send them each a Bible to save time.

By February 20, the sixteenth day of shooting, the production was eight days behind the original forty-eight-day schedule, and Eric Stacey had no idea what to expect coming out of the typewriters every morning. Lasky assured him the script was ready, but a completed draft was still not forthcoming. Stacey saw through Lasky's feint. In his daily production and progress report, he wrote, "They want Hawks to look it over and are afraid to send it out without his approval since he will change it all anyway." At the end of the day he still had no firm idea how many of Thursday's twelve actors, twenty-four chickens, two dogs, and seven horses he would need on Friday.

On February 26, the final 308-page script was approved, though that did not keep Lasky, Hawks, and the writers from continuing to rewrite on the set. Looking at the rushes of the previous day's shoot each night, Hawks would decide something wasn't working about a scene, rewrite it that night, and re-shoot it the next day. One scene in particular bothering the director was the discussion between York and Pastor Pile when Pile promises to write an application for a draft exemption on religious grounds. "This is one of the most important scenes in the picture," Hawks commented and he had it redone until he was satisfied.

With a complete, if still metamorphosing, script in hand at last, the company was divided into two units. The first unit would continue with its work in Burbank and on several exterior sets around Los Angeles. The second unit would shoot the war sequences.

The second unit leased an eighty-acre barley field outside Santa Susana in the Simi Valley and three hundred men set to work with tractors, dump trucks, and five tons of dynamite to recreate the Argonne Forest. Yielding to the myth, now well-ingrained, that the battle on Hill 223 involved trench warfare, the set designers ordered two miles of zig-zagging trenches dug and sandbagged. To save money and keep the war scenes in perspective, Wallis, Hawks, and Jack Warner discussed the possibility of having some of the battle story presented in a newsreel footage style.

The shooting schedule was reset at seventy-six days once the script was finished and the production moved more or less steadily ahead with a few stumbles here and there. During the first week of shooting, special effects thunder and lightning spooked the horses and mules, causing a small stampede and ruining the set. Later, a seasoned and normally reliable day player kept inexplicably blowing his lines with Coop, requiring thirteen takes of one scene and sixteen of the next.

There were also delays when Hawks changed his mind in the middle of something. He specified how he wanted a certain shot set up of Cooper and Brennan riding in a prop car. When he saw the set, he decided to change the camera angle, requiring the camera and all the lights to be struck and repositioned, a two-hour job.

In one dramatic scene, Cooper was to come out of the rain into a little country church where Brennan and the congregation of extras were singing "Give Me That Old Time Religion." Hawks planned to shoot it from one side, but when he saw the set, decided to shoot it from the opposite angle instead. This required not only repositioning the camera and relighting a large area but taking down a wall where the new camera position was and putting a wall up where the camera had been.

Since the process would take the rest of the day, the actors spent two hours rehearsing and running lines, then went over to the audio department to record the hymn, thinking that would save time later. The new setup was ready the next morning but it turned out Brennan had never lip synched before. He worked diligently to match his movements to the recorded track played back during each take but he simply couldn't do it. The scene was reshot with live sound. The reshoot also gave Hawks a chance to make another improvement. A few days before, Hal Wallis sent a memo to Hawks. "I saw last night's dailies of Sgt. York and Brennan looked very much like Groucho Marx." Hawks had makeup artist Ernie Westmore tone down the offending eyebrows.

Hawks and Wallis convinced Warners to hire the best film composer in the business for Sergeant York. Acclaimed for his triumphant score in Gone with the Wind, Max Steiner agreed to take the assignment. The new picture had much of the sweep of Gone with the Wind but would give him a completely different historical context to work with. Steiner started scoring the picture on March 28, working with completed segments without knowing exactly what would come before or after, or even if that scene would be in the final film.

Coop developed a rash below his nose and Hawks had to shoot around him for three days beginning April 5. That day the second unit came in from the Simi Valley to shoot a battalion headquarters scene. Hawks' unit used the stage from 9:00 a.m. until 5:00 p.m. for the listening post and Hill 223 scenes, then the second unit, under B. Reaves "Breezy" Eason, shot from 6:00 p.m. until after midnight.

April 9 was the most complicated day of the entire production, with fifteen players, thirty-five crew members, and 282 extras on location at City Hall for the scene in which General Pershing presented York with the Congressional Medal of Honor. In real life Pershing presented the sergeant with the Distinguished Service Cross, his Medal of Honor not yet having been authorized. But as in the question of trenches, popular myth made good theater.

The Medal of Honor is unique in that its reproduction is a violation of federal law, somewhat in the same league with coining money or printing postage stamps. It is also a federal offense to buy or sell one. The prop department was stymied, so Jack Warner wrote to Washington in February and asked to borrow one. He received a medal directly from the adjutant general of the army with the request to return it as soon as the scene was shot.

Cooper was sidelined again for a day with a sore throat on April 15, but the production went on. The second unit continued to be frustrated by rain with an average of one day in three curtailed or canceled because of the weather. Still they were making good progress under Breezy Eason. Stacey wisely suggested a meeting before Eason's first day of shooting to make sure he came back with what Hawks was expecting. Otherwise, Stacey predicted, "we are liable to have all kinds of criticisms when Eason's first day's work comes in. The people will be too muddy, or not muddy enough."

Eason did reshoot at least one of scene at the studio's request. The script called for a group of German soldiers to come walking by under York's supervision as he marched them back to American lines. The extras had the right amount of mud, as well as military bearing and menacingly dashing Teutonic features (Eason had advertised his casting call in the fraternity houses of the University of Southern California and UCLA, selecting the tallest and blondest to be enemy soldiers). But the drama and the victory somehow weren't there. Jack Warner sent down the message, "this scene is one of the main reasons I bought this story. We need additional scenes to show it wasn't just a walk in the park."

The real Sergeant York was not involved in discussions of changes in the screenplay or problems with the squad members. He left those matters to Lasky. He did visit the set in Burbank at least once at Lasky's invitation and was excited and pleased with what he saw. There was one awkward moment when York accidentally surprised Cooper behind the set smoking a cigarette. Cooper knew the sergeant didn't approve of smoking and hastily put his smoke out like a youngster caught behind the garage. Cooper later sent York a picture of himself in his *Sergeant York* costume, inscribed with an apology.

The first unit finished shooting on Thursday, May 1. The second unit wrapped two days later, the last shot being German machine gun nests and soldiers running out in surrender. They worked seventy of seventy-six shooting days in all, with the Second Unit concurrently shooting twenty days of thirty-three scheduled. The company used 123 sets to film forty-four speaking parts, including twenty-six representing living people—all Hollywood records. They exposed 201,616 feet of film and spent $1,389,000 of Harry Warner's money, including the purchase of forty acres of trampled and exploded barley from their eighty-acre battlefield.

Howard Hawks was not on the set to wish his company farewell. He left town earlier in the week to attend the Kentucky Derby.

Chapter Twenty-Three

Triumph

The Great White Way had disappeared. The usual nighttime New York traffic still darted and cascaded down the street, headlights gleaming, stoplights and streetlights still glowing; but the huge, garish, blinding lights of the Broadway theaters sharing the world's most famous show business address were gone. Broadway's northwest-southeast swath through Times Square was always the brightest in midtown Manhattan, casting shadows over the lesser streets flanking it. Now it was a mysterious cavern of darkness and anticipation.

On the sidewalk and in the street in front of the Astor Theater, a large crowd waited impatiently. It was nearly midnight and the city air was cool and refreshing at that hour, even in the summer. The blackout lasted thirty seconds and when it was over, Broadway burst to brilliant life again to welcome a new jewel in its luminous crown.

Above the Astor marquee, as the crowd roared, one of the biggest signs in the history of Broadway blazed to life. Four stories high and half a block long, it was actually two superimposed images alternating every few seconds. In one, a forty-five-foot tall Gary Cooper, dressed in mountain homespun, held a squirrel gun in his hand; in the other Cooper appeared as a soldier in battle dress, sighting down his infantry rifle. To the side, the largest letters ever seen on Broadway read, "Gary Cooper in Sergeant York."

Alvin York left Pall Mall July 1 and arrived in New York the next day for the premiere of his picture. Pennsylvania Station was packed with cheering spectators, soldiers, color guards, and bands to welcome him. The burly veteran was besieged by reporters before he could even step onto the platform. They clambered onto the train and ambushed York in his compartment with questions, not about the movie, but about what America should do concerning the war in Europe. Paris had fallen and the British were barely hanging on against the devastating night bombing raids on London. Lend-Lease made American industrial power available to Great Britain but German submarines were exacting a heavy toll.

York believed sending war matériel in protected convoys was the answer. "It's nonsense to make our material here and then have it go to the bottom," he commented. "We ought to convoy even if we have to take the goods right over to the other shores." When reminded of former President Hoover's non-interventionist stance, York replied, "Hoover doesn't know the temper of the people. That's why he's ex-president." America, he said, needed "Minute Men, not Munich Men."

Lasky was in town of course and so was Gary Cooper. They all met at the Ritz Towers, where Lasky had an apartment, then went together to the premiere the night of July 2. Lasky and Warner Bros. were encouraged by the advance ticket sales, which were the biggest for any Hollywood picture since *Gone with the Wind*. As they made their way by limousine to the Astor, Lasky and York recalled earlier triumphal journeys down the same street—Lasky in his heyday when critics were calling him the "Ziegfeld of the Movies," and York in the parade that bright May day more than twenty-two years before.

Ushers and police cleared a path between the car and the theater entrance as the limousine stopped at the curb. York glanced up at the huge sign and Lasky reminded him the Warner Bros. publicity department figured that with its fifteen thousand lights, it had ten times as many bulbs as the town of Pall Mall. Smiling and waving, York, Lasky, and Cooper walked inside together and took their seats. This was the first time for York and Cooper to see the finished work. Lasky had seen the rough cut three weeks before, making occasional suggestions as Howard Hawks made the final edits in Burbank.

The picture was an unqualified triumph. *Variety* predicted it would be the biggest moneymaker of the year. Walter Winchell called it "a Yankee Doodle Dandy that I encourage everyone to see." Other critics agreed. Dorothy Kilgallen: "One of the greatest entertainments of all time." Louella Parsons: "One of the finest pictures of any year."

The studio ran ads for the movie in *Life*, *Look*, and *Redbook*, as well as in fan magazines and theater industry press. There were color features in *The American Weekly* and *This Week*. Warner Bros. spent seventy-six thousand dollars advertising the release of *Sergeant York*, of which Lasky paid 25 percent.

The day after the premiere, York attended a breakfast sponsored by the Gold Star Mothers of America, women whose sons were killed on active military duty. At noon he was the guest of the Tennessee Society at a luncheon in the Hotel Astor. *Sergeant York* put York back in the center of the spotlight and he eagerly expounded on his interventionist views. "England does not need our manpower over there. What she needs is our manpower over here, producing planes and guns and tanks and boats. American equipment smoldering in rust at the bottom of the Atlantic will not stop Hitler." York also told his audience he hoped the recent German offensive against Russia did not succeed. "A speedy German victory would give fuel to such isolationists and appeasers as our friends Senator [Burton K.] Wheeler [a Montana isolationist] and ex-Colonel Lindbergh."

Despite his insistence on helping England, York denied he was in favor of war. "No one can possibly hate war as much as a soldier who has tried to catch his breath with the mud of the trenches caked on his face."

Days after York's return to Pall Mall on July 5, he got another invitation from Lasky, this time to attend the Washington premiere of *Sergeant York* at the Earle Theater on July 31. Miss Gracie, sixteen-year-old Woodrow, and Arthur Bushing's son, Arthur Story Bushing, went along this time, arriving at Union Station a little after noon on July 30.

York's Washington reception had all the pomp and exuberance of a state visit, eclipsing even the greeting he received in New York. Tennessee

Governor Cooper, Lasky, and York were welcomed by Undersecretary of War Robert P. Patterson, along with Tennessee Senators Tom Stewart and Kenneth McKellar, Senator Robert B. Reynolds, chairman of the Senate Military Affairs Committee, and a contingent of Tennessee representatives. York's old division commander, General Duncan, traveled from his retirement home in Lexington, Kentucky, to join in the occasion. The Tennessee State Society, Veterans of Foreign Wars, American War Mothers, Gold Star Mothers, Sons of American Legionnaires, and the Boy Scouts were in attendance.

The VFW and American Legion supplied honor guards and music was presented by the United States Marine Band, VFW Band, and a drum and bugle corps. A huge "Welcome Sergeant York" banner hung over the scene, and in the background were hundreds of ordinary citizens straining for a look at the famous hero and movie subject. Those who couldn't attend listened to the whole ceremony broadcast live over station WWDC.

At the conclusion of the welcome, York spoke a few words of thanks. Then, with Miss Gracie, Woodrow, and the rest of his party, he got into one of a line of cars that paraded down Constitution Avenue to Pennsylvania Avenue and turned in at the White House gate. The York family and Lasky were ushered into President Roosevelt's office and presented to him by Senator McKellar and Representative Estes Kefauver.

Roosevelt had seen the picture at a private showing about ten days before and he told York he was "really thrilled. The picture comes at a good time," the president continued, "although I didn't like that part of it showing so much killing. I guess you felt that way too."

"I certainly did," replied the Tennessean.

Roosevelt's only suggestion, made with a laugh, was they should have made "old Cordell" play himself. As he listened to the president, Lasky felt a tug at his sleeve. It was Woodrow. "Where's the bathroom?" he whispered. With a word and a look, Lasky tried to communicate that White House visitors didn't saunter off to the bathroom when the president was addressing them, even those who were named after one of the chief executive's predecessors. About that time, Roosevelt signaled the waiting photographers and reporters to be let in. In the swirl of activity, young Woodrow was able to slip away without a breach of etiquette.

The rest of the day included interviews, a test by York of the new Garand infantry rifle (of which he previously said, "It's sort of frail looking to me.") and autographing defense bond albums at the Treasury Department.

July 31 was Sergeant Alvin York Day at the Capitol. So many legislators wanted to speak with him at breakfast he missed a scheduled appearance to open the House of Representatives with a prayer. Following another whirlwind day, a reception was held at the Willard Hotel, after which the guests of honor got in a car for the short trip to the Earle Theater. As the sergeant and his family slowly pulled away, the reception guests spontaneously followed alongside them on the sidewalk. The impromptu parade lasted all the way to the theater, men in their tuxedos (a few, this being Washington, in tails) and ladies in evening gowns puffing up the walk.

The congressmen and generals cheered as wildly as the Broadway audience when the picture was over. York and Miss Gracie walked down the aisle to the front of the theater and the room exploded in shouts and applause. In a telegram to Jack Warner the next morning, Lasky described it as the "greatest evening I have ever witnessed in a theater. Notices and publicity sensational."

After a promotional jaunt to Philadelphia from Washington and back, Lasky returned to Hollywood, and the York family went home to Pall Mall. At the train station in Crossville on the way, young Arthur Bushing observed York talking with an old gentleman in work clothes and a battered hat. Bushing learned the man was a cattle trader York did business with occasionally who happened to be at the station. The boy noted Sergeant York's manner: open, friendly, completely at ease— exactly the same way York was when talking with President Roosevelt days before. As far as the sergeant was concerned, there was no difference between one conversation and the other.

There was still one more premiere on York's mind. A year earlier Lasky promised *Sergeant York* would open in Nashville. "Washington is really applying pressure to have the premiere there, and other cities are competing for the honor," he said at the time. "But I have promised Governor Cooper that the premiere will be in Nashville, and I intend to keep that promise."

Lasky did not keep his promise, easily discarding a smallish southern city in favor of the entertainment capital of the country as the place to launch his comeback masterpiece. So York, Governor Cooper, and Nashville Mayor Thomas L. Cummings decided to have a premiere of their own on Thursday, September 18. When Lasky was informed of the plan, he immediately began trying to convince them to reschedule their event. Lasky had set up a Hollywood premiere party at the Masquers Club for September 17 and assured its planners Sergeant York would be there as the guest of honor.

Lasky offered to come himself and "bring one or two members of the cast" if the Nashville date could be changed. To plead his case, he sent York a program of the September 17 dinner, with Sergeant Alvin C. York first and most prominent on a list of honorees including Lasky, Cooper, Walter Brennan, Jack Warner, Hal Wallis, and Howard Hawks. Lasky also wrote that invitations were sent to Charles Laughton, Bert Lahr, Edgar Bergen, Ray Bolger, Jimmy Durante, Orson Welles, Dick Powell, Phil Silvers, and many others. But Sergeant York was unswayed. He had other commitments. Lasky had no choice but to cancel his celebration.

At midday on September 18, Alvin York arrived in Nashville. At 1:00 p.m. he presented the Nashville Hospitality Cup to the Clarksville High School Band, which provided entertainment for the occasion. Outside the Hermitage Hotel, Governor Cooper read a proclamation renaming Sixth Avenue in the sergeant's honor. For the duration of *Sergeant York's* run at the Knickerbocker Theater in town, the street would be officially known as York Avenue.

In the afternoon York attended the Tennessee State Fair, constantly at the center of a cluster of admirers. He took particular notice of the livestock and bought a polished hickory walking stick for a dollar. At 8:00 p.m., York, Gracie, Alvin Jr., Pastor Pile, York's brother George, and his old friend Tom Conatser attended a reception at the hotel, then walked down the street to the Knickerbocker, where the sergeant cut a ribbon across the theater entrance, signaling the beginning of ticket sales.

At 9:00 p.m. Joan Leslie called the theater from Hollywood, her voice and York's piped through the theater's sound system. York stood in front of the stage curtain with a telephone and spoke with the actress. "You'd get to see the real Gracie if you were here tonight," York observed, to tremendous applause.

"That would be wonderful," Leslie replied. "Tell her how much I'd like to be there."

"You can tell her yourself if you like," the sergeant said, handing the telephone to his wife. "Are you very excited? I know you are," said Leslie.

"Oh no, I'm used to this," Gracie answered softly, having been entertained recently by movie stars, generals, and President Roosevelt.

Though he previously repented of his last trip to a Nashville movie theater, Pastor Pile seemed delighted with the film and with Brennan's portrayal of him. "I am glad to be here," he told reporters. "If I have been a small instrument in God's hands to help Sergeant York to a nobler, broader life, I thank God. And I hope this picture show of him helps to lead young people and others upward and finally to that beautiful city from where there is no return."

After the show Gracie remarked at how incredibly close to Pastor Pile's voice Brennan's was. "I don't see how he can imitate your voice so well," she said. "The speaking part is pretty good," Pile agreed, then added with a grin, "But goodness, I never was as ugly as that fellow." Possibly another vote against the eyebrows.

While the Knickerbocker was selling out five shows a day at fifty-five cents a ticket (50¢ before 5:00 p.m., children always a quarter), the Astor in New York was turning patrons away at every showing as well. Box office receipts nationwide were more than $20,000 a week and growing. Decca Records released the "Sergeant York" collection of hymns including "In the Sweet By and By," "Church in the Wildwood," "Give Me That Old Time Religion," and "Nearer My God to Thee." Clothing retailers renamed their regimental stripe neckties "York Stripes." Even Sam Cowan got on the bandwagon with Grossett & Dunlap publishing a new edition of *Sergeant York and His People*, priced at fifty cents, with Gary Cooper as York on the cover.

As the accolades and box office receipts tumbled in, the Cowan book continued to be an irritation to the Warner Bros. legal department. Studio lawyers referred to it as that book "which we are staying religiously away from;" the screenwriters never had it as an information source. Cowan's attorneys were informed by the studio in a letter dated June 7, 1940, that the picture would not include anything from Cowan's book.

When the movie came out, Cowan changed lawyers and wrote again. His new counsel sent the studio a letter claiming that after seeing the movie, the author was surprised to see—

> *not only does the production reflect the color and atmosphere painted by his book, but a number of incidents were lifted bodily from his book and used in the picture. Many scenes are based on original literary work in his book, that could not have been obtained from Sergeant York. . . . It can be clearly established that these incidents are productions of Mr. Cowan's own literary talent, and their connection with the York story are solely due to his authorship.*

Despite the fervor of the claims, there were no specific examples of plagiarism in the letter.

Otis Merrithew was also back in the news. The publicity surrounding the release of *Sergeant York* fanned the flames of his anger at what he considered York's undeserved wealth and notoriety. Interviewed by the *Boston Globe* two weeks after the movie opened on Broadway, Merrithew lashed out savagely at the claims made on behalf of his famous comrade:

> *None of the survivors are in agreement with Sergeant York's version of what really happened over there. . . . We never recall signing any affidavit. . . . That would be against our grain as we always had figured Sergeant York out to be "yellow" and not a commanding officer. . . . One morning as we were to go over the top, York was stark mad with fear. He jumped up on top of the parapet and started to holler, "I want to go home! For God's sake, why isn't this war over?" Sergeant Early rushed up to him and pushed his automatic pistol to his head and said, "If you*

don't shut up, I'll blow your brains out," as we all knew that
York was exposing our whereabouts to the enemy.

These fantastic tales made barely a ripple as the film continued to break attendance and box office records across the country.

York reveled in the spotlight. Through the 1930s he had been in steady demand as a speaker but the movie made him a national hero all over again. As he used his notoriety in 1919 and afterward to promote his belief in God and the value of a good education, he used it now to rail against those who said the new war in Europe was not America's affair. As late as 1939 York was somewhat ambivalent about the need for intervention, mixing his warnings against Hitler with offhand comments, widely reported, that he "didn't know what the last war was about" and didn't see "why we need to get tangled up with any foreign row." Such musings did not keep him from continuing to prod his old superiors at the Civilian Conservation Corps to drill their men in military maneuvers.

As the war escalated in Europe, York became a leading spokesman for the interventionist viewpoint. Eleven days before the fall of Paris on June 14, 1940, he sent a telegram to Senator McKellar, encouraging him to support Roosevelt's proposal to call the National Guard to active duty. York also warned, "In view of the fast approaching danger to our country and the crying need for a strong national defense, I think there should be compulsory military training in all CCC camps in the USA at once."

The boldest and most eloquent expression of the sergeant's views on the growing international crisis was a Memorial Day speech given at the invitation of the Veterans of Foreign Wars at the Tomb of the Unknown Soldier on May 30, 1941. As the prerelease publicity surrounding *Sergeant York* was nearing its peak, York continued his public battle against pacifist Charles Lindbergh and against Senator Wheeler. His appearance at Arlington National Cemetery was York's chance to take his opponents to task publicly and fully explain his position.

York was fifty-three. His moustache drooped, his shoulders sagged, his six-foot frame labored under the weight of 275 pounds. His old sharpshooter eyes required glasses to read the text before him. But his voice rang strong and true out over the crowd gathered above the Potomac.

He began by thanking the VFW for inviting him. "They could have chosen many far better speakers. There is a famous transatlantic aviator, for one. And a United States senator whose favorite bird must be the ostrich." Perhaps, he went on, his hosts had a specific reason for inviting him.

> *You see, but for the grace of Almighty God, in this consecrated tomb might be the mortal remains of one whose name is Alvin C. York. Both the aviator and the senator were denied that privilege. . . .*
>
> *There is a line in Scripture which says that if a man doth die, his spirit shall nevertheless live on. How true that is, you here today have seen with your very own eyes, for the spirit of this soldier lives on in the heart of every real American.*
>
> *There are those in our country today who ask me, "You fought to make the world safe for democracy. What did it get you?"*
>
> *Let me answer them now. It got me twenty-three years of living in an America where a humble citizen from the mountains of Tennessee can participate in the same ceremonies with the president of the United States. It got me twenty-three years of living in a country where the goddess of liberty is stamped on men's hearts, as well as the coins in their pockets. . . .*
>
> *By our victory in the last war, we won a lease on liberty, not a deed to it. Now, after twenty-three years, Adolf Hitler tells us that lease is expiring, and after the manner of all leases, we have the privilege of renewing it, or letting it go by default. I have no doubt that the American people choose to renew it, Senator Wheeler to the contrary. . . . France let Germany into the Rhineland because there was a large group of isolationists in the French government. They weren't afraid, because they were protected by the Maginot Line, beyond which no invader could*

possibly advance. They forgot that there are more doors to every
house—even every house of cards—than the front one. . . .

If Hitler wins in Europe, we Americans will find ourselves
surrounded by hostile nations who will not, even if we choose,
let us keep to ourselves. The evil combination of Germany,
Italy, Russia, and Japan will then operate against us even more
openly than it does now. . . . [If we Americans are willing to
let that aggression continue without a fight,] then let us stop
making guns, and let us surrender to Hitler right now, while
we can still do so on our own terms.

The boy whose remains are in this unknown soldier's grave
wouldn't recognize that kind of an American. England is
fighting for her very life—for the right of her people to be free.
We have always fought for that right. If we have stopped, then
we owe the memory of George Washington an apology, for if we
have stopped, then he wasted his time at Valley Forge.

We are standing at a crossroads in history. The important
capitals of the world in a few years will either be Berlin and
Moscow, or Washington and London. I, for one, prefer Congress
and Parliament to Hitler's Reichstag and Stalin's Kremlin. And
because we were, for a time, side by side, I know this unknown
soldier does, too.

We owe it to him to renew that lease on liberty he helped
us get.

May God help us to be equal to the task.

Senator Wheeler's fellow isolationist, North Dakota Senator Gerald
P. Nye, spoke at a rally of the America First Committee in St. Louis
the night after *Sergeant York* opened in Washington. "We all go to the
movies," he reminded his audience. "We know how the silver screen has
been flooded with picture after picture designed to rouse us to a state
of war hysteria."

Here he read a list of recent movies, including *Convoy, Flight Command, I Married a Nazi,* and *Sergeant York.* "At least twenty pictures
have been produced in the last year, all designed to drug the reason
of the American people." The senator referred to press reports of the

meeting between President Roosevelt and York and the president's comment that he didn't like so much killing. "Yet," said Nye, "he is glad to see that picture and a score of others rousing the American people to be killed on a real battlefield, not a movie lot."

Nye initiated a Senate investigation of the movie industry as a monopoly and propaganda agency, but York still had no qualms about the message in his life story. Later in the summer of 1941, as he prepared to leave Pall Mall for the annual American Legion convention in Milwaukee, Sergeant York offered a simple solution to the whole affair. Nye and Lindbergh, he said, "ought to be shut up by throwing them square into jail. Today, not tomorrow."

"If the lives of American Legion members are propaganda," York continued, "then Senator Nye should start tearing up all the history books in the country. It seems to me that men like Harry Warner, Jesse Lasky, and Louis B. Meyer are being persecuted not because they hate Hitler, but because they are being unfair to him."

Harry Warner traveled to Washington from Hollywood to defend his picture in person. On September 26, he took the stand and explained before the Senate committee how producers had wanted to make *Sergeant York* since 1919, so it could hardly be a propaganda ploy for interventionists. He insisted the movie was an accurate portrayal of the life of a great American, "and if that is propaganda, then I plead guilty to the charge."

Senator Wayland Brooks, an Illinois isolationist and member of the committee, responded to Warner's remarks. "I want to say that I didn't find any propaganda in *Sergeant York* unless it was propaganda for allegiance to our country and glorification of a great hero. I thought it was well done, and I say it from the experience of one who fought overseas in the last war."

Later in the session, the committee chairman, Senator Clark of Idaho, recalled Brooks's remarks and said, "I agree with you on *Sergeant York*. I don't know how it ever got into this investigation. I think it's a grand picture."

Senator Nye sat glumly in a corner. He couldn't respond to the senators' remarks with any degree of accuracy, since he had not yet seen the movie in question.

Lindbergh saw *Sergeant York* in New York on September 13. In his diary he wrote, "It was, of course, good propaganda for war—glorification of war, etc. However, I do not think a picture of this type is at all objectionable and dangerous." He was himself under fire for a speech days before in which he said the only people who wanted war were "the British, the Jews, and the Roosevelt administration."

Propaganda or not, the armed forces requested prints of *Sergeant York* to show to troops stationed around the world. It reminded them of home, and of faith, and of one of the great military heroes in whose footsteps they followed. One appreciative audience was the crew of the USS *Enterprise*, a massive carrier and pride of the American Pacific Fleet. On the night of December 6, the crew members cheered the screen exploits of the famous world war doughboy as their magnificent ship sailed off the coast of Pearl Harbor, Hawaii.

Within a few hours, Senator Nye's arguments would be academic.

Chapter Twenty-Four

Under Siege

Alvin York endured considerable public ridicule for opposing the dashing and handsome Lindbergh. After the publication of his comments suggesting the flyer should be thrown in jail, he got letters calling him "skunk" and "ignoramus." A letter from Minneapolis, signed "Just an Average American Citizen," accused him of participating in Hollywood's "juicy warmongering propaganda," adding, "We will fight to defend America. We will not go abroad to fight ignorant negroes in Timbuctoo in the hope that someday someone will make a moving picture of us butchering our game." Another critic wrote, "Just because a Jewish motion picture company made you a 'hero' for a few lousy 'grands,' you think you are an authority, but really you are just a *nobody* standing besides Lindy."

After the first Sunday in December 1941, letters in that vein ceased abruptly. York was suddenly in greater demand than he had been in years, with a new generation of Americans learning of his story through *Sergeant York*. As the country struggled back from the disaster at Pearl Harbor and various government agencies began passing the blame around, York was almost constantly in print and on the air-waves with a message of optimism and hope. He became, as he was immediately after the Great War, a symbol of bedrock American values, speaking several times a week on behalf of the Red Cross, defense bonds, and other war efforts.

York accepted an offer to write a syndicated column six days a week for the new Chicago *Sun.* The three-year contract paid him 40 percent of syndication rights after expenses, with a guarantee of ten thousand dollars per year. Longsuffering Arthur Bushing received one hundred dollars per month to assist him and was authorized to approve copy for publication in the sergeant's absence. The column was to begin on December 1, but the first installment of "Sergeant York Says" did not appear until Monday, December 15.

The picture beside the article, of a grandfatherly gentleman with wire-rimmed glasses, double chin, and an ample moustache, could have been of a midwestern college professor. But there was no professorial reserve in the words: "Now the Japs have proven on our own flesh and blood that, like Hitler and Mussolini, they will stop at nothing. I had to be persuaded to fight last time. Nobody needs that today. At one blow, the Japs have welded every last American into one solid chunk of steel. They have forged the sledgehammer that will smash them."

On Christmas Day Sergeant York had his customary crowd of relatives, friends, and neighbors for dinner. There was a church service in the morning, where the second elder doubled as song leader and Santa Claus. Then all helped themselves to Miss Gracie's legendary feast. "Everybody had gotten aplenty," the sergeant wrote in his next day's column. "Nobody was afraid to have his say. I thought how different it must be in some other countries. I thought, 'it's just things like this, things we take for granted, that we're fighting this war to keep.'"

The next morning York revisited his old training ground at Camp Gordon. He mingled with the recruits, pronouncing them ready to fight against "Hitler and his yellow cronies." He made a speech to hospital patients in the post auditorium then walked through the wards speaking with men who were too sick to attend his presentation. On December 30, the day after York returned to Pall Mall, the wire services announced Charles Lindbergh had volunteered his services in the Army Air Corps.

In addition to his daily column, York broadcast an inspirational message every Sunday from the auditorium of the York Agricultural

Institute, which radio station WNOX in Knoxville fed to regional out-
lets and, on special occasions, to the network. Looking toward the year
ahead in his program of January 25, 1942, he painted Hitler and Japanese commander Tojo as "Powers of Darkness—madmen and crimi-
nals" who ignored the warning the apostle Paul gave in his letter to the
Galatians. "'God is not mocked; for whatever a man soweth, that shall
he also reap.'

"Those who have attacked us have sowed to the flesh entirely," he
went on. "The world as they see it is made up of material things only—
of flesh, of tanks, planes, guns, marching men. They deny God or force
their cowed people to worship their leader as a god. And they deny the
spirit of religion which is the spirit of mankind. They have willfully
blinded themselves to the barrier that they cannot pass: The body of
man can be crushed and nations swallowed up, but the Christian spirit
can never be destroyed." The program concluded, as it began, with a
chorus of the sergeant's favorite hymn, "Onward, Christian Soldiers."

In another of his columns, York gave a somewhat more earthly
suggestion of how America should set its war strategy. "We know that
whatever Japan does comes from higher up the fork. Trace the dirty
water back to the head and you'll find Hitler's Germany bubbling. It's
like when a man finds a gap in his fence-wire and somebody's pigs root-
ing in his garden patch. The man gets busy and drives those pigs out,
but he don't stop there. He looks for the fellow who cut the wire. You
can herd pigs out, but if you leave the fence cutter loose, they'll keep
coming back. So my notion is, the big job we and our Allies have is to
put up Hitler's meat above all. It'll be hog-killing weather for the others
mighty soon after that."

Soon after the new year began, York wrote to Jesse Lasky in Burbank for an accounting of the income from *Sergeant York* and some idea
of when he might expect more money. York had received his second
twenty-five-thousand-dollar payment in July but no royalties. Lasky
replied to York and to John Hale that as of the end of the year, *Sergeant
York* had not grossed $3 million, the threshold required for York's roy-
alty stream to begin.

The movie had, however, been the biggest grossing film of 1941.
Cooper won the New York Film Critics award for best actor and the

picture received nominations for eleven Academy Awards. Cooper got his nomination as predicted, with other nominations including best picture, best supporting actor (Walter Brennan), supporting actress (Margaret Wycherly as Mother York), director (Howard Hawks), screenplay, music, sound recording, editing, black-and-white art direction, and black-and-white cinematography.

The Academy Awards ceremony was held at the Biltmore Hotel in Los Angeles on Thursday, February 26, 1942, with Bob Hope as master of ceremonies. The ten nominations for best picture included *The Little Foxes* (Bette Davis's film for Goldwyn while Cooper was shooting *Sergeant York*), *The Maltese Falcon* (screenwriter John Huston's debut as a director), and *Citizen Kane*. *Sergeant York* lost the best picture award to *How Green Was My Valley*, but Cooper won for best actor, outpolling Orson Welles, heavily favored in the title role of *Citizen Kane*. Coop received his statuette from James Stewart, who won the award the year before playing opposite Katherine Hepburn in *The Philadelphia Story*. Stewart, one of the first Hollywood stars to join the military, appeared onstage in his Army Air Corps uniform and embraced Cooper as he stepped to the microphone.

In accepting the award, Coop was characteristically brief. "It wasn't Gary Cooper who won this award, it was Sergeant York. Because to the best of my ability, I tried to be Sergeant York."

William Holmes picked up *Sergeant York*'s second Oscar for editing.

Alvin York's first royalty check from Warner Bros. was issued February 28, 1942, in the amount of $32,617.55, a little more than fourteen years' salary for a CCC camp superintendent. There was plenty to be done with it. York Institute was building its gym, and there were future plans for a principal's home, dormitory, and vocational shop. In 1940, the school formed a band but had only a ragtag collection of instruments. York took the would-be musicians to Nashville and filled his truck with new trumpets, clarinets, flutes, saxophones, and drums.

The Bible school building was well underway, with York paying for nearly all of it. Thwarted for so many years by other interests as he struggled to build York Institute—and then ultimately being forced out as its head—the sergeant was determined to build this time with his own money and operate according to his own vision. York constructed the

Bible school entirely of flagstone, with large, elegant French windows, fine tongue-and-groove paneling, and electric lights in every room. Of the forty-thousand-dollar cost, York provided thirty-eight thousand.

He also brought innovations to his own house on the York Highway. Steam radiators were installed under windows in every room, upstairs and down. And two rooms—the bedroom to the right at the top of the stairs and a coat closet under the stairs—were converted into bathrooms. A sink and electric stove were installed in the busy kitchen, bringing an end to a 160-year era of spring water and kindling.

The downstairs closet-turned-bathroom retained one of its old traditions. Not wanting the children or any guests present to see them kissing, York and Miss Gracie had always slipped into the front closet for a minute when Alvin was on his way out the door. Even after its conversion, the new bathroom continued to be their rendezvous for a tender goodbye whenever the sergeant left home.

By the time *Sergeant York* was re-released at popular prices on July 4, 1942, its subject had earned more than most Fentress County residents could expect to see in a lifetime. A year-end accounting showed Alvin York's royalty payments for 1942 totaling $134,338.14. Warner Bros. originally withheld $10,000 from the February check against whatever settlement the company might have to make with Tom Skeyhill's estate. On June 3, the studio received a letter from York advising he might consider legal action if the money were not forthcoming. The studio, in reviewing the original agreement between York and Lasky, determined York was responsible for supplying clear title to his story to them, but feared the prospect of unfavorable publicity. Two days later Warner Bros. sent York his $10,000.

Other legal disagreements were gradually ironed out as well. The Skeyhill estate settled with the studio on August 4, 1942. York, feeling Skeyhill's common-law wife had absolutely no legitimate claim, insisted the studio settle for $3,500 or less, and Lasky reported an agreement was reached. Having all received their $250, York's old squad members quieted. Donoho Hall, a Tennessee veteran hired as a technical consultant for $100 per week during the shooting, reconsidered the importance of his contribution and sued Warners for $15,000. He settled that summer for $500. That only left Sam Cowan, now on his third attorney and without the thread of a claim as far as the studio legal department could see.

One outstanding debt got Lasky's immediate attention. Jack Moss, Gary Cooper's agent, wrote to Jack Warner in September claiming the studio never reimbursed him for $734 in long distance calls made from Sun Valley, Idaho, to Coop during contract negotiations. Since Cooper's participation in *Sergeant York* was the result of a trade for Bette Davis, the only contract involving Cooper was between Warner Bros. and Goldwyn; Cooper's agent was little more than a long-distance bystander. Nevertheless, Warner dashed off one of his dark blue memos to Lasky insisting Warner would not be thought of as a man who didn't pay his bills, and to take care of Moss's check at once.

York's $134,000 for the year was less than Gary Cooper's $150,000 guaranteed for twelve weeks on the picture. Together those figures paled compared to the bonanza Jesse Lasky engineered for himself. Signing his rights to the York story over to Warners had earned him $40,000, plus $1,500 per week in salary with forty weeks guaranteed. In addition, his original contract called for 20 percent of the gross over $1.6 million and 25 percent of everything over $2.5 million. The last week of 1941, the agreement was amended to give Lasky a cash payment of $85,000 with royalties beginning at $2.1 million; a second change raised the cash amount to $90,000 and the royalty threshold to $2,580,000.

Still not satisfied with his cash flow arrangement, Lasky made a remarkably deceitful arrangement that fortunately York, in all likelihood, never knew about.

Largely thanks to the energy and creativity of Howard Hawks, Jesse Lasky produced an Academy Award-winning box office sensation. All that aside, Lasky decided to raise some quick cash by selling his interest in the picture to a studio competitor. On December 4, 1942, Lasky sold his interest in *Sergeant York* to United Artists studio, one of his old employers, for $805,000 cash. On December 22, Warner Bros. quietly rescued Lasky's share from United Artists for $820,000, yielding his new business cronies a profit of $15,000 in eighteen days, and costing his old colleagues almost two-thirds the price of the picture's original production budget.

For all his newfound wealth, Alvin York lived the same way he had for the past twenty years on his bottomland farm in Pall Mall. He rose early, dressed in khaki work pants, khaki shirt, necktie, and hat. He saw to the farm operations with the help of his brother Joe and checked in on his general store in Pall Mall and his other properties around the county. York kept an office at York Institute, where the old battles seemed forgotten for the most part, and he presided at the weekly devotional service there which was broadcast over the radio.

Though he no longer had any management responsibilities at the institute, York spoke at assemblies frequently during the year and handed out diplomas every spring at commencement. Children who never knew Fentress County without York Institute crossed the stage to accept a diploma, shake the sergeant's huge hand, and hear a proud word of congratulation. (Students got a school holiday to go to the movie when *Sergeant York* opened in Jamestown; the admission was a piece of scrap iron for the war effort.) York remained devoted to the school he founded, and the school valued him as a symbol of patriotism and morality, and an unsurpassed public relations tool.

York continued expanding his livestock operations, adding more black angus cattle and Poland China hogs. With his neighbors, he set up the community's first livestock co-op. With the help of his checks from Warner Bros., the sergeant eventually controlled the mineral rights to thousands of acres in and around Fentress County, where exploration companies tested for barite, oil, and gas.

Still another business interest was the York Mill, a fine old wooden structure built on tall pillars of stacked rock just across the Wolf River and across York Highway from the family homestead. The mill was built about the time Alvin was born and patronized by generations of Pall Mall residents. York already had a small mill wheel in a side room of his store, but this additional enterprise was a large two-story building, painted red, with a mill wheel that took two men to reach around. Instead of a traditional water wheel, power was provided by a water-driven turbine, rotating around a vertical axis and completely submerged in the millrace. A shaft came up from the turbine, out of the water, through the floor of the mill, and into the driving gears. After

York bought the mill in December of 1942, friends and passersby frequently saw him standing on the porch in front of the entrance, passing the time with customers or watching the road through the window of the tiny office with its cheerful and inviting woodstove.

Obesity and arthritis began to have an effect on Sergeant York. Struggles with pneumonia and rheumatic fever sapped his strength; nevertheless, he kept up his full schedule of traveling and speaking engagements. In spite of his health, York was eager to register for the draft. When Senators Wheeler and Nye were still preaching isolationism, York said the draft should be revived at once to eliminate the "chasm of shame" separating dutiful enlisted troops from the rest of young America. When Roosevelt signed the draft into law on October 17, 1940, York heartily approved, saying it was the best way to defend the country.

York was appointed head of the Fentress County Draft Board, with Bushing as clerk, and on April 27, 1942, the sergeant himself registered for the draft. It was the fourth national selective service registration and required the thirteen million American men between the ages of forty-five and sixty-four to fill out an occupational questionnaire; they would not be called into combat service. With reporters and a *Life* magazine photographer standing by, Sergeant York was registered by Pastor Pile at the same desk in Pile's store where he registered in 1917. "If they want me for active duty, I'm ready to go," declared the sergeant, despite spending the last week of March and first week of April in bed with pneumonia on doctor's orders.

York also responded to reports about five thousand drafted Tennesseans rejected by the army because they were illiterate, and others turned down for service because they had bad teeth. York offered to raise a battalion of these rejects and lead them into combat. Whether they could read or not, he knew his fellow mountaineers to be true patriots and good shots, and that was what really mattered. Furthermore, he reminded the authorities, "George Washington had store teeth, and they didn't even fit."

York came to the defense of another group receiving some attention in the press. Black American soldiers were being encouraged by enemy propagandists to rise up against their white rulers and join the

Axis cause. York had always accepted the social division of the races prescribed by his time and place. This challenge to American solidarity made him rethink his position. In his newspaper column he wrote, ". . . the most part of us, colored and white, know and are proud that our country was built up by both races and belongs to us all. Shoulder to shoulder, we've spilled our blood wherever America was threatened. That's a tie no lie can cut. We've come a far piece together and crossed some mighty rough territory to get where we are. There's room for more improvement. We're fighting and working for that chance to go on making America a better place for everybody to live in."

Sergeant York was commissioned an honorary major in the infantry in order to assist with training infantry soldiers. He continued to visit military installations in Georgia, Louisiana, Texas, Washington, and elsewhere, talking with new recruits, soothing their homesickness and fear of what lay ahead. He wrote about the trips in his columns: selling defense bonds in front of the Alamo, complimenting the training at Fort Oglethorpe, describing the sort of sendoff every soldier deserved as he watched a bus pull away from a small town near Alexandria, Louisiana.

As always, Tennessee celebrations received York's special attention. A defense bond victory rally in Nashville was one of many he attended during the year. Held on March 10 at the Ryman Auditorium, it featured York as the sole speaker and a special appearance by a local singer originally named Fannye Rose. Fannye had gone to high school a few blocks up Broadway from the Ryman and achieved national stardom under the stage name Dinah Shore. Miss Shore was the most popular female vocalist in the country, a featured soloist with Eddie Cantor, host of her own radio program, and under contract to the Waldorf-Astoria. Admission to the show was a dollar's worth of defense stamps, which patrons were allowed to keep.

On July 2, the first anniversary of the opening of *Sergeant York*, the sergeant took part in a special broadcast from Knoxville, with Gary Cooper again playing a scene from the movie in a Hollywood broadcasting studio. York was heard on national radio broadcasts almost every week. His speeches continued along the same thread as his proclamation at the Tomb of the Unknown Soldier a year earlier: patriotism, Christian faith, and sacrifice would triumph in the end. He appeared on "Hello, America," and "Letters from the Front," and a special international tribute to Douglas MacArthur, still waiting in Australia for an opportunity to retake the Philippines. The sergeant promoted the Red Cross's $65 million national fund drive and endorsed the Treasury Department's program requesting every American to buy defense bonds equal to a day's pay. York encouraged his fellow farmers to do as he was doing and set aside the income from an acre of land to support America's defense.

The Bible school York chartered in 1939 opened in the summer of 1942. His Hollywood fortune allowed the sergeant to realize the dream of providing a place for children (and any adults so inclined) to learn about the gospel without the interference of school board politics or limitations of state budgets.

The first session was less than a month long but well attended and a success by any measure. Children came from all over the county, arriving late in the long summer afternoons after their chores were done, scrubbed, combed, and dressed for a party, with girls in pastel summer dresses, the boys in jeans or khaki pants and bright cotton shirts.

York, Pastor Pile or visiting guest speakers preached in the main hall, with York leading hymns in his fine strong voice, taking full advantage of the room's superb acoustics. After a dinner break the children returned, many accompanied by their parents, for teaching, preaching, singing, and praying until bedtime, their voices carrying along the creek to the Wolf River and up and down the valley.

On some days outdoor picnics were held on the lawn in front of the flagstone porch. The men set up tables and chairs on the grass as the women busied themselves in the school kitchen preparing food they brought from home—cold fried chicken, cornbread and biscuits, relishes and chow-chow, salad greens, cakes, pies, and ice cream, with spring water (there was no plumbing in the school) or lemonade to wash it all down.

By the middle of 1943, the tide of the war shifted in favor of the Allies. The American Pacific Fleet was pushing the Japanese westward one bloody island at a time, from Midway the summer before, to Guadalcanal, the Russell Islands, and the Solomons. Russia was on the offensive against Hitler, and America began a series of unprecedented daylight bombing raids against Germany's industrial heartland along the Ruhr with the new Boeing Flying Fortress. (Among the American pilots overseas was B-24 bomber group commander James Stewart, who'd handed Gary Cooper his Oscar a year and a half before.) Mussolini was on the run as British and American forces headed for Sicily and the Italian mainland.

Sergeant York continued as a popular morale booster and found special favor in official quarters—a far cry from the earlier charges of propagandism. The State Department requested several prints, including versions the studio dubbed in Spanish and French, to give to friendly nations in embassies around the world. Chinese Nationalist leader Chiang Kai-Shek asked for and received a copy to show his troops in the field.

Day-to-day life in Pall Mall was little affected by the war. Except for their young men being called away, the families of the community went on as always, spared the suffering city folks endured without their accustomed stock of foodstuffs, tires, gasoline, and store-bought clothes. Meat, butter, and eggs were plentiful in the valley, and the demand for tires was low. The ladies pieced quilts, sewed skirts, and knitted socks whenever they needed them. One of the few panics was caused by a shortage of hairpins, whose price skyrocketed from nineteen cents to sixty cents a pound, when they were available at all. Old celluloid hairpins, hunted up in closets, burst into flames in the presence of newfangled curling irons and hair dryers. Some women made do with toothpicks.

One rationed commodity everyone missed at first was sugar, which not only flavored coffee but was an important ingredient for canning and curing. By the time the 1943 planting season came around, farmers solved the problem by growing more sorghum, a cane whose juice was pressed and rendered by boiling into a thick molasses that tasted something like brown sugar, only, some declared, much better. Old cane presses were repaired and new ones built, their gears turned by a horse or mule walking in a circle around the machine.

The reintroduction of old ways was fine with Mother York. Blind now and bedridden, she knew no reason why rationing and the draft should keep the community from carrying on as always. "Women will just have to roll up their sleeves and pitch in," she told a visitor. "It is not going to hurt them to do a little work. Won't hurt them near as bad as traipsing around to this, that, and the other place and seeing things they would be better off not seeing."

Having carded and spun wool from her own sheep, raised her own cotton, plowed her own field with a team, and cleared timber in knee-deep snow, Mother York had little patience with women who complained about the inconveniences of rationing. "Lots of women nowadays have been spoiled by having things come too easy for them. But [while the men are at war] they will have to take care of things at home. They ought to be thankful they've got something to take care of."

Mary York expected little out of life and took her third son's notoriety in stride. His heroism only proved he did his duty as God called him. She was proud of Alvin, certainly, but as she told one of the many reporters standing in the grape arbor in front of her cabin on Alvin's wedding day, "I'm proud of all my children." Her recipe for success in raising a family, she declared, was to "praise 'em some once in a while, whup 'em when they need it, and leave the rest to God."

The night of May 20, 1943, Mother York died peacefully in her sleep at the age of seventy-seven. Her funeral was held in York Chapel by Reverend R. D. Brown of Ohio, one of her and Alvin's favorite preachers and a regular guest at the York Bible School.

That summer another series of programs was held at the Bible school, completely funded by Sergeant York. He also paid for improvements to the York Chapel building and continued his donations to York Institute for tools, sporting goods, kitchen equipment, and other needs.

The York Institute Class of '43 numbered only thirty-six, its size reduced by world events and Sergeant York's draft board. The band and the football team were temporarily disbanded, but the school continued to flourish under state supervision and principal C. W. Davis. (P. B. Stephens transferred to a new state position supervising rehabilitation for the handicapped in Chattanooga.) Governor Cooper accepted York's invitation to speak at graduation exercises on May 14. York was there to introduce the governor and, as was the custom, to hand out the diplomas.

Sergeant York's son George entered the military in the summer of 1943 and York wrote to the chief of chaplains to have him appointed an army minister. George had attended seminary for two years and planned to be a preacher, but according to Chaplain William R. Arnold, the young York lacked official qualifications. First, he was four years shy of the minimum age of twenty-four; second, he had to be established as a professional minister; and third, he needed a degree and two years of experience. (The issue was soon moot. George developed a hernia, underwent surgery in a military hospital, and received a medical discharge after eight months in uniform.)

The week York was requesting a chaplain's appointment for his son, Sam Cowan made one final attempt to wring some cash out of Warner Bros. On July 9 he wrote to Lasky—who cared not at all by this time—in what he deemed "a last effort to avoid a lawsuit."

After retracing his claims to episodes in the movie, still never offering specific examples, he revealed a new development:

> *I have received, Mr. Lasky, from the editor of an Eastern magazine with national circulation a request to debunk York—show what he really is today and some of the things he has done for money that differ from the sentiments expressed upon his return. I have not accepted the editor's offer for I still feel kindly disposed towards York. . . . This, Mr. Lasky, is a friendly letter. If I hear from you personally with an offer I could accept, I will proceed no further with the editor's proposition and will write you releasing you from all obligations in connection with your movie and my book.*

Lasky ignored the threat. Cowan had fired his last and biggest gun, to no effect.

Chapter Twenty-Five

Mammon's Revenge

By the time President Roosevelt signed a bill instituting "pay as you go" payroll deductions for federal income tax payments, effective July 1, 1943, Alvin York had already exchanged several letters with the Treasury Department over his tax liability for 1940 and 1941. His income ballooned in those years because of the two $25,000 payments from Jesse Lasky for film rights to the story of his life. York claimed the money was not regular income but a capital gain and figured his taxes accordingly.

For 1940 York declared $600 in government salary from the CCC, offset by a $531 loss on farm operations. He also declared "Income from Capital Assets Held for More Than Twenty-four Months" of $25,000. As a capital gain, only half the $25,000 was taxable. With his deductions for dependents and an earned income credit of $300, he figured his tax liability at $473.98. The government, figuring his film income fully taxable, claimed the correct tax was $2,984.00.

In 1941 he had a combined net loss of $548.11 on total income from salary and farming of $1,245.17, plus another disputed $25,000. He paid $1,137.52 in taxes; the Treasury countered that he owed $5,361.98 instead.

York filed a protest with the Internal Revenue Service on May 11, 1943, though subsequently he did send another payment. On a single supplemental 1040 form, York refigured his tax liability for every year from 1918 to 1941 and wrote a check to the IRS for $9,381.62 in all. The government agency informed him he could only file a single year's claim on a 1040 but the agency would hold the payment against his 1942 taxes owed.

The IRS claim for 1942 rendered all previous arguments inconsequential. Along with net income of $6,794.57, York listed a capital gain that year of $134,338.14, representing his film royalties. The sergeant figured his tax at $37,273.74; the government argued the correct total was $91,880.69.

That meant taxpayer York had to come up with a minimum of more than $54,000 plus accruing interest, assuming no criminal penalties were added. Having spent freely on the York Institute, the York Bible School, a household of eleven, and a large contingent of friends and relatives whose requests for money he never refused, it was a sum he had no way of paying. The government was happy to have the war hero traveling to military bases, raising money for the Red Cross, hawking war bonds, and otherwise helping the war effort. Other than some expenses, he was never paid anything for his part in raising millions. But as far as the IRS was concerned, none of York's work on behalf of the government offset his tax liability.

George Edward Buxton York received his medical discharge on December 31, 1943. Within a week his brother Woodrow Wilson York was denied a deferment to keep him out of the service. Woodrow, Sergeant York suspected, would not fare well under military discipline. He and Alvin Jr. were the most unruly of the children growing up, inclined to drinking and playing cards in the image of their father before his religious conversion. (In 1940, Woodrow almost killed Junior, cracking his skull with a metal pole used to open high windows at York Institute. Newspaper reports called it a "farm accident.")

Because he was a farmer, married, and had a young son, Alvin Jr. received a deferment. Woodrow applied for an occupational deferment, which many farmers were awarded, their civilian jobs being crucial to the war effort. It fell to Arthur Bushing, as clerk of the local draft board, to inform Woodrow his request was denied, since the farm he worked on had plenty of other help.

The sergeant's concern for Woodrow's safety was tempered by good news from the fronts in Europe and the Pacific. Japan and the Axis powers were in full retreat. York shared his optimism with fresh recruits on another tour of training camps in Georgia, Alabama, Louisiana, and Tennessee. He told the men they were getting the finest military training in U.S. history. He reminded them, with a sense of pride, how in spite of Flying Fortresses and all the other advantages of modern warfare, "the infantry will have to go in and dig the Germans out before victory will be completely ours." York also praised the fighting spirit of America's British and Russian allies, who proved, "sheer courage and fighting spirit are the match for even the most destructive military force ever loosed in Europe."

A reporter asked the famous guest what Davy Crockett and Daniel Boone would think if they could see how modern wars were fought. "They'd stand straight up in their graves," the sergeant answered.

Woodrow entered the service in March 1944, leaving his wife and infant son behind (though Alvin Jr. got a deferment under similar circumstances), and prepared to ship out for the Pacific Theater after basic training; George Edward returned to his seminary studies, this time in Florida; and Alvin Jr. continued working with his younger brothers and sisters on the family farm, living with his wife and son in a house Sergeant York built for them across York Highway from the family homeplace.

York Bible School sessions in the summer of 1944 were low-key events. Many of the prospective participants were serving in the military. Even if there was a ready congregation, Sergeant York would have been pressed to fund another summer's programs. He agreed to pay the Internal Revenue Service $8,345.98 plus interest to settle the claims against him for 1940 and 1941. He also paid $9,381.62 to settle earlier claims and $37,273.74 as the undisputed portion of the tax on his 1942 income. The issue of the additional $54,000 for 1942 was not settled and now there was also the question of the tax on his 1943 film royalties of $15,301.15.

In little more than two years, Alvin York paid $55,001.34 in federal income tax. By the end of 1944, according to government calculations, he owed them that much again.

York and his Jamestown lawyer, John Hale, enlisted the aid of an energetic, ambitious young Nashville attorney named John J. Hooker to guide the sergeant's protests and appeals through the tax courts. York then turned his attentions to another serious concern closer to home.

True to his premonitions, his son Woodrow proved ill-suited for military life. Woody chafed at the discipline and labored in the shadow of his famous father. Miss Gracie was at a loss for how to reach her son at times. When he was fifteen, she wrote Sergeant York on tour that she had caught Woodrow with "a nother deck of cards in his pocket this morning. I taken they from him oh how mad he got. Well I don't know what he thinks about. Maby he will change after a while."

He didn't change, hadn't found a career that interested him, and entered the army unhappy and adrift. His parents indulged him out of love but the army had no patience for a malcontent, even one who had a famous father, famous namesake, and once used the White House bathroom.

After only a few months Woodrow was admitted to the hospital at Camp Maxey, Texas, for psychological testing and observation. His letters home were confused; his father said they "didn't read right." Woodrow's commanders thought a hospital stay would give him time to adjust and orient his thinking.

After five months the young soldier was released from the hospital proper and transferred to the reconditioning annex, where soldiers drilled, exercised, and prepared to resume active duty after an illness. Rather than return to his unit, Woodrow headed for Tennessee, absent without official leave. Military police picked him up in Memphis on January 24, 1945, and wired Camp Maxey for instructions. The commander and the executive officer of the hospital discussed their decision. They could have young York brought back to Texas under armed guard at his own expense or trust him to return without them.

The officers wired the MPs to let him go and ordered him back to Camp Maxey. Woodrow York disappeared. The executive officer of the hospital, Lieutenant Colonel Leroy Simmons, wrote a warm and sympathetic letter of encouragement to Miss Gracie on January 29. "I trusted him," he said of Woodrow. "I still trust him. I think he will come back. He is the son of an honest God-fearing man, and I can't help but think he has some of the qualities of his parents."

Private York returned to his parents' house in Pall Mall about three weeks later, hiding at first in the basement, then revealing himself to his family members, who were at the same time relieved and concerned. Sergeant York felt his son was ill and still needed help but told him he had an obligation to fulfill, drove him to Jamestown, and put him on the bus. Two days later Woodrow was back, claiming he was afraid to travel without a military pass. Sergeant York took him this time to the military authorities in Crossville, who sent him back to Texas and the military stockade.

"There is something wrong and bad wrong with this boy," the worried father wrote Woodrow's commander. "And I sometimes doubt the wisdom of confining this kid in the stockade as sick as he has been. I think if you will check this boy's record you will find that all this trouble has happened since he was put in the hospital."

With the end of the war, Sergeant York completed his service as head of the local draft board, though he kept leasing the board space in his Jamestown building for a few dollars a month. Life changed little in the county as the war concluded, as it had changed little when it began.

The sergeant continued to feed everyone within earshot twice a day. One occasional visitor noted it was "like going to a big hotel, but you never had to pay, and didn't have to be invited." When word got out York would be making a trip into Jamestown from Pall Mall, anyone who wanted a ride walked over to the house or the store where his car was, got in, and waited for the sergeant to take the wheel and depart. When they finished their business in town, passengers ambled to the courthouse square where the car was parked, got back in, and waited for the ride home.

Rationing ended in October and farmers cut back on their sorghum crop. York Institute welcomed five veterans back to the senior class as the school year began and York's old friend Cordell Hull received the Nobel Peace Prize for his role in organizing the United Nations.

York continued to be dogged, however, by one of Hull's earlier career milestones. On February 25, 1913, the Sixteenth Amendment to the Constitution, allowing the government to assess an individual income tax, was passed, due in part to the aggressive support it received from the Tennessee congressman. York and his lawyers, Hale and Hooker, continued their protracted discussions in an attempt to reach a settlement on the sergeant's tax liability with Washington.

The final tally, according to IRS figures, was a debt of $85,442.03 on film royalties paid in 1942 and 1943, plus interest and penalties. The government refused to allow York to deduct any of the money he raised for York Institute or donated to it over the years because he could produce no record of it. Likewise, any deduction for the construction or operation of the York Bible School was not allowed, as it was not a duly registered tax-exempt entity. None of the time spent traveling and speaking on behalf of the military training effort or defense bonds or the Red Cross was deductible. Convinced they could prepare a compelling case given the time, Hale and Hooker received continuances to allow them to plan a defense.

Hoping for a windfall, York tripled the acreage of his mineral leases, controlling the rights to six thousand acres of land in Tennessee and Kentucky where companies continued searching for oil, gas, and barite. Several small strikes encouraged York there might be a gusher ahead, which would enable him to pay his debts and put his tax troubles behind him. He even spent two thousand dollars on a rickety wooden drilling derrick of his own in hopes of establishing a new income source.

One summer afternoon in 1946, Sergeant York leaned over a wagon tongue and couldn't straighten up. He weaved unsteadily for a moment, then sat down on the tongue, propping himself up against the front of the wagon. He refused to go to the hospital and stumbled inside to his bed with the help of two cousins who were in the yard. He lay in his room for a few days, then resumed his regular rounds at the store and in Jamestown; but it was clear to Miss Gracie and Dr. Guy Pinckley, his doctor and friend, York had suffered a mild stroke. The right side of his face remained partly numb and tingling and numbness came and went up and down the whole right side of his body. Sometimes at night he would awaken suddenly with the sensation he was smothering and would sit up on the edge of the bed, joints aching with arthritis, to try and catch his breath.

The sergeant's disability meant Miss Gracie would temporarily have to take over the task of getting her son Woodrow out of the army. He was on duty in the Philippines, where he contracted malaria and spent still more time in army hospitals. She wrote to him regularly with news from home and admonitions about his drinking. One letter read in part:

> Well honey I sure you hope you are feeling good tonight and hope your head is O. K. But honey please take good care of yourself. If you need some money just let me know at once. And don't drink any and be careful with your money for some one might try to rob you if you do get to drinking. . . . I am still keeping your watch for you so you can have it when you come home . . . Well I am praying for you and that you won't drink and that the Lord will spare your life to return home safe so keep looking up and please pray for yourself. With love from your loving mother. Write when you can. I love to hear from you.

Miss Gracie also contacted the authorities to explain Sergeant York's illness and asked that her son be discharged to come home and help the family. She wrote to the War Department on August 1, 1946, to say her husband "hasn't seen a well day for months" and if her son could come home, "it might be he could keep from going astray." Later in the year, after a minor auto accident left the sergeant with injuries to his abdomen and right shoulder, the numbness on his right side increased.

Private First Class Woodrow York returned from the Philippines to Fort Dix, New Jersey. There a personnel officer explained he could apply for a dependency discharge. In mid-October Dr. Pinckley and the pastor at York Chapel, B. R. Kean, sent notarized statements to the army affirming Sergeant York's frail condition. Miss Gracie wrote the sergeant's old friend Senator McKellar to enlist his help, and McKellar contacted Major General Edward F. Witsell, the adjutant general of the army, for assistance.

Private York went AWOL again on November 15, was taken into custody on December 4, and held until after the turn of the new year. He left Fort Dix for Pall Mall February 13, this time with official permission, and was discharged on the last day of the month.

Meanwhile, his brother Alvin Jr. was spending three months in the federal penitentiary in Montgomery, Alabama, for selling moonshine. Neither of these York boys was in a position to ease their ailing father's difficulties.

Though spells of dizziness bothered him from time to time after his stroke, Sergeant York felt well enough to hand out diplomas at the York Institute graduation in the spring of 1947, and continued writing letters to influential friends on behalf of acquaintances and strangers alike. A woman wrote asking if York would intercede with the new governor of Tennessee, Jim Nance McCord, to grant a stay of execution for her son. Others wanted appointments to the welfare board or the school board or had a nephew who needed a job. York responded to as many as he could and sent handwritten requests to senators, governors, and anyone else he thought might be able to help.

The rickety, second-hand derrick York set up the year before struck oil in August of 1947, with a flow of fourteen barrels an hour estimated to generate $572 a day in production royalties. He had drilled seventeen hundred feet into the Knox Dolomite formation on a leased 507-acre tract along the Pickett County line belonging to his neighbor Prent Huff. His oil was purchased by the Atomic Producing and Refining Company of Albany, Kentucky, under contract with Southern Oil Service in Nashville, whose drivers had strict instructions the sergeant allowed no loading or hauling on Sundays.

News of the strike brought a flurry of photographers to snap York posing on one knee, smiling broadly, washing his hands in the greenish-black crude. It also prompted a wave of letters from strangers looking for help and advice. Eager landowners in the vicinity, those elsewhere above the Knox Dolomite formation, and some who thought they might possibly be somewhere near the Knox Dolomite formation, wrote to inquire what drilling techniques York used, how he selected the spot, and if he could offer any direction on how they might duplicate his success.

The oil flow was impressive but short-lived. After a few weeks, a neighboring well in the same layer of rock was acidized—flushed with an acid solution to dissolve the rock and release more oil. Instead of opening an underground channel and bringing on a gusher, the acidizing process blocked off the flow. Pressure dropped and the rate of production slowed. York eventually had six producing wells on his leases but together they generated a profit of less than two thousand dollars per year.

Continuing health and financial problems did nothing to dampen Alvin York's enthusiasm for living or his interest in people and politics. His sixtieth birthday, on December 13, 1947, was as lively as ever. Miss Gracie served table after table of neighbors, friends, family, dignitaries, and perfect strangers. The sergeant loved to talk—his two favorite subjects were hunting and politics—and he still kept a Savage .22 rifle near at hand to plunk at an old can or tree stump or take an occasional short foray into the woods. He also remained interested in what the youngsters were doing, visiting York Institute almost every day.

In good weather the sergeant sat on the big side porch of his house, ready for a chat with anyone who happened to drive or walk by. Saturday afternoon, if a group of teenagers came walking by on their way to the movies in Jamestown, York would hail them and they would pause at the front gate or around by the barn lot to speak with him. That night, returning by lantern light, the boys and girls would call out, "We're back, Sergeant York! Good night!" to the old gentlemen who by that time might be inside reading, listening to the radio, or already in bed.

In earlier days York said the only books he ever read were the Bible and a biography of Jesse James. By his sixtieth birthday his library was filled to the rafters with more than three thousand books and he read a dozen or more magazines regularly. *Progressive Farmer* and *American Cattleman* were favorites, along with *Life*, *Look*, and *Perspective*, published by the Church of Christ in Christian Union.

Though his world was growing somewhat smaller, the sergeant was still very interested in current events. He eyed the Russians' actions in Eastern Europe with suspicion. "It looks like we've got to take a firm stand with Russia," he told a visitor as the Soviets tightened their grip on the war-ravaged countries along their border. "We found out what appeasement got us from Japan. If we don't stand firm, we'll have to let the atom bomb do the job." Despite the friction, his outlook was optimistic. "I don't think the bomb will ever be necessary, because I am sure that if we stand firm Russia will back down."

He allowed this was a regrettable stance to have to take but force was the only language a nation that forgot God could understand. The Bible, not bullets, would ultimately be "the only real solution" for achieving world peace.

As the sergeant aged, Dr. Guy Pinckley had his hands full. York despised hospitals and medical treatment but his friend Pinckley was always a welcome sight at the door, even if the visit was a professional one. Dr. Pinckley had moved to Jamestown in 1941 and married Wilma Reagan, the member of the institute's first graduating class who became the first popularly elected superintendent of Fentress County schools.

The Pinckleys and Yorks grew closer still after Pastor Pile's death in 1948 and as the sergeant's condition required more of the doctor's attention. Sergeant York had blood pressure so erratic at times Dr. Pinckley would take it in both arms and average the two readings. In late 1948 and again in early May of 1949, York had more strokes leaving the right side of his face partially paralyzed. He refused all efforts to get him to the hospital. "Nobody else's needles are as sharp as Pinckley's," he explained. "Couldn't have anyone else giving me a shot."

Following the 1949 stroke, Sergeant York walked with the help of what he called his "cattle stick," a rough staff he kept in his car for prodding his prized Herefords. He was in the habit of carrying his stick around the house during the day and on his travels to Jamestown or the local cattle auctions. These days he leaned on it more heavily and tired more easily. Still he bombarded his steady stream of visitors with questions and comments about politics, current events or a neighbor's new coon dog. And when he got ready to drive to the auction barn, he'd give a yell; whatever children could make it to the car in time were treated to the sight of a shrewd bargainer and fine judge of livestock in action, with the prospect of a cold soft drink from the store afterward.

Drinks were a nickel at Sergeant Alvin C. York & Son General Merchandise and Groceries, Home of "York's Special" Bolted Meal.

Bologna was forty cents a roll, bleach twenty cents a bottle, bread sixteen cents a loaf, and matches seven cents a box. However many people
were inside, there were always as many or more out on the porch, swap-
ping stories and catching up on the news. Likely as not the sergeant
would be there, if he wasn't sitting on his side porch or under one of
the maples across the street. Comfortably settled on a straight-backed
kitchen chair, his thinning hair covered by an ancient and shapeless hat,
York invariably attracted a circle of listeners eager for a word about the
triumphs of the past or pronouncements on current news.

Military developments remained a special interest. The Commu-
nists were agitating in Korea, and President Truman decided to send
Americans to keep a lid on the conflict. From his chair under the maple
tree, York said he hoped two world wars taught the country a lesson.
"Made a bad mistake in the First World War. We should of went right
on to Berlin. But we stopped, so we had another war to fight. Second
War we made the same big mistake. Shouldn't of sat down on the Elbe
to wait for the Russians. So now we got another war to fight. This time
I hope we don't make no mistake."

The one topic he never discussed was his increasingly desperate
financial condition. His lawyers were unable to work out any sort of
compromise with the Internal Revenue Service and were preparing documents to take the case to trial in Nashville. The greatest problem was
the lack of definitive records. Sergeant York's charitable donations, net
worth, and liabilities were impossible for the attorneys to figure. The
truth was a moving target besides, because the tender-hearted sergeant
continued to give money away to relatives and friends, and cosign notes
with little chance of being repaid.

To make a compelling case, John Hale and John J. Hooker needed
more information as well as the sergeant's presence in court to answer
questions and clarify the facts. Besides the facial paralysis due to his
strokes, York continued battling pneumonia, arthritis, and colitis,
making the prospect of travel to Nashville unlikely.

The tax trial date was finally set for December 12, 1951. With each
passing month since the battle was joined back in 1943, the stakes rose
for York and his lawyers; interest was steadily increasing the amount
he would have to pay if they lost. During the flush of patriotism and

resolve following Pearl Harbor, Sergeant York wrote a "Sergeant York Says" column shaming citizens who squirmed at paying income taxes when there was a war to win. On January 8, 1942, he upbraided all the "bone-heads with the audacious nerve to complain because they make enough to be taxed."

But 1951 was another world. America enjoyed peace and unprecedented prosperity after surviving a mortal threat Sergeant York had done his part to disarm. York's generosity and love of country made him a pauper, yet the government saw only its numbers, and numbers were all that mattered. It made some observers wonder who the real boneheads were. Members of York's family were convinced the tax authorities in Nashville were giving the sergeant a hard time only because his old political opponents were jealous of him.

On December 12, York's tax lawyers received another continuance.

Change was working its way into Fentress County. The York home and most every other home in the valley had electricity by the time Gary Cooper won his second Oscar for *High Noon* in 1952. There were more indoor toilets and fewer outhouses in the country, though still plenty of the latter. (People who lived all their lives treading out to the privy didn't see the point in spending all that money for something they considered a city convenience—like air conditioning—rather than a necessity. This resulted in households with a car in the lot, a tractor in the barn, fine china in the corner cupboard, and an outhouse in the downhill corner of the back yard.)

Gary Cooper accepted his Oscar on television, the first time the ceremony was telecast, though Pall Mall residents were too far away and too isolated by mountains to pick up the WSM Television signal from Nashville.

By 1952 county-wide telephone service progressed to the stage where the principal of York Institute, Ernest Buck, could implement a system for calling students when bad weather closed the school. Before then the lack of phones made it impossible to reach everyone; if enough students braved the icy mountain roads, and enough teachers were there, school went on. The first test of the system was prompted not by snow but by the measles, which closed the institute for several days. The first county-wide cancellation of classes on account of snow took place the following year.

County phone service replaced the Vick's Salve Line, built ten or twelve years before by local residents to connect hand-cranked telephones for those who wanted them. Lacking glass insulators to place atop the poles carrying wires from house to house, the men discovered empty Vick's Salve jars were just the right size and shape for the job.

The York Institute football team, disbanded in 1942, was revived in 1948. The band, discontinued the same year had to wait until 1953 for its renaissance. The school was thriving then, with an enrollment of more than four hundred and a graduating class that year of fifty-two. The handsome brick main building never received its proposed stone towers and lancet windows but it was expanded by the addition of a pair of two-story extensions, one on each end.

The student body elected its Miss York Institute, prince of personality, bachelor of ugliness, and other traditional honorees, and presented a senior class play titled *Aunt Tillie Goes to Town*. The evening of May 27, 1953, as he had for a quarter of a century, Sergeant York handed out diplomas on the stage of the auditorium beneath the fragrant pines.

Chapter Twenty-Six

Another World

It seemed at first to be another of his dizzy spells. Miss Gracie soon realized though, this time it was much worse. The sergeant fell to the floor, disoriented and in pain, then lost consciousness. She called Dr. Pinckley and, with her sons' help eased Sergeant York into the car for the half-day drive to the hospital in Nashville. It was February 24, 1954, a Wednesday. Sergeant Alvin C. York had suffered a cerebral hemorrhage and the doctors couldn't tell at first whether he would live or if he did, whether he would have his senses about him when he came to.

Through the following days, Miss Gracie stayed at the hospital while Dr. Pinckley and members of the family shuttled back and forth along U.S. 70, then north to York Highway and the Wolf River Valley. The old soldier's condition was upgraded to "satisfactory" on March 9 and he was allowed to go home to Pall Mall later in the month.

The question still remained whether Sergeant York would recover. When he first returned to his ground floor bedroom with its large windows looking out through walnut and maple trees where the sun rose over the valley rim, York walked a little, shuffling from his bed to the living room couch or out to the side porch. It wasn't long, however, before he spent his whole day in bed. One day he couldn't get up at all. The infantry hero had taken his last step.

Paralysis did not dim his interest in local and world affairs and certainly did not dissuade visitors from dropping by. (On his sixty-seventh birthday in 1954, the York Institute band formed up under his window to play "Happy Birthday.") Once his condition was stable, people resumed coming to the door—neighbors, politicians, students from the institute, tourists, children, favor seekers. Miss Gracie would answer a knock at the door. "Who is it, Gracie?" Alvin would ask. It didn't matter what the answer was; his response was always the same. "Tell 'em to come in." However he felt that day, he never turned a guest away. A lunch or dinner invitation was automatic.

Even if he wasn't on tour any more or assailing Charles Lindbergh, Alvin York still made national news. The February 26, 1956, issue of *Newsweek* ran a photo with caption of the family's youngest son, Thomas Jefferson York, signing Air Force enlistment papers as a recruiting officer and Sergeant York looked on. The trio gathered around a small table in the sergeant's bedroom against a backdrop of painted wainscoting and flowered drapes. It was one of the first pictures taken after York suffered an aneurysm, blinding his trusty shooting eye and prompting him sometimes to wear dark glasses.

Other than a wheelchair ride to the side porch or the living room, Sergeant York found it too painful to travel, even as far as the square in Jamestown or to the institute, where a large color photograph of him, a gift of the class of '44, hung in the entrance hall. It was hard to reconcile the man of the photograph—husky, smiling, with luxuriant red hair—with the tired old gentleman living out on the Wolf River. What didn't change were hidden things: patriotism, Christian faith, a generous heart, a love for every brick, plank, and nail in that elegant school building under the pines.

York did make one more trip to the school. The night before had been a painful, sleepless one and he wasn't sure he could stand the drive south over the mountain along the smooth black ribbon of the York Highway. He had no intention, though, of disappointing the students at the York Institute or the men of the 82nd Airborne Infantry Division, successor to his old unit, who came to honor him.

August 21, 1957, was a hot day and the sergeant wore a white dress shirt, tie, and his Sunday Stetson. A reviewing stand large enough for his wheelchair stood on the institute grounds facing the football field, a stone's throw from where York turned the first shovel of dirt one October morning long ago to signal the building of the institute had begun.

From his wheelchair on the platform, York looked out over the hundreds of students—most of whose parents went to the school as well—the teachers and, straight ahead, an honor guard and forty-piece band from the 82nd Airborne. These were the men who inherited the traditions of the All-American Division. The campaign ribbon from Meuse-Argonne flew with dozens more from their standard.

The soldiers flew in from Fort Bragg, North Carolina, under the sponsorship of the 82nd Division Association. The division commander, Major General John W. Bowen, said his outfit "stands ready today, still inspired by the example of Sergeant York." York smiled weakly as the band played "Over There" and "It's a Long Way to Tipperary," then signaled he would have to leave. Cutting the ceremony short, representatives from the 82nd presented him with the keys to a sporty new black Pontiac Star Chief. The right half of its front seat had been removed and the floorboard fitted with special tracks for his wheelchair.

His voice barely audible, York said, "I certainly thank you."

Four muscular paratroopers picked him up from his wheelchair and carried him to a litter. "Don't drop me, boys," the sergeant grinned. The soldiers smiled back, gently placing him in a waiting ambulance for the ride home.

Sergeant York's Nashville attorney, John J. Hooker, thought the deadlock with the IRS might be broken at last. Hooker, with York's old friend John Hale, prepared a stipulation—an agreement on the facts of the case—which government lawyers signed during their court appearance in 1951. It would allow Hooker to try the case in Nashville, based on facts the government accepted as true, without the sergeant being present. After discussing matters, however, York asked that the case be continued in hopes of finally reaching a more favorable compromise. York and Hale promised to prepare a detailed financial statement to present the next time the case came up.

By the time of the new court term, Hooker still had no financial statement and in York's absence, he proposed a settlement based on the stipulation the government agreed to the year before. The new group of government lawyers refused to accept the old stipulation, which they had the right to do, and drew up a different, shorter stipulation. Hooker saw it would not fairly present his case unless supplemented by York's and Hale's testimony.

Stalling for time, Hooker asked for and received another continuance due to Sergeant York's illness. As the years passed York remained too sick to come to Nashville, failed to provide the financial statement as promised, and refused to let Hooker settle unless York was present. The pattern repeated until January 28, 1957, when the court granted what the judge said would be the final continuance. At the next session Hooker had to present a defense or lose by default.

Bringing the sergeant to Nashville was out of the question and by 1957 Hale was deceased. Hooker had heard that York's farm and other property were mortgaged and he might actually owe more than he was worth. But he didn't have the documentation he needed. York, he was told, had virtually no net income, a small veteran's pension of fifty or sixty dollars a month, and since finally applying for it at the end of 1955, the traditional Medal of Honor pension of ten dollars a month.

The day after his 1957 tax court appearance, Hooker's partner, David Keeble, wrote to York, with a copy to Dr. Pinckley, hoping the doctor could impress the seriousness of the situation on his patient. He also explained his firm's belief that the case should be handled by someone else:

> *. . . In view of Sergeant York's desire that the case not be tried unless he is present, a position which we can thoroughly understand, and with which we are in entire accord, it just simply isn't feasible for us to continue to represent Sergeant York. We therefore request a Jamestown attorney be employed to take the matter over. If this is done, we will make absolutely no charge for any work that we have already done, and we will send our complete file to the new attorney and will be glad to talk with him if he will come to Nashville.*

Miss Gracie took over the sergeant's correspondence duties after his hemorrhage. The letter from Hooker's office was disturbing because she had none of the answers he needed, didn't know where to get them, and despaired of putting the case in the hands of a stranger after so many years. She wrote them back asking them not to desert her, still not indicating when or whether she would prepare the financial statement they had waited for more than five years.

Keeble wrote again on March 26:

> *It is not that we do not want to help you and Sergeant York, but there is nothing that we can do from this end of the line. . . . If you will arrange to get that detailed signed audit and then advise us what amount of cash Sergeant York could put up to settle the case, we will see what we can do with the Government. Without that information our hands are tied. . . . Frankly, it has always surprised me that the Government has been as tough and as hard-boiled in this case as it has been, but that is something that we can't do anything about.*

Further exchanges of letters did no good. Miss Gracie continued to express the hope that Hooker would not give up, and Hooker continued to explain that without basic information he could not prepare a case.

As the next tax court date approached, Sergeant York dictated a letter to Gracie. Even if there was a Republican in the White House, he put his trust in his "good Democrat friends" in Congress. York wrote to Senator Estes Kefauver asking him if he could help. (Mr. Hooker received another continuance after all.) Senator Kefauver spoke twice with the IRS Deputy Commissioner and once with Hooker, offering to help settle the matter himself. What the senator would need, he explained, was authorization to act on the sergeant's behalf, and he sent Sergeant York a simple one-paragraph authorization to sign. Befuddled by the paperwork and working through Miss Gracie, York wrote back to Kefauver but did not include the authorization form. Hooker prepared a second form and sent it to York. Kefauver, by then, saw he would have to go ahead without it as best he could.

Continuances were a relief, but the interest clock had been tick-
ing for years, and Alvin York was out of time. The original government claim against York was for $85,442 in additional tax. By the time
Kefauver got involved, interest totaled more than the tax, $87,155.
York's cumulative indebtedness, assuming no penalties were assessed,
was now fixed at $172,597.

Joe L. Evins represented the Fourth District of Tennessee in the
House of Representatives, holding the position Cordell Hull left to
become Roosevelt's Secretary of State. Of course Evins knew his famous
constituent from Fentress County. He visited the sergeant in Pall Mall
and got an occasional letter from him, dictated to Miss Gracie, reminding him of York's position on a legislative issue or asking for an appointment on behalf of a friend. Hearing that the Tennessee legislature had
formally requested the IRS go easy on York and reading other press coverage of the long-running battle between the sergeant and the government, Congressman Evins wrote to the commissioner of the Internal
Revenue Service to see if any sort of compromise were possible.

The acting commissioner, Charles I. Fox, replied that York agreed
he owed taxes on $56,301.15 more income than originally claimed,
which, if the IRS concurred, would mean a tax liability of $29,140.80,
not counting interest or penalty. "As you can see," the commissioner
wrote Evins on April 21, 1959, "this case involves a legal question
which admittedly is not free from doubt," the doubt being whether the
disputed capital gain could be claimed when it was stretched out over
several years, rather than being earned in a lump sum. Fox also assured
Evins that York would be given every legal right to prove his claim,
acknowledging, "determination of taxable income often involves con-
troversies over which reasonable men may disagree." The authorities in
Washington seemed far more inclined to compromise than the "hard-
boiled" agents and lawyers Hooker faced in Nashville.

As he continued his informal investigation, Evins was particularly
curious to find out why York's cinematic "memoirs" were considered
different from the printed memoirs of former president Truman and
President Eisenhower. Both men received special dispensation to count
their book income as a capital gain. Of his million-dollar advance,
President Eisenhower paid $260,000 in income tax, rather than the

$500,000 he would have paid on the amount as regular income. The fact York had received payments over a number of years and continued receiving occasional checks (now from United Artists—who ended up with the picture after all when Warner Bros. sold off the rights to many of their old films in the mid-1950s), blurred the distinction in the government's view. There was no specific event or moment to mark the capital gain.

Another question Evins had for the IRS was why the service could not forgive Sergeant York's income tax liability but could forgive Joe Louis. The "Brown Bomber" was the world heavyweight boxing champion when World War II began and enlisted in the army in 1942 to give boxing exhibitions around the world. Retiring from the ring undefeated in 1949, he tried unsuccessfully to regain the title the following year. In 1956 the government sued Louis for $1,210,789 in back taxes, which the champ could not pay. Louis continued to live the lavish lifestyle of a sports celebrity in spite of his debt and the tax claim was eventually forgiven by the IRS in light of Louis's contribution to the war effort. Why was Sergeant York's lifetime of service to his country any less valuable?

Representative Evins also read with interest a syndicated column by Inez Robb on April 24, in the wake of the 1959 tax filing deadline. She wrote how Sergeant York, bedridden, nearly destitute, and in danger of losing his farm, applied for Social Security benefits the month before. Briefly tracing the story of his battle in the Argonne, the success of the film, and York's financial dilemma, she concluded, "I wish Uncle Sam could find it in his heart to forgive the sergeant his alleged tax indebtedness, a sum the government doesn't really need, and let the old hero end his days in peace and honor."

Joe Evins wrote to Sergeant York and explained that he was going to talk with the IRS on the sergeant's behalf. Evins also scheduled meetings with Attorney General Robert Kennedy, and with House Speaker Sam Rayburn, who had been a member of the welcoming committee on the dock in Hoboken when York returned from France.

In the spring of 1960 the IRS received its long-awaited financial statement from Alvin York, which showed selling everything he owned wouldn't cover even the proposed $29,000 compromise amount, much less the original $172,000. His net worth was $24,813, including $2.20

in a checking account, fifty head of cattle worth $2,750, a 1957 Pontiac Star Chief valued at $750, and miscellaneous machinery and furniture. The farm was appraised at $25,750 but had a $5,300 mortgage. There were also doctor bills, past due real estate taxes, and other debts.

His income for 1959 was $5,739.15, reported as follows:

Sergeant York royalties	$2,662.00
Rental income	$1,249.25
Oil royalties	$329.72
Farm operations—loss	($697.82)
Veteran's pension	$135/month
Social security	$38/month
Medal of Honor pension	$10/month

Evins continued his efforts to find some legal recourse for the sergeant and the new IRS commissioner, Dana Latham, was also trying to come to a settlement with York. The commissioner soon discovered, as York's own lawyer had, that getting a timely or accurate response from Sergeant York was a difficult task at best.

Congressman Evins found a couple of encouraging precedents on the questions of tax relief and the extension of veteran's benefits under extraordinary conditions. Mrs. Eldrey L. Whaley was a widow whose husband, an army major, died in a prisoner of war camp in Korea in 1951. A total of $484.80 was withheld from her husband's pay for taxes during his two years of imprisonment. She successfully petitioned Congress for a refund, even though the Secretary of the Treasury refused her claim because it was not filed in a "timely" manner. Congress therefore could, under special circumstances, override the Treasury on issues related to individual tax claims.

The other precedent dated from 1955 and established that the Veterans Administration could in some cases pay for disabilities not related to military service, such as Sergeant York's. A veteran named Albert Woolson lived in Duluth, Minnesota, 160 miles from the nearest VA hospital in Minneapolis. He was treated several times at a private hospital in Duluth and the VA, citing regulations and the availability of the facility in Minneapolis, refused to reimburse charges estimated at $1,200. Woolson's senators, Edward Thye and Hubert Humphrey, introduced a bill for Woolson's relief, insisting the regulations should be discounted in this case, as Mr. Woolson was 108 years old and the last survivor of the Grand Army of the Republic. The bill passed and the old veteran had all his charges reimbursed, as well as permission to continue receiving treatment at the private hospital.

Buoyed with optimism, Evins introduced two bills in the House during May of 1960. HR 12022, introduced May 2, would treat all of Sergeant York's physical infirmities as service-connected disabilities; HR 12224, introduced ten days later, would relieve him of all tax liability for 1942 and 1943. Both bills were rejected by a judiciary subcommittee because they dealt with issues "covered by general statutes." Evins's precedents required the committee to waive the general statutes rule, also known as Rule 12. In the case of Sergeant York, the committee refused to do so.

Evins sent Commissioner Latham a copy of the April 24 column by Inez Robb. "The debt the Nation owes this hero, not only for his service during the war but through the fact that his life has been a model of patriotic behavior, cannot be estimated in dollars and cents," Evins wrote, and went on to point out York's philanthropic work, the inestimable morale building value of the movie, and the precedents involving capital gains from memoirs of Truman and Eisenhower, which were not set when the York case was enjoined in 1951.

"Regardless of technicalities there is no question that from the point of simple equity this transaction . . . is comparable to that through which President Eisenhower and former President Truman disposed of their life stories and were granted the capital gains privilege." Furthermore, he noted, "Sergeant York is not in a position to pay this tax liability and there is no hope of collecting it since his means are rapidly being dissipated and he is nearly destitute."

The IRS remained unmoved on the capital gains question, though the agency accepted the revised settlement amount of $29,140.80 as the most it could expect under the circumstances. News of his financial crisis brought Sergeant York back into the national headlines. The trickle of reporters and interviewers never stopped over the years; with

Congressman Evins's bills on the floor of the House, the pace of their visits increased.

Visitors from a generation ago would have seen few changes in the house. Except for the radiators, electric stove, and indoor plumbing, York, Miss Gracie, and Gracie's sister Kansas lived as they had when they moved in on Valentine's Day, 1922. A knock at the door was answered by Miss Gracie, still slender and graceful, and still with the long braids Alvin loved so much coiled on each side of her head, though they were gray now instead of honey blonde.

Alvin received visitors sitting on the edge of his bed with a blanket in his lap or in a wheelchair in his room. His vision was poor, the right eye completely blind and the left weak but he still delighted in company. His handshake was strong and firm; to one visitor it was more like gripping a baseball glove than a hand. His voice was still firm. The invitation to supper still inevitable.

To a new generation of reporters, Alvin York was the last remnant of another world. These reporters lived in a world of transistors, air conditioning, and jet airplanes. In Huntsville, Alabama, a day's drive from Pall Mall, men were working on a rocket to send an astronaut into outer space. Here in the Valley of the Three Forks of the Wolf, the old soldier they'd come to see was born in a log cabin, plowed a field with mules, and fought a war without radios, C-rations, or atomic bombs.

York had little to say about his tax troubles. "I gave the government half of it," he said of his movie royalties, "and told 'em the other half was mine." He told visitors why he refused the offers made to him early on. "I could see how far our mountain country was behind the times. Not having any learning myself, I wanted it for the boys coming up. We needed schools and roads, and because I could get in to see governors, I made schools and roads—and the Bible—my life work.

"I raised all the money I could, and as fast as it come in, I spent it. I never had enough." He admitted poor bookkeeping was partly responsible for his situation. "I got no education, so I never tried to understand all that stuff."

He knew President Truman as a legionnaire before World War II and thought he was a good leader. But York had little respect for Eisenhower because he thought he knuckled under to Soviet Premier Nikita

Khrushchev in negotiations. "Eisenhower ought to quit trying to give
Russia everything we've got. You can't buy friendship! . . . When Khrushchev called him a liar in Paris, he should have mashed his mouth. I don't
believe Khrushchev would have called MacArthur a liar, or Patton, or
Harry Truman."

A group of soldiers from the 82nd Division came to call. York
entertained them sitting on his bed, demonstrating his form with an
old muzzle-loader and on request, taking his Medal of Honor and other
awards out of a locker at the foot of his bed to pass them around. York
asked the men what they thought of Castro, whose exploits were much
in the news. The old sergeant had no patience with the Communist
guerrillas. Staring at a master sergeant sitting beside him with his good
eye, York asked suddenly, "When are you gonna take a battalion of
Airborne down there and settle Castro's hash?" There was, after all, a
weapon that would blow Castro and his regime sky high. "Next war
we get into, we'd better do it with the A-bomb. And if they can't get
anybody else to push the button, I will."

In an article for *Cavalier* magazine, William Bradford Huie wrote
of his visit with Sergeant York in the summer of 1960. Joe Evins was
moved enough by it to have the entire article entered into the appendix
of the *Congressional Record* for August 26. Huie's solution to the sergeant's tax problem was a novel one. "Why don't we figure those dead
Germans at $1,000 apiece, then allow an extra $1,000 for all those prisoners? . . . The Defense Department should then pay Sergeant York a
sergeant's wages for 4 years for all that morale work he did in the camps
during the Second World War. . . . then add interest at six percent." The
result, Huie figured, would allow the sergeant to live the rest of his life
"in peace and dignity."

"We'd better take care of the sergeant," Huie warned. "For when
we sound Taps over him on a Cumberland mountainside, his breed
will end. Suburbia doesn't grow heroes; and we can't write ballads about
Americans who bolt wheels onto Chevrolets, drink beer, and watch
Gunsmoke."

Chapter Twenty-Seven

A Great Country

Joe Evins continued working to reduce Alvin York's debt to the government. Meanwhile, a small American Legion post devised a plan to pay it. The Jere Cooper Post in Dyersburg, Tennessee, undertook to raise the funds for retiring the sergeant's debt by soliciting members and encouraging Legion posts throughout the state to do the same. As the drive gathered momentum through the summer of 1960, more than twenty posts passed resolutions and joined in the campaign.

The Legion's target date for raising the necessary twenty-nine thousand dollars to pay York's compromise settlement was Armistice Day, November 11. Tennessee posts, along with national Legion leadership, began planning an Argonne anniversary celebration for October 8, to honor York and tell him about the progress of the fund-raising. As the date drew nearer, plans for the event grew more elaborate. Tennessee Governor Buford Ellington and other state dignitaries would attend. There would also be a special presentation by Dr. Homer H. Stryker, a member of American Legion Post 332 in Kalamazoo, Michigan. Dr. Stryker was the inventor of the Circ-O-Lectric Bed, a hospital bed mounted between two parallel six-foot metal circles. With the touch of a few buttons, the bed would articulate like a regular hospital bed and would also track around the circle to a sitting position or to a leaning position to help Miss Gracie get her husband (still at two hundred pounds after six years of paralysis) in and out of bed.

Three hundred well-wishers waited in the front yard that cool October afternoon as four legionnaires gingerly worked the big, high frame of the bed through the front door and onto the porch of Sergeant York's house. The sergeant talked easily with old friends, reporters, and passersby, answering questions about current events in his still-big voice. Yes, the United Nations was helping ease world tensions. No, he didn't like Vice President Nixon as a candidate for president any more than he liked Eisenhower. Always a faithful Democrat, Sergeant York would be voting for Kennedy.

He demonstrated his new bed using the hand-held push-button unit. He grinned broadly at his audience as the bed moved through its paces, observing, "Just about everything seems to be push-button these days, including me."

The fund-raising campaign, which started so auspiciously, was turning into a disappointment for Dyersburg Legion members. By Veteran's Day, 1960, total contributions statewide stood at less than three thousand dollars. The group doggedly pursued its goal regardless, hoping a big donation or prominent sponsor would reignite the drive.

York wrote to the Veterans Administration in another attempt to be certified to receive nonservice related disability benefits. Required to answer specific questions about his condition, the old soldier swallowed his pride and complied:

> *I am unable to dress or undress myself unassisted, not able to get in and out of bed without assistance, unable to feed myself without help, unable to attend the normal wants of nature unassisted. . . . I am truly a helpless invalid and feel that I am entitled to benefits commensurate with my condition and am trusting in your wisdom to so decide.*

Joe Evins pressed forward with energy and determination, looking for some sort of crack in the bureaucratic Washington defenses. By the first week of January 1961, Evins introduced yet another "Bill for the Relief of Sergeant Alvin York." He met again with IRS Commissioner

Latham, with Speaker Sam Rayburn, and with Attorney General Robert Kennedy, who suggested the incoming president, his brother John (who sent the sergeant a personal invitation to the Inaugural Ball), might consider an executive order relieving York of his liability.

Evins took this idea to the Treasury and Justice Departments and discussed it with legal counsel of the House of Representatives. The overwhelming opinion was that the need and justification for such an order was certainly there, but the legal issue of the president's authority for such an action was very much in question. Besides, such a precedent could be disastrous for a future chief executive. They advised against it and Attorney General Kennedy and Evins did not ask the president for help.

In a later meeting with Speaker Rayburn to ask for his support on the most recent House bill to help York, Evins listened with interest as the Speaker proposed another approach. Rayburn suggested the two of them assemble a private fund-raising committee to solicit contributions nationwide for York's tax bill. If they couldn't erase the liability, perhaps they could pay it off.

On March 18, 1961, Speaker Rayburn announced the formation of the Help Sergeant York Committee, with himself as chairman. Evins was treasurer, with other members including Attorney General Kennedy, Silliman Evans Jr., publisher of the Nashville *Tennessean*, Gary Cooper, and Evins's assistant Robert Moore as executive secretary. Rayburn made the first donation himself, a check for $1,000, and Evins matched it.

The Help Sergeant York Committee gave Americans a way to do something for the old hero they had been reading about in both history books and newspapers the past few months. Evins sent a note to the postmaster general's office asking the department to be on the lookout for any envelopes addressed to Sergeant York and sent to Washington. Within days the floodgates of thanks opened wide.

C. Douglas Dillon, Secretary of the Treasury, donated one thousand dollars. Oveta Culp Hobby, a Houston newspaper publisher who founded the Women's Army Corps during World War II, sent another thousand, as did Eastern Air Lines president and World War I ace Eddie Rickenbacker. Warner Bros. donated $2,500.

When told the Help Sergeant York Committee was up and running, the sergeant leaned back in his push-button bed and let out a long sigh of relief. "I'm mighty grateful," he said simply. "Those tax folks have been a-houndin' me so long and I been a-fightin' them so long I just thought it'd never end."

When informed the government had finally agreed to settle for twenty-five thousand dollars, down from the twenty-nine thousand previously proposed (and only a fraction of the original $172,000), he replied, "Seems funny, talking about reducin' something I don't owe." Without irony or bitterness, he continued. "This tax business has been troubling us a long time and we really worried about it. We sure appreciate everything these fine people have done for us and are doing."

He settled back in the sheets, glancing out the window at the river and the mountains beyond. "You know," he said almost nonchalantly, "this is a great country."

Sergeant York's favorite television program was *The Ed Sullivan Show*, a Sunday night institution for millions of families across the country. Sullivan was a newspaper columnist turned impresario, whose wooden presence before the television cameras made him the butt of frequent jokes. But as host of a weekly network variety show, broadcast live from New York, he had a remarkable sense of what America wanted to see and hear and gave it to them, whether it was trick dogs or Elvis Presley (from the waist up).

The Help Sergeant York Committee contacted Sullivan and asked him to make an appeal for their cause on his show. After checking with the FCC to make sure there was no legal impediment, Sullivan gladly agreed. At the beginning of his broadcast on Sunday night March 26, Sullivan stood alone in front of the stage curtain and told York's story, simply and with genuine conviction. As the studio orchestra softly played "Over There," Sullivan ad-libbed the essential facts about York's heroic deeds and his current financial troubles. Then: "If all of you throughout the country agree with me that this is a cruel, ironic, and heartbreaking thing to happen to one of America's greatest heroes, won't you sit down with me tonight after our show and send whatever small or large sum of money you can afford to the Sergeant York Fund, Washington, D.C."

Sullivan got his musical cue that the time allotted for the appeal was up. A Colgate Dental Creme commercial was ready to air. He continued. "Never let it be said that when the chips were down for Sergeant York, we pulled away from him. Because certainly, with the chips down, he never pulled away from us."

In its first week the committee took in more than thirteen thousand dollars. After Ed Sullivan's heartfelt speech, the money came in even faster, much of it one or two dollars at a time, the cash stuffed in envelopes and mailed with handwritten notes. Network television did more for the beleaguered sergeant in two minutes than the American Legion and Joe Evins were able to do in a year. Eventually more than eight thousand letters were received. Evins kept every one and his office sent each donor a reply. The comments reflected the love Americans still harbored for their humble hero.

"From one vet to another. Wish it could be more."

"If I had money, I'd pay it all for him."

"If each WWI vet paid his share of Sgt. York's tax bill it would be less than ⅞ of 1 cent so I will pay my share & make up for a few that can't pay. I'll always remember what Pershing told the boys of the 36th Div when he inspected them before coming home—to take an active part in politics and let no one push you around."

"I am a boy of 13 enclosing just one dollar. Its not much compared to what Sgt. York gave, but I hope it helps."

"I don't care for the Russians but I don't think they would have used Sgt. York as rotten as we have."

"Enclosed is a very, very small tribute to Sgt. York and my only apprehension is that it may pay part of someone's salary in the Internal Revenue Department. Instead of Sgt. York owing us $25,000, we owe him $25,000—at least. We were by his

side when he was paraded down 5th Avenue as a hero. We
should be more willing to be by his side now."

"When I am your age I will tell about my biggest honor.
That is that I wrote to you and I realy mean it Mr. York! And I
am enclosing 25¢ to help you. I saw a movie about your young
manhood about when you became close to God. I cried I was so
happy I realy did."

By April 8, the Help Sergeant York Committee received $27,000, with envelopes continuing to pour in. On April 19, Joe Evins presented a check for twenty-five thousand dollars to IRS Commissioner Mortimer C. Caplin. The commissioner had to field a few questions concerning whether or not he was letting the old soldier off too easy and insisted there was "no special advantage" involved. In a letter to the sergeant announcing the settlement of his case, Caplin wrote, "The response of the American people in helping you dispose of this matter is a genuine tribute to you and what you did for your great country."

Hearing the news brought another wide grin to the sergeant's face. "I'm tickled to death to hear about this," he said. "Anybody would be. You know, every time somebody makes the load of life a little lighter, it's good to hear about it."

By the time Congressman Evins turned the balance of the Help Sergeant York Committee funds over to John J. Hooker in Nashville to deposit on York's behalf, there was a surplus of almost twenty-five thousand dollars. Hooker set up a trust fund designed to pay the sergeant and Miss Gracie about $200 a month as long as they lived.

In May, Evins received a letter from attorneys representing S. Hallock du Pont, a financier and member of the great Delaware industrial dynasty, informing him Mr. du Pont wanted to help and honor Sergeant York and was setting up a trust fund to do so. The fund, holding stock and paying out dividends, would provide York $300 a month for the rest of his life.

On behalf of Sergeant York, Congressman Evins accepted du Pont's gracious gift. Getting wind of the du Pont fund, representatives of the Veterans Administration contacted Evins to say they would be forced to review Sergeant York's eligibility for his $138 monthly pension, since his income now put him above the threshold for receiving benefits. The VA subsequently stopped York's June check. He never got another one.

York suffered an intestinal hemorrhage on May 26, 1961, and spent Memorial Day in the hospital at Jamestown. Dr. Pinckley assured the public there was no cause to "get too alarmed" and was able to stop the internal bleeding and send his patient home in time to celebrate his forty-second wedding anniversary. The end of his tax troubles after so many years made the celebration that June 7 all the more festive, with the accustomed crowd of reporters, politicians, strangers, and friends all on hand to pay their respects and wish the couple well. Alvin and Miss Gracie posed for pictures, she standing beside the bed, the sergeant propped up and holding a big anniversary cake on his lap baked by his niece, Elva Jean Clouse. The cake was decorated with a large waving American flag rendered in icing.

One of the photographers said, "Give him a kiss, Miss Gracie." She leaned over and pressed her lips to her husband's cheek. Cameras flashed and there was a smattering of applause as she stood up straight again. Her children watched in astonishment at this simple demonstration of affection. Since the couple always shared affectionate moments either alone or hiding in the front closet, none of the family ever saw them kiss before.

The Circ-O-Lectric bed, affectionately called the "Ferris wheel bed," was a genuine comfort to York and a help to Miss Gracie in assisting him. Its only liability was it barely fit on the front porch. Once it was worked through the door, there was no room outside to maneuver and no room for anyone else to walk from the top of the porch steps to the threshold. His friends solved this inconvenience by removing the porch and replacing it with a large veranda running completely across the front of the house. The roofline of the house was extended overhead and a row of square two-story columns ran from the eaves down to the front edge of a wide, smooth cement surface the bed could roll across easily.

Sergeant York faded from the national headlines and spent a quiet year in Pall Mall. He was completely confined to bed now and spent most of his time in his bedroom, with occasional visits to the new veranda or to the side porch, which was now screened in. His pneumonia reappeared from time to time and intestinal bleeding and inflammation came and went. He never complained and continued to receive visitors eagerly, discussing current events and prospects for the hay crop.

One visitor was Ike Hatfield. Ike and the sergeant hadn't spoken in years, and York asked his friend Leo Hatfield, Ike's nephew, if he would invite Ike to come over. When Leo extended the invitation, his uncle replied, "Well, let me get a clean shirt on." The two Hatfields returned to the sergeant's house later the same day, and Ike sat down beside the bed in York's room.

The two old friends talked late into the night about their long-ago afternoons on the hillsides, crouched beside a campfire among a circle of friends, listening for the glorious chorus signaling their hunting dogs were on the scent.

"Mine got it first," came the shout.

"I believe yours was second," was the expected reply.

"Boys, your hearing can't be what it used to be. That dog's mine!" another would say as they all grabbed their hog rifles and took off through the brush.

The crickets kept up their commotion outside the bedroom window as the old farmers recalled the good times and bad in their long lives: the corn shuckings and square dances; the weddings and funerals; the children and friends who died too soon. When Ike stood to leave, it was after midnight. Tears ran freely down his cheeks, as they did down his friend's; neither reached up to wipe them away. He shook Alvin's hand—both men's hands big and thick, the handshake firm—and walked outside across the cement veranda into the mild night air.

By the summer of 1962, Dr. Pinckley was sending his most famous patient to the hospital in Nashville with increasing frequency. On June 29, Sergeant York underwent prostate surgery. The surgery was successful, but the hospital stay aggravated his pneumonia. His blood pressure remained erratic, his intestinal bleeding persisted, and doctors suspected a blood clot in his lung. Gracie brought him home after the operation but soon found herself on the way to Nashville with him again, her husband short of breath and in pain.

Gracie's sister Kansas, nearing eighty, still lived with the family, as did the two youngest sons, Andrew and Thomas, their wives, and six grandchildren. Andy and Tommy helped around the farm, but it fell to Miss Gracie to attend to her husband and manage the family's affairs. Apart from signing an occasional picture or letter, the sergeant didn't write any more. Gracie kept the books, corresponded with the doctors, and kept in touch with John J. Hooker regarding the annuity they now enjoyed.

She wrote to Joe Evins on November 23, 1962, asking whether any of the money he took care of for them could be used to pay her 1961 property taxes. The check was overdue at the county tax assessor's office and she hoped the fund could be used to settle the debt before the interest built up too much more. Her cash shortage was compounded by a barn fire on September 3 that destroyed all her hay for the winter. "Sgt. York is not feeling much good and I don't want to have him worried about these taxes unpaid," she wrote. "As that money was put there for him to use as he needed it I hate to bother you about this but sure would love to know if his taxes could be paid out of that fund." She also still owed the surgeon $275 for her husband's prostate surgery the summer before.

Evins forwarded the letter to Hooker in Nashville and he wrote explaining the bank might not be able legally to pay the taxes. Hooker asked Miss Gracie for an accounting of taxes owed and a letter signed by herself and all the children authorizing the bank to pay on their behalf. She sent the paperwork and the taxes were eventually paid out of the account.

Astronaut John Glenn became the first American to orbit the earth; the Russians sent nuclear missiles to Cuba and took them back again; the New York Yankees won the American League pennant for the eleventh time in thirteen years but lost the World Series to their transplanted former crosstown rivals, the San Francisco Giants. President Kennedy enjoyed a rest stop in the same Houston hotel where York stayed on his speaking tour in 1920, then died the next day in Dallas at the hands of an assassin. The American military began turning its attention to the ruins of French Indochina and the new regime in Vietnam.

Alvin York kept up with current events in a world he could never have imagined as a youngster. He continued to watch television, read the newspapers, and pump friends for information and opinions about all that was going on. He sent Colonel Glenn a telegram congratulating him on his space voyage, saying he did more for peace in one day than the rest of the world did in twenty years. He also said he thought the space program was a good idea but the government was spending too much money on it. His cure for the evils of the world was the same as always. December 13, 1963, was his seventy-sixth birthday and he explained to the customary large crowd that respect for freedom and righteousness weren't what they used to be in America.

"If this country ever falls," he told his birthday revelers, "it will fall from within. I think we've just got to go back to the old time religion, shouting as though the world is on fire. Maybe people will realize we've gotten onto some wrong roads and return to the old paths."

Between hospital stays he was as curious and as cordial as ever but the trips became more frequent. A kidney infection in April restricted him to a liquid diet. From the hospital, Gracie wrote to her niece Elva Jean in Jamestown. "I sure would hate real bad if I was to haft to give him up but if the Lord wants him to come on home to live with him of course he will haft to go. He said today that if he did not go back home that he would go to Heaven."

York and Gracie were able to return to Pall Mall, where they spent a few peaceful months. Gradually weakening, he still gleefully gave his grandchildren rides on his electric bed, letting them push the buttons raising it to a sitting position and back down again. He lapsed into a coma on January 29, 1964, and recovered in a Jamestown hospital. Intestinal bleeding and pneumonia sent him back to Nashville in June.

On August 29, 1964, Sergeant Alvin York entered Veterans Hospital in Nashville with an acute urinary tract infection. It was his fourth hospital confinement of the year, his eleventh in two years. Despite antibiotics and life support equipment, York's condition continued to decline. Gracie and her son George Edward, now a Nazarene minister, kept watch in the sergeant's room. The patient's eyes followed Ed around the hospital room. Though York could no longer speak or move, Ed was sure his father could hear and understand him. The sergeant fell into a coma the next day; it was clear the old hero's last hours were near at hand. At lunch with his mother, Ed York voiced what he and Miss Gracie were both thinking. "Dad's not going home this time. We may as well shape up for it."

On his last birthday someone had asked him how he felt. "The Lord's been good to me despite everything," he answered. "I'm seventy-six now and I believe I'll still make it to a hundred. I just ought to be able to coast that far." Wednesday morning, September 2, Miss Gracie and George took a break from their hospital vigil to go for a drive and do a little shopping. A nurse called the store and had them paged. Before they got back, Sergeant York died peacefully without regaining consciousness.

An honor guard from the Nashville American Legion lined Gracie's path as she walked beside her husband's casket from the hospital door to a hearse. Governor Frank Clement offered to have the body lie in state at the Tennessee Capitol; President Johnson sent word that York could be buried with full military honors at Arlington Cemetery. But the sergeant had made his wishes plain on the matter. "When I die they'll put me away with the rest of the folks in the old family graveyard," he said. Now Miss Gracie was taking him back to lie with the rest of Old Coonrod's people.

On Friday morning Sergeant York's open casket, draped with the Stars and Stripes, was placed on the side porch of the big white house on the Wolf River. People lined up outside the door, through the yard, and on down York Highway, quietly waiting in the warm summer sun for their turn to pay their last respects. People who knew Sergeant York all their lives passed the time in line with those who never saw him before, sharing their thoughts, crying unashamed. Six hundred students from the York Agricultural Institute signed a special register after filing by. Neighbors, observing the traditional southern custom, slipped up the back steps with a casserole or a pot of beans to keep Miss Gracie out of the kitchen for a few days.

The next morning was clear and warm, as was Friday, with a cloudless light-blue sky. As the sun cleared the mountain rim behind the house, the casket was moved to York Chapel a mile up the road, where a large crowd waited outside. The small church quickly filled with family members and dignitaries. Arriving later, Lorene Cargile, a daughter of York's sister Lucy, was stopped with other relatives at the door and told no more room was available. "It's not too crowded for us. We're family." The doorkeeper stepped aside.

Reverend R. D. Brown, former pastor of York Chapel, drove down from Wilkesville, Ohio, to conduct the funeral. As he prepared to begin the service, loudspeakers were set up outside the church so everyone could hear. Thousands gathered around York Chapel, with thousands more beginning to congregate at the York family cemetery plot across from the Methodist church back across the river. Tennessee Highway Patrol officers supplemented the troops of the Jamestown police in an effort to keep traffic moving through the valley. Cars were parked by the hundreds in fields and along the road.

A fence across the street from the chapel was taken down to make more parking room. Local residents established an informal shuttle service, offering rides in their trucks and wagons to those who decided to park at the valley's edge and walk the rest of the way, men trailing hay from the cuffs of their Sunday suits, women picking their way through tobacco fields with their high heels in their hands.

President Lyndon Johnson sent Lieutenant General Matthew B. Ridgway, commander of the 82nd Division during World War II and later NATO commander, as his personal representative. The 82nd also sent a band and full honor guard. Eight thousand people watched as the casket was carried to the gravesite by six members of the 82nd in crisp khakis and gleaming jump boots, a sergeant in the lead on each side. Gracie followed immediately behind, leaning on her son George, with Reverend Brown close beside. Dressed in black, Gracie wore a hat covered with black ribbon and cried quietly into a white lace handkerchief as she watched the soldiers.

The band played hymns the sergeant requested, "Fairest Lord Jesus," "Faith of Our Fathers," and his favorite, "Onward, Christian Soldiers." A twenty-one gun salute echoed across the valley. Into the enormous following silence, a bugler sent the slow, measured notes of Taps. The casket was lowered and the pallbearers pulled taut the draped flag, creasing its length and folding the prescribed triangle shape with military precision. Sergeant Major Paul Huff, a close friend and Medal of Honor recipient in World War II, presented the flag to Miss Gracie.

Accompanying its account of the funeral, the *Fentress County Leader-Times* ran a large photograph of the sergeant on the front page. He was standing in his living room in late middle age, bespectacled and portly, dressed in wrinkled work clothes, and had an intent expression on his face as he ran a ramrod down the bore of his beloved muzzle loader. No doubt he was a war hero. But this was the man his friends knew and lost. This was the memory they would always cherish.

In the fall of 1965, Gracie York wrote to Sam M. Fleming, chairman of Third National Bank in Nashville, where the Help Sergeant York Committee trust fund was set up. York died without a will; court filings showed his net worth to be $5,000. Gracie wanted to know if any of the trust fund money could be used to buy the sergeant a grave monument. "I sure think he deserves a nice one," she said.

The fund could not legally be used for a monument, he answered, but Fleming had another idea. He sent Gracie's letter to his friend and fellow Third National board member Lipscomb Davis, who had traveled with York on his first fund-raising tours in 1919 and 1920. Davis built a successful furniture manufacturing business over the years and kept in touch with the York family from time to time.

Davis wrote to Miss Gracie to say he would be pleased to take on the task of raising the money for an appropriate memorial. He said he never forgot the joy of their travels together. "My life was made much richer by the year I spent traveling with you and with the Sergeant," he wrote on October 8, 1965. "It was a great opportunity for a young man. . . ."

A monument worthy of the sergeant's memory, Gracie learned, would cost between forty-five hundred and five thousand dollars. "I don't think that is too much money for Mr. York for he deserves all I can do for him," she wrote to Davis. She also shared the depth of her loneliness a year after her husband's death. "I have had plenty of wearies since Mr. York passed away beside wearing about his absence. Oh Lipscomb I just could not tell you how much I do miss him. And of course I always will miss him as I had him to go to for advice and to comfort me until he got so sick. . . . Even if he did have to stay in bed I could talk with him. But the good Lord called him away from this old world of suffering and sorrow to a world of peace and happiness where suffering will be no more."

Davis immediately wrote to Governor Clement to ask whether the state would consider appropriating the money. The governor replied the state had already appropriated fifty thousand dollars for the Tennessee Historical Commission to fund a statue of Sergeant York for the capitol grounds. Clement suggested that any surplus not needed for the statue could be used for the gravesite monument. The procurement request would have to work its way through proper channels and the money set aside.

Miss Gracie was not inclined to wait. She wanted the monument completed by Memorial Day, 1966. So she took out a sixty-five-hundred-dollar mortgage loan on her farm, most of which was to purchase the monument. Eager to reimburse her, Lipscomb Davis took up the matter of fund-raising with the American Legion. Surely, he thought, they would contribute to so worthy a project for such a hero, who also happened to be one of their charter members.

The Legion replied it was one of the first and largest donors to the Help Sergeant York Committee and informed Davis the membership "would not be receptive" to another plea for funds on the sergeant's behalf.

Davis then contacted the Veterans of Foreign Wars, explaining his long acquaintance with Sergeant York and his conviction that a campaign for the monument would require little effort from so large and active a membership. "If each of your posts would merely publicize the fact that funds were being solicited on a voluntary basis, I believe the amount could be raised."

The VFW also had its plate full in terms of solicitations and projects. On Memorial Day, 1966, the organization was dedicating the Tennessee Cottage at the VFW National Home in Eaton Rapids, Michigan, marking the conclusion of a sixty-thousand-dollar fund-raising effort. The members felt they could not take on another significant project but would be glad to make a contribution.

Two dead ends sent Davis back to one of his original prospects, the Tennessee Historical Society (a separate entity from the Tennessee Historical Commission, which funded the statue). He suggested the Society solicit contributions from the public as tax-deductible gifts and use them to reimburse Miss Gracie.

The president of the Society, Henry Goodpasture, said he didn't think his group's participation would be a good idea. First, he thought soliciting donations might hamper an ongoing drive for new members, as there seemed to be no precedent for such an appeal. Second, if the Society could not endorse the effort directly, they should not support it indirectly. Third, Goodpasture misunderstood Davis's earlier inquiry; the Society was more enthusiastic at first because Goodpasture thought Davis was asking if he could make a special gift to the Society and have it handled as a tax deduction.

Davis's reply was uncharacteristically tart, though characteristically on point. "I would find myself in agreement with the conclusion which you and the others reached. It would be unfortunate if the Society did start a program of solicitation of funds for various historically worthwhile projects. Quite understanding, I will look elsewhere for a sponsor for my project."

Meanwhile, Miss Gracie watched proudly as the monument to her husband took form in the Wolf River Cemetery. Its two most prominent features were a ten-foot Georgia granite cross and an angel of Italian marble kneeling in prayer. Sergeant York's headstone was incised with a World War I helmet, rifle, and Medal of Honor. A twenty-foot flagpole rose to one side, and the ground around the area was paved with marble chips. There was a stack of granite books symbolizing the sergeant's love of education with the inscription, "Proverbs 14:34," his favorite Bible verse. Visitors noticing the Scripture notation turned their eyes expectantly to Gracie, waiting for her to quote it. Her eyes invariably met theirs with a wry smile. "Look it up," was all she would say.

The York statue on the capitol grounds consumed all the funding set aside for it; there would be no surplus for the Pall Mall memorial. The solution came at last from the office of the new governor, Buford Ellington. Money from the state's annual miscellaneous appropriations bill could be used to repay Mrs. York for her expenses. On November 9, 1967, the state issued a check for five thousand dollars to Citizens Bank of Albany, Kentucky, to the credit of Mrs. Alvin C. York. She was able to pay off the rest of the mortgage balance, about fourteen hundred dollars, and soon reclaimed the deed to four hundred acres of fine Tennessee farmland.

Chapter Twenty-Eight

A Hero's Legacy

Miss Gracie continued to live in the old homeplace with Kansas, Tommy, and Tommy's wife and two children. Visitors to the gravesite stopped frequently at the house, thinking it was a museum. As always, Gracie opened her door to everyone and talked freely about the sergeant.

Gracie sold the York Mill and eight acres surrounding it to the Tennessee State Conservation Department for ten thousand dollars and watched with delight as it was restored. Picnic grounds were added, playground equipment installed, and open air pavilions built. Engineers said the mill, though needing a roof and a coat of paint, was as sturdy as the day Sergeant York bought it. After its dedication as a state park on October 11, 1967, Gracie's son Andrew was appointed park ranger to oversee his father's old enterprise.

The next year Gracie attended the unveiling of her husband's statue on the capitol grounds in Nashville. The Tennessee Historical Commission conducted extensive research and gave detailed consideration to sculptors around the world who might qualify for the job at hand. One member of the committee mentioned the Iwo Jima memorial and its seven marines hoisting the American flag on the battlefield. It was the largest cast bronze statue in the world. It was also historically accurate, classically proportioned, and instilled with an admirable combination of immediacy and timelessness.

The sculptor was Felix de Weldon, Austrian born, who worked in a Washington, DC studio built originally for artisans who had decorated the Capitol. De Weldon was a naturalized American citizen and navy veteran who previously sculpted three English kings and two American presidents. He also completed two World War I projects: a monument at the American cemetery in Belleau Wood and an equestrian statue of General Pershing to replace one in Paris destroyed by the Germans during World War II.

After the commission awarded de Weldon the project, he visited the capitol lawn in the spring of 1967, eventually producing sketches and models of a ten-foot standing bronze of York poised for action, left foot forward, right foot braced behind him, sighting down his rifle. He was dressed in battle gear including helmet, web belt, and wrapped leggings. ("Those things always came undone the first hour," the sergeant noted, pleased to see his World War II counterparts had laced leggings.)

The sculpture was completed in Washington, then sent to the Francesco Bruni Foundry in Rome for casting. The original plan was to dedicate the statue on October 8, 1968, the fiftieth anniversary of York's Argonne battle, but the statue was not shipped from Italy in time. Arriving in Baltimore by sea and continuing by rail to Nashville, it was unveiled on December 13, which would have been the sergeant's eighty-first birthday. Miss Gracie, Governor Ellington, and Sergeant Major Huff joined the crowd gathered at the southeast corner of the capitol grounds on a bluff above the Cumberland River. The statue stood covered by an enormous red velvet drape billowing in the cold wind beneath a dark, overcast sky. Gracie pulled a rope and the drape cascaded to the ground, revealing the towering image, mounted atop a block of black Norwegian granite.

Robert McGaw, a member of the monument committee, recalled York's heroic victory and remarked on the rarity of such courage. "Common sense tells us that one man armed with a rifle and pistol could not defeat a battalion of machine guns. But the monument is there and we are here because Alvin York did it. . . . There is considerable doubt that any other man could have done it."

By the time Sergeant York died, Gracie had survived three of her children—her first son, who lived only four days in 1920; Sam Houston, who died before his second birthday in 1929; and an unnamed daughter who was born and died November 2, 1940, as production on *Sergeant York* was about to begin in Hollywood.

Her youngest, Thomas, returned to Pall Mall from a tour in the Air Force and resumed his responsibilities on the farm. He also took a job as a park ranger at the York Mill and another as a Fentress County constable. He was on duty just after midnight the morning of May 7, 1972, when he was called to investigate a one-car accident on York Highway at Buzzard's Roost Road, about a mile from the Kentucky line. Leaving a local nightspot called the Candlelight Inn, the driver ran off the road and hit a tree. Constable York arrived at the scene to find the man uninjured but highly intoxicated.

He arrested the man and put him in the back seat of his patrol car. As York drove back toward Jamestown, his passenger became more and more violent. He stopped on the shoulder of the road, got out, and opened the rear passenger door to settle his prisoner. The man pulled a .38 Derringer and fired. Constable York drew his service revolver and fired three shots. The prisoner, a car salesman from Albany, Kentucky, was shot twice in the arm and once in the chest. York was shot once in the face at point blank range. When a passerby stopped a few minutes later, both men were dead.

An investigation concluded York and his prisoner fought alone, but Miss Gracie continued to insist there was an ambush or some other element to the story. The case was closed officially, though Gracie refused to accepted the inquiry's findings.

Miss Gracie never accompanied Sergeant York on his trips to California. Pregnancy, illness, or responsibilities at home always prevented her from accepting invitations from Warner Bros. and others to ride west on the Santa Fe *Chief* with her husband. In 1983 she went at last, though by air rather than rail. The army had developed a new air defense system for armored columns, officially designated the Division Air Defense Gun but known as the Sergeant York gun. Miss Gracie was invited to attend its rollout on September 1, 1983. Even though Alvin Jr. died the week before after a long battle with lung cancer, Gracie was determined to make the trip as a gesture of thanks to those who wanted to honor her husband.

At the reception, hosted by Ford Aerospace, the project contractor, Gracie had a surprise waiting in the person of Joan Leslie, whom she had never met in person. Leslie heard Gracie's voice on the records she and the sergeant made to help the actors with their Tennessee accents and the two women spoke by phone the night of the Nashville movie premiere. Now they were introduced at last and spent much of the evening together reminiscing about the movie and its impact on their lives.

The York gun consisted of two forty-millimeter cannon linked to special radar and computer systems and mounted on a modified tank chassis. The system was supposed to calculate the path of enemy aircraft, then aim the cannon so their shells would intersect the plane's flight path. Initial trials were promising, but further testing disclosed unreliable guns and ineffective radar. Some critics later said the York was no better than the much cheaper Vulcan system—a mobile twenty-millimeter gatling gun—it was designed to replace. The York was eventually abandoned after seven years and $1.5 billion in costs, one of the largest weapons programs ever stopped in midstream.

A little more than a year after her California trip, Miss Gracie went to the hospital in Jamestown for tests to see why she wasn't feeling well. Discharged after six days, she became violently ill the day after returning to Pall Mall and was taken to a bigger hospital in Crossville. She was then transferred to Park View Hospital in Nashville, only a short distance from the Veterans Hospital where the sergeant went so often in his final years.

Miss Gracie's condition gradually deteriorated and she died at Park View on September 27, 1984, at the age of eighty-four. Her funeral was held in York Chapel; she was buried in the evening gown she wore during her California trip, laid to rest beside the husband she missed so dearly, beneath the fine and fitting monument she designed herself. She also selected her own epitaph: "Mother of 10 children 'Therefore be ye also ready; for in such an hour as ye think not the Son of Man cometh,' Matt. 24:44." The marble walks were neat as always, the shrubs grown tall and lush around them. Planting the hedge with their own hands eighteen years before saved Gracie and the children two hundred dollars.

Gracie had turned down an offer of $250,000 for her farm from a Memphis businessman and offered it to the state in memory of her husband instead. The state proposed a purchase price of $175,000. Gracie asked the state at least to consider $225,000, allowing for the historical value of the property and the thousands of pines recently planted. The state, unmoved by her generous gesture or delicate financial condition, held firm. She eventually settled for $180,000 and turned all the land over to the state except for the house and five surrounding acres, upon which she continued to pay property tax for the rest of her life. (The state declined to waive the assessment, and she was too proud to request it.) After her death the house became property of the state. Ten years later a modest display of family photos and furniture was opened on the ground floor. A hiking trail and other features were added to the site over the years.

The Bible School did not survive beyond the first year of Sergeant York's paralysis. Deprived of prospective participants by the war and denied York's involvement because of his health and financial troubles, the school never established a regular curriculum or season. Pastor Pile, George York, Arthur Bushing, R. D. Brown, and others preached and taught there intermittently until about 1954, after which the school was abandoned. The limestone building, solid, beautiful, and desolate, stands empty today on state property a stone's throw from the site of York's birthplace, patiently awaiting a new purpose and a new benefactor.

Pine trees survived on the grounds of the Alvin C. York Agricultural Institute, thanks to the only fit of anger anyone remembers the sergeant exhibiting in public. One afternoon in 1950, York was riding with a reporter from Pall Mall to Jamestown. As they drove by York Institute, the sergeant noticed a crew of men unloading saws and axes from a truck. He had the reporter stop the car and walked over to ask the men what they were doing.

"I don't know what business it is of yours, mister," said the crew boss, "but we're fixing to cut down these trees. The state has done sold the timber to the railroad. We work for the railroad."

Sergeant York, the reporter recalled, turned "fire-red." Pointing his finger "like a pistol," he said, "Drop those saws and axes!"

The crew boss turned to him. "Who says so, Old Buddy?"

"My name is Sergeant Alvin York and I say so!" He was shaking with anger. "I give those trees to the state so the school children will know what a real full-grown pine looks like. I'll break half in two any man that touches an ax or saw to one of those trees. Hear me?"

The men froze, then packed their tools and left. The trees remained until a blight destroyed them years later and replacements were planted.

Today just north of Jamestown, the Alvin C. York Agricultural Institute, the only state-supported high school in Tennessee, continues its work. Under the leadership of Dr. Douglas Young, the York Institute was designated one of the 140 best rural schools in America by *Redbook* magazine in 1992. At the time, it served as a model for rural education in thirty-nine school systems in three states; it sponsored a popular and wide ranging adult education program; and it extended its reach through a five-county fiber optic television network and the internet. Enrollment for the 2020 school year was 483, down from a high near 700 in 2008.

A hundred yards from the spot where Sergeant York turned his first spade of dirt in 1925, hangs a York Institute flag that spent eight days in orbit on the space shuttle in 1992. Down the hall is the handsome portrait of the sergeant donated by the Class of '44.

Some institute students enjoy a work-study program funded from an unusual source. In 1967 Miss Gracie received a curious notice from the town of Easthampton, in Suffolk County, New York. The property taxes for 1965 and 1966 were due on her lot the notice said and the total was $43.17. Gracie paid the taxes, then set about finding out exactly what land in Suffolk County these people were talking about.

A bit of detective work revealed the lot was the one Carl Fisher gave the York Industrial Institute more than forty years before. In the various transfers of property among the agricultural institute, the industrial institute, and the state, its presence was forgotten. The sergeant paid property tax on it for a generation without evidently realizing what it was.

The vacant half acre on Montauk Peninsula was eventually sold in 1985 for thirty-five thousand dollars. Wilma Reagan Pinckley, former school superintendent and widow of York's physician, pledged an additional thirty thousand dollars, and the combined total was used to establish a program to provide students with jobs at the school. Dozens of jobs as cafeteria servers, maintenance workers, groundskeepers, and similar tasks continued to be available each year as a result of the program.

The original York Institute building, adjacent to the present facilities, is a sad shell, deserted and decrepit, a casualty of modern economics. When the campus needed upgrading, it was less expensive to build a new building than to add fire prevention systems, remove asbestos, and modernize electrical and plumbing in the old. The running water fixtures that so amazed students in 1929 were hopelessly behind the times. An engineering consultant, hired to recommend ways to preserve the building, advised tearing it down. In 1981 the school moved into expansive, though architecturally uninspiring, new quarters next door.

In 2008 the state transferred ownership of the original building to the Sergeant York Patriotic Foundation along with $500,000 appropriated for its demolition. The foundation raised roughly the same amount of money and by the following year shored up the facade with angle iron braces and made the structure weather tight. Their ambitious plan to restore the structure as a museum, archive, study center, meeting venue, and home of the foundation-supported Center for Valor and Peace awaits further development. Meanwhile the structure remains surrounded by a wire fence to protect passersby from falling bricks.

Today's York Institute complex hums with activity, boys and girls rushing through the halls, darting in and out of doorways at the sound of the bell. With computers and fax machines near at hand, they could no more imagine a school with nothing but a teacher, a room, and a bench made from half a log, than their redheaded benefactor could imagine words and pictures flying from one video screen to another at the speed of light.

Modern culture is quick to label anyone a hero, to the point where the word has all but lost its meaning. Successful athletes are heroes. Honest politicians are heroes. People who return lost purses with the money still in them are heroes. As columnist and writer Florence King observed, all anyone has to do to become a hero in America today is fall in a hole and live to tell about it.

Such dilution of the title results from two forces opposing each other to an unprecedented extent. One is that the world is desperate for heroes. It always has been. We want someone we can hold up as an example to inspire us. We want to be part of a race that produces great people who accomplish heroic things; we want to be able to look at a hero and imagine, with dedication and strength of character, we can be heroes too.

The opposing force, stronger now than ever, is a culture that discourages heroism. While we crave it as always, heroism, so rare in the first place, has become increasingly difficult to find. A society embracing relativism and multiculturalism is hard pressed to produce a hero. If every view of the world is equally acceptable, there can be no absolute standards of bravery, sacrifice, patriotism, faith, truth, fairness, fidelity, and honor.

And without absolutes, there can be no heroes.

Real heroes are not now and were never defined by degrees of success; or by doing something they should do anyway even if most people don't; or except in rare cases by a single awe-inspiring moment of courage. Rather they are those people blessed and burdened with a God-given vision for improving their world that requires them to make a conscious, voluntary, life-changing sacrifice, which they make unhesitantly, and without complaint.

Sergeant York is not a hero only because he killed about two dozen Germans, captured 132, and saved the lives of eleven American soldiers, including himself, one autumn morning in France. That proved his patriotism, bravery, and resourcefulness, not his heroism.

He is a hero because he felt a burden to use his fame for the benefit of the mountain children of Tennessee—rather than for his own comfort and security—and acted on that burden. He is a hero because, with a third grade education, he chose to take on the entrenched educational bureaucracies of Fentress County and Tennessee to get his school built. He is a hero because, after being stripped of his title and control at York Institute, he returned the next spring to hand out diplomas and continued supporting the school for the rest of his life.

He is a hero because he traveled throughout the country before and during World War II selling war bonds, raising money for the Red Cross, and lifting the spirits of American soldiers, all the while receiving—and asking—nothing but expense reimbursements. He is a hero because, sick and nearly destitute, he could endure the withering attacks of the IRS, avoiding financial ruin at the eleventh hour, and say only, "You know, this is a great country."

He is a hero because he had the moral foundation to be a hero. Certainly he had his faults and shortcomings; even heroes are fallen creatures. But his life was guided by unshakable absolutes founded on the teachings of the Bible, which taught him what was right, and taught him his responsibility in seeing that right was done, regardless of the sacrifice.

The lifetime of sacrifices Sergeant York made between his first fundraising trip in 1919 and his disabling illness in 1954 still bear fruit today. Students at the York Institute this year are great-great-grandchildren of its first pupils, the fourth generation to enjoy a more successful, productive life through the realization of Sergeant York's heroic vision. Hundreds of others have found employment there over the years as teachers, administrators, and support staff. They and their families can thank the sergeant for their livelihoods.

Most important, Sergeant York is a hero because not only his school, but his inspiring example, transcend time and place. His story still moves us. His life is still an encouragement to all who feel the tug of their own blessing and burden for building a better world. One look at this backwoods Tennessee farmer with a third grade education and we find ourselves persuaded that, if he can leave such a legacy, so might some of us who follow.

A Note on Sources

Sergeant York's personal papers remain in the hands of his family and until recently were stored in the second floor bedrooms of the York homeplace in Pall Mall. Efforts have been made to catalog and preserve them and future plans call for the papers to be made available for research.

Fortunately, several thousand pages of these documents have been photocopied and are available in the library archives of Tennessee Technological University in Cookeville, Tennessee. The York files are catalogued as Research Group 20. Tennessee Tech also has a collection of videotaped interviews with various York relatives and friends which were made by the Upper Cumberland Historical Society in 1988.

There have been four previous biographies of Sergeant York. The first, *Sergeant York and His People* (New York and London: Funk & Wagnalls Company, 1922; reprinted in pamphlet form, Jamestown, Tennessee: Wolf River Cemetery Association, n.d.), is valuable for being written so soon after York's return from the war and before work on the school began. It is also the oldest detailed portrayal of life in Fentress County and the Wolf River Valley. The factual errors concerning York's war experiences (such as Pershing supposedly awarding York his Medal of Honor) and the florid writing style do not diminish the value of Sam Cowan's eyewitness accounts of life in Pall Mall when it was still relatively isolated.

Sergeant York: His Own Life Story and War Diary (Garden City, NY: Doubleday, Doran & Company, Inc., 1928) is out of print but is the best source of reliable information about York's early life and war experiences. The first half of the book gives an interesting and insightful account of Tom Skeyhill's trips to Pall Mall, participation in shooting matches, description of a moonshine still and other local attractions, and his talks with York. The second half consists of long excerpts from York's war diary, with additional commentary by York added for the book.

Sergeant York: Last of the Long Hunters (Philadelphia: The John C. Winston Company, 1930; reprinted St. John, Indiana: Larry Harrison, n.d.) was originally intended by Skeyhill and York as a book for boys, though it has taken on the aura of a definitive reference book over the years. The book is long on adventure, including Revolutionary War battles and Indian torture techniques but not a reliable source of facts. York family members insist Skeyhill's portrayal of Tennessee mountain slang here is comically overdone. In its reprinted form, which includes the original photos and paintings, this may be the most widely distributed book about York currently in circulation.

Sergeant York: An American Hero by David D. Lee (Lexington: The University Press of Kentucky, 1985) is the only previous book about York written after his death. It is more an analysis of York as a heroic figure than a detailed biography of his life. This book has a scholarly and responsible approach to the facts and includes many quotes about York as well as those by him.

There is a manuscript fragment among York's papers titled *An American Idyll*, probably by Skeyhill, which is a collection of the letters York and Gracie wrote to each other while the sergeant was overseas. The work was evidently never completed but is a treasury of correspondence unavailable elsewhere—there are no letters in the research files from the period before the sergeant's marriage.

York's war diary remains in family hands and because of its fragile condition and historical importance, stays locked away in a bank vault. The text of the diary, however, is on the internet, courtesy of the Alvin C. York Agricultural Institute.

Between the summer of 1996 and the summer of 1997, I conducted a series of interviews in Pall Mall, Allardt, Jamestown, and
surrounding communities in Fentress County. Audio recordings were
made on micro cassette. The people I interviewed and whom I thank
most kindly for their time, were:

George Edward Buxton York	Andrew Jackson York
Betsy Ross York Lowrey	Helen Lowrey York
Elva Jean York Clouse	Bradley Cook
Ernest Buck	Leo Hatfield
Ova Blair	Edith Pile
Janice Lee	Dr. Douglas Young
Wilma Reagan Pinckley	Dr. Arthur Story Bushing
Lorene Cargile	Jewelene Hinds
Maxene Rains	Colene Holt
Ella Jeanne Frogge Leonard	Jim Taylor
Leva Pile	Emogene Smith

Scrapbooks seldom receive recognition as a source, but this project
has benefited greatly from two of them. One was compiled by W. Lipscomb Davis Sr. when he accompanied Sergeant York on his speaking
trips in 1919 and 1920, and was graciously loaned to me by his son,
Lipscomb Davis Jr. Though the newspaper names and cities have all
been trimmed off, it is possible to reconstruct the locations and chronology from the texts of the clippings. The scrapbook also contains calling
cards from hotel managers, lapel ribbons, programs, ticket stubs, and
other wonderful memorabilia. The second scrapbook is in the library of
the York Institute and consists mostly of articles about the early history
of the institution. It is possibly the most complete reference anywhere
on the school's first decade.

Of the hundreds of periodical features on York, the most pivotal
is the one on the front page of *The Saturday Evening Post* for April
26, 1919. This was the report revealing to the world York's exploit in

the Argonne Forest. It was reprinted as a fund-raising brochure during York's early speaking tours and was later entered into the *Congressional Record* to justify requests for retirement benefits for the sergeant.

Bibliography

Alvin C. York Agricultural Institute. Records.

——. Scrapbooks.

——. Vertical File. Alvin C. York.

"Alvin C. York Presses Aim." *New York Times* (18 Sept. 1927): II 6:8.

"Alvin York Is to Boost Own Your Home Meeting." *Tennessean* (5 June 1919).

"Applauds Sergeant York on Armistice Eve." *New York Times* (11 Nov. 1928): 28:2.

"Approves York Pension." *New York Times* (5 March 1937): 23:4.

"Are You a U.S. Hero? Public's Mood Decides." *Tennessean* (18 June 1995): 14A.

Aswell, James R. "Hi, Alvin." *Scholastic* (9 Nov. 1942): 2.

Baker, David. *Flight and Flying: A Chronology*. New York: Facts on File, Inc., 1994.

"Baseball Is 'Fine' Says Mother York." *Tennessean* (12 June 1919): 15.

Batey, Carol. "York's Wife Urges State to Fund School." *Nashville Banner* (7 Jan. 1983).

"The Battling Yorks." *Newsweek* (20 Feb. 1956): 47:31.

"Beaty Family, of Fentress County, Stops Here." *Tennessean* (18 July 1941).

"Bedside Tribute to the Old Hero." *Life* (24 Oct. 1960): 49:99 +.

Biographical Directory of the American Congress 1774–1996. Joel D. Tresse, ed. Alexandria, VA: Congressional Quarterly Staff Directories, 1996.

Birdwell, Michael E. "The Making of the Film *Sergeant York*." Cookeville, TN: Tennessee Technological University, 1989.

Black, Norman. "Army Gun Development in Danger." *Tennessean* (26 Aug. 1985).

Brandt, Nat. "Sergeant York." *American Heritage* (Aug/Sept. 1981): 56–64.

Brannen, Lynne. "Sergeant Alvin York Believes Nazis to Fall before the Allies in Summer." *Chattanooga News* (9 Feb. 1944).

"Bride of a Hero a Hard Job Thinks Mrs. York." *Tennessean* (10 June 1919): 1 +.

Burt, Jesse Clifton. *Your Tennessee.* Austin, TX: Steck-Vaughn Co., © 1979.

Butler, La Crisha. "Hero York's Son Seeks Lost Copy of Pistol." *Tennessean* (1 March 1989).

——. "Replica of York's Pistol Found, Now at Museum." *Tennessean* (2 March 1989).

Buxton, G. Edward, Jr. *Official History of 82nd Division American Expeditionary Forces, "All-American" Division, 1917–1919.* Bobbs-Merrill Co., 1919.

"Calls Sergeant York 'Bravest of Men.'" *New York Times* (22 March 1919): 6:2.

Carpozi, George. *The Gary Cooper Story.* New Rochelle, NY: Arlington House, 1970.

Chant, Christopher. *Aviation: An Illustrated History.* New York: Crescent Books, 1978.

Chase, Joseph Cummings. "Corporal York, General Pershing, and Others." *World's Work* (April 1919), 636 +.

"A Child of Nature and Grace." *Literary Digest* (21 June 1919), 61:33–4.

Chronicle of the Cinema: 100 Years of the Movies. New York: Dorling Kindersley, 1995.

"Churches Make Appeal." *New York Times* (9 Nov. 1936): 11:1.

"Commission Makes York a Real Colonel." *Tennessean* (10 June 1919): 1 +.

"Conscience Plus Red Hair Are Bad for Germans." *Literary Digest* (14 June 1919), 61:42–48.

Corlew, Robert E. *Tennessee: A Short History.* Knoxville: UT Press, 1989.

Cornwell, Ilene J. *Biographical Directory of Tennessee General Assembly v. III–V.* Nashville: The Tennessee Historical Commission, 1990.

Cowan, Sam. *Sergeant York and His People.* New York: Funk & Wagnalls, 1922.

Crutchfield, James A. *Tennesseans at War.* Nashville: Rutledge Hill Press, 1987.

"Daily 'War' at Capital." *New York Times* (5 Oct. 1929): 21:7.

"Draftee York on the Other side of the fence this time." *Nashville Banner* (17 Oct. 1940).

"Drys Draft York. He Refuses to Run." *New York Times* (8 May 1936): 2:7.

Eames, John Douglas. *The Paramount Story.* New York: Crown Publish ers, Inc., 1985.

Ed Sullivan Show, The. (26 March 1961) Courtesy of Sofa Entertainment.

Epstein, Lawrence J. *Samuel Goldwyn.* Boston: Twayne Publishers, 1981.

Fann, Gina. "Family, Friends Honor Memory, Valor of York." *Nashville Banner* (9 Aug. 1985).

"Fentress Feud." *Time* (25 May 1936): 26 +.

Flair, Sharon Curtis. "Alvin York Kin a Lad after Ancestor's Own Heart." *Nashville Banner* (27 Aug. 1988).

"Floor Fight Is Looked For." *New York Times* (15 Sept. 1941): 3:1.

Fontenay, Charles L. "Sergeant York's Widow Dies; Rites Set." *Tennessean* (28 Sept. 1984).

"Funds for York's School." *New York Times* (16 Oct. 1927): II 1:3.

"Girl Cured by Iron Lung to Lead March with York." *New York Times* (25 July 1939): 12:2.

"Give Great Ovation to Sergeant York." *New York Times* (22 March 1919): 6:2.

Gelernter, David Hillel. *1939, the Lost World of the Fair.* New York: Free Press, 1995.

Glaenzer, B. "The Ballad of Redhead's Day." *New York Times* (24 May 1919): 12:7.

Goldhurst, Richard. *Pipe Clay and Drill John J. Pershing: The Classic American Soldier.* New York: Reader's Digest Press, 1977.

"Goldstar Mothers Honor Sergeant York." *New York Times* (4 July 1941): 16:2.

"Governor and Staff Leave on Visit to York." *Tennessean* (6 June 1919).

"Governor, National, and State Legion Heads to Honor Sergeant York at Pall Mall Home" *Tennessee Legionnaire* (Sept.–Oct. 1960): 3.

"Governor Roberts to Tie Nuptial Knot for York." *Tennessean* (5 June 1919): 1.

"Hillbilly Is the Best." *Nashville Banner* (10 June 1969).

"Hits 'Calamity Howlers.'" *New York Times* (18 May 1941): 33:3.

Hogue, Albert R. *Davy Crockett and Others in Fentress County Who Have Given the Country a Prominent Place in History.* Crossville, TN: Chronicle Publishing Company, 1955.

"Home Guard Post for York." *New York Times* (20 March 1941): 23:5.

"Honor Read and York." *New York Times* (13 July 1919): 8:2.

Horn, Blinkey. "Sergeant York to Pitch First Ball in Second Half of Vol-Pelican Twin Duel." *Tennessean* (11 June 1919).

"House Resolution in Honor of Sgt. York." *Fentress Countian* (3 April 1925).

Hugh, Walker. "York's Rifle: Enfield or Springfield?" *Tennessean* (12 Oct. 1969).

"Hull 'Nominated' on Tennessee Day." *New York Times* (23 July 1939): 26:1.

Humble, R. G. *Sgt. Alvin C. York. A Christian Patriot.* Circleville, OH: Advocate Publishing House, 1966.

Isenberg, Michael T. War *on Film: The American Cinema and World War 1, 1914–1941.* Farleigh Dickinson University Press, 1981.

Jungmann, A. M. "What Did Alvin C. York Do?" *Ladies Home Journal* (Oct. 1919), 36:64.

Kane, Joseph Nathan. *Facts about the Presidents.* New York: H. W. Wilson Co., 1993.

"Lasky Arrives to Speed York Film Production." *Nashville Banner* (22 April 1940).

Lasky, Jesse L. and Don Weldon. *I Blow My Own Horn.* Garden City, NY: Doubleday & Co., 1957.

Lasky, Jesse L. Jr. *Whatever Happened to Hollywood?.* New York: Funk & Wagnalls, 1975.

"Lasky Visits York; Film Offer Reported; $50,000 Said Demand." *Tennessean* (10 March 1940): 1 +.

Lee, David D. *Sergeant York: An American Hero.* Lexington: The University Press of Kentucky, 1985.

Lee, Janice Pile and Darlene P Brannon. *The View of the Valley of the Three Forks of Wolf.* May 1986.

"Life Goes to the World's Fair: It Turns Out to Be a Wonderful Place." *Life* (3 July 1939): 54 +, (31 July 1939): 24, (18 Sept. 1939): 87.

Lindbergh, Charles A. *The Wartime Journals of Charles A. Lindbergh.* New York: Harcourt Brace Jovanovich, Inc., 1970.

"Lindbergh Scored by Sergeant York." *New York Times* (12 Nov. 1941): 2:7 +.

Linger, O. A. *Sergeant Alvin York.* Lexington, KY: Georgetown Quarterly (Jan. 1927).

Lipman, Walter. "Day at the World's Fair." *Current History* (July 1939): 50–51.

"Looking Backward." *Newsweek* (25 April 1955): 45:54.

Lord, Lewis. "A Slaughter No One Knew How to Stop: PBS's Searing New Look at the Great War." *U.S. News and World Report* (11 Nov. 1996): 52–53.

"MacArthur Aids Flag Body." *New York Times* (19 Feb. 1942): 11:2.

"MacArthur, York Honored." *New York Times* (7 April 1942): 10:4.

"Major Heroes." *Newsweek* (18 May 1942): 19:30.

"Man Who Sent York Overseas Writes of War's Great Hero." *Tennessean* (1 June 1919): 1.

Martin, Dan. "Murfreesboro VA Hospital Named After Alvin C. York." *Tennessean* (9 Aug. 1985).

"Mary York Is Sworn." *New York Times* (4 Jan. 1962): 35:5.

McBride, Joseph. *Hawks on Hawks*. Berkley: University of California Press, 1982.

McGaw, Robert A. "A Likeness of Sergeant York." *Tennessee Historical Quarterly* 27.4 (1968): 329 +.

McHenry, Robert, ed. *Webster's American Military Biographies*. Springfield, MA: G. & C. Merriam Co., 1978.

The Medal of Honor of the United States Army. Washington, DC: The United States Government Printing Office, 1948.

Medal of Honor Recipients 1863–1978. Washington: U.S. Government Printing Office, 1979.

Middlebrook, Martin. *The First Day on the Somme, 1 July 1916*. New York: W. W. Norton, 1972.

"'Miss Gracie' Didn't Seek Fame." *Nashville Banner* (28 Sept. 1984).

"Mr. Chase and the Sergeant." *The New Yorker* (12 July 1941), 17:10–11.

"More Yorks Want to Do 'Some Shooting.'" *New York Times* (25 Feb. 1944): 9:2.

Moutoux, John T. "Senators See York Movie and Say It's Grand Film" *Knoxville News Sentinel.* (30 Sept. 1941).

Mullen, Michael. *Historical Dictionary of World's Fairs and Expositions, 1851–1988*. John E. Findling and Kimberly D. Pelle, eds. New York: Greenwood Press, 1990: 293–300.

"Must Fight to Keep Liberty, Says York." *New York Times* (31 May 1941): 6:2.

Nashville: A Short History and Selected Buildings. Eleanor Graham, ed. Historical Commission of Nashville-Davidson County, TN, 1974.

"Nashville Honors York." *New York Times* (11 June 1919): 3:6.

"New Sgt. York Bio Adds Fresh Perspective." *Tennessean* (27 Oct. 1985).

"Nimitz Is Honored in South." *New York Times* (24 Nov. 1944): 12:3.

Normand, Tom. "World War I Hero Sgt. Alvin York's Widow Gracie Dies." *Nashville Banner* (27 Sept. 1984).

"Nye Says Films Spread War Waves." *New York Times* (2 Aug. 1941): 16:6.

"'Obey' Omitted in Rites Which Joined Couple." *Tennessean* (8 June 1919): 1.

"Offers Commission to York." *New York Times* (30 May 1919): 7:1.

"Old Soldiers." *Time* (18 May 1942): 39:63.

"One Day's Work." *Time* (11 Sept. 1964): 84:26.

Parsons, Louella O. "Tall Lanky Gary Cooper Gets Sgt. Alvin York Role in Movie." *Tennessean* (7 Sept. 1940): 1 +.

"Passes Bill Rewarding York." *New York Times* (13 Feb. 1935): 20:6.

Pattullo, George. "The Second Elder Gives Battle." *The Saturday Evening Post* (26 April 1919): 191:1, 2, 71, 73, 74.

Patureau, Alan. "Sergeant York: The Legacy Moves On." *Dixie Living* (28 June 1987).

Perry, Hamilton Darby. *The Panay Incident.* New York: The MacMillan Company, 1969.

"Picture Will Be Based on Life and Exploits of Alvin C. York." *Tennessean* (13 March 1940): 1 +.

Pinckley, Wilma. *Fentress County History as I Reviewed It.* Jamestown, TN: *Fentress Courier*, 1987.

———. *Hill Country History as I Renewed It.* Jamestown, TN: *Fentress Courier*, 1989.

———. *Journeys Down Memory Lane.* Jamestown, TN: *Fentress Courier*, 1994.

———. *Local History as I Pursued It.* Jamestown, TN: *Fentress Courier*, 1988.

———. *Mountain History as I Rescued It.* Jamestown, TN: *Fentress Courier*, 1990.

———. *Treasured Memories.* Jamestown, TN: *Fentress Courier*, 1992.

Pitt, Barrie. *The Last Act.* London: Macmillan, 1984.

"Plane Ride Refused by Sergeant York." *New York Times* (22 Sept. 1929): 18:2.

Plumb, Beatrice. *Lives that Inspire.* Minneapolis: T. S. Denison & Co., 1962.

"Pneumonia Threatens York." *New York Times* (18 April 1963): 12:8.

"Praised by Sergeant York." *New York Times* (7 Jan. 1941): 6:1.

Price, Ed. "The Making of a Legend: Alvin Cullom [sic] York." *Now and Then* (Fall 1987): 5–8.

Priest, J. Percy. "Sergeant York to Discuss Movie Contract with Producer Here." *Tennessean* (14 March 1940).

———. "World War Hero to Learn Whether He Will Go to Hollywood for Film Production Based on Life." *Tennessean* (14 March 1940): 1.

"'Ready to Go,' Says York." *New York Times* (28 April 1942): 10:6.

"Reception for Alvin York Is Planned Here." *Tennessean* (28 May 1919): 1.

"Refused $1,000 Night." *New York Times* (31 May 1922): 7:5.

"Replaces York on Dry Ticket." *New York Times* (27 June 1936): 7:2.

"Returning Fighter Is Welcomed by Pastor." *Tennessean* (2 June 1919).

"Roberts Plans Visit to York at Oglethorpe." *Tennessean* (29 May 1919).

Scott, Jim. "Courageous York Forced to Leave Jamestown Fete." *Nashville Banner* (22 Aug. 1957): 10.

"Sergeant Alvin C. York Will Give Views on World Affairs, Issues through Daily Newspaper Column." *Tennessean* (2 Dec. 1941): 1.

"Sergeant of Screen, Sergeant in Person." *New York Times* (2 July 1941): 12:3.

"Sergeant York Balks at Lasky Film Offer, Like Trading for a Mule Says War Hero." *New York Times* (16 March 1940): 9:2.

"Sergeant York, Both Picture, Hero to Be Welcomed Today." *Tennessean* (18 Sept. 1941).

"Sergeant York Dies At 76 but the Legend of His WWI Exploits Live On." *Chattanooga Times* (3 Sept. 1964): 7.

"Sergeant York for Draft." *New York Times* (23 Aug. 1940): 9:6.

"Sergeant York Grows Old . . . but Tax Stew Continues." *Tennessean* (12 March 1961).

"Sergeant York Here in School Fund Drive." *New York Times* (4 Feb. 1928): 2:3.

"Sergeant York Ill with Pneumonia." *New York Times* (3 July 1950): 17:4.

"Sergeant York in Critical Condition." *New York Times* (31 Aug. 1964): 4:8. "Sergeant York in Fight at Law." *New York Times* (24 July 1927): II 7:6.

"Sergeant York in Films." *New York Times* (24 March 1940): 30:6.

"Sergeant York in Hospital." *New York Times* (23 May 1964): 8:5.

"Sergeant York Is a Happy Man." *Memphis Commercial Appeal* (28 Aug. 1960): IV: 1.

"Sergeant York Is Feted." *New York Times* (26 May 1919): 10:2.

"Sergeant York Is in Semicoma." *New York Times* (30 Jan. 1964): 12:7.

"Sergeant York Is Made Major in Infantry." *New York Times* (8 May 1942): 11:6.

"Sergeant York Home, His Girl Says, 'Yes.'" *New York Times* (1 June 1919): II 1:6.

"Sergeant York Hopes We Will Avoid Wars." *New York Times* (11 Nov. 1934): 2:6.

"Sergeant York Laid to Rest." *Fentress County Leader-Times* (10 Sept. 1964): 1 +.

"Sergeant York Marries Boyhood Sweetheart." *New York Times* (8 June 1919): 13:3.

"Sergeant York Movie Premiere to Be Held Here Early in 1942." *Tennessean* (9 Sept. 1940): 1:1 +.

"Sergeant York Offers Plan to Stop Hitler." *New York Times* (9 Oct. 1938): 41:6.

"Sergeant York Portrait to Be Unveiled." *Nashville Banner* (16 Oct. 1987): C7.

"Sergeant York Premieres as Color Classic on TBS." *Tennessean* (15 May 1988).

"Sergeant York Quits School." *New York Times* (9 May 1936): 5:5.

"Sergeant York Ready to Join War on Japan." *New York Times* (12 Nov. 1937): 3:6.

"'Sergeant York' Said 'Dangdest' Thing Seen Here." *Tennessean* (19 Sept 1941).

"Sergeant York Seeks $2,000,000 Fund." *New York Times* (1 Dec. 1925): 19:4.

"Sergeant York Signs Up Again." *Life* (11 May 1942): 12: 26 +.

"Sergeant York Surrenders." *Time* (1 April 1940): 35: 69.

"Sergeant York Takes Bad Turn." *New York Times* (24 June 1964): 27:7.

"Sergeant York to Visit Here." *New York Times* (25 July 1919): 7:2.

"Sergeant York to See Polo." *New York Times* (3 July 1941): 26:2.

"Sergeant York, 74, 'Acutely Ill' with Intestinal Hemorrhage." *New York Times* (28 May 1961).

"Sergeant York Undergoes Surgery on Prostate Gland." *New York Times* (30 June 1962): 6:2.

"Sergeant York Urges Aid for Red Cross." *New York Times* (19 Feb. 1942): 11:2.

"Sergeant York 'Very Sick.'" *New York Times* (14 April 1963): 81:5.

"Sergeant York Visits Nashville." *Tennessean* (4 July 1919).

"Sergeant York Visits with the President." *New York Times* (31 July): 13:5.

"Sergeant York, War Hero, Dies." *New York Times* (3 Sept. 1964): 1:6 +.

"Sergeant York Welcomed Here as Premiere of Picture Begins." *Nashville Banner* (18 Sept. 1941.)

"Sergeant York Winces." *New York Times* (19 Jan. 1927): 4:5.

"Sergeant York: Yesterday's Hero." *Newsweek* (18 Nov. 1957): 50:19.

"Sergeant York's Barn Burns." *New York Times* (4 Sept. 1962): 67:4.

"Sergeant York's Exploit." *New York Times* (7 Oct. 1929): 24:4.

"Sergeant York's Greatest Fight." *Literary Digest* (3 July 1926): 90:26.

"Sergeant York's Legendary Exploits Told in Rare Book." *Tennessean* (7 June 1987).

"Sergeant York's Own Story." *Literary Digest* (13 May 1922): 73:40 +.

"Sergeant York's Son Slain." *Tennessean* (8 May 1972): 1.

"Sergeant York's Widow Gives Museum Site." *Tennessean* (3 Dec. 1967): 6B.

Shackford, James Atkins. "The Autobiography of David Crockett: An Annotated Edition with Portraits, Maps, and Appendices" (dissertation). Nashville, TN: Vanderbilt University, 1948.

Shackford, James A. and Stanley J. Folmsbee. *A Narrative of the Life of David Crockett of the State of Tennessee.* Knoxville: UT Press, 1973.

Shanks, Maudean Wright. *History of Alvin C. York Agricultural Institute.* Jamestown, TN, 1994.

Skeyhill, Tom. *Sergeant York: The Last of the Long Hunters.* New York: Doubleday & Co., 1930.

Smith, Charles W. "Turkey Shoot Staged for Movie Producer and Party." *Tennessean* (28 April 1940).

Smythe, Donald. *Pershing: General of the Armies.* Bloomington, IN: Indiana University Press, 1986.

"Son Tells Tales of Hero Father." *Tennessean* (18 Oct. 1991).

Sparks, Andrew. "Sergeant York Is Still a Fighter." *Atlanta Journal and Constitution* (14 May 1961): 6 +.

Spiller, Roger J. *Dictionary of American Military Biography Vol. III Q-Z.* Westport, CT: Greenwood Press, 1984.

Stallings, Laurence. *The Doughboys: The Story of the AEF, 1917–1918.* New York: Harper & Row, 1960.

Storms, Roger C. *Partisan Prophets: A History of the Prohibition Party.* Denver, CO: National Prohibition Foundation, 1972.

Swindell, Larry. *The Last Hero.* Garden City, NY: Doubleday, 1980.

Talley, James. "'I'm Mighty Grateful' Says Sergeant York." *Tennessean* (19 March 1961): 16A.

Tennessee State Library and Archives. John Trotwood Papers, V-H-4. Box 59, f. 14.

——. Scrapbook Collection. V-J-6, Ac. no. 1857.

——. Small Collection. Letters (to Sgt. Alvin York), 1939–1943. V-L-4. Box 2, Ac. no. 7342.

——. Tennessee Federal Writers Project. Tennesseans: From the Beginning of Tennessee History until 1941. VI-B-1-5, Ac. no. 1776.

——. Tennessee Historical Society. Speeches. VI-A-1-5, Ac. no. 455.

——. Vertical File. Alvin C. York.

——. William Henry McRaven Papers, 1851–1964. III-H-3. Box 36, Ac. no. 67–30.

Thompson, Jerry. "York Statue Unveiled at Capitol." *Tennessean* (14 Dec. 1968), 1–2.

Tidwell, Mary Louise Lea. *Luke Lea of Tennessee*. Bowling Green, KY: Bowling Green State University Popular Press, 1993.

"Tired of Posing as a Hero." *New York Times* (13 June 1919): 14:5.

Townsend, Jimmy. "Sergeant York Inspired Better GI Treatment." *Nashville Banner* (21 Aug. 1985).

Twain, Mark and Charles D. Warner. *The Gilded Age*. Philadelphia: American Publishing Co., 1874.

"Upholds Sergeant York." *New York Times* (13 Aug. 1935): 8:1.

"Victory Is Due to Hand of God Says Hero York." *Tennessean* (23 May 1919): 1 +.

"Visiting." *Newsweek* (24 July 1939): 14:31.

"Want Helen Wood in York Picture." *Nashville Banner* (30 March 1940).

"War Hero's Dream Now Coming True." *New York Times* (6 June 1926): IX, 6:1.

Warner Bros. Archives. Burbank, CA: University of Southern California.

"Washington Hails Brave Sergeant York." *New York Times* (25 May 1919): 14:3.

Wayne, Jane Ellen. *Cooper's Women*. New York: Prentice Hall Press, 1988.

Welch, Pat. "Sergeant York's Monument to Put Family in Debt." *Tennessean* (1 May 1966): 1 +.

"What Did It Get You?" *Time* (9 June 1941): 37:21.

"What Shall It Profit a Man? Says Sgt. York." *Tennessean* (8 June 1919).

Who Was Who in America Vol. III 1951–1960. Chicago: A. N. Marquis Co., 1960.

Williams, Gladys. *Alvin Cullom* [sic] *York*. "Http://www.voyager.rtd.utk. edu/VolWeb/Schools/York/york.html" (August 22, 1996)

Winchell, Walter. "On Broadway." *Tennessean* (5 July 1941).

Woodward, David R. and Robert Franklin Maddox. *America and World War I: A Selected Annotated Bibliography of English-language Sources.* New York: Garland Publishing, Inc., 1985.

Wolf, S. J. "Sergeant York—Then and Now." *New York Times* (15 Aug. 1948): VI 48:3.

"Workers Named for 1,000,000 York School Drive." *Knoxville News-Sentinel* (17 Jan 1927): 12.

"World's Fairs." *Time* (12 June 1939): 11–12.

Yarbrough, William. "York Institute Treated as 'Stepchild.'" *Knoxville Journal* (Feb. 1969): C1.

York, Alvin C. *Sergeant York: His Own Life Story and War Diary.* Tom Skeyhill, ed. Garden City, NJ: Doubleday, Doran and Co., 1928.

———. "Sergeant York Says." *Tennessean* (15 Dec. 1941 to 3 July 1942).

———. *Sergeant York's War Diary.* "Http://www.voyager.rtd.utk.edu/ VolWeb/Schools/York/york.html" (August 22, 1996).

"York Abandons Field after Defeat." *Knoxville Journal* (29 Jan. 1927): 1 +.

"York Assails Legion." *New York Times* (31 May 1930): 19:2.

"York Back Home, Still Farmer; No Agreement; Lasky Optimistic." *Tennessean* (17 March 1940): 1 +.

"York Balks at Camera." *New York Times* (26 Jan. 1922): 36:3.

"York Declines to Comment." *New York Times* (11 Aug. 1935): 8:1.

"York, Dinah Shore to Appear in Big Defense Rally Here." *Nashville Banner* (5 March 1942).

"York Drive Depends on Knoxville." *Knoxville Journal* (28 Jan. 1927).

"York Explains Lecture Mix-Up." *New York Times* (17 Feb. 1935): 29:6.

"York Fails to Visit Subway His Only Wish." *Tennessean* (24 May 1919): 1.

"York Film to Inspire Nation Says Hannah." *Tennessean* (26 June 1919).

"York Gives Up Honeymoon." *New York Times* (12 June 1919): 18:5.

York, Gracie Williams. "The Reminiscences of Mrs. Alvin 'Sgt.' York" *Tennessee Regional Oral History Collection of the Memphis Public Library.* Glen Rock, NJ: Microfilming Corporation of America, 1976, © 1977.

"York Has Busy Day Taking in Local Sights." *Tennessean* (11 June 1919).

"York, Hero of War, Welcomed by City." *New York Times* (10 November 1928): 16:8.

"York Holds on to School." *New York Times* (16 July 1936): 19:2.

"York Institute Bill Passes." *Fentress Countian* (16 April 1925).

"York Is Cleared in Suit." *New York Times* (20 Nov. 1941): 29:3.

"York Is Going to Hollywood." *Nashville Banner* (13 March 1940).

"York Makes Plea for Homeless Soldiers." *Tennessean* (11 June 1919).

"York May Run for Congress." *New York Times* (13 May 1942): 7:5.

"York Not Going to Stick around Mountain Home." *Tennessean* (4 June 1919).

"York Operated On." *New York Times* (29 Sept. 1928): 2:2.

"York Party See Vaudeville and Movie Shows." *Tennessean* (12 June 1919).

"York Quits School Presidency Charging 'Lack of Cooperation.'" *Tennessean* (9 May 1936).

"York Rushed Out of Army in Home State." *Tennessean* (30 May 1919).

"York Says Garand Rifle 'Sort of Frail Looking' in Discussing New, WWI Armies." *Tennessean* (27 June 1941).

"York Says He Is Considering Congress Race." *Tennessean* (21 March 1940).

"York Says Paratroopers on Berlin Could Win." *New York Times* (2 Sept. 1944): 4:5.

"York School in Dispute." *New York Times* (26 July 1927): 37:2.

"York Sees Subway and Tours City with Belle." *Tennessean* (27 May 1919): 1.

"York Sees Subway from Private Car." *New York Times* (27 May 1919): 7:3.

"York Spies on Fair, Early for Tribute." *New York Times* (13 July 1939): 15:6.

"York Sues Over School." *New York Times* (17 Sept. 1927): 16:8.

"York Takes Peep at Theater and Movies." *Tennessean* (12 June 1919).

"York Thinks of Mother While Capital Cheers." *Tennessean* (25 May 1919).

"York to Build Own School." *New York Times* (17 March 1926); 11:2.

"York to Pose for Historical Picture." *Tennessean* (15 June 1919).

"York to Uplift Mountaineers." *Literary Digest* (30 Aug. 1919): 62:35.

"York's Party Will Arrive Here Tonight." *Tennessean* (9 June 1919).

"York's Pastor Repents." *New York Times* (18 June 1919): 22:2.

Zim, Larry, Mel Lerner, and Herbert Rolfes. *The World of Tomorrow: The 1939 New York World's Fair*. New York: Harper & Row, 1988.